D0848509

37653013394948
McMath ▮▮▮▮▮ NonFiction
940.542 McMANUS
Alamo in the Ardennes : the
untold story of the
American soldiers who made

APR   2007

CENTRAL ARKANSAS LIBRARY SYSTEM
SIDNEY S. McMATH BRANCH LIBRARY
LITTLE ROCK, ARKANSAS

Additional Advance Praise for *Alamo in the Ardennes*

"John McManus shines a light on the lesser-known battles that made the historic defense of Bastogne possible. His excellent research puts the reader on the icy battlefields of Belgium, where threadbare American retrograde fighting frustrated Hitler's last offensive in the west."

—Kevin M. Hymel, author of *Patton's Photographs*

"John McManus has deftly woven a wide range of previously untapped sources into a dramatic and finely detailed account of events that set the stage for the successful defense of Bastogne during the Ardennes counteroffensive. In doing so, McManus pays a long overdue and heartfelt tribute to the brave men of the 110th Infantry Regiment, Combat Command R, 9th Armored Division, and CCD, 10th Armored Division, without detracting from the epic stand of the 'Screaming Eagles' of the 101st Airborne Division."

—Lieutenant Colonel (Ret.) Mark J. Reardon, U.S. army historian and author of *Victory at Mortain*

ALAMO IN THE ARDENNES

Also by John C. McManus

The Americans at Normandy: The Summer of 1944—
the American War from the Normandy Beaches to Falaise

The Americans at D-Day:
The American Experience at the Normandy Invasion

Deadly Sky: The American Combat Airman in World War II

The Deadly Brotherhood:
The American Combat Soldier in World War II

ALAMO IN THE ARDENNES

THE UNTOLD STORY OF THE AMERICAN SOLDIERS WHO MADE THE DEFENSE OF BASTOGNE POSSIBLE

JOHN C. McMANUS

BICENTENNIAL
BICENTENNIAL
1807
WILEY
2007
BICENTENNIAL
BICENTENNIAL

John Wiley & Sons, Inc.

This book is printed on acid-free paper. ∞

Copyright © 2007 by John C. McManus. All rights reserved

Maps on pages xxx–xxxv © 2007 by Rick Britton

Wiley Bicentennial Logo: Richard J. Pacifico

Published by John Wiley & Sons, Inc., Hoboken, New Jersey
Published simultaneously in Canada

No part of this publication may be reproduced, stored in a retrieval system, or trans-
mitted in any form or by any means, electronic, mechanical, photocopying, recording,
scanning, or otherwise, except as permitted under Section 107 or 108 of the 1976
United States Copyright Act, without either the prior written permission of the Publisher, or authorization through payment of the appropriate per-copy fee to the Copyright Clearance Center, 222 Rosewood Drive, Danvers, MA 01923, (978) 750-8400, fax
(978) 646-8600, or on the web at www.copyright.com. Requests to the Publisher for
permission should be addressed to the Permissions Department, John Wiley & Sons,
Inc., 111 River Street, Hoboken, NJ 07030, (201) 748-6011, fax (201) 748-6008, or
online at http://www.wiley.com/go/permissions.

Limit of Liability/Disclaimer of Warranty: While the publisher and the author have
used their best efforts in preparing this book, they make no representations or warranties with respect to the accuracy or completeness of the contents of this book and
specifically disclaim any implied warranties of merchantability or fitness for a particular purpose. No warranty may be created or extended by sales representatives or
written sales materials. The advice and strategies contained herein may not be suitable for your situation. You should consult with a professional where appropriate. Neither the publisher nor the author shall be liable for any loss of profit or any other commercial damages, including but not limited to special, incidental, consequential, or
other damages.

For general information about our other products and services, please contact our
Customer Care Department within the United States at (800) 762-2974, outside the
United States at (317) 572-3993 or fax (317) 572-4002.

Wiley also publishes its books in a variety of electronic formats. Some content that
appears in print may not be available in electronic books. For more information about
Wiley products, visit our web site at www.wiley.com.

Library of Congress Cataloging-in-Publication Data:

McManus, John C., date.
    Alamo in the Ardennes : the untold story of the American soldiers who
made the defense of Bastogne possible / John C. McManus.
        p.   cm.
    Includes index.
    ISBN 978-0-471-73905-0 (cloth : alk. paper)
    1. Ardennes, Battle of the, 1944–1945. 2. Bastogne (Belgium)—History,
Military—20th century. 3. United States. Army—History—World War,
1939–1945. I. Title.
    D756.5.A7M35 2007
    940.54′219348—dc22   2006019135

Printed in the United States of America

10 9 8 7 6 5 4 3 2 1

To Nancy, with all my love

CENTRAL ARKANSAS LIBRARY SYSTEM
SIDNEY S. McMATH BRANCH LIBRARY
LITTLE ROCK, ARKANSAS

CONTENTS

Illustrations begin on page 123.

PREFACE

Bastogne. The very name conjures up familiar images: deep snow; bitter cold; the 101st Airborne surrounded, fighting a desperate battle; Patton's armor breaking the siege. All of these images are seared into the memories of anyone who has ever heard or read about what took place at Bastogne, Belgium, in the winter of 1944–1945. The 101st Airborne Division's epic defense of the town during the Battle of the Bulge is well known, as is the 4th Armored Division's triumphal relief of the town on December 26, 1944.

All of this is only part of the story, however. None of these heroics ever would have happened if not for the self-sacrificing efforts of a ragtag, battered collection of American soldiers who absorbed the brunt of the German offensive along the Ardennes frontier east of Bastogne. Over the course of several days in December 1944, numerous outfits, including the 28th Infantry Division, Combat Command Reserve (CCR) of the 9th Armored Division, Combat Command B (CCB) of the 10th Armored Division, plus various other smaller units, including elements of the 101st Airborne, fought a bloody delaying action against powerful, numerically superior enemy forces. If these Americans had not detained the vanguard of the German offensive, the 101st Airborne Division in its entirety could not have made it to Bastogne before the Germans, thus denying them control of this crossroads town, and the Battle of the Bulge might have turned out much differently.

In making this statement, I do not mean to suggest that the successful defense of Bastogne won the Battle of the Bulge for the Allies. Far from it. Indeed, one could argue that the most vital fighting took place on the northern shoulder of the Bulge in such places as Elsenborn Ridge, St. Vith, Werbomont, and along the Meuse River approaches. The goal of the German offensive, after all, was to cross the Meuse and make a dash for Antwerp. They failed to do so because Allied soldiers on the northern shoulder kept them from crossing the Meuse. In a larger sense, hundreds of thousands of Allied soldiers and not any group in any one sector fighting within a large battle area over the course of six weeks, collectively won the battle.

That said, there is no question that capturing Bastogne was crucial for the Germans. They needed the town for its road net and for its communications. They needed it as a place to bring up supplies and reinforcements. They needed it because whoever controlled Bastogne controlled the Ardennes. So if they had taken the town by the second day of their offensive, as they originally planned, they would have achieved a crucial element for success. Obviously the German offensive was a major gamble. Its success depended almost entirely on speed. German armored formations needed to move quickly through the Ardennes, turn north, cross the Meuse, and get to Antwerp as quickly as their wheels or tracks could carry them. All of this had to be done before the Allies could counterattack with their numerically superior air and ground forces. For the Germans, Bastogne was the vital pivot point they needed to exit the Ardennes swiftly, but they failed to take it.

The Germans' failure to occupy this strategic location was the work of two distinct groups of American soldiers. History has largely focused on the group that endured the siege from the evening of December 20 through December 26. Most of these siege defenders were members of the 101st Airborne Division, and they fought with tenacity and resolve. But I would argue that the contributions of another group—those who fought east of Bastogne and in its outskirts from December 16 through December 20—were every bit as vital and noteworthy. Some of these men were from the 101st Airborne Division, but the vast majority were not. Most were members of the 28th Division, CCR of the 9th Armored or CCB of the 10th Armored. These soldiers fought a desperate delaying action. They were outnumbered and outgunned. In some cases the odds were ten-to-one against them. They absorbed the brunt of Hitler's last-ditch gamble in the West.

They fought in what I term the Bastogne corridor, the area roughly along the twenty-five-mile front that the 28th Infantry Division held when the battle began. This front stretched from Lutzkampen in the north all along the Luxembourg side of the Our River, through such towns as Heinerscheid, Marnach, and Hosingen, down to Bettendorf and Reisdorf. The most vital objectives were in the sectors held by the 110th and 112th Infantry Regiments. Any sustained and rapid breakthrough in those sectors would lead the Germans west on roads that inevitably led to Bastogne, some twenty miles to the west. Over the course of five furious days, the fighting that took place in this part of the Ardennes decided the race for Bastogne. Those five days are the primary focus of this book.

I contend that, in a way, the siege of Bastogne was anticlimactic. By that time, the German timetable was blown, American reinforcements were rushing to the Ardennes, and the Germans found themselves enmeshed in a bitter battle of attrition they could not win. In saying this, I am not minimizing the exploits of those Americans who held off the Germans during the siege of Bastogne. I am simply saying that Bastogne was much more valuable to the Germans on December 17 than on December 25.

Even as the Germans attempted to destroy the stubborn defenders of Bastogne during the siege, the bulk of their forces were west and north of the town, running into strengthening Allied armies before the Meuse. By that time Bastogne was little more than a prestige objective for the enemy. The garrison there was a defiant bone in the throat that now had to be eliminated out of sheer hatred, or perhaps outright embarrassment that it was still there at all. Conversely, if the Germans had captured Bastogne at any time between December 16 and 19, it would have been a vital pivot point, a kind of springboard toward their ultimate objective of splitting the Allied armies in two. For the Germans, then, their timetable was everything. In the Bastogne corridor, over the course of several violent days, several unlucky groups of American soldiers destroyed that delicate timetable. In so doing, they helped save Bastogne for the Allies. This is their story.

ACKNOWLEDGMENTS

My first word of thanks goes to the veterans of the 101st Airborne Division. In the summer of 2004, I served as a historian for a sixty-year anniversary European battlefield tour that began in Normandy and ended in Berchtesgaden. At Bastogne, I had the privilege of hearing several 101st Airborne veterans, including Bud Lubutka and Jack Agnew, speak of their experiences there. Time and again, the Screamin' Eagle veterans alluded to the vital battles that other units like the 28th Division had fought east of Bastogne, thus buying them enough time to get to the city. As a World War II historian, I had heard of these battles, but I did not know a great deal about them. My curiosity was piqued.

After I returned to the States, I was browsing through a bookstore one day when I happened to spot a copy of Bob Phillips's *To Save Bastogne*. This seminal book tells the history of one regiment of the 28th Division in the Bulge. I bought the book and devoured it. At that point, I was hooked on the story of the race for Bastogne. The siege, I realized, was well chronicled, but the race was not. *Alamo in the Ardennes* grew from my desire to tell the story of this race and perhaps broaden our understanding of the Battle of Bastogne.

I contacted Bob Phillips, and he could not have been more helpful. He shared much insight on his research, generously described his own experiences in the battle, and put me in touch with dozens of other veterans of the 110th Infantry. I don't think I can thank him enough.

There are many other people to thank. Stephen S. Power, my editor at Wiley, believed in this project from the start. He has the editor's gift of knowing how to make a manuscript better but without a heavy hand. He's also a fellow fantasy baseball geek whose only shortcoming that I can see is his affinity for the New York Yankees. His assistant, Naomi Rothwell, did an outstanding job on the numerous procedural and logistical issues that go into the writing of a book. My literary agent, Ted Chichak, recognized the great potential of this story, encouraged me to pursue it, and found a great home for it. As ever, I am grateful for his experience and wisdom.

At the University of Missouri–Rolla, where I am a professor of U.S. military history, many people provided daily support (some without even knowing it). The interlibrary loan staff was always helpful and efficient in acquiring the many books and articles I needed for my research. The university helped fund some of my research travels. A word of thanks goes to my colleagues in the Department of History and Political Science: Diana Ahmad, Tseggai Isaac, Michael Meagher, Shannon Fogg, Petra DeWitt, Pat Huber, Jeff Schramm, Wayne Bledsoe, Lawrence Christenson, Don Oster, Lance Williams, Harry Eisenman, and Robin Collier, the greatest secretary of all time. I would like to especially thank Larry Gragg, our department chair, for being a daily guide on what it means to be a professional and, at the same time, a good person. Russ Buhite has been my mentor for years, and I would like to thank him for his friendship and the many things he has taught me over the years. The same goes for Tom Fleming.

During my research travels, I was fortunate to receive help from a great many people. At the Center for the Study of War and Society in Knoxville, Tennessee—my old place of employment—Cynthia Tinker made the center's vast collection of firsthand accounts from World War II available to me. She also indulged my trips down memory lane. She has a passion for the American experience in World War II, and it shows in the excellent job she does. Down the hall from the center, Nick Wyman at the Special Collections library made sure that I got the most out of my visit there.

At the United States Army Military History Institute in Carlisle, Pennsylvania, Dr. Richard Sommers and his staff were as accommodating as could be. Their archive is basically the Holy Grail for historians of the modern army, especially now that the archive is housed in a new state-of-the-art facility. Just up the road at Fort Indiantown Gap, Charlie Oellig gave of his own time and expertise so that I could find everything I needed at the Pennsylvania National Guard Museum. Charlie dug around in the archives and prepared every relevant veteran's memoir for me. Thank you, Charlie. Elsewhere in the Keystone State, Joe Horvath of the Pennsylvania Military Museum found and made copies of several 28th Division letters for me.

At the National Archives in College Park, Maryland, Ken Schlesinger helped me navigate the archive's vast holdings. Frank Shirer at the U.S. Army Center of Military History took the time to point me on the trail of several productive leads. I would like to thank Daun Van E at the Manuscripts Division of the Library of Congress. He was prompt, professional, and knowledgeable in preparing me to research the extensive John Toland

Papers. Elsewhere at the Library of Congress, Sarah Bradley Leighton helped me get the most out of the burgeoning Veterans Oral History Project collection. Her courtesy and patience are much appreciated. Much thanks go to Joellen Bland at the George Marshall Foundation Library and Archives, Virginia Military Institute. She helped track down several useful memoirs within their growing collection.

There were so many people who sent me important material or helped me track down veterans that it is impossible to thank them all individually. But I would like to single a few out. Gus Hickok gave me much good background information on the 28th Division in the Bulge. Demetri "Dee" Paris did everything he could to fortify me with information on Combat Command Reserve (CCR) of the 9th Armored Division. Robert Peterson sent me excellent firsthand material from the 2nd Tank Battalion. Les Grover put me in touch with many of his buddies from the 52nd Armored Infantry Battalion. Without the help of these four gentlemen, this book probably would have been very thin on the story of CCR.

George Bunnell of the 109th Infantry Regiment Veteran's Association facilitated contact with many veterans of that unit. He also was kind enough to include my ad in the association newsletter. John Pollick sought me out and facilitated a fascinating interview with his father, Sid, who was a squad leader in the 109th. George Thieleman sent me an extensive list of Bulge veterans that produced many good interviews. Rufus Lewis gave me an illuminating after-action report and history of his unit, the 420th Armored Field Artillery Battalion, as well as an interview about his own experiences. John Andrew did the same for the 705th Tank Destroyer Battalion. He even loaned me his only copy of the unit's history, for which I am grateful. Neil Garson prepared a long list of fellow 10th Armored Division vets and helped me track down several men who were not on the list. He also gave of his time and memories in an interview.

Lou Dersch did everything he possibly could to provide me with good information on the experiences of the 687th Field Artillery Battalion in the Bulge. He gave me a contact list, assented to a couple of interviews, and sent me copies of several firsthand accounts from members of the unit. He even made me an honorary gunner corporal of the unit, something that makes me very proud.

I would like to thank John Westover, an eminent combat historian and World War II veteran. We are generations apart, but I like to think that we are kindred spirits. John loaned me a copy of his multivolume memoir chronicling his experiences as an army combat historian (among many other things, including his service as an artillery officer). He also graciously subjected himself to a long interview discussing his life and career, particularly the World War II combat interviews he conducted with S. L. A. Marshall at Bastogne. Because of the efforts of Westover, Marshall, and Joe Webber, the third member of their Bastogne team, we have a valuable contemporary record of the battle, seen through the eyes of the soldiers themselves. John himself conducted the combat interviews with Teams Desobry, Cherry, and O'Hara. He was nice enough to explain exactly how he went about his work. Needless to say, this added much to my understanding of the battle.

Rick Britton, a talented cartographer, created excellent maps that have strengthened the book immeasurably. Thank you, Rick.

Two other military historians were particularly helpful in the preparation of this work. Roger Cirillo of the Association of the United States Army is an incredible font of knowledge on the Bastogne corridor. He gave me much vital background information and consistently pointed me in the right direction. Chris Anderson, the editor of *World War II* magazine and a leading military historian, has given me over the years a better understanding of his beloved 101st Airborne Division's history. Plus, he's a good friend and a good guy.

There were friends across the sea as well. Frank Kieffer is the curator of the Battle of the Bulge Museum in the restored Clervaux castle. He befriended my wife, Nancy, and me, and gave us a guided tour of his museum's first-rate collection. Pierre Eicher is in a class by himself. He is the leading local authority on the Bastogne corridor and, more specifically, the 28th Division in Luxembourg. He lived through that time, so the history is personal to him. Pierre gave fully of his time and his considerable intellect, guiding us over the battlefield and telling stories. His home library is unparalleled, and he allowed me access to it. I thank Pierre and his lovely sister, Maria, for their kindness, friendship, and hospitality.

A very special word of thanks goes to Kevin Hymel, a good buddy and fellow military historian (yes, Kevin, you get your own paragraph!). During my visit to Washington, Kevin shared his home with me. Besides being one of the most upbeat people in existence, he was a constant source of insight, encouragement, and companionship. He embodies true friendship. He also knows the photo archives inside and out. Because of his efforts, this book is illustrated better than it ever would have been without him. Thank you, Kevin!

Other good friends also helped by just being themselves: Mark Williams, Sean Roarty, Joe Carcagno, Ron Kurtz, Bob Kaemmerlen, John Villier, Steve Kutheis, Mike Chopp, Dave Cohen, and Ed Laughlin, a distinguished veteran of the 82nd Airborne Division.

I would like to convey my deep appreciation to the Woody family, the greatest in-laws a guy could ever want. Ruth and Nelson have always treated me like their own son, and I am very grateful for that. They have brought much good to my world and many others. The same is true for Doug, Tonya, and the boys, David, Angee, and the girls, along with Nancy and Charlie. Thank you for everything.

My own family is a constant source of love and friendship. Fortune has certainly smiled upon me. I'd like to thank Mike, a financial wizard who shares my passion for history and sports, for being a great big brother. My sister, Nancy, and her husband, John, are not just family—they are the best of friends. My nephew, Michael, and my nieces, Kelly and Erin, add much joy to my life. My parents, Michael and Mary Jane, are, quite simply, the best parents of all time. I can't repay them. I can only honor them.

As always, the last word of appreciation goes to my amazing wife, Nancy. I have dedicated this book to her, and this is appropriate. This book is hers as much as mine (although I am responsible for any errors or omissions). She was there every step of the way, trawling around battlegrounds, ferreting out interesting stories, chasing the ghosts of the past, searching for good photographs. She truly understands my passion for my work. But I hope she knows that none of it means anything without her. She is the greatest. I am very lucky to be her husband.

STAFF POSITIONS IN THE U.S. ARMY

Division Level or Above

G1 = Personnel   G4 = Supply
G2 = Intelligence   G5 = Civil Affairs
G3 = Operations

Below Division Level

S1 = Personnel   S4 = Supply
S2 = Intelligence   S5 = Civil Affairs
S3 = Operations

TYPICAL UNIT STRUCTURE IN THE WORLD WAR II U.S. ARMY

These are approximations. Strength levels, attached units, and command structure often varied.

Squad—12 soldiers, commanded by a buck sergeant; three squads per platoon

Platoon—40 soldiers, commanded by a second lieutenant; four platoons per company

Company—190 soldiers, commanded by a first lieutenant or a captain; four companies per battalion

Battalion—900 soldiers, commanded by a major or a lieutenant colonel, three battalions per regiment

Regiment—3,500 soldiers, commanded by a colonel, three regiments per division

Division—14,000 soldiers, commanded by a major (two-star) general, two or more divisions per corps

Corps—Between 30,000 and 60,000 soldiers, commanded by a senior-level major general

Army—Between 60,000 and 120,000 soldiers, commanded by a lieutenant (three-star) general

Army Group—Between 250,000 and 600,000 soldiers, commanded by a four-star general

CAST OF CHARACTERS

Twelfth Army Group

General Omar Bradley, CO
Brigadier General Edwin Sibert, G2

First Army

Lieutenant General Courtney Hodges, CO
Colonel Benjamin "Monk" Dickson, G2

VIII Corps

Major General Troy Middleton, CO
Colonel Andrew Reeves, G2
Major Malcolm Wilkey, Assistant G2

28th Infantry Division

Major General Norman "Dutch" Cota, CO
Colonel Jesse Gibney, Chief of Staff
Lieutenant Colonel Thomas Hoban, Commandant
Sergeant Jerry DeMaria, Communications, Signal Company
Private George Mergenthaler, Machine Gunner, Mechanized
    Reconnaissance Troop
T/5 John Noon, Percussionist, Division Band
Sergeant Robert Milbier, Jeep Driver for General Cota

109th Infantry Regiment

Lieutenant Colonel James Earl Rudder, CO
PFC Amos Meyers, Rifleman
Private David Skelly, Machine Gunner, D Company
Lieutenant Bedford Davis, 2nd Battalion Surgeon
PFC Bill Alexander, Intelligence and Reconnaissance Section,
    2nd Battalion
Private Robert Jackson, Rifleman, F Company
Lieutenant William Pena, Executive Officer, I Company

110th Infantry Regiment

Colonel Hurley Fuller, CO
Colonel Ted Seely, Temporary CO
Lieutenant Colonel Daniel Strickler, Executive Officer and later CO
Captain John Aiken, Communications Officer
Captain Gerald Harwell, Adjutant
Captain Lloyd Mackey
Captain Edwin Rensmeyer, S2
Captain Rowland Koskamp, Chaplain
Chief Warrant Officer Ralph Johnson, S1 Section
Staff Sergeant Clarence Johnson, S1 Section
Staff Sergeant Bob Miller, S1 Section
Staff Sergeant Bob Kalish
Staff Sergeant Frank Kusnir, Intelligence and Reconnaissance
Corporal Carl Montgomery, Chaplain's Assistant
T/Sergeant James Pelletier, Machine Gunner, Headquarters Company
Private Harold Snedden
Private Harold Walter
Private Gabe Carson, Antitank Company
Sergeant Jacob Welc, Squad Leader, Antitank Company
Captain Irving Warden, CO, Cannon Company
Lieutenant Colonel Donald Paul, CO, 1st Battalion
Captain Jimmy Burns, S3, 1st Battalion
Captain Wesley Rose, S1, 1st Battalion
Captain Lawrence Woodley, Surgeon, 1st Battalion
Lieutenant Raymond Beaucar, 1st Battalion
Lieutenant Frank Richwine, Communications Officer, 1st Battalion
Captain LeVoe Rinehart, CO, A Company
PFC Walter Dayhuff, Rifleman, A Company
Corporal Cecil Hannaford, Assistant Squad Leader, A Company
Lieutenant Thomas "Kit" Carson, CO, B Company
T/Sergeant JJ Kuhn, Ranking NCO, B Company
Private Joe Norris, Rifleman, B Company
Sergeant Morris Pettit, Squad Leader, B Company
Private Leroy "Whitey" Schaller, Rifleman, B Company
T/Sergeant Stanley Showman, Platoon Sergeant, B Company
PFC Ed Uzemack, Runner, B Company
Lieutenant Jack Haisley, Platoon Leader, C Company
Lieutenant John Maher, Platoon Leader, C Company
Captain Andrew Carter, CO, D Company
Lieutenant Glen Vannatta, Executive Officer, D Company
Lieutenant Harry Mason, Platoon Leader, D Company

Lieutenant Colonel James Hughes, Executive Officer, 2nd Battalion
Lieutenant Kenneth Maddox, Headquarters Company, 2nd Battalion
Private Bob Pocklington, Headquarters Company, 2nd Battalion
Lieutenant Dana Speer, Platoon Leader, E Company
Sergeant Bob Bradicich, NCO, E Company
Private Bob Phillips, Medic, F Company
PFC Robert Probach, Rifleman, F Company
Corporal Frank Stepnick, Mortarman, F Company
Major Harold Milton, CO, 3rd Battalion
Captain Floyd McCutchan, CO, I Company
Lieutenant Edward Jenkins, Executive Officer, I Company
PFC Chester Kuzminski, Rifleman, I Company
Sergeant William Meller, Squad Leader, I Company
PFC Thomas Myers, Rifleman, I Company
Sergeant Fred Pruett, Machine Gun Squad Leader, I Company
Captain Frederick Feiker, CO, K Company
Lieutenant Thomas Flynn, Executive Officer, K Company
Lieutenant Bernie Porter, K Company
Sergeant James Arbella, Mortar Section Leader, K Company
PFC Edwin Cornell, Rifleman, K Company
Sergeant John Forsell, Squad Leader, K Company
PFC Edward Gasper, Rifleman, K Company
T/4 Robert Tucker, Medic, K Company
Lieutenant Bert Saymon, CO, L Company

112th Infantry Regiment

Colonel Gustin Nelson, CO
Captain William Cowan, S1 Section
Captain Paul Troup, CO, Headquarters Company
First Sergeant Wayne Kugler, Headquarters Company
First Sergeant George Mortimer, Cannon Company
Lieutenant Colonel William Allen, CO, 1st Battalion
Sergeant Lamoine "Frank" Olsen, Platoon Sergeant, A Company
Captain Stanley Dec, CO, B Company
Private Cliff Hackett, Rifleman, B Company
Private Alexander Hadden, Rifleman, B Company
Private Charles Haug, Runner, B Company
Lieutenant Charles Hogzett, Platoon Leader, B Company
Private George Knaphus, Rifleman, B Company
First Sergeant George McGeoch, B Company
Sergeant Peter Friscan, Squad Leader, C Company
PFC Linford Lilly, Rifleman, C Company

Lieutenant Colonel Joseph MacSalka, CO, 2nd Battalion
PFC John Allard, Rifleman, F Company
Captain Charles Crain, CO, H Company
Lieutenant Ralph Larson, Platoon Leader, K Company
PFC Buck Bloomer, Rifleman, K Company
Captain Guy Piercey, CO, M Company
PFC Clarence Blakeslee, Mortarman, M Company
Sergeant Murray Shapiro, Machine Gun Squad Leader, M Company

707th Tank Battalion

Lieutenant Colonel R. W. Ripple, CO
Major R. S. Garner, Executive Officer
Lieutenant Richard Payne, Platoon Leader, A Company
Private John Marshall, M4 Sherman Tank Crewman, B Company
Captain Herbert Ellison, CO, D Company
Lieutenant Thomas Byerly, Platoon Leader, D Company
Lieutenant Orville Nicholas, Platoon Leader, D Company

35th Engineer Combat Battalion

Private Bernard Michin, Bazookaman

44th Engineer Combat Battalion

Captain Thomas Johnson, CO, B Company

103rd Engineer Combat Battalion

Captain William Jarrett, CO, B Company
Corporal George Stevenson, Machine Gunner, B Company

103rd Medical Battalion

Sergeant Andrew Puchany, Medic, D Company
Sergeant Paul Luther, Medic, D Company
Sergeant Gene Fasig, Medic, D Company

107th Field Artillery Battalion

Private Frank LoVuolo

109th Field Artillery Battalion

Sergeant Charles Johnson, Forward Observer, B Battery

229th Field Artillery Battalion

Corporal William Kelley, Forward Observer, A Battery
Private Jack Chavez, B Battery

687th Field Artillery Battalion

Lieutenant Colonel Max Billingsley, CO
Lieutenant Les Eames, Survey Section, Headquarters Battery
T/Sergeant Gene Fleury, Radioman, Headquarters Battery
Corporal Clifford Iwig, Headquarters Battery
PFC Lou Dersch, Gunner, B Battery

Combat Command Reserve (CCR), 9th Armored Division

Colonel Joseph "Duke" Gilbreth, CO
Sergeant James Fink, Sherman Tank Commander, B Company,
    2nd Tank Battalion
Sergeant Wayne Wichert, Squad Leader, C Company, 55th Armored
    Engineer Battalion

Task Force Rose

Captain Lyle Rose, CO

Task Force Harper

Lieutenant Colonel Ralph Harper, CO

Task Force Booth

Lieutenant Colonel Robert Booth, CO
Major Eugene Watts, S3
Sergeant Herman "Ham" Kramer, Radioman
Corporal Elmer Oakes, Assistant Squad Leader
Corporal Ray Stoker, Truck Driver
PFC Carlton Willey, Intelligence and Reconnaissance

Combat Command B (CCB), 10th Armored Division

Colonel William Roberts, CO

Team Cherry

Lieutenant Colonel Henry Cherry, CO
Captain William Ryerson, Task Force CO

Lieutenant Edward Hyduke, Task Force CO

Lieutenant Carl Moot, 420th AFA Forward Observer attached
  to Team Cherry

Corporal Mike Heyman, Reconnaissance Section Leader

PFC Spurgeon Van Hoose, Radioman

Team O'Hara

Lieutenant Colonel Jim O'Hara, CO

Captain Ed Carrigo, S2

Captain John Devereaux, CO, B Company, 54th Armored Infantry
  Battalion

Lieutenant Ted Hamer, 420th AFA Forward Observer attached
  to Team O'Hara

T/Sergeant Tom Holmes, Platoon Leader, Intelligence and
  Reconnaissance

T/Sergeant John McCambridge, Communications

Private Ken Kauffman, Communications

Team Desobry

Major William Desobry, CO

Major Charles Hustead, Executive Officer

Captain Gordon Geiger, CO, Headquarters Company

Captain Omar "Bud" Billett, CO, B Company, 20th Armored Infantry
  Battalion

Captain William Schultz, CO, B Company, 3rd Tank Battalion

Lieutenant Pete Greene, 420th AFA Forward Observer attached
  to Team Desobry

Lieutenant Jack Prior, Surgeon

Captain I. Lee Naftulin, Dentist

Lieutenant George Rice, S4

Sergeant Larry Stein, Intelligence and Reconnaissance

Staff Sergeant Bill Kerby, Mortar Platoon Leader

Sergeant Leon Gantt, Squad Leader

Sergeant Major Jones, Squad Leader

Corporal Colby Ricker, M18 Hellcat Tank Destroyer Gunner

PFC Donald Addor, Radioman

Private Lou Cerutti, Rifleman

PFC Boyd Etters, Rifleman

PFC Jack Garrity, Rifleman

PFC Jerry Goolkasian, M4 Sherman Tank Loader

PFC Delmer Hildoer, M4 Sherman Tank Gunner

420th Armored Field Artillery Battalion

Staff Sergeant Rufus Lewis, Computer, Headquarters Battery

80th Medical Battalion

PFC Neil Garson, Medic, Clearing Platoon

101st Airborne Division

Brigadier General Anthony McAuliffe, Acting CO
Brigadier General Gerald Higgins, Executive Officer
Colonel Thomas Sherburne, Acting Artillery Commander
Lieutenant Colonel Harry Kinnard, G3
Corporal Arlo Butcher, Battery F, 81st Airborne Antiaircraft Battalion
Private Cleto Leone, Rifleman
PFC Don Dobbins
Captain Willis McKee, Physician, 326th Airborne Medical Company
PFC Elmer Lucas, Medic, 326th Airborne Medical Company
Private William Stone, Radioman, Forward Observer Team, 321st Glider
    Field Artillery Battalion

327th Glider Infantry Regiment

Colonel Joseph Harper, CO
Major R. B. Galbraieth, Battalion Executive Officer
PFC Charles Fisher, Headquarters Company, 2nd Battalion
Lieutenant Alfred Regenburg, Platoon Leader, G Company
PFC David Rich, Bazookaman, G Company
PFC John Sherman, Rifleman, G Company

501st Parachute Infantry Regiment

Lieutenant Colonel Julian Ewell, CO
Captain Francis Sampson, Chaplain
T/5 Leon Jedziniak, Medic
PFC Robert Wickham, Intelligence and Reconnaissance
PFC John Trowbridge, Machine Gunner, Headquarters Company
Major Ray Bottomly, CO, 1st Battalion
Captain Claude Wallace, CO, I Company
Lieutenant Leonard Witkin, Platoon Leader, I Company
Staff Sergeant Erminio Calderan, Platoon Sergeant, I Company
Staff Sergeant Robert Houston, Platoon Sergeant, I Company
Sergeant Buck Ketsdever, I Company
PFC Marvin Wolfe, Rifleman, I Company

PFC Frank Guzy, Radioman, I Company
Private Richard Hahlbohm, Rifleman, I Company
PFC William McMahon, Machine Gunner, I Company

506th Parachute Infantry Regiment

Colonel Bob Sink, CO
Lieutenant Colonel James LaPrade, CO, 1st Battalion
Major Robert Harwick, Executive Officer, 1st Battalion
Private Ewell Martin, Rifleman
Private James Simms, Assistant Bazookaman
Private Donald Burgett, Rifleman, A Company
Private Harold Phillips, Rifleman, A Company
PFC Steven Polander, Rifleman, A Company
Private Donald Straith, Rifleman, A Company
Lieutenant Joe Reed, Platoon Leader, C Company
PFC Robert Wiatt, Rifleman, C Company
Private Bob Dunning, Headquarters Company, 3rd Battalion

705th Tank Destroyer Battalion

Lieutenant Colonel Clifford Templeton, CO
Major Worth Curtiss, S3
T/5 Larry Tanber, M8 Armored Car Gunner

Civilians

Elise Dele, Bivels
Marguerite Lindenmeyer, Bivels
Jean Serve, Clervaux
Emil Frere, Mageret

Germans

General Hasso von Manteuffel, CO, 5th Panzer Army
Lieutenant General Fritz Bayerlein, CO, Panzer Lehr Division
Captain Heinz Novak, CO, Armored Reconnaissance, Abteilung 2,
    2nd Panzer Division
Lieutenant Rudolph Siebert, Platoon Leader, Abteilung 2

MAPS

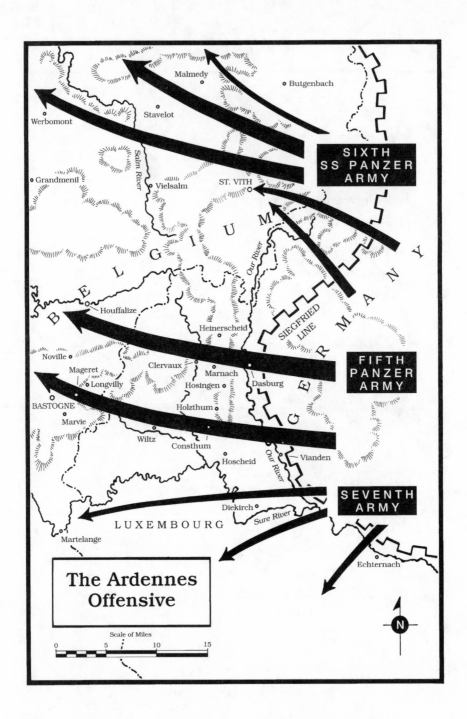

The Ardennes
Offensive

Scale of Miles

0   5   10   15

XXX

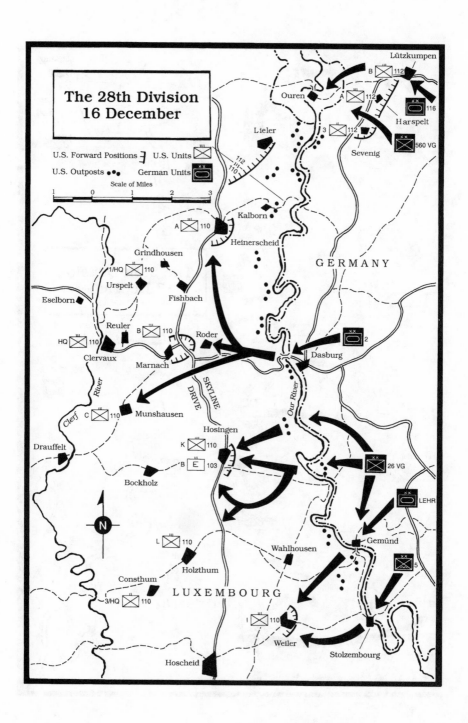

The 28th Division
16 December

U.S. Forward Positions ⊐ U.S. Units
U.S. Outposts •●• German Units
Scale of Miles
1   0   1   2   3

Lützkumpen
B ⊠ 112
Ouren
A ⊠ 112
⬜ 116
Harspelt
Lieler
3 ⊠ 112
Sevenig
560 VG

Kalborn
A ⊠ 110
Heinerscheid
GERMANY

Grindhousen
1/HQ ⊠ 110
Urspelt
Fishbach
Eselborn
Reuler
B ⊠ 110
Roder
HQ ⊠ 110
Dasburg
⬜ 2
Clervaux
Marnach
SKYLINE DRIVE
Our River
Clerf River
C ⊠ 110
Munshausen
Hosingen
K ⊠ 110
B E 103
26 VG
LEHR
Drauffelt
Bockholz
N
Gemünd
⬜ 5
L ⊠ 110
Wahlhousen
Holzthum
Consthum
LUXEMBOURG
3/HQ ⊠ 110
I ⊠ 110
Weiler
Stolzembourg
Hoscheid

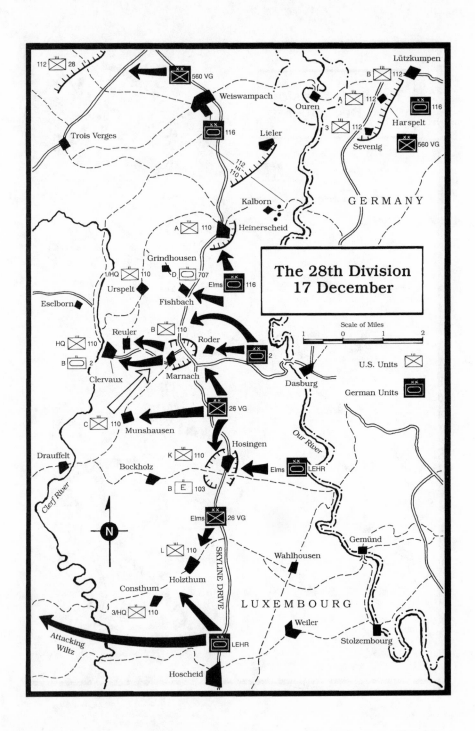

The 28th Division
17 December

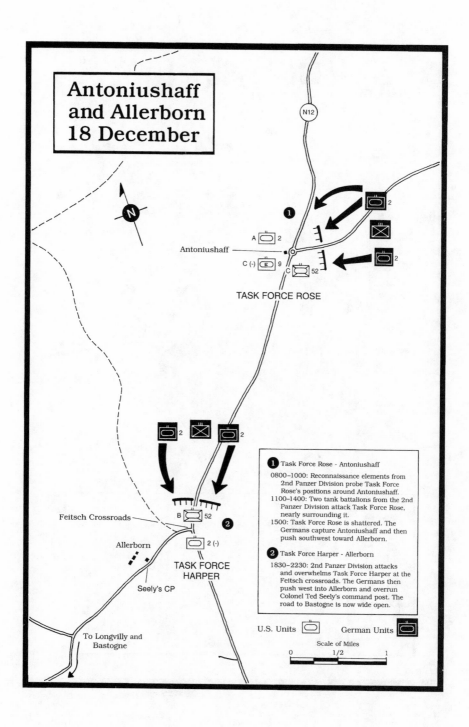

Antoniushaff and Allerborn 18 December

N12

Antoniushaff

A 2

C (-) 9   C 52

TASK FORCE ROSE

Feitsch Crossroads

B 52   2

2 (-)

Allerborn

TASK FORCE HARPER

Seely's CP

To Longvilly and Bastogne

1 Task Force Rose - Antoniushaff

0800–1000: Reconnaissance elements from 2nd Panzer Division probe Task Force Rose's positions around Antoniushaff.

1100–1400: Two tank battalions from the 2nd Panzer Division attack Task Force Rose, nearly surrounding it.

1500: Task Force Rose is shattered. The Germans capture Antoniushaff and then push southwest toward Allerborn.

2 Task Force Harper - Allerborn

1830–2230: 2nd Panzer Division attacks and overwhelms Task Force Harper at the Feitsch crossroads. The Germans then push west into Allerborn and overrun Colonel Ted Seely's command post. The road to Bastogne is now wide open.

U.S. Units   German Units

Scale of Miles

0   1/2   1

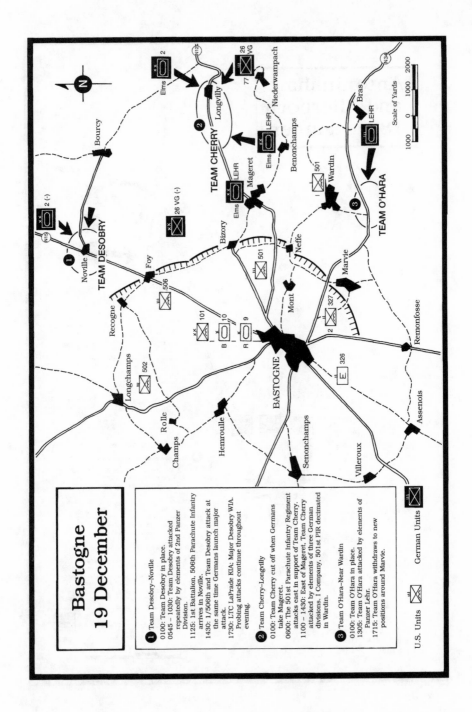

Bastogne 19 December

1 Team Desobry-Noville

0100: Team Desobry in place.
0545 – 1030: Team Desobry attacked repeatedly by elements of 2nd Panzer Division.
1125: 1st Battalion, 506th Parachute Infantry arrives in Noville.
1430: 1/506th and Team Desobry attack at the same time Germans launch major attack.
1730: LTC LaPrade KIA; Major Desobry WIA. Probing attacks continue throughout evening.

2 Team Cherry-Longvilly

0100: Team Cherry cut off when Germans take Mageret.
0600: The 501st Parachute Infantry Regiment attacks east in support of Team Cherry.
1100 – 1430: East of Mageret, Team Cherry attacked by elements of three German divisions. I Company, 501st PIR decimated in Wardin.

3 Team O'Hara–Near Wardin

0100: Team O'Hara in place.
1305: Team O'Hara attacked by elements of Panzer Lehr.
1715: Team O'Hara withdraws to new positions around Marvie.

U.S. Units   German Units

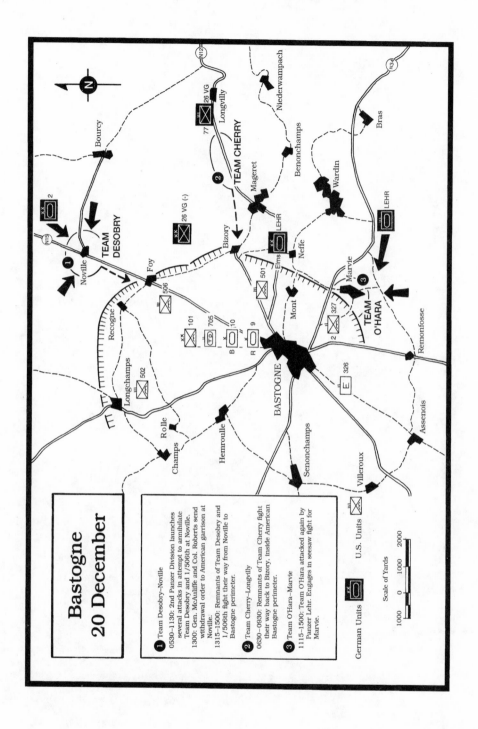

Bastogne 20 December

1 Team Desobry–Noville

0530–1130: 2nd Panzer Division launches several attacks in attempt to annihilate Team Desobry and 1/506th at Noville.

1300: Gen. McAuliffe and Col. Roberts send withdrawal order to American garrison at Noville.

1315–1500: Remnants of Team Desobry and 1/506th fight their way from Noville to Bastogne perimeter.

2 Team Cherry–Longvilly

0630–0930: Remnants of Team Cherry fight their way back to Bizory, inside American Bastogne perimeter.

3 Team O'Hara–Marvie

1115–1500: Team O'Hara attacked again by Panzer Lehr. Engages in seesaw fight for Marvie.

German Units

U.S. Units

Scale of Yards

1000 0 1000 2000

INTRODUCTION

Colonel Hurley Fuller was angry, scared, and exhausted. The past thirty-six hours had been the most horrendous and stressful of his life, and he had been through plenty of bad situations. Long ago, back in his native Texas, his parents had separated. Young Hurley had attended the University of Texas but never finished his degree, opting instead to join the army in 1916 at the age of twenty. Two years later, as a freshly minted lieutenant with the 9th Infantry Division, he endured the horrors of trench warfare in the Argonne Forest. The memories of what he had seen there never left him. The Argonne was a wasteland of shattered trees and shattered men, seemingly nothing there but gray-green corpses, their skin soaked to putrefaction by the steady, cold rains. Combat in the Argonne had been very disillusioning to a young officer like Hurley. Nonetheless, he stayed in the army during the interwar period.

His career was steady, if rather unspectacular. He had earned a reputation as being irascible but competent. The most common adjective used to describe him was cantankerous. He had no West Point pedigree, no brilliant war record, and absolutely no political skills. He had a tendency to talk back to superiors. He was not the type of officer to attract the attention of General George Marshall's notebook, the one he used to record the names of officers who impressed him. That book was too crowded with such names as Eisenhower, Bradley, Patton, and Collins to include someone like Fuller. In this second world war, Fuller had seen many of his peers receive general's stars while he was slotted for field-grade assignments.

His worst moment came in Normandy, when he was in command of the 23rd Infantry Regiment of the 2nd Infantry Division. In June, his regiment was in the middle of a maze of hedgerows, several miles north of

1

Saint-Lô, pushing for that town but getting nowhere. Fuller was not much of a tactical innovator. He was so enamored of the World War I–era bolt-action Springfield rifle, that he arranged for his entire regiment to be armed with them, thus ensuring that his riflemen would have little personal firepower.

As in 1918, Fuller witnessed the product of bloody stalemate there in the hedgerows. He was losing hundreds of men to gain half a mile. Day after day, the wounded streamed back, on foot or on litters, to the aid stations. It was all so hellish, so hopeless, such a nightmare. Actually, it was all so reminiscent of 1918, except for one thing: this time Fuller was in a position of senior command. He was responsible for more than just a platoon or a company. He was in command of three thousand soldiers, and they were all, seemingly, getting killed, getting wounded, or losing their minds to psychoneurosis. Try as he might, Fuller could not figure a way to break that stalemate in Normandy. Even in the best of times, Fuller was not much of a talker, nor was he very inspirational. He tended to retreat behind a gruff exterior and keep his men at a distance. This tendency only deepened during the horrible days in Normandy. He withdrew behind his hard shell, his ever-present pipe firmly in his mouth as he pored over maps, looking for a solution.

Then came the most painful memory of all. One day, at the division command post (CP), Fuller's two immediate superiors, General Walter Robertson, the division commander, and General Leonard "Gee" Gerow, the corps commander, fired him on the spot. It had been yet another unproductive, bloody day in the *bocage*. Fuller's battalions were in disarray. Everything was a mess, and he was not sure what to do about it.

At the division CP, General Gerow was mad as a hornet, and he decided to make an example of Fuller. He pounded on a map board and demanded an explanation from Fuller as to why his forces had scattered in the face of the enemy. Gerow stretched to his full height, well over six feet tall, and towered over Fuller, who stood no more than five feet, five inches. At that moment, Fuller froze. Try as he might, he did not know what to say. Gerow fired question after question at him. Even when the general shouted, "Goddamn it, Colonel, I'm talking to you! Now, you answer me!" Fuller could not bring himself to speak. With that, Gerow and Robertson relieved him. Stunned and bewildered, Fuller felt involuntary tears roll down his cheeks as a young captain led him away.

He spent the next few months in limbo, hanging around General Omar Bradley's headquarters, enduring the humiliation of his relief, hoping for another command. Finally, in November he got his break. His old friend Major General Troy Middleton, commander of VIII Corps, was looking out for him. The two had known each other since World War I. Colonel Ted Seely, commander of the 110th Infantry, 28th Infantry Division, was hospitalized for shrapnel wounds. Seely had led the 110th through Normandy, the Siegfried Line, and Hurtgen Forest. He was well liked in the regiment, but for the time being, he was in the hospital. The 28th Division was part of Middleton's VIII Corps. Middleton seized on the regimental opening created by Seely's infirmity and suggested to General Norman "Dutch" Cota, the division commander, that he appoint Fuller as commanding officer (CO) of the 110th. Cota could hardly refuse such a coercive suggestion from his boss.

Fuller took command on November 24, just three days before his fiftieth birthday. Even in this moment of vindication, satisfaction eluded Hurley. He found himself in a tough spot, replacing a popular commander who fully intended to return to the regiment. What's more, Fuller's new executive officer, Lieutenant Colonel Daniel Strickler, wanted his job. Strickler was a fine officer who had guided another of the division's regiments, the 109th, through the misery of Hurtgen Forest. As such, he had proven himself and felt he deserved to command the 110th. (In an ideal political environment, he probably would have been Cota's choice.)

Fuller knew he was an outsider in this National Guard division. He had not been with these men of the 110th in Normandy and the Hurtgen, so he had much to prove to them. Some of his soldiers even thought he came from a desk job in Washington. One rumor had it that he had been a POW in World War I. All of this was, of course, false, but Fuller could do little to debunk such canards. Never much of a communicator, he had trouble establishing a rapport with the troops of his new command. He made very little impression on most of them.

Nor did he have any opportunity to ease his way into combat with them. Throughout the first two weeks of December, Fuller had worried incessantly over the vulnerability of his regiment. At that time, the 110th was spread so thin along the Our River that it covered the distance ordinarily assigned to an entire division. He had no continuous front line. He could do little more than establish company-sized "strong points" in strategically located towns such as Heinerscheid, Marnach, Hosingen, Holzthum, and Weiler. The Germans were just across the Our River, in Germany itself, close enough to cause all sorts of problems, Fuller knew.

On December 13, he moved his regimental command post from Consthum, a few miles from the Our, to Clervaux, a delightful resort town located several miles northwest of Consthum and farther away from the front. This was a good decision. Clervaux was ten times the size of Consthum. Most of Clervaux was nestled into low, flat ground between two prominent, pine-covered ridges. The narrow streets were lined with dense rows of two- and three-story houses. Charming shops and boutiques honeycombed the town. The Claravallis Hotel anchored Clervaux's western exits. At the southeastern edge of town, a medieval monastery and a medieval castle, both built on prominent hills, towered above even the tallest pines. Clervaux was the perfect, centrally located place for Fuller's headquarters. But the town's picturesque beauty made little impression on the practical colonel. If the Germans ever came across the Our River in force, with a full-scale attack, Fuller knew his regiment would be in serious trouble.

At 0530 on December 16, that very thing happened. The Germans launched a powerful counteroffensive. Their tanks, troops, and artillery were everywhere. For a solid day and a half, they had been battering away at the 110th, slicing through the thinly held front, advancing west. In all that time, Colonel Fuller had been here, in his little office on the second floor of the Claravallis Hotel, trying to manage the battle. Communications were intermittent. Sometimes he had been able to talk with commanders by telephone or radio, sometimes not. Bad news had been steadily pouring in: the Germans had overrun Heinerscheid, they were past Marnach, they were roaring past the 3rd Battalion's strong points at Hosingen and Consthum. The eastern side of Clervaux was dominated by a ridge, over which lay the little town of Reuler. All day long, Fuller had heard the sounds of fighting from over there, even as he received spotty reports from the town's American defenders. Somewhere over that ridge, his soldiers were fighting and dying. Every minute the situation seemed to deteriorate further. Indeed, fighting had been going on all day in Clervaux itself, and Fuller knew that it would be only a matter of time until the Germans attacked his command post.

This made Normandy seem like a picnic. After all, the Americans had been the ones on the offensive in Normandy. The fighting there had been awful, but the Americans could call off their attacks at any time without much fear of a major German offensive. This situation in the Ardennes was different and much more perilous, Fuller knew. Since the prior morning, he had understood that his unit was at the epicenter of a massive and ambitious enemy offensive. It was a bit like being in the middle of a hurricane. The whole German army seemed to be attacking his lonely regiment. Time after time, he had tried to impress his superiors with the gravity of the situation, but they did not seem to understand. General Cota, from the division CP at Wiltz, ten miles to the southwest, had told him several times to "hold at all costs." Fuller had done his best to comply, but Cota had given him precious little help.

Now, at 1825 hours on Sunday, December 17, Colonel Fuller eyed the field telephone that rested on his little desk and contemplated his next move. His office reeked of the sickly sweet smell of pipe smoke. Outside in the hallway and in the lobby one floor below, all he heard was chaos. Wounded men were groaning and wailing. Medics were rushing about, doing anything they could to help the wounded. Staff officers and NCOs were hollering back and forth in a cacophony of confusing voices. One of his intelligence officers was deliberating as to whether he should burn the regimental codes and signals instructions.

The Claravallis Hotel, rectangular in shape but ornate in a charming, resort-town sort of way, now stank of mud, cordite, and fear. Fuller could hear small arms fire outside and a distant rumbling, too. He knew the source of the rumbling. Moments before, Lieutenant Colonel James Hughes, executive officer of the 2nd Battalion, had reported from Reuler and told Fuller that several German tanks had roared past his position on the way to Clervaux. The enemy tanks were on the way. After a day and a half of bitter fighting, Fuller had little left with which to stop them. In a matter of minutes, they would drive into town from the northwest and roll right up to the Claravallis.

The colonel knew that he and his headquarters group were in serious jeopardy. For thirty-six hours he had done his best to hold at all costs, as his orders stated, but now he knew he had to retreat or die. For several hours he had actually been pleading with division for permission to withdraw (many of his subordinates were doing the same with him), but to no avail. Now he knew for certain that if he did not withdraw, the 110th command group, and whatever else was left of this fine regiment, would face complete annihilation. If they got out of Clervaux right now, though, they just might be able to set up a new defensive line along the road to Bastogne.

Fuller picked up the phone and called the division CP in Wiltz. He got Colonel Jesse Gibney, Cota's chief of staff. Outside, Fuller heard the rumbling grow louder. The tanks were getting closer. He quickly described the desperate situation at Clervaux and asked for permission to withdraw to a new position on the Bastogne road.

Gibney cut Fuller off: "Your orders are positively to defend in place and give up no ground."

Never one to use much tact in dealing with superiors (or anyone else), Fuller was nearing a breaking point and replied, "Let me talk to General Cota about this."

"General Cota is at dinner and can't be reached by phone," Gibney responded.

The quick-tempered Fuller could feel anger welling inside him. For some time now, tension had been brewing between Gibney and him. He sensed that the chief of staff did not respect his assessment of the situation, and that Gibney had little understanding of the crisis they all faced.

The tanks outside were getting closer by the second. The ominous noise of their engines filled the hallways of the Claravallis. A staff officer popped into Fuller's office and reported that six German tanks were in the street, right outside.

Fuller's anger gave way to a mixture of sadness and fear as he resumed his conversation with Gibney: "Since you're transmitting the general's orders, I have no choice but obey them and fight in place." He could not resist adding a flourish, one that emanated from his Texas roots. "I should tell you that we're basically in the same predicament that Colonel Travis found himself in at the Alamo. We will never surrender or retreat."

No sooner had those words left Fuller's mouth when a volley of three German tank shells crashed into the S1 office on the first floor, right below him. The noise of the explosions was overwhelming. It felt as though the entire hotel would come crashing down. The enemy tanks were shooting point-blank, probably from a distance of only fifteen yards outside the hotel.

"What was that?" Gibney asked.

"German tanks," Fuller replied. He could not help but feel a bit of vindication. Yes, the situation was *this* bad. Why hadn't Gibney and Cota been able to understand that? Now it was too late. Fuller had no more time to talk. Gibney was saying something, but Fuller cut him off and hung up the phone. Somewhere downstairs German soldiers were yelling. Orders or not, Fuller knew he had to get his people out of there.

This really is like the Alamo, Fuller thought, but on a much larger scale and with many more lives at stake. Clearly the Germans now controlled Clervaux, but could anyone stop them from capturing Bastogne? Fuller did not know. Even as he scrambled into action at the Claravallis, thousands of other American soldiers all over the Bastogne corridor were dealing with the same furious German onslaught, fighting for their lives. Somewhere out there in the darkness, each and every one of them was experiencing his own Alamo in the Ardennes.[1]

1

BEFORE THE FURY

1

The Hurtgen Forest was a horrible nightmare, but it was over now. For some it was over because they were dead. But for the living, Hurtgen was now just a bitter memory, albeit one that would never really fade. In the middle of November 1944, the 28th Infantry Division left the Hurtgen Forest and convoyed south to the Ardennes.

In just two weeks in the Hurtgen, the division had suffered over six thousand casualties. Now platoons were the size of squads. Companies were the size of platoons. Battalions were the size of companies. The unit had been fighting since July in Normandy and it badly needed rest and replacements. Veterans needed time to rebuild their shattered nerves, put the misery of the forest behind them, and maybe enjoy life again. New arrivals needed a chance to ease into their new assignments, make friends, feel a part of something, and learn how to survive in combat.

The Ardennes, everyone thought, was the ideal place for this rest. The Ardennes was quiet. This was the ghost sector, a place where the war was taking a holiday. The soldiers of the 28th Division, nicknamed the Bloody Bucket for its distinctive divisional symbol, fanned out all over the Bastogne corridor in Luxembourg. They settled into towns, manned outposts, and did some training. More than anything, though, they rested. The Germans seemed to be doing the same.

Thanksgiving came on November 23 that year. For survivors and replacements alike, there was much to be thankful for—security, warmth, and some wonderful food. The cooks prepared turkey, gravy, potatoes, cranberry sauce, and everything else that goes with a traditional Thanksgiving dinner. There was more food than even these hungry men could eat.

One company in the 112th Infantry received "four hundred pounds of turkey complete with trimmings. That day we all could say we had something to be thankful for," a soldier recalled.

Some GIs even had Thanksgiving dinner with Luxembourgers. Sergeant Herman "Ham" Kramer ate dinner in Colmar-Berg at the home of a local tavern keeper: "He had squirreled away some wine from the Germans. He brought out that wine." With a flourish, the tavern keeper first poured a small bit of wine in his glass and then larger portions into the glasses of the Americans. Somebody asked him why he did that. "It's a local tradition," he replied. "If there's any impurity or cork, I will take that in my glass." Kramer and his friends were impressed: "The people there in Luxembourg were just great. They admired us and were so grateful to us."[1]

Indeed they were, and the admiration cut both ways. The Germans had swallowed up the tiny, beautiful country in May 1940. The ensuing occupation was difficult for the rebellious and independence-minded Luxembourgers. The Germans impressed private citizens into work as laborers and conscripted young men for their army. Anyone who opposed the Germans risked being hauled away to a concentration camp. On September 10, 1944, the Americans had liberated Luxembourg, ending four years of tyranny and restoring freedom to a people who yearned for it. September 10 is to most Luxembourgers what July 14 is to the French or July 4 to the Americans: a day of liberty and celebration.

So it was only natural that the 28th Division soldiers quickly established strong, enduring ties of friendship with the Luxembourgers of the Ardennes. In Clervaux, Sergeant Bob Bradicich, a squad leader in E Company, 110th Infantry, found several surrogate families: "We could get some food from the 'mess hall,' and I gave it to the civilian families and sometimes would eat with them at their house. This went on for a couple of weeks."

One night a young girl, in response to his kindness, gave him a card that had a soldier's prayer written on it. Bradicich was touched. He had lived through the Hurtgen Forest, and he knew that a soldier needed every bit of help he could get—temporal or spiritual—to survive. He tucked the card away and resolved to carry it with him everywhere.

Just down the street from Bradicich, medics like Sergeant Andrew Puchany had plenty of time to treat local patients because of the absence of combat casualties. Puchany and his buddies had a couple of favorite patients, including a "sweet girl of eighteen who had ulcers on her legs" and a "bearded lady friend." Sergeant Gene Fasig was a medic in D Company of the 103rd Medical Battalion, part of which was at Ettelbruck, far behind the frontline outposts. He and the twenty-one other medics, in the course of their duties, met and befriended plenty of locals: "The civilian population was very good to us, and we will never forget the friends we made there. We planned to show our appreciation by giving a party for as many of the local children as we could cram into our living quarters. Candy and foodstuffs were donated by every man who received a package from home . . . a program of entertainment was being whipped into shape. Already we had a Christmas tree up in our OR [operating room] trimmed with anything and everything that had color." As the citizens of Ettelbruck strolled by, many of them donated ornaments for the tree.

The scene was much the same to the north in Wiltz, a picturesque river town of some four thousand people where General Cota had set up his division headquarters. Sergeant Paul Luther and another small group of D Company, 103rd Battalion medics, set up their hospital in a school building in the middle of town. He and six other men slept on the upper floor of a nearby bakery: "We slept on the floor on our own blankets and even had access to a toilet. Across the street was a pub operated by a very nice family. They always had pastry snacks and drinks available and were friendly to everyone." As in Ettelbruck, the Americans were planning a nice Christmas party with a tree and plenty of goodies for the kids.[2]

Even frontline soldiers like Private David Skelly, a machine gunner in D Company, 109th Infantry, got the chance to experience the festive atmosphere. The line companies of his regiment rotated back and forth from the front, affording soldiers like Skelly the opportunity to rest in Diekirch, a small town located four miles east of Ettelbruck: "We were sent to . . . quarters in a hotel, where I immediately made friends with several civilians. We were constantly surrounded by children who always asked us for chewing gum and chocolate. To my astonishment, there was among them a ten-year-old girl who understood a little English and even spoke it. I became especially fond of her and often brought her something to eat."

Two miles north of Wiltz, at Eschweiler, the soldiers of the 28th Division Mechanized Reconnaissance Troop grew especially close to the people. One of the recon troopers, Private George Mergenthaler, forged such deep friendships that he made a permanent impression on the town's history. Mergenthaler was a child of privilege, heir to a printing fortune, and a graduate of Princeton University. He had chosen to serve in combat as a private soldier. Urbane, witty, and kind, he spoke both German and French. Quick with a smile or a joke, he made friends rapidly. "He was helping us always," Michel Huberty, a resident of Eschweiler, remembered. "He was cutting wood and carrying the hay to the cattle. He was a fine lad."

Perhaps his best friend in town was Father Antoine Bodson, the local priest. Mergenthaler was a Catholic kid. He and Father Bodson enjoyed conversing in both English and French. For a short time, Private Mergenthaler even lived in the rectory before moving to the home of a local family. Father Bodson enjoyed the companionship of this American: "He felt in my house like at home. He was treated like a brother and after a few days we were the best friends. Every night we sat together, listening to the broadcasting. Sometimes he dined . . . with me. Out of my library he got books . . . to read. Every morning he went with me to Holy Mass and Communion."

Mergenthaler and his buddies, like Private Cletus LaFond, often ate with the people of Eschweiler: "At mealtimes many times, the boys were invited to share the home cooking of their hosts, and reciprocated by bringing some of their GI food, chocolate and fruit juices to the kindly people." Private Mergenthaler spent much of his spare time helping the villagers with chores or dispensing care package items his wealthy family had sent him.[3]

Of course, most of the GIs were not as pure of heart as Mergenthaler. Plenty of them were on the make. In Wiltz, Clervaux, and several other places, American soldiers prowled the streets looking for willing women. There were dances and movies. Rest-center hotels in the larger towns teemed with GIs who were looking for a good time anywhere they could find it. There was also plenty of beer hall carousing. Sergeant Gene Fasig and several other medics drank most of their nights away with Ettelbruck women: "Our group took advantage of the recreation offered by this quiet Luxembourg town and almost immediately female connections were made and the beachheads of love were well established."

At Knaposcheid, a little burg half a mile north of Eschweiler, Private E. C. Wilson, a truck driver in the 630th Tank Destroyer Battalion, marveled at the skill with which his buddy Sam Christopher pursued women. The 630th had been in Europe since the previous summer, and everywhere women fell for Chris, as Wilson and the other soldiers called him. "I don't care where we went, what town, what nationality, the women took to him." Here at Knaposcheid they were billeted in the home of a farm family that had a teenage daughter. "She had already attracted Christopher. She was already making a play for him." The close proximity of the girl's parents kept the prospective lovers apart for the time being, but Wilson knew it was just a matter of time until Chris and the girl got together.

In frontline towns like Weiler, civilians had long since been evacuated to safer areas, but there were exceptions. Sometimes the Americans permitted local farmers to harvest their crops on quiet days. On one such day, Private First Class Thomas Myers of I Company, 110th Infantry, noticed two young women harvesting potatoes in a nearby field. He and an NCO buddy walked over to them and checked their passes to make sure they were authorized to be in the area. "At close hand, we could see that under the bandannas, the heavy woolen sweaters, skirts, and stockings were two quite attractive young women." Myers and his sergeant were pressed for time, so they checked the passes, made some small talk, found out that the two were sisters, and moved on.

But the sergeant did not forget what he had seen. A few days later, the women were back. The sergeant said to PFC Myers, "Let's go check some civilian passes." The two soldiers walked toward the potato field. "Watch my style," the sergeant said. "I'm going to talk one of those gals into 'going for a walk' with me." Myers knew exactly what "going for a walk" meant. He was happily married with a two-year-old daughter at home, and he had no intention of "going for a walk."

The sergeant was his buddy, though, and Myers was curious to see how this would turn out: "The . . . Luxembourgers accepted our gifts of chewing gum and 'D' bars while my friend turned his charm on the younger of the two sisters. The language barrier . . . was great, but I am sure that she understood by his gestures that he wanted her to go for a walk with him." She refused to go anywhere.

PFC Myers was amazed to see the older sister start walking away, beckoning for him to follow. Curious, he followed her over a hill to the end of the field. She unpacked a homemade bacon sandwich and handed it to him. They sat down and began to eat. Myers was not sure what else to do: "It then became obvious that all she wanted was to hear about America and my family."

They had trouble communicating but spent a pleasant half hour doing their best to understand each other. When they finished eating, they got up and went back over the hill. The sergeant was still trying to make time with the kid sister, but with no more luck than before. Admitting defeat, he gave up and went back to Weiler with Myers. All the way there, he fumed while an amused Myers tried to keep from laughing: "[He] began cursing about his bad luck and my good luck. I never told him what we did but let him assume what happened."[4]

Movie star Marlene Dietrich and her USO troupe were making the rounds of the Ardennes that December, entertaining the troops. The German-born but fully Americanized actress could not have been very popular with the Nazis, so it was fairly courageous of her to entertain soldiers that close to the front.

Lieutenant William Pena attended a dinner on the evening of Saturday, December 9, 1944, in which Dietrich was the guest of honor. He and his unit, I Company, 109th Infantry, were fresh off the front lines, resting now in Diekirch: "Our men were grouped in unoccupied homes and buildings, and the officers roomed at the hotels." Pena was staying in the Hotel des Ardennes right in the middle of town. A native of Houston,

Texas, he was the executive officer of the company. He had been fighting since September, and he was ready for some fun.

That night he and the other battalion officers gathered at a smaller
hotel just down the street for the dinner. Everyone wore dress uniforms
and polished boots. Several female nurses from a nearby medical unit also
attended. Lieutenant Pena sat at a table in the front of the room, right
next to Dietrich's head table: "[She] looked a bit older than I remembered her in the movies, and she seemed tired from traveling, but then
with us she was not onstage. Still, her glamour permeated the room."
Every table was draped with long tablecloths that nearly touched the
floor. Pena and his friends spent much of the dinner bemoaning the fact
that they "couldn't see her beautiful legs."

After the dinner, Pena and the other officers went back to their hotel
for a dance with the nurses, while Dietrich and her troupe went to a
nearby recreation hall to entertain the enlisted men. The evening was a
success. She planned to come back to Diekirch and perform for the officers in less than a week.

The next day, December 10, she was a few miles to the northwest visiting the 687th Field Artillery Battalion at the Hotel du Moulin near
Bourscheid. Like Pena the night before, Lieutenant Les Eames, a young
officer in the survey section of Headquarters Battery, was looking forward
to seeing the movie star's legs (and much of the rest of her). He too was
disappointed. Dietrich showed up for lunch in a loose-fitting paratrooper's
uniform. To make matters worse, she was "impatient as the devil . . . sat
down to eat w/o introductions or how-do-you-do, bitched, crabbed, took
off zzzzip! Saw her show later in the PM, not good, but not too bad."[5]

2

A few miles east of where Dietrich and her supporting cast were perform-
ing, the war was still going on. Quiet sector or not, the men at the front
were dealing with all the usual privations of combat: exposure to the elements, fatigue, and constant danger. General Norman "Dutch" Cota's
overwrought division was stretched along a thin line of outposts and
strong points that paralleled either side of the Our River. The division's
northern neighbor was initially the 2nd Infantry Division, but a few days
before the German offensive, the brand-new, raw 106th Infantry Division
replaced the 2nd. To the south, the 9th Armored Division bordered the
28th. The 28th had so much ground to defend that Cota was forced to
keep all three of his regiments on the line.

In the north, the 112th Infantry held the smallest sector but was actually in the midst of the Siegfried Line, east of the Our, in Germany itself.

From Lutzkampen in the north through Harspelt in the center, to Sevenig in the south, the regiment covered a reasonable distance of three and a half miles. "Since my sector was closest to the enemy lines, in some cases not over 140 yards, it was the shortest of the division front," Colonel Gustin Nelson, the CO, later explained. He was a bald, energetic, courageous West Pointer. His class of 1921, with only seventeen graduates, had been the smallest in the history of the academy.

He and his officers made sure that the troops dug in well, set up interlocking fields of fire, and protected their holes against the possibility of tree bursts. Nelson even devised several contingency plans in the event of a German attack. He placed his command post at Ouren, a little town that hugged the western banks of the Our. The 112th was the only 28th Division regiment with a continuous, fully defended front.

To the south, Hurley Fuller's 110th Infantry was covering more than thirteen miles of Ardennes territory. So overstretched was the 110th that Fuller could place his companies only in strong points astride the strategically situated towns of Heinerscheid, Marnach, Hosingen, Holzthum, and Weiler. A paved, ridge-lined road, dubbed the Skyline Drive by the Americans, stretched from north to south, connecting many of the strongpoint towns.

While the companies did have some support from an eclectic mix of tanks, tank destroyers, self-propelled artillery, and engineers, they could not hope to man an uninterrupted line. Small groups of soldiers would outpost the Our, a couple of miles to the east, during the day and return to their towns at night. Fuller's companies were constantly running contact patrols to stay in touch. One can scarcely imagine a more thinly held sector. The 110th was responsible for twice as much territory as any regiment could be expected to control, yet it had only two of its battalions at the front. Much to Fuller's chagrin, the other battalion was behind the lines, in division reserve, and he was miffed at Cota about that. "Very dangerous gaps in our lines existed," Fuller said. "This plan of defense, however, was what was ordered by . . . Norman D. Cota."

Farther to the south, the 109th Infantry was in a similar situation, patrolling more than ten miles of rolling country west of the Our. As with the 110th, there was no bona fide defensive line, only town- and crossroads-centered strong points in the vicinity of Walsdorf, Fouhren, Longsdorf, Hoesdorf, and Reisdorf. Here, too, soldiers often outposted the Our during the day and pulled back at night.

The division after-action report described the area quite succinctly: "The terrain along the entire division front is extremely hilly, much of it covered with pine forests. Observation is difficult because of the many wooded draws. The road net is fair." Actually the roads were everything in the Ardennes. The terrain was so hilly, so studded with woods and deep draws, that mechanized forces were often road-bound. The 110th and 112th Infantry Regiments held the most vital road routes of advance to Bastogne. This was the Bastogne corridor.[6]

For the combat soldiers of the 28th Division, life at the front in December was a series of routines. Private Charles Haug's B Company, 112th Infantry, was clustered in foxholes on a hillside overlooking Lutzkampen. The town was ghostly, its residents long gone. At any given time, the Germans or the Americans might be in the town, using the buildings for observation. Beyond Lutzkampen, Private Haug, a platoon runner, could just make out pillboxes and dragon's teeth on the Siegfried Line. The pillboxes were enormous concrete bunkers, bristling with machine guns or artillery pieces. They dotted the landscape seemingly in a haphazard fashion, but actually they were expertly set up to support one another. The dragon's teeth were foot-high lumps of concrete, laid out in tight, even rows, carpeting the countryside in hopes of impeding Allied tanks. Outside of a few shells flying back and forth, little was happening. "Our kitchen crew moved up . . . just behind our hill. We were fed two meals a day. One at about four o'clock in the morning and one about nine o'clock at night. We had to eat during the darkness because we couldn't take the chance of getting out of our holes and moving during the daylight."

Occasionally the men could get out of their holes and move around in the daytime. Lieutenant Charles Hogzett, a platoon leader, even allowed his soldiers to have a little fun: "We . . . let them go back down into the valley behind our defensive positions, where there was an open area about a hundred yards square, where they exercised by running and throwing a football around."

Private Alexander Hadden, a rifleman in B Company, was new to the world of combat. He was a bright nineteen-year-old who had once been enrolled in the Army Specialized Training Program, or ASTP. The program afforded young men who did well on aptitude tests the opportunity to go to college on the army's dime. Secretary of War Henry Stimson had designed the program in hopes of attracting intelligent youngsters to the army and ultimately protecting them from frontline combat. But the program did not survive the voracious needs of the war machine. By 1944 the army was in dire need of more combat troops, so the ASTP was disbanded. Hadden and thousands of others like him ended up in frontline infantry units.

Day by day, he adjusted to life on the front line: "Activity centered around standing guard at whichever of the company positions we happened to be occupying at the time. While there were a few sunny days—much relished of course—the skies hung low and were mostly gray, with rain or snow from time to time. Endless time was devoted to keeping warm, fed, and dry, though very little could be done about keeping clean." Hadden and his buddies rotated "two hours in [a] covered foxhole sleeping and trying to keep warm, and two hours maintaining vigil towards the east and being cold. It was a mind-numbing routine of course." Sometimes at night a flare or a star shell would burst over the lines, illuminating the whole area for a few spooky minutes. Then things would get quiet again.

In no time, Private Hadden came down with a nasty diarrhea problem, a common malady for frontline troops. "Thus began a months-long intimacy with diarrhea, and its close and malevolent cousin, dysentery. I don't think I ever shook them altogether." When the urge came, Hadden crawled, crab-walked, or ran to a nearby slit trench that served as a latrine, and did his business.

By and large, the front was very quiet. Sergeant Murray Shapiro, a machine gunner, was holed up in a position near Sevenig, a mile south of Lutzkampen. He received "rations of beer or coke . . . tobacco . . . reading material consisting of daily issues of *Stars and Stripes* . . . *Yank*, and all kinds of paperback books . . . as well as occasional handouts of razors, pens etc." They also got plenty of mail from home, including Christmas care packages.[7]

At times, neither side seemed very interested in maintaining hostilities. Bedford Davis, the surgeon for 2nd Battalion, 109th Infantry, was visiting the front with General Cota one sunny day when he observed a humorous, and revealing, conversation between the general and a soldier: "Some of the men were lying on the ground outside their foxholes and slit trenches to absorb the welcome sunshine. German soldiers about two hundred yards away were doing the same."

As Dr. Davis watched, the general began talking to one of the sunbathing men: "Son, do you see that man over there wearing a gray uniform?"

"Yes sir," the soldier replied.

"Don't you know he is your enemy?"

"Yes sir."

"Why don't you shoot at him then?"

"Sir, he might shoot back!"

Everybody laughed, including General Cota. He wanted his troops to be aggressive, but he knew, in this quiet sector, the man was right. Why shoot at someone if he was not shooting at you?

Occasionally German patrols would slip across the Our River, look around for a bit, and quickly go back. Rarely was there much shooting. Troops from the 109th were amazed and amused to see what went on in some of the Siegfried Line fortifications across the Our. "Pillbox defense appeared to have its romantic moments," one regimental officer wrote, "as female figures could occasionally be seen in the dusk entering the 'boxes,' and then leaving at dawn to return to the small villages in the rear."

Several miles to the north, Private First Class Robert Probach witnessed the same kind of permissive environment. He had been wounded two and a half months before, and he was just now returning to his unit, F Company of the 110th Infantry: "We would drive about three miles to the high banks overlooking the Our River. We would wave to the Germans on the other side. Sometimes we would shout good morning and they would respond the same way." At times, just to satisfy their superiors, the two sides would squeeze off a few playful, unaimed shots at one another. Naturally, no one ever got hurt.[8]

Of course, there was still plenty of danger, especially for those who participated in the ongoing routine of patrolling. Throughout the first couple of weeks of December, soldiers of the frontline companies spent much of their time on patrols, usually at night. Commanders constantly needed fresh information on the enemy's whereabouts, his intentions, and his strength. Sometimes, since the American front was so thinly held, the brass simply wanted to maintain contact with friendly units on their flanks. Only patrols could gather this kind of information. "All we did was cut telephone lines, throw grenades, terrorize the German troops, then wade the river and return before we were discovered," a rifleman explained.

But most patrols were more involved than that. Small groups of frightened men had to find their way through the frigid darkness, in places where the enemy might be, and still complete their missions. The whole thing took nerves of steel, patience, and more than anything else, awareness of one's surroundings. The numerous new replacements in the 28th Division learned quickly or they did not live.

One of those replacements, Private Hadden, participated in several squad-sized forays into eerie Lutzkampen. "We would assemble in the CP . . . to plan the excursion. Someone—usually with a little experience—would be designated a 'point man,' and he would lead the group into the town, with the next men slinking into the village at intervals of five to ten yards on alternating sides of the street. A couple of others would be outriders, walking parallel in adjacent fields. We would try to be sure that only one man would move at a time so that the others could cover him in case of trouble. My heart would be in my throat the entire time. A barn door would creak in the wind and bang shut, and [my heart] would leap into my mouth." Sometimes they rummaged through the houses in search of food, souvenirs, and maybe some intelligence on the Germans. "Nothing of any real value was ever found."

The Germans were often out there, though, conducting patrols of their own. One night PFC Probach was with a ten-man patrol. As an experienced man, he was unnerved that the patrol included a new guy who was generally considered to be slow and unfit for frontline duty. The rookie was of Native American descent, and everyone simply called him the Indian.

The little group set out into the December pitch darkness. "The Indian had been placed at the front of the patrol to keep him from falling behind," Probach said. The men were spread out, making it difficult to talk to or see anyone else. Probach was near the rear of the patrol. After a short advance, the patrol stopped. Everyone took cover and waited by the side of the road. Probach had no idea why they were doing this. Several minutes passed until someone whispered an explanation to him. "The Indian insisted a German patrol . . . was near." Neither Probach nor anyone else had heard anything, so they were quite skeptical, especially in light of the new man's low status within the unit. "Reluctantly, we flattened ourselves on the ground and waited quietly. In less than ten minutes a German patrol passed by." The Americans waited, watched, and then went back to their company positions. The new man had won the respect of Probach and the other soldiers. "[He] had an uncanny sense of sight and sound at night." From then on, he was inevitably known as Chief and was always in great demand for night patrols.

The job of most patrols was to avoid contact with the enemy, gather information, and come back. But at times in December, American commanders ordered raids to destroy Siegfried Line pillboxes. Some of Cota's division was training for pillbox busting in anticipation of going on the attack sometime after Christmas. Thus the raids provided a dangerous sort of on-the-job training.

One crisp winter morning, three platoons from F Company, 112th Infantry, drew such a mission. Under cover of an artillery barrage, the platoon worked their way close enough to shoot at the targeted pillbox. "The BAR [Browning automatic rifle] men delivered a steady stream of bullets into the embrasure, forcing them to button up," one soldier recalled. "Sergeant Wendt, then a private, sneaked up in the back of the pillbox and caught some of the Germans in the doorway. With accurate BAR fire, he forced them to scatter and leave the door open. Then the engineers placed 600 pounds of TNT inside the opening and blew it to pieces." One man was killed and two more wounded in the process of destroying this pillbox. General Cota personally commended the survivors.[9]

Perhaps the most terrifying frontline chore that December was duty on an outpost or observation post (OP)—both terms were widely used— out there beyond the lines, in no-man's-land. The job of a soldier on OP was to watch, listen, and report. OP duty was a leap of faith. A man's entire survival depended on the hope (and expectation) that the enemy would never attack in strength. If they did, he was finished.

Depending on the terrain and tactical situation, the OP could be a foxhole dug into a prominent ridge, a house at the edge of a town or even, in the case of Private First Class Bill Alexander, a medieval castle. Alexander was a member of the Intelligence and Reconnaissance (I and R) section, 2nd Battalion, 109th Infantry. He spent days at a time in a castle that loomed over Vianden, a pretty medieval town nestled against the west bank of the Our River: "From the castle, we could look across the Our River on the side of the hill where there is a sanatorium, which turned out to be the Germans' observation post. They were watching us and we were watching them watching us. Usually there were two men in the castle for twenty-four hours and then they were relieved the following day." Most OP soldiers had phones or radios, but not Alexander. He had to communicate through a small detachment that was staying in Hotel Heintz in Vianden.

Artillery forward observers were constantly on OP duty. Sergeant Charles Johnson was part of a four-man observation team from B Battery, 109th Field Artillery. His unit was based in Reuler, supporting the 110th Infantry. Each day he and the three other soldiers on the team piled into a jeep and drove a mile north to Fischbach, a town that neither side really controlled. "It was unoccupied by soldiers or civilians." Johnson's team would get to the town and "search it carefully for enemy presence, and settle down to observing whatever enemy activity was going on." Johnson was certain that the Germans came into town at nightfall. One of the houses had a cellar containing a pile of potatoes. Johnson swore that the pile shrank each day. Sure enough, one morning they saw German soldiers "leaving one side of town as we came in on the other side. They were in small-arms range but we didn't fire on them because we wanted to protect our own mission."

North of where Sergeant Johnson was, the 3rd Battalion, 112th Infantry, maintained its OP in a two-story house at Sevenig, a tiny farm village adjacent to the Siegfried Line. Anyone wanting to go in there had to do so at night, for obvious reasons. Even in the dark, it was not hard for the Americans to find their way to the building because the path to it was littered with mattresses and chairs that had been pilfered by soldiers going back to their foxholes.

Lieutenant Ralph Larson's 2nd Platoon, K Company, moved into the OP after dark on December 10. Larson was a Minnesota native and thus accustomed to the kind of cold that was settling into the Ardennes, but it was nice to get some shelter for a change. "We had not had such comforts since our arrival from the States. We stayed in a German house—living quarters were upstairs and the barn below. We could sleep in regular beds when not on duty."

Lieutenant Larson spent much of his time in the attic, with a pair of binoculars, looking east out of a window. "We had an exceptional vantage point. Also we had direct telephone contact with the company CP." At times he could see a lone German soldier leave his pillbox for some fresh air, but other than that, not much seemed to be happening.

Private First Class Clarence Blakeslee was often in the attic, too. The thirty-year-old Michigan native was a mortar forward observer from M Company. Before coming up to the OP, he had just received a big batch of letters from his wife and family: "It was my first mail since leaving home in July." He read his letters by the light of a "wine bottle with gasoline with a sock for a wick." In the attic he found a good spot to do his job. "We observed through a ventilator in the roof. The enemy snipers knew we were using it and fired at it so often it was literally pulverized with bullets. We did not put our faces in the opening but stood on a box, back where they couldn't see us." Blakeslee heard that a few days earlier, an artillery captain had had his helmet shot off by a sniper. The captain did not have a scratch on him.

Blakeslee and Larson were lucky in that they could stay in the house all day and night. By contrast, each rifleman had to take his turn outside on listening-post duty. Every night Lieutenant Larson picked three of his men for this dangerous task. The job of a soldier on listening post was to leave the house, crawl a couple hundred yards closer to enemy lines, lie there, remain absolutely quiet, and just listen. If the enemy was coming, the man on listening post was supposed to warn his comrades in the house. Chances were good that he would die in the next instant. Listening-post duty usually lasted two or three hours. The fact that there was snow on the ground for much of December only added to the misery of being on listening post.

Private First Class Vernon "Buck" Bloomer, a twenty-one-year-old midwesterner from Rantoul, Kansas, never looked forward to leaving the comparative security of the house to lie in the snow for hours. "You'd just lay there quiet on the bare ground. It was pretty cold and miserable. If anybody even coughed, they couldn't go out on a listening post." As he lay there, he often heard the enemy somewhere out there in the winter night. "You could hear them having conversations. We were that close." Most likely, the Germans were not more than two or three hundred feet away.

Inevitably with antagonists this close together, somebody would get hurt from time to time. For several days, B Company of the 112th outposted Lutzkampen and saw nothing, but the Germans apparently were still interested in the town. One of Private Haug's best buddies, Private Bud Kunz, got lulled into a false sense of security. He went into the town during daylight hours looking for souvenirs. "He was walking all by himself close to the edge of town. He ran smack into three Krauts . . . walking directly into our little town. He became terrified. He made no effort to shoot, but instead turned on his heel and ran as fast as he could for the basement where we had our dugout." The enemy soldiers opened up on him with their burp guns. "Bud dropped to the street right before our eyes. They . . . hit him about ten times in the neck and back, and a big pool of blood soon gathered around his body. He must have been dead before he hit the ground."

Haug and the other Americans opened fire on the Germans. "Two of them dropped to the street." One was killed, one was wounded with a broken leg, and the other one got away. The B Company soldiers captured the wounded German, gave him care, and interrogated him, but he would not say what he was doing there. They sent him to the rear in a jeep. Haug and another soldier drew the undesirable mission of retrieving Kunz's body. "[He] was still laying on the muddy street where he had fallen. I'll always remember the expression on his face. His head was laying in the mud, and there was a big pool of bloody water all around his body. His mouth and eyes were wide open and his face had the pale color of a wax dummy." As the two men carried their dead comrade, Haug tripped and the body fell right on top of him. His pants were covered with blood for the next two months.[10]

3

On the surface, the front seemed quiet enough, but for the combat soldiers who were there day and night, living near the enemy, watching his every move, something was strange. Gradually, as December unfolded, many of the frontline soldiers began to sense that the Germans were up to something. It was an ominous feeling, disquieting, troubling, slippery but distinct. There was a new and very serious danger brewing out there, and the perceptive 28th Division soldiers were sensing it.

The Germans, after all, were moving more than a quarter of a million soldiers and thousands of vehicles into position. It was hard to conceal that kind of movement for long. At Roder, a tiny village half a mile east of Marnach (itself a town of no more than three dozen buildings), Private Joe Norris and several of his buddies from B Company, 110th Infantry, were on patrol one day when they distinctly heard the sound of multiple vehicles from the direction of the German lines: "We heard this massive noise just like trucks in a depot that were getting ready to leave. You could hear the squeak of tank treads." On one foray near the Our, Private First Class Probach and his squad mates heard "the Germans moving heavy equipment and tanks up near the opposite bank of the river." Just east of

Fouhren, Private First Class Amos Meyers was on OP duty overlooking the Our one night when a wall of sound engulfed the German side: "Throughout the night we heard engines running and noisy equipment moving about, but all was hidden behind the hills." At Hosingen, Sergeant John Forsell and many other soldiers from K Company, 110th Infantry, heard "plenty of movement of vehicles and heavy equipment." Another K Company soldier, Private First Class Edwin Cornell, even saw the enemy preparing to cross the Our: "On patrol . . . we observed the enemy building a bridge across the Our River that separated the two sides."[11]

Some of the combat patrols were returning with POWs who had interesting stories to tell. At Lutzkampen, a few nights before the German offensive, Lieutenant Hogzett's platoon captured several enemy soldiers. He took them back to the platoon CP, and Hogzett watched while his CO, Captain Stanley Dec, interrogated them: "They were obviously frightened and were extremely courteous and most anxious to cooperate. They stated that they had been on the Russian front for the past year and that they had been brought into the Siegfried Line approximately one month ago." They willingly told the Americans the name of their commander and, more important, that an offensive was in the offing. They themselves had seen "considerable movement of troops into the line in anticipation of an offensive thrust on the part of the Germans."

To the south, at Hosingen, Private First Class Edward Gasper, a K Company, 110th Infantry, rifleman, was sitting in a foxhole with his buddy, looking to the east when they saw movement: "Here comes this German soldier coming in. He was deserting from his outfit. We sat him down on a piece of ground, a stump or something, gave him a cigarette. He could talk good English. He said he was a schoolteacher. He was about twenty-five, thirty, years old. He had had enough. He said he was gonna get the hell out of it. He said there was gonna be a big push before Christmas. We sent him down to the company commander there [Captain Frederick Feiker]. I never saw him again. I hope to hell he got out."[12]

A few Luxembourgers even saw the German buildup firsthand, crossed the lines, and attempted to warn the Americans. Marguerite Lindenmeyer, her brother, and two other people were in their hometown of Bivels, outside of Vianden, when a German patrol picked them up one night. "Bivels is no-man's-land," the Germans said. "No civilians are allowed to stay here anymore." The Germans took them to their side of the river. For several days they interrogated them, politely but intensely. They wanted to know how many Americans were in Vianden and what kinds of weapons they had.

Eventually, after extracting as much information as possible, the German soldiers lost interest in them. The German-speaking Lindenmeyer managed to slip away and wander around in the Bitburg area for several days, meeting and talking to a growing herd of German soldiers. She saw "a great assemblage of guns, plus towing tractors and tanks, in camouflaged positions along the streets. Something was going on—lots of German military everywhere in the streets, but not on the main roads. There were machine guns, tanks, trucks, cannons. You can't name it all, but lots and lots of equipment." And plenty of fresh German soldiers. One of them, "a fanatic young soldier," told her, "By Christmas we'll be in Paris again."

Lindenmeyer was not under any scrutiny by the German soldiers, as they considered her one of their own. She left the town, forded the Our, and made contact with two Vianden resistance fighters. They put her in touch with the police, who in turn sent her to the Americans. Someone in the 109th Infantry interrogated her at Diekirch, but in her words, "Despite my honest eyewitness reports of troops and tanks gathered near the border, the Americans seemed very skeptical."

Another Bivels woman had a similar experience, although the Americans did take her more seriously. A little more than a week before the German offensive, Elise Dele, a plain-faced, forty-one-year-old woman, risked an expedition into Bivels with her teenage son. The weather was getting colder, and they had left their warm clothes at home several weeks before, when they had been evacuated. As they approached their house, German soldiers appeared. Dele and her son tried to run away. The boy escaped, but not Elise. The Germans took her across the river and questioned her as they had Lindenmeyer. Like Lindenmeyer, Dele had only so much information, and limited supervision by the Germans. She slipped away and tried to get back across the Our. Along the way, she saw the massive German buildup. There were troops, tanks, trucks, guns, pontoon bridging equipment, and boats. During her odyssey, she dodged mines, evaded German patrols, made her way through barbed wire, and on December 14, crossed the Our by boat.

In Vianden, she told two resistance fighters what she had seen. Immediately they took her to the 109th Infantry Intelligence and Reconnaissance (I and R) soldiers at the Hotel Heintz. They gave her coffee and food. She told them what she had seen. These frontline soldiers were highly impressed. When she finished, she wanted to go find her son, but the soldiers, knowing the importance of what Dele had told them, would not allow that.

Instead, they put her in a jeep bound for Diekirch. In Diekirch, the regimental S2 officer interrogated her. He, too, was impressed, so much so that he sent her to division headquarters at Wiltz. From there, her story went up the chain of command to VIII Corps and then to First Army, whose G2 section added the comment that "large numbers of engineers with bridging equipment suggests preparation for offensive rather than defensive operations." In response to these reports, a few more patrols went out, but that was about it. Dele remained in Wiltz, still separated from her son.[13]

Among those who headed up American units in the Ardennes, there was a sort of bureaucratic inertia mixed with pervasive skepticism at such ominous intelligence reports. The prevailing mood was that the Germans were close to defeat and incapable of a major attack. It seemed that the farther up the chain of command, the less concern, or perhaps more accurately, the less action, there was in response to the evidence of a serious German offensive. The frontline troops were seeing the signs of an impending enemy attack right before their very eyes and ears. To them the coming assault was no secret; it was a matter of when, not if, it would happen. They passed this information up to their superiors, who in turn did the same. It was a sort of collective buck-passing: privates and sergeants expected their captains to do something, captains expected their colonels to do something; and colonels expected the same from their generals.

Nowhere was this more evident than in the 110th Infantry, the unit that would soon find itself squarely beneath the coming avalanche. At Marnach, Sergeant JJ Kuhn was convinced by December 12 that the Germans were coming. Kuhn was from Milwaukee, Wisconsin. He had been in B Company of the 110th Infantry for several years now. The thirty-year-old senior NCO had taken a hunk of shrapnel in the hip a couple of months earlier and was just now returning to the outfit.

He and the other B Company men had been told that this was a quiet sector, but they didn't buy that: "[We] did not accept the idea the German Army was just going to sit still for the winter." He worked closely with the company commander, Lieutenant Thomas "Kit" Carson, to set up good defensible positions. On the evening of December 12, Sergeant Kuhn and several other men sat in a farmhouse east of Marnach, watching German vehicle traffic move toward the Our River. This traffic, combined with numerous other sightings of large numbers of enemy troops moving for the river, could only mean that an attack was imminent. "We were sure the Germans weren't bringing all that machinery up just to sit for the winter." Kuhn got on the phone and reported what he had seen to his battalion commander, Lieutenant Colonel Donald Paul. Paul told him to call Colonel Fuller, in Clervaux. Sergeant Kuhn did so and "talked to Colonel Fuller, who told me he needed positive evidence."

Kuhn was a bit perturbed. He sensed that Fuller did not believe him. Plus, he did not like the colonel. A few days before, Fuller had chewed him out for not saluting him, in a combat zone no less. Kuhn wondered what it would take to stir this damned colonel into action. If Fuller needed positive evidence, then Kuhn was only too happy to provide it.

Before sunrise the next day, Sergeant Kuhn and another soldier went down to the river's edge. There were no Germans around, but there was irrefutable evidence that they had been there: "We found two turds and some German toilet paper. They used old paper cut into sheets about eight inches square. We picked up the two pieces of excrement and soiled paper and took it back to battalion."

They showed their messy evidence to Lieutenant Colonel Paul and Captain Wesley Rose, the battalion S1. Paul confirmed Kuhn's suspicion that Fuller did not believe his reports from the night before. Captain Rose, a good-humored officer who resembled the actor Cesar Romero, was no fan of Colonel Fuller. With a wry smirk, Rose typed up Kuhn's report and put it and the feces in a manila envelope and marked it "Exhibit 1."

Sergeant Kuhn took the envelope to Lieutenant Carson, his CO, and asked permission to take it to Fuller. "Hey, Kuhn, you're on your own," Carson replied.

The sergeant hitched a ride back to regimental headquarters at the Claravallis in Clervaux. "They let me in, but a major . . . told me I couldn't see the colonel. He took the manila envelope with my report and my 'evidence' into another room. I sat in the lobby and put my helmet on the bench beside me."

Kuhn sat for several minutes waiting. Finally he heard Fuller bellow, "Who's the son of a bitch that sent me this shit?!"

With anger surging within him, and fully prepared for a confrontation, Kuhn stood and started for the sound of Fuller's voice, but an officer stopped him: "You better not. The colonel would shoot you for sending him that exhibit of your findings." Kuhn said he wanted to tell the colonel about all the tanks and trucks he had seen, but the officer ushered him out with a wink. "We cannot do anything without the colonel's orders." Convinced that Fuller had no clue what was in the offing, Sergeant Kuhn returned to Marnach.

Elsewhere in Clervaux, another NCO, Staff Sergeant Frank Kusnir, was also sniffing trouble. The New Brighton, Pennsylvania, native was in the I and R section of the 110th. It was his job to gather reports from patrols, interrogate prisoners, and analyze the enemy's intentions. Kusnir, along with the rest of Headquarters Company, was stationed in a medieval castle that dominated the town of Clervaux. In the basement of the castle, he had a couple of POWs he was trying to interrogate through an interpreter: "They were very smug and very confident, so we sort of sensed something was in the air." The attitude of these Germans, combined with numerous reports of vehicle noise from the German lines, convinced Sergeant Kusnir that something was cooking. When he expressed this concern to his boss, Major Robert Gaynor, the regimental S2, the major was not convinced: "Oh, they're only trying to keep you guys awake," he said dismissively.

Like Kuhn, Kusnir held a low opinion of Colonel Fuller and believed that the colonel did not understand or appreciate the gravity of the threat: "Fuller was a joke." One day in early December he had accompanied the colonel on an inspection of frontline positions. At one point, they paused to get their bearings: "We checked the map. He looked out and saw some flowers blooming along the road. So he said to the driver: 'Oh . . . I've got to get those flowers and send 'em to my wife 'cause she collects and dries 'em and puts 'em between the Bible.'" Kusnir and the driver exchanged puzzled glances. The sergeant thought to himself, "What kind of a guy is this?" Kusnir was the hardened son of Slovakian immigrants and a veteran army man who had joined the National Guard in 1936. Fair or not, he viewed the colonel's preoccupation with flowers as a sign of weakness, and he had little respect for him. Kusnir had no idea that Fuller had fought in World War I. To Kusnir, Fuller seemed like a desk soldier out of his element.

Sergeants like Kuhn and Kusnir were obviously right to be agitated about German intentions. They, and many others like them, did the best they could to sound the alarm to their superiors. They hoped that their commanders would call in air strikes on the German troop concentrations, beef up the front lines, or just do something constructive. When none of those things happened, they assumed that senior officers like Fuller were in a fog.[14]

But this was not necessarily fair. From the moment Fuller took command of the 110th, he was very concerned about the vulnerability of his regiment. That concern only deepened as December unfolded. For instance, on December 12, Fuller had lunch with his old friend General Troy Middleton, the commander of the VIII Corps. He spent much of the lunch haranguing Middleton, whose VIII Corps included the 28th Division, about the danger of his thinly held line: "I pointed out to him my concern about such an overextended front, and particularly to the fact that the main Dasburg-Bastogne road ran right through the middle of my sector. General Middleton did not seem at all concerned about it."

Nor was the colonel ignoring reports like Sergeant Kuhn's: "For five days prior to the German attack on December 16, our patrols and OPs had noted unusual activity across the Our River . . . and had constantly reported this to Division HQ. I personally discussed this with General Cota. He, however, displayed no particular interest in it and gave me the impression that he did not expect anything stronger than a raid, probably in battalion strength."

So Fuller was passing the buck to his immediate superiors, Cota and Middleton, both of whom disavowed any lack of concern. Cota later denied having received any disquieting reports from Fuller. He claimed that he had ordered Fuller to investigate German activities by sending patrols across the Our and that Fuller had not done this.

Then again, Cota also stated in his division's after-action report that "all available G-2 information pointed to the fact that Fortress Bn [Battalions] and reorganizing units were manning this sector of the Siegfried Line." This was patently untrue, so much so that the report contradicted itself a few pages later in mentioning Elise Dele's eyewitness account of German tanks, engineers, and assault infantry. What's more, another division report, prepared in the G2 section, acknowledged knowing about "motor movement along the East bank of the Our . . . heavier than heretofore. During the same period [the Germans] made a number of small, portable, wooden foot bridges. Activity was particularly heavy during the hours of darkness with much movement of bridging materials. New units were apparently on our front." In spite of the existence of this report from his own G2 people, Cota contended that the only indications of an enemy attack came from civilian reports like Dele's and certainly not "from any higher headquarters."

Thus, Cota placed the buck firmly into Middleton's palm. Middleton, of course, wanted no part of it. Major General Middleton's corps had been in this sector since October. Since then, he had constantly lobbied for more troops to bolster his dangerously thin Ardennes front. On several occasions he addressed the subject with his immediate superior, Lieutenant General Courtney Hodges, commander of the First Army and the next higher commander, General Omar Bradley, commander of the Twelfth Army Group. "Frankly, I was very concerned about the front," Middleton later said.

During a tour of the Ardennes with Bradley, Middeleton communicated that concern. In response Bradley said, "Don't worry, Troy. They won't come through here."

"Maybe not, Brad, but they've come through this area several times before."

On another occasion, Middleton heard that two German deserters were predicting an imminent attack in the Ardennes. He went to the front and interrogated them himself. He also ordered more patrols.

On the other hand, Middleton did downplay the warning of another one of his division commanders who was jumpy about the increased German activity on his front. When this general anxiously called Middleton late at night to report the enemy buildup, Middleton told him to "go back to sleep . . . you've been having a bad dream." One of Middleton's intelligence officers, Major Malcolm Wilkey, believed that the general was not all that concerned about an enemy offensive in his sector. Wilkey had the impression that "the staff were more concerned and had voiced their impressions to Middleton, and that Middleton had brushed them aside." One time Middleton even told Wilkey and the other G2 officers, "I have never based any decision on a G2 estimate yet." Wilkey was deeply insulted.

Basically, in the weeks leading up to the Battle of the Bulge, no one at Middleton's level or below wanted to take the risk of predicting a German offensive and demanding requisite action from the highest Allied commanders.[15]

In the 28th Division sector, then, there were plenty of indicators of the enemy offensive. That being the case, how did the Germans pull off such a surprise attack? There were three factors: bad weather, bad intelligence analysis, and a bad mind-set among American commanders.

From late November onward, foggy, rainy, snowy, drizzly weather concealed the German buildup from the prying eyes of Allied pilots. The weather was so bad that in the first two weeks of December, the Air Force flew a grand total of eight reconnaissance sorties in the entire VIII Corps sector. Half of those flights were aborted because of poor weather. The other four were hampered by fog and low clouds. These flights produced nothing of value, negating one of the best tools intelligence officers had in gathering information about the enemy.[16]

Nor were high-level intelligence officers doing much with the information they were getting. At the company and battalion levels, the troops were doing what they could. They were gathering good information on the enemy's suspicious activities and passing it up the chain. At the highest level, Ultra, the Allied system for cracking sensitive German codes, yielded more good indicators of German troop movements, albeit without specific evidence of German intentions. For any of this to be useful, intelligence officers at the corps, army, and army group level had to interpret the alarming troop reports correctly and inform their superiors so that they could take appropriate action. By and large, this did not happen.

To be sure, some of them voiced concerns, the most famous being the warnings of Colonel Benjamin "Monk" Dickson, G2, of Hodges's First Army. Several times in the fall, Dickson had anxiously trumpeted the evidence of the German buildup. In a staff meeting he once blurted, "It's the Ardennes." All of this made good latter-day copy for reporters and filmmakers, especially when the self-promoting Dickson claimed to be a prophet of sorts. But in reality, he never actually predicted a German offensive in the Ardennes (indeed, after claiming an attack would come somewhere in the West on November 11 and being proven wrong, he then said the Germans would attack in April for Hitler's birthday). Moreover, Dickson's supposed prophetic concern about a German offensive did not keep him, on the eve of the Bulge, from going to Paris on leave.

More than anything, Colonel Dickson was reacting to what he thought of as blandly optimistic reports coming from General Bradley's Twelfth Army Group G2, General Edwin Sibert. Dickson and Sibert did not get along. Dickson was bright but headstrong and volatile. He resented Sibert and wanted his job. Sibert thought Dickson was hard to work with and too secretive. By December 1944 these two men—arguably the two most important G2's in the army—were feuding to the point where they rarely spoke. This meant that coordination between the intelligence staffs of First Army and Twelfth Army was nonexistent. They were competitors, not partners.

Nor did the U.S. Army place enough emphasis on intelligence gathering. Up and coming officers became S3s (operations), not S2s. Most intelligence officers, whether at the battalion, regiment, division, corps, army, or army group level tended to be outsiders. Seldom were they slotted for command. "G2 people were not well thought of in the Army," General Sibert said, "Many people had a habit of saying, 'I wonder what is wrong with him that he is in G2.'" Considering the pervasiveness of this unfortunate attitude, it was not surprising that American intelligence would, at times, fail miserably (Pearl Harbor and the Bulge being the most notorious examples).

In the final analysis, the Americans did not know the Germans were coming in the Ardennes because they did not want to know. High-level commanders and intelligence officers could not imagine that the Germans had the capability or the audacity for a major offensive. Charles B. MacDonald, author of one of the best books ever written on the Bulge, summed the failures up perfectly: "In no way did the intelligence officers alert their commanders to a threat in the Ardennes serious enough or imminent enough to warrant any change in Eisenhower's . . . plans north and south of the region. Allied intelligence officers had committed the most grievous sin of which a G-2 is capable. They had looked in the mirror for the enemy and seen only the reflection of their own intentions."[17]

Bradley called the weak Ardennes sector a "calculated risk." He and Eisenhower knew that the Allies could not be strong everywhere. Some portions of the two-hundred-mile front had to be deemphasized, and the Ardennes seemed like the best place. This was not unreasonable. Hitler, as in 1940 during his invasion of France, chose the Ardennes because it did not seem to be a likely place for an offensive.

If somehow the Allies had figured out German designs, they could have redeployed troops to the Ardennes. In doing this, Bradley might well have ended the tragic, wasteful, foolish campaign he was fighting in the Hurtgen Forest. Regardless, the Allies would not have avoided a major battle in the Ardennes. They simply would have been better prepared.

2

FRIDAY, DECEMBER 15

1

The clock was ticking. All over the Ardennes, timepieces were grinding on, marking the last quiet hours, oblivious to what lay ahead. As they had done for so many days in this quiet sector, American soldiers carried on with their routines, at times casually glancing at their wristwatches, none of them knowing that these were the last precious hours of surcease. The Ardennes was about to change forever. The soldiers were, too.

On the other side of the Our, a mighty German war machine was also waiting out these final hours. Hitler had assembled three entire armies: the 6th SS Panzer under SS General Josef "Sepp" Dietrich, the 5th Panzer under General Hasso von Manteuffel, and the 7th Army under General Erich Brandenberger. The three armies comprised thirty divisions, some of which were the best-armored formations the Germans had left. There were a quarter of a million men, hundreds of tanks, hundreds of self-propelled guns, thousands of trucks, half-tracks, armored cars, and other vehicles. The Luftwaffe had even assembled one thousand planes for this operation.

The German plan was ambitious but basic. In the northern sector of the offensive, Dietrich's 6th SS Panzer Army, including four ruthless SS panzer divisions, would drive through Monschau, Malmedy, and Werbomont; breach the Meuse between Huy and Liege; and dash north for Antwerp. Dietrich was an old party crony of Hitler's. Like the führer, he had been an NCO in World War I and had no formal military education. In the early 1930s, Dietrich had formed Hitler's personal bodyguard. The hard-drinking SS man had fought on many fronts in this war, earning a reputation for being pitiless and cunning. Hitler trusted him as much as he trusted anyone these days.

Immediately to the south of the 6th SS Panzer, Manteuffel's 5th Panzer was to make an equally potent attack. Manteuffel had four panzer and four infantry divisions, plus assorted heavy-artillery batteries, engineers, and the like. He had begun the war as a lieutenant colonel, risen to command a division in North Africa and another one on the eastern front, and had emerged as one of Germany's leading mechanized commanders. Intense, good-humored, and thoroughly professional, Manteuffel was entrusted with a task similar to Dietrich's. In its northern sector, the 5th Panzer Army was supposed to envelop the lightly held Schnee Eifel, push through Elsenborn ridge, capture St. Vith, and roll northwest. To the south, Manteuffel's formations would cross the Our, infiltrate, overwhelm, and surround or bypass the 28th Division strong points at such places as Heinerscheid, Marnach, Hosingen, and Weiler.

They would then surge west through the entire Bastogne corridor. "The success or failure of the operation depends on an incessant and stubborn drive to the west and northwest," Manteuffel told his commanders. "The forward waves of the attack must not be delayed or tied down by any form of resistance. Bastogne should fall on the second day of the operation, or at least be encircled by then." Once this was done, they would then turn north, cross the Meuse, roar farther north, and envelop Antwerp from the west. The brunt of this powerful attack would hit three American infantry divisions: the 99th at Elsenborn, the 106th at the Schnee Eifel, and the 28th in the Bastogne corridor. The latter would be especially hard-pressed. In fact, on the eve of the attack, the 28th was unknowingly facing parts of eight German divisions, most of which belonged to Manteuffel's army. As Manteuffel himself stated, his best chance for victory was speed. Any delay or deviation from his precise timetable would invite failure.

Brandenberger's 7th Army was located to the south of the 5th Panzer Army. The 7th had the mission of defending the southern flank of the operation. Brandenberger had eight infantry divisions. Many of them were new *Volksgrenadier* formations, consisting of new recruits, "retrained" air force or navy men, over-age men, young boys, or Europeans recruited from around Germany's crumbling empire. The 7th Army's job was to cross the Our and capture Vianden, Diekirch, and Ettelbruck. They would then push west to Neufchateau and protect the flank of the German offensive from an inevitable U.S. counterattack. The 28th Division's 109th Infantry was squarely in the way of the 7th Army's route of attack. Brandenberger figured he would eliminate the 109th in short order.

The overall objective of Operation Wacht am Rhein ("Watch on the Rhine"), as Hitler initially called it, was to split the Allied armies in two, cut off the entire British Twenty-First Army Group, retake Antwerp, and, ultimately, force the Western Allies into a negotiated peace. At that point, Hitler could then deal with the Soviet Union; maybe the British and Americans would even join the fight against the communist colossus. It was an ambitious, risky plan, a long shot, really. But then Hitler was not the type to play it safe. A gambler at heart, he dreamed big dreams and courted major failures. Everything now depended on speed. It also depended on an assumption that was, for Hitler, an article of faith: American soldiers would crumble in the face of adversity.[1]

2

On the American side of the Our, this Friday was just another quiet day. On the fringes of Lutzkampen, Private Charles Haug, the young runner in B Company, 112th Infantry, was in the Christmas spirit. Just outside of town, he and two of his buddies were sitting in a basement dugout, talking about Christmas, when they suddenly realized it was only ten days away. "So we decided to do something about it. The way everything looked, we would be sitting in this town for the rest of the winter. We cut ourself [sic] a little evergreen tree from the edge of town and set it up." With the front quiet, they went into Lutzkampen in search of something to put on the tree: "We went through the rooms in a couple of houses . . . and we soon came across a whole box of [Christmas] tree decorations. We loaded this little tree with everything possible." They sat back, admired their tree, and thought of home. Outside, the afternoon shadows were already lengthening.

Gradually the late afternoon gloom gave way to pitch darkness. These were the shortest days of the year in the Ardennes, offering, at most, nine hours of daylight.

A few hundred yards east of Harspelt, Sergeant Lamoine "Frank" Olsen was in an abandoned house that served as his command post. He was a platoon sergeant in A Company, 112th Infantry. He and his men were out in no-man's-land, on OP duty. Many of his soldiers were out lying in the darkness, either in holes or on the level ground, listening for enemy movement. Now, a runner came into the house, lit up by only a few candles, and handed him a slip of paper. Preoccupied with a hundred details of command, Sergeant Olsen merely glanced at the paper. It was a telegram for Corporal Green, one of the men who were outside. Olsen did not have time to give it to him now. He resolved to do it later, after Green came back inside.

Back in Harspelt, Corporal William Kelley was using the darkness for concealment as he made his way into another OP. He was part of an artillery forward observer team. Their unit, A Battery of the 229th Field

Artillery Battalion, was supporting the 112th Infantry up here. He and the two other men on his team, Lieutenant Bryant and Corporal Peterson, walked as quietly as they could down a Harspelt street. "The OP was in a thick stone house," Kelley recalled. They went inside and relieved another observer team.

Kelley and the other two soldiers were thrilled to see that the house contained comfortable beds and a sturdy roof overhead. Several infantrymen were there to provide security for Kelley's team. For the artillerymen, their duties would begin in earnest the next morning, after daylight, when they could watch for enemy activity, call down some fire, or maybe just pick out likely targets. Nothing much seemed to be happening up here. Corporal Kelley could hardly believe his good fortune in drawing this "soft" duty. He picked out a bed, settled in, and thought of how lucky he was to be in this quiet spot, sleeping in comfort.

Three miles to the west, at Heinerscheid, Corporal Cecil Hannaford was nowhere near as happy. An assistant squad leader in the 3rd Platoon, A Company, 110th Infantry, he had just found out that his platoon had been ordered to leave the shelter of their buildings in Heinerscheid and go set up a roadblock OP near Kalborn, a mile to the east.

Sullenly, Hannaford and the others slogged out into the cold night: "We strung a telephone line on the ground to our outpost as our only communication with the Company Command Post" in Heinerscheid. When they got to their OP position, at an intersection, Hannaford was dismayed to see that it was "in plain view of the paved road on the next hill a . . . mile . . . away." The Mississippi native felt vulnerable there, not to mention cold. As he and his foxhole buddy, Lowell Coats, dug in and set up their position, Corporal Hannaford could only think of the rest of the company, warm and dry back in Heinerscheid: "The guys back in the village could . . . have a roof over their heads. We had to go out in the open, in the snow and ice . . . and dig foxholes, guard an intersection, not very fun."

They finished digging in, and Hannaford took the first watch. Oh well, he thought, at least it's quiet here.

A couple of miles over the eastern horizon, at the little agricultural village of Sevenig, Lieutenant Ralph Larson and his men were in much better spirits. Larson and his 2nd Platoon, K Company, 112th Infantry, soldiers had been up here on OP duty for six days. Tonight a platoon from L Company was taking over for them. When L Company arrived, Larson's men were spread among five houses and a few outside listening posts. In veritable silence, the L Company soldiers changed places with them. Private First Class Buck Bloomer, a rifleman in Larson's platoon, noticed the sour faces of the L Company men. They did not look very happy to be there, and Bloomer could not blame them. He had spent plenty of time lying outside in the snow on listening post, and he was glad to leave that chore to someone else. Bloomer was looking forward to leaving here and getting some rest. Lieutenant Larson quietly gathered Bloomer and the other men together and pointed them west: "We trudged across the open field past the frontline positions . . . crossed the crest of Sevenig Hill, and found our way to the Company K area."

They set up at the edge of a wooded draw, near a kitchen area, in earthen bunkers. The rest of the company was clustered around some captured Siegfried Line pillboxes. The good news was that the 2nd Platoon was off OP duty and slightly behind the lines now. The bad news was that they were earmarked to assault a couple of pillboxes the next day. In the meantime, they had some time to rest. Private First Class Bloomer and his comrades immediately got to work improving their bunker: "In our bunker there was three [men]. We put pine needles on the ground as a mattress." Lieutenant Larson made sure his people were settled in. Then he allowed himself to catch some sleep.[2]

3

At nearly the same time that Lieutenant Larson drifted off to sleep, some of his fellow 28th Division officers were miles away at the Diekirch Hotel, enjoying a musical performance. Marlene Dietrich, true to her word, was back with the 109th Infantry, entertaining a group that consisted mostly of officers. She and her USO troupe were putting on a variety show. The room where they performed was smoky and crowded, but festive. She was singing and dancing, in sultry attire (no paratrooper uniform tonight), all the while showing off her legs. Several members of the 28th Division band, including T/5 John Noon, accompanied her: "I played drums and xylophones." Noon had a fine time, as did everyone else. Dietrich was on her game tonight. The entertainment went on for at least two hours. When it was done, the officers went back to their hotels, the enlisted men to their billets. Dietrich went to sleep. She and the troupe were scheduled to visit the 99th Division, in the northern Ardennes, the very next day.[3]

Twenty miles to the north, in Clervaux, Sergeant Bob Bradicich was also enjoying music, but in a more private setting. Over the last few weeks, Bradicich and several other soldiers had befriended numerous locals. Tonight they were enjoying one another's company: "We got together with some of the townspeople and actually had a dance. Somebody got a record player and played some music. It was great."

Just across town, at the Claravallis Hotel, home of the 110th Infantry headquarters, Captain Edwin Rensmeyer was returning from the hospital.

He had been wounded several weeks before but had recuperated enough for the doctors to send him back to the 110th. Rensmeyer still had bandages on wounds that had not completely healed.

With only the clothes on his back and a few personal items, he walked into the Claravallis and reported to Colonel Hurley Fuller, who looked a bit old to the youthful captain. The colonel welcomed him back and immediately assigned him to the S2 section. Captain Rensmeyer saluted and left, and told Captain Jerry "Pop" Harwell, the regimental S1, about his new job: "He advised me that since I was well rested I would start my tour of duty . . . as the [S2] Duty Officer that night. I . . . sat down in the Lobby of the Claravelle [*sic*] Hotel and took over the duties of the Duty Officer."

Everything was so quiet that Rensmeyer quickly despaired of getting any real intelligence work done. No reports were coming in, no phones ringing; hardly a soul was stirring. Basically his job that night was to stay awake in case something happened. He shrugged his shoulders and resolved to make the best of it: "I spent the night writing letters to my wife, my parents, and my wife's parents. It had been almost a month since I had had an opportunity to do this."

As Captain Rensmeyer sat at his little desk writing letters, two courageous German soldiers were infiltrating Clervaux. The two men made up an artillery observation team. They slipped into Clervaux from a forested hill at Reuler. From there they worked their way behind the Parc Hotel, located on a hillside overlooking the center of town and the medieval castle. With practiced stealth, the Germans hid out in a stable, waiting for the right moment to penetrate deeper into Clervaux. They were not spies. Both of these men were in uniform. When the coast was clear, they left the stable and cautiously walked a couple of blocks until they reached the Pharmacie Moletor. As quietly as possible, they picked the lock and went inside. The pharmacy was an excellent observation point, opposite the Hotel Central, right in the middle of town. The Germans set up their radio in a back room and waited for the right moment to call down artillery fire on Clervaux.[4]

Fifteen miles to the west, at Bastogne, Major Malcolm Wilkey, an intelligence officer on General Middleton's VIII Corps staff, had an uneasy feeling in the pit of his stomach. The G2 staff, along with the rest of VIII Corps headquarters, was in an old Belgian Army barracks, just west of Bastogne. This barracks building was anything but spacious. "There was a corridor down one side like an English railroad car." The G2 section occupied a few small offices just down the corridor from the G3 group.

Wilkey was a Harvard graduate and a former artillery officer who had chosen to transfer to corps intelligence six weeks earlier. His job was to supervise the numerous special intelligence teams that were attached to VIII Corps. His domain included interrogators, counterintelligence teams, and military intelligence experts who circulated among the local population in search of fresh information. He also spent much of his time coordinating with G2 officers from the various divisions that were part of VIII Corps.

Earlier today he had been in Luxembourg City working with the 4th Division. On the way back, he had debated whether to visit a friend of his in Clervaux, but decided against it. He had returned to headquarters and eaten a good dinner at the officer's mess hall. Now he was in the G2 office talking with Major Rudolph Sherrick, the night duty officer, catching up on what had happened that day. Sherrick was sitting at a table, with several reports scattered around him. In Sherrick's opinion, the reports added up to something very menacing. He looked up at Wilkey and fixed him with an earnest look: "You know, Wilkey, we are going to get hit in the face by the biggest counterattack ever, and probably real soon, too."

At that moment, something clicked in Wilkey's mind. He agreed completely with Sherrick. The Germans were about to attack. When they did, it would not be a local push; it would be a massive offensive. For several days now, Wilkey had felt jittery about German intentions but had not said much. It was as if he had needed someone else to verbalize what he was already thinking. Wilkey left the G2 office and discussed his concerns with several G3 officers. They were unmoved. One of them said that the Germans would not dare attack "because of the greatly superior American air power."

These nonchalant assurances did nothing to assuage Major Wilkey's concerns. One overarching thought kept popping into his mind: "This was the psychological time for Hitler to do something if he was going to survive. It wasn't whether Hitler could win by a counteroffensive; it was that every other course of action open to him would lead to disaster." Wilkey returned to the G2 office and told Sherrick that the G3 men were not particularly alarmed.

The two intelligence officers shook their heads in frustration. Coupled with the fact that the Allied armies were stymied on every front, it seemed to Wilkey and Sherrick that the Germans could win a psychological victory by launching an offensive of their own. The logical place for such an attack had to be the thinly held Ardennes. As each minute passed and the two majors mulled this over some more, they became even more convinced that something big was about to happen.

Wilkey left the office and visited Lieutenant Colonel Hauge, the assistant G2, at his billet to voice his concerns. The two men had been friends for nearly two years. Hauge listened carefully. He respected Wilkey's opinion but did not share his urgency: "Come back in the morning and we'll talk it over with Colonel [Andrew] Reeves," the VIII Corps G2.

Disappointed, Wilkey left Hauge's room, returned to the office, and sifted through more intelligence reports. More than ever, Wilkey was convinced that VIII Corps was about to be attacked. Despairing of getting any action from his superiors, Wilkey decided to sound some warnings himself. He hopped into his jeep and attempted to visit his old unit, the 174th Field Artillery Group, at the Schnee Eifel. He could not get through. The night was too dark, and communications were not good enough. Exasperated, he drove back to Bastogne. It had been a long day for Wilkey. He was exhausted and frustrated. He collapsed into bed, all the while determined to renew his warnings in the morning.[5]

Time was just too short. Even if Wilkey had succeeded in galvanizing his fellow VIII Corps officers into action, there was little that could have been done outside of putting the sparsely held Ardennes front on full alert. Intelligence is perishable. If Wilkey and others like him had sounded such warnings a week or two before, troops could have been redeployed to VIII Corps, beefing up the Ardennes defenses. But by the evening of December 15, it was too late for that. The troops at the front were, for the moment, on their own against an overwhelming force that was right at their doorstep.

As the last hours of December 15 ticked away, some of the frontline GIs were seeing and hearing indicators of that titanic enemy force. Just outside of Hosingen, Lieutenant Thomas Flynn, the executive officer of K Company, 110th Infantry, was at his company's southernmost OP, listening to engine noises in the distance. The engines sounded like "motorcycles used by couriers," and they seemed to be a couple miles away, at the Our River. Flynn and the OP soldiers listened for several minutes, but the noise faded. The wooded draws around their position made it very difficult to pinpoint the location of these distant sounds. Eventually the sounds dissipated, and quiet returned to the area. Puzzled, Lieutenant Flynn told the men to stay alert. He returned to the CP back in Hosingen. All around the town and in the company OPs outside of town, the men of K Company stayed in their positions and alternated watch in the usual manner.

Twenty miles to the northeast, on the other side of the Our, Private First Class John Allard was sitting in a Siegfried Line pillbox with nine other American soldiers of F Company, 112th Infantry. The night before, they had crossed the river and captured this pillbox and several enemy soldiers. Allard had volunteered for this patrol because of his twin brother,

Howard. The two young men were very close. Back home on the family ranch in Willows, California, they had spent much of their youth hauling large sacks of rice. When the war came, they joined the army together. For a time, they were both in the Army Specialized Training Program (ASTP). When the program was abolished, the Allard brothers were both assigned to the 28th Division, albeit in different companies. John went to F Company and Howard to G Company of the 110th.

Both of them fought in the Hurtgen Forest. On December 13, just two days earlier, John had received a letter from his father saying that his brother was listed as missing in action in the Hurtgen. He might be a prisoner, or he might be dead. John believed the latter, and he was seething with anger about it. He had volunteered for this dangerous patrol in the hopes of hurting those who had hurt his brother.

Now he and the other men were in quite a spot, right in the middle of swarms of Germans. The night before, the patrol leader, Lieutenant Donald Nikkel, had sent two men back to the American lines with the German prisoners, while the rest of the patrol waited in the pillbox. They had sat there all day listening to large numbers of enemy soldiers and vehicles outside. For now they were safe and hidden in this dank concrete box, yet they knew they could not stay there much longer. Somehow they had to get through the enemy legions and make it back to their company, not just for their own safety but to pass on the word of this enemy buildup.

When things seemed to quiet down a bit, Lieutenant Nikkel ordered them to get moving. Ever so quietly, they left the pillbox and started moving, in staggered formation, through the darkness. Seemingly every direction they went, they saw or heard German soldiers. Finally, Nikkel ordered them into a remote patch of woods, figuring they could make it down to the river along this concealed route. "Everything went well until we reached [a] clearing which was filled with two-man tents, many with candles burning in them," Allard recalled. They had to go right through this enemy camp. Allard and the others knew there was no other way back. Terrified, with adrenaline surging through their veins, they set out as silently as they could: "As quietly and quickly as possible, we walked between the rows of tents, all the way through the clearing to the woods at the edge of the river." To their immense relief, none of the Germans in those tents stirred. The patrol tiptoed through the woods, plunged into the cold river, waded across, and made it back to F Company near Ouren. Allard watched as Lieutenant Nikkel made his report to Captain Rice, the company commander. They made arrangements to call down artillery on the German marshaling areas. For now, that was all they could do.

At that moment, twenty-five miles to the south, another group of American soldiers was on patrol, overlooking the Our. These men were from F Company of the 109th Infantry. The company was defending a two-mile front in and around the town of Walsdorf. The mission of this patrol was to keep the river under observation near Gemund, just in case the Germans were doing anything.

The patrol was squad-sized. Among this scared little group of men was Private Robert Jackson, a native of the Upper Peninsula in Michigan. Jackson had joined the unit about a month before and had participated in several patrols. On one of them, a few weeks earlier, he had killed a German soldier with his bare hands. The memory of the man's warm blood on his hands, and the liquid gurgling sounds of his death throes, had still not left Jackson.

Now in the chilly quiet of late evening, they found a brushy hillside, concealed themselves, and kept their eyes on the rushing river below them: "The sky is clear and stars light the darkness," Jackson wrote in a present-tense account, "giving us the ability to plainly see across on the German side."

For about an hour, they waited and watched, seeing nothing. The patrol leader then moved them to a different spot, closer to the river. All at once the leader stopped, told them to seek cover, and pointed at the river. "Slipping quietly into the protective brush, we move forward to gain a view of the riverside activities. Fog is covering the far side of the river where motors are idling but in the middle of the stream, men are working on a submerged bridge. It is six inches below the water and the muffled sounds of their construction now reach our ears clearly." Awestruck, they watched as the Germans brought a truck up to the river's edge and dumped off some timber. With practiced urgency, groups of men picked up the timbers and put them in place.

Jackson and the other patrol members knew there was only one reason the Germans would build a bridge here: they were about to attack. The Americans did not linger long. In no time, they hustled back to the company CP in Walsdorf and reported their findings to the CO, Captain Ronnet. "Good job, men," he said, "we'll have demolition teams blow it up and bomb it. Send a messenger back to battalion in the morning informing them of this new development." Satisfied that he had done his job, Private Jackson went back to his foxhole, jumped in, and drifted off to sleep.

At 2300, an hour after Jackson's patrol returned to Walsdorf, Private Leroy "Whitey" Schaller and four other members of B Company, 110th Infantry, left the warm safety of their house in Marnach and set out on a recon patrol of the Our River. The wind whipped around Schaller and the other soldiers. The temperature seemed to be dropping by the minute. There was just enough snow underfoot to make Schaller worry about the crunching sounds their boots made as they walked. A wispy layer of fog coated the ground.

Schaller had felt uneasy for several days now. Two civilian electricians had restored power in Marnach, and that was great, but Schaller wondered who these guys were and how they had suddenly materialized in the area. One of them was husky, blond, and blue-eyed, a veritable poster child for the Nazi superman myth. Every time Schaller asked if the electricians had been checked out, he was told "probably so." The whole thing seemed strange, and he wondered why no one else was as concerned as he was.

Now, as he and the four others patrolled with wary stealth, Schaller simply hoped that nothing dangerous was out here. The night was quiet, almost eerie, but that was nothing new. A German could be waiting behind every tree along this road that led to the Our. Private Schaller kept his eyes straight ahead, searching for trouble.

Soon he found it. Somewhere in the darkness, he was sure he saw movement. Then he heard the sound of boots. German soldiers were approaching rapidly: "I stopped the patrol and we stood fast as [a] large German combat patrol passed within 30 feet of our path." Schaller and the others hugged the ground, watching, waiting, holding their collective breath. In all, there were sixteen enemy soldiers. On they went, out of sight, somewhere toward Marnach.

Schaller and the others waited for another hour while the sergeant pondered what to do. "[He] was totally shaken." At last, he gave the order to abort the patrol. As quietly as possible, grateful to be alive, they headed back to Marnach.[6]

They did not know it at the time, but they had just witnessed the first moves of Hitler's offensive.

3

SATURDAY, DECEMBER 16

1

At 0400 the Ardennes front was dark. The air was cold, crisp, and moist, but not freezing. Blankets and clumps of snow covered parts of the Bastogne corridor. Naturally there was more snow in the higher elevations. The lower ground tended toward a sodden mixture of dew and melting snow. The roads were wet but clear. A steady shroud of fog coated most of the area. Clouds obscured the moon.

The German side of the Bastogne corridor was pregnant with danger. As quietly as possible, thousands of German soldiers were crossing the Our in small boats, building bridges across that river (such as the one Private Robert Jackson had seen at Gemund), moving into assembly areas and infiltrating through or around American lines.

In late November, General Hasso von Manteuffel had visited this area, seen firsthand just how thinly held it was, and developed appropriate tactics. He wanted his infantry soldiers to infiltrate under cover of darkness, wait in safety while their own artillery pounded American positions, then encircle the 28th Division strong points, push past them, and dash west. Later, when the engineers had finished building bridges over the Our, the infantry would be joined by Manteuffel's powerful armored forces. Right now the infantry were slowly on the move, like bogeymen in the night. Most of them kept well hidden, but some did not.

At Weiler, a tiny town located two miles west of the Our, Private First Class Chester Kuzminski was standing guard near the village church. His unit, I Company of the 110th Infantry, formed Colonel Hurley Fuller's strong-point defense in this section of the thin regimental line. Kuzminski had been asleep only half an hour earlier. He was still shaking off the cobwebs of slumber. Before he knew it, he heard what sounded like machinery noises somewhere in the darkness, beyond Weiler. He wondered if he was hearing things, but no, the noises continued. Kuzminski hollered to another guard twenty-five yards away, told him what he was hearing, and decided to report this to someone else. "I'm going to wake the radio operator," he told the other guard.

Kuzminski turned and headed for the house where the radioman was sleeping. "I heard movement close by again, and sure enough, a Jerry came out of the bushes. I opened up on him and he fell down." When Kuzminski was sure the German posed no further threat, he ran into the house and woke his buddies: "We're being attacked. Get on the radio and warn the CP to be alert. Wake up everybody."

Nine miles to the northeast, at Harspelt, Sergeant Frank Olsen of A Company, 112th Infantry, was checking on his OP soldiers. Hours earlier he had received a telegram for one of his men, Corporal Green, but that was far from his mind now. Sergeant Olsen was an experienced National Guardsman who had joined this unit several years before, back in his hometown of Union City, Pennsylvania. He had fought with this outfit since Normandy. He had seen a lot of men come and go, and he knew the dangers and discomforts of OP duty.

Now he was walking among the foxholes, checking on the men, talking to them, making sure they were awake and thawed out: "All of a sudden everyone started shooting and I found myself among German soldiers all around me." Sergeant Olsen was confused and frightened, but he knew he had to make it back to the stone farmhouse that served as his command post. Only there could he report what was going on to his superiors. "The Germans couldn't distinguish me from their own in the dark, so I removed my helmet and tucked it under my arm like a football and ran through them as fast as I could."

He was almost at the farmhouse when he collided with a couple of other dark shapes. They all fell heavily to the ground. From only a few feet away, Olsen heard a voice cursing him in German. "Being a prudent man, I kept my mouth shut, got up and continued on my way." He made it to the farmhouse but quickly got involved in a firefight with two Germans in a nearby outhouse.

A little less than a mile to the north, near Lutzkampen, Private Charles Haug, one of the B Company, 112th Infantry, runners, was standing guard in a dugout, wondering why the Germans had not fired any flares that night. Haug had been on this front for many weeks, and every other night the Germans had shot flares, but not tonight. That seemed strange.

In another hole not far away, Private George Knaphus was pondering the same question. The company first sergeant, Ralph McGeoch, stopped by Knaphus's hole and asked him how things were going. "Awfully quiet," Private Knaphus replied.

"How quiet?"

"Nothing."

"They're up to something," McGeoch replied. He trotted off to the CP, in a nearby stone house, to alert his CO, Captain Stanley Dec.

Several yards away, Private Alexander Hadden, the former-ASTPer, was staring east, toward the German lines, while his foxhole buddy slept next to him. "I became aware of a growing rumble—clearly not artillery—emanating from the east. It soon grew loud enough that I woke my buddy, who grumbled his way out" of his sleep. The two young soldiers listened as the noises grew louder by the second. "It was continuous and sounded like motor noise." Puzzled, they simply stood still and listened some more.

Roughly one hundred yards to their rear, Lieutenant Charles Hogzett was sleeping soundly in the crude dugout that served as his CP. At 0500, the hissing sound of his field telephone awakened him: "I recognized the voice of the sergeant who was manning the telephone in Lutzkampen." The sergeant was on a listening post in one of the buildings at the edges of the town. Now he was "obviously distressed." In an urgent tone, he said to Lieutenant Hogzett: "Lieutenant, there are at least five hundred German troops down here, and I can hear tanks east of town."

Hogzett told him to pack up and get out as best he could. Then he called Captain Dec, who had already been alerted by First Sergeant McGeoch. Dec told the young lieutenant to get his platoon ready and make sure his two machine guns were covering both sides of the road that led out of Lutzkampen.

A few minutes later, the Germans turned on searchlights and bounced them off the clouds. They were using this artificial moonlight to help their troops infiltrate the American positions, especially in the 112th Infantry sector, where Manteuffel did not even have an artillery barrage planned.

But the Americans had no way of knowing this. The sudden light was bizarre and disorienting. "What the hell? Who turned on the lights?" Private Haug thought, as he squinted at the beams. Private Hadden wondered the same thing: "There were no clearly defined beams which would have served to identify the source of the light. We were totally mystified!"

Several hundred yards to the south, Sergeant Murray Shapiro, a machine gunner in M Company, 112th Infantry, was transfixed, staring at the eerie shafts of light. As he watched, he heard the overwhelming noise that Hadden had noticed a few minutes before: "We were engulfed with the unnaturalness of steady, loud sound and light, not unlike an American high school dance of the seventies and eighties." Private First Class Charles Blakeslee and another 81-millimeter mortar man in M Company were nearby, peeking over the lip of their dugout, trying to see something in the light: "The lights criscrossed [*sic*] on the clouds over our positions and cast an eerie light around us. When we looked toward the German lines, we were blinded, much like looking into the headlights of a car." A nervous type, Blakeslee sensed that something very bad was about to happen.

At Sergeant Olsen's Harspelt OP, the lights came at a perfect time. Since his initial encounter with the Germans in the dark, he had made it into his CP. Now he and his men were picking off several Germans who were bathed in light and caught in an open field: "It got light as day. Then we could really knock 'em down. As far as you could see [the land] was dotted all over with 'em. We had good fire." The enemy soldiers went down in heaps and lay lifeless in the shadows of the artificial light. For the moment, Olsen's men were holding off the infiltrating Germans.[1]

In spite of the searchlights, the noises in front of the 112th Infantry, and these early skirmishes, most of the Bastogne corridor was still quiet. At the northeastern edge of Hosingen, two observers from K Company, 110th Infantry, were sitting atop the town's concrete water tower, peering east into Germany. As the clock struck 0530 precisely, the observers saw something incredible. The entire German horizon glowed with the pinpoints of hundreds of lights. One of the men picked up his nearby phone and started to place a call to Captain Frederick Feiker in the company CP. Seconds later, enemy artillery rounds shrieked into the town. Multiple explosions erupted at the same time. The phone line went dead.

Just down the street from the water tower, T/4 Robert Tucker, a medic, was in a three-story building that had once been someone's store and home. A shell scored a direct hit on the building, starting a fire. "We gathered what we could and ran across the small town square to a former hotel. Our jeep had been hit and was in ruins." Tucker and the other medics set up an aid station in the basement of the former hotel.

By now five houses were on fire, and the shells were coming down en masse. "The town was pretty well lit up," Lieutenant Thomas Flynn, the executive officer, recalled. He and Captain Feiker did not know what was going on, but they figured it was prudent to prepare for an enemy attack. They ordered some of the men out of their buildings and into their prepared positions. Flynn went to the northern end of the town, jumped into a foxhole with two machine gunners, and kept an eye on the Skyline Drive.[2]

A few miles to the south, just outside of Walsdorf, Private Robert Jackson and his buddy were curled up in their foxhole, getting some much-needed sleep. The previous evening Jackson and several other soldiers from F Company, 109th Infantry, had discovered a nocturnal German bridge-building project near Gemund. Now Private Jackson awoke with a start as the world erupted around him: "The booming explosions rock the earth and shower us with dirt. Our ears are hurting from the deafening sound and the concussion gives us a headache. We crouch down in our foxhole and pray for the pounding to cease. It doesn't." They simply lay still and prayed that nothing would hit them. The very ground seemed to tremble around them.[3]

A few miles to the west, at picturesque Bourscheid, Lieutenant Les Eames, the artillery officer who had not been much impressed with Marlene Dietrich the week before, was sleeping soundly at the Hotel du Moulin, the headquarters of his 687th Field Artillery Battalion. All of a sudden he was "startled into consciousness" by the sound of eight shells simultaneously whizzing right over the hotel and exploding nearby. He rolled out of bed, put on his boots, and went to the lobby, the location of the CP, to see what was happening. The 687th served as an artillery support unit for the 109th and 110th Infantry Regiments. Eames listened as reports of intense shelling came in from all the batteries, situated slightly behind the frontline infantry companies.

A couple of floors above Eames, in the attic, T/Sergeant Gene "Jock" Fleury, a radio operator, was sleeping on a cot. The twenty-two-year-old Fleury awoke to a shell burst somewhere above the roof, far too close for comfort. "It was the type of shell that burst when it got so many feet above the targets. Here came the shrapnel through the rafters and through the shingles."

Fleury had lived a tough life in Seattle. His bootlegger father had left when Jock was four. His mother had shuttled him among thirteen different grade schools. Sometimes he had lived with her. Other times he had boarded at school. The family had very little to eat during the Depression. Young Jock managed to graduate from high school and went to work for the Civilian Conservation Corps. Through all the tough times, Fleury prided himself on his sense of humor. But now as he listened to yet another shell bearing down on the roof, he knew this was no laughing matter. He got up and "made a beeline for the stairs. It was real narrow, like a funnel. I don't think I even hit the steps."

Not far from Fleury, Corporal Clifford Iwig was just coming off guard duty, watching the cooks prepare breakfast, when the shells hit: "My first thought was that one of the cooks' stoves blew up." That fleeting thought passed as the reality of the enemy barrage set in. He saw pieces getting knocked off the hotel as the shells exploded just outside or above it. He wisely took cover. Iwig did not know it, but the German barrage was also pounding other 28th Division artillery units—the 107th, the 108th, and the 109th Field Artillery Battalions.[4]

* * *

Ten miles to the north along the Skyline Drive from Bourscheid, the enemy artillery tore into Marnach, no doubt in an attempt to soften up B Company of the 110th Infantry. Sergeant JJ Kuhn, the NCO who had clashed with Colonel Fuller a few days before, was just going inside the hotel that housed the company CP "when all hell broke loose. German artillery fire was falling all over the town. One building after another collapsed from the shelling."

A few doors down from the CP, Sergeant Morris Pettit jolted awake. He and his squad were billeted in this humble two-story house. Pettit was on the second floor. He heard a shell scream in and hit the house: "The house . . . was set on fire. I was the last man down the steps to the first level. As I got to the bottom of the stairs, the roof of the house began to fall in flames." Luckily, no one was hurt. With shells exploding all over the place, Sergeant Pettit led his squad to prepared foxhole positions just east of town. Like so many other experienced men, he expected an attack to follow the barrage.

T/Sergeant Stanley Showman, platoon sergeant of the 3rd Platoon, was wide awake inside a drafty old stone house. He was a nineteen-year-old farm kid from Virginia who had never even finished school. He had served with B Company all the way through Normandy and had been badly wounded in mid-September during the initial push into Germany. Along the way, he had worked his way up from rifleman to ranking NCO in this platoon.

Now he had the lives of thirty-five men in his hands. He peeked outside and saw much of Marnach burning. He immediately ordered his men out of their buildings, including his own: "I made it out of that house in nothing flat. We went around some other buildings to . . . get the men organized . . . in slit trenches and stuff." In a few minutes, Showman ended up with a small group in a slit trench about one hundred yards east of town.

Not far from Sergeant Showman, PFC Whitey Schaller was in a house, trying to unwind after the harrowing night patrol he had experienced a few hours before. He heard the enemy artillery pounding the whole town and sought cover. As he did so, he noticed a group of men going through a breakfast chow line in an adjoining house: "[An] incendiary round hit and some of the men were almost caught inside the conflagration. Our house was temporarily overlooked, and we hastened to shake everybody out."

Schaller and his buddies vacated their house and ran to their prepared positions, slightly outside of town. On the way, Schaller noticed the immense damage the shelling was doing to little Marnach: "The barrage thoroughly renovated the town. All but one building that sheltered a gun, or a vehicle, or troops was destroyed by incendiary shells." Flames flickered, lighting up the night, reflecting off the thin blanket of snow that coated the ground. Smoke billowed straight up in clumps from rooftops. The fire scorched stone buildings and consumed wooden barns. Amazingly, neither the fire nor the explosions killed anyone.

Lieutenant Kit Carson, the B Company CO, was sure that an attack was imminent. He and his experienced sergeants like Kuhn, Pettit, and Showman did everything they could to get the men in position to repel the coming onslaught.

A mile and a half north of Marnach, at Grindhausen, Lieutenant Glen Vannatta heard the shells falling in Marnach. Vannatta was the executive officer of D Company, a heavy weapons company that parceled out mortar and machine-gun support to the rifle companies. Vannatta was warmly bundled underneath a down comforter, lying in a real bed. The constant rumble of explosions awakened him. He turned to his CO, Captain Andrew Carter, who was sleeping in another bed across the room and asked, "Captain, are you awake?"

"Yeah, Van, what do you make of it?" Carter asked in his New Orleans accent.

"It's incoming mail. Sounds like it's up around Marnach."

The two officers listened some more. Vannatta was sure that Marnach was getting hit hard: "The guns were quite far away, no firing noise, just the whistle and shell burst." Puzzled but alarmed, Vannatta and Carter got up, went downstairs, and called the 1st Battalion CP at Urspelt. They did not know anything either. For now, the D Company command group could only cluster around a map, listen to the distant explosions, and anticipate what might happen next.[5]

Even as Vannatta and the other leaders of D Company studied their maps, the two German artillery observers who had snuck into the Pharmacie Moletor at Clervaux the day before were scanning the town for targets. The Germans placed a call on their radio.

Moments later, large-caliber, long-range artillery shells began to fall all over town. In a small room on the second floor of the Claravallis Hotel, Lieutenant Colonel Daniel Strickler, the executive officer of the 110th Infantry, immediately woke up. He listened for a few seconds as explosions rocked the whole town with concussion. Some of the shells were landing very close to the Claravallis.

Strickler decided he had better get up and check in with Colonel Fuller. He hurriedly dressed and knocked on the door of Room 10 next door, where Fuller was sleeping. The latter had also been awake, listening. With no preamble, he greeted Strickler with a question: "What do you make of this?"

"Something is cooking," Strickler replied. "All this big stuff dropping in here is a sure sign that we are in for a fight."

"Let's check with the battalions," Fuller said.

They walked downstairs to the operations room. Colonel Fuller picked up the phone there and attempted to get in touch with his battalions: "I was unable to reach a single battalion by telephone. Telephone communications with Division HQ were also out." Somebody was jamming the radios, too. Fuller and Strickler exchanged an apprehensive glance. "Only then did we realize how thoroughly the Germans had planned this offensive, stopping at nothing to achieve the greatest degree of surprise," Strickler wrote.

Outside, the explosions continued their monotonous cadence. The shells were tearing into numerous buildings, setting fires, ripping off facades, destroying rooftops. All over town, hundreds of American soldiers were experiencing a rude awakening. Many of them were here on R & R. Clervaux was supposed to be a rest center, but it was very rapidly turning into a combat zone.

The day before, Private Gabe Carson (no relation to Lieutenant Kit Carson) had gotten an R & R pass to take a few days off from his duties as a 57-millimeter antitank gunner. Upon getting to Clervaux, he had bought some steaks, and since he had no refrigerator, he had "put them between the door and storm door" of his billet to keep them cold. "Because of the shelling . . . the storm door was all broken and the steaks were full of glass." Carson was, of course, frustrated and angry at the spoiling of his beautiful steaks.

Across town, Private Frank LoVuolo was standing guard outside of the Villa Prum, near the Wiltz road. Like Carson, LoVuolo was on R & R. He was an artilleryman from the 107th Field Artillery Battalion. Private LoVuolo was standing at the end of the villa driveway, with shells hitting all over the place: "The . . . exploding shells became so intense that I could hear shell fragments strike the pavement near the building. I was forced to race for the protection of the villa. Crawling, running, crawling, I finally reached the villa front door." Someone slammed the door shut behind him. LoVuolo and the others took refuge in the basement. From the cellar, the explosions sounded like rolling thunder.

A few blocks away, Private Jack Chavez, a vacationing artilleryman from Battery B, 229th Field Artillery Battalion, was inside the Commerce Hotel listening to the terrifying sound of the blasts. He could hear buildings crumbling, then the lights in the Commerce Hotel went out, as Clervaux's power plant took a direct hit. Soon there were several explosions right outside of the Commerce: "A number of windows in our hotel were broken." An officer came along and ordered Chavez and several other men to stay inside. Hundreds of others, both soldiers and civilians, were doing the same thing.

This initial enemy barrage at Clervaux and many other towns lasted about an hour. By 0630 most of the shelling had slackened or petered out altogether. It caused very few casualties, although it did destroy many buildings in towns like Heinerscheid, Munshausen, Marnach, Hosingen, Urspelt, Reuler, Clervaux, and even Wiltz, the home of 28th Division headquarters. The biggest impact of the artillery barrage was on telephone communications. They were almost completely knocked out in the 109th and 110th Infantry sectors (the Germans chose not to shell the 112th in favor of infiltration). More than anything, the shelling served to alert many of the Americans that something big was coming.[6]

2

At 0615, nearly an hour before sunrise, thousands of German infantry soldiers began their attacks all over the Bastogne corridor. At Holzthum, Lieutenant Bert Saymon, the commander of L Company, 110th Infantry, was at his CP in a schoolhouse at the western edge of town. That morning he had planned to send out an infantry squad with some 81-millimeter mortar men from the battalion's heavy weapons company. Their mission was to pound Gemund. But when the German barrage began, Saymon's superior officer, Major Harold Milton, commander of the 3rd Battalion, had canceled the order. Just now Saymon was sending out a jeep to retrieve the men who were to participate in the fire mission.

East of Holzthum, at the Café Schincker–Skyline Drive crossroads, where L Company's 1st Platoon was manning a roadblock, the platoon's soldiers watched as the jeep glided by and disappeared into the foggy mist. A few moments later, they heard the sound of small arms fire and squealing brakes. The shooting ceased, and they saw ghostly figures in the fog. Not knowing whether the shapes were Germans or simply their returning buddies, they held fire.

The figures were German, and in no time, they opened fire on the roadblock. Tracers stabbed through the mist. The firefight was inconclusive, but the Americans could tell that a large number of Germans were crossing the road to the north and the south, working their way deeper into the American sector at Holzthum and even Consthum, home to Major Milton's 3rd Battalion CP. These Germans were from the 26th Volksgrenadier Division. Their orders, straight from Manteuffel, were to infiltrate, envelop American strong points, avoid major battles, and head for Clervaux.[7]

A few miles east of Weiler, Staff Sergeant William Meller was in the middle of a sweaty nightmare. He was the ranking noncom in the 2nd

Platoon of I Company, 110th Infantry. He and a glorified squad that passed for a platoon (twelve men) were deployed in a forward position some three-quarters of a mile west of the Our, right in the pathway of the 39th Fusiliers Regiment, 26th Volksgrenadiers Division. Miller and his people were deployed in and around an old house and barn, near the T of an intersection.

In Meller's dream, he was back in the Hurtgen Forest, staring at the faceless, bloody, bone-shattered lump of what had once been "someone's son . . . crying for the mother that will never hear his voice again." A few months before, Meller had been a raw nineteen-year-old. This morning he was still nineteen, but he seemed much older somehow.

His field phone rang. Meller woke with a start and answered it. "Sarge, the field in front of us is filled with krauts, armed to the teeth. They don't see us," one of Meller's men reported. "What should we do?"

Fear knifed through Sergeant Meller. He swallowed hard: "Open up with your machine gun, short bursts for the next five minutes, then fire only when you see something." He ordered the accompanying BAR (Browning automatic rifle) man, Red, to add his fire to the machine-gun team, and signed off. Meller got to his feet, glanced outside, and saw that it was still pitch dark. He checked his watch: 0630. He woke his assistant squad leader and told him to tell the 60-millimeter mortar team, located just behind a barn near this house, to start dropping some shells on the enemy troops. Then he spent several minutes just listening: "We've been taking return fire from the Germans . . . small arms, burp guns, machine pistols, and rifles. There's no mistaking the sound. They are firing at the sound of our machine guns," he later wrote. "The high pitch of the German burp guns and machine pistols sounds like a dentist's drill grinding my teeth. It seems closer in the dark of night." Sergeant Meller shuddered. God, how he hated the sound of those things. The fire from the American machine gun was slowing down.

He left the house and carefully made his way through the foggy dark to his machine-gun team. The gunner nodded a greeting. "We can't see anything in this soup, Sarge. I don't know where they are," he complained.

"Don't fire unless you see something. They aren't sure where we are . . . so be careful, they may be right out there in front of you. They can crawl right up to the edge of this foxhole before you see them." The gunner nodded fearfully. Meller moved on to check on another one of his men.

A few hundred yards away, on a ridge that overlooked the Our River, another young I Company noncom, Sergeant Fred Pruett, was at a machine gun, seeing movement in front of his position. Since the moment Private First Class Chester Kuzminski had shot a German soldier in Weiler an hour before, I Company had been fully alert. The ensuing artillery barrage had only added to this high level of readiness. Sergeant Pruett and his squad had been ordered to this position. He and his men were dug into the ridge, well hidden from what looked like swarms of Germans who were crossing the river in boats and ascending the ridge. Somewhere in the distance, he heard a few popcornlike explosions and some screams. The Germans were apparently running into at least one of the minefields U.S. engineers had sown in this area.

Now there were numerous shapes moving closer in the darkness. Pruett tensed over his gun and prepared to fire, as did an adjacent gun team. He had wisely ordered his team to remove the tracer rounds from their ammo belts so as not to give away their position. He spotted a target and fired. "We stayed there . . . holding that position and firing on the Germans." Enemy soldiers went down like bowling pins. Their return fire was inaccurate, and they were obviously confused. "The Germans never really found out where we were." Pruett and the other machine gunners rationed their fire, pinning down anyone they saw. Down by the river, many enemy soldiers were wounded, crying for help. Then things quieted down. Pruett and his machine-gun squad did not know what was going on, but for the moment, they seemed to have foiled this enemy attack—or whatever it was.

Even as Pruett's machine guns laced through the ranks of the enemy Volksgrenadiers near the river, hundreds more were closing in on Weiler itself. It was impossible to contain them. They were out in the darkness moving around in organized or confused clumps, here and there running into American positions, taking casualties, but always on the move.

At the eastern edge of Weiler, Private First Class Thomas Myers, the married man who had enjoyed a platonic lunch with an attractive Luxembourg girl a few weeks earlier, was standing in a foxhole, shoulder to shoulder with the old man of I Company. Myers was in his early twenties, while Private Thorne, the tall, redheaded man next to him, was all of forty years old. To most men of Myers's youthful age, people of Thorne's age seemed impossibly old. Myers asked how in the world someone as old as Thorne ended up in an infantry company, of all places. As Thorne started to answer, they noticed movement in front of them. The two riflemen were on a patch of high ground just beyond Weiler. The ground in front of them sloped down into a draw before rising again into another ridge. German soldiers were advancing over that ridge. Thorne and Myers exchanged shots with the Germans, and then the enemy seemed to go away.

Neither soldier had any clue that a major German offensive had just started, so they returned to their conversation. "He was a married bookkeeper with a bad back," Myers recalled, "and had been rated 4F by his draft board. But early in 1944, his rating was changed, and he was drafted into the army. He was told that he would only see limited service. However, by some mixup of orders, he was sent for . . . infantry training." Thorne could not make it through the training, and army doctors promised to discharge him. Nonetheless, he had gotten orders to ship overseas as an infantry replacement, and here he was in a rifle company at the front, waiting for his discharge papers to come through. Myers was amazed that a man of Thorne's advanced years and obvious infirmities had slipped through the cracks in such a way.

The Germans started attacking again. An enemy bullet creased through the dirt, right between their heads. They glanced at each other and then toward the enemy. The shot came from very close. In one awful second, Myers realized that there was an enemy soldier hiding behind a clump of bushes some ten yards to their front. This "brave (or foolish)" German had crawled through the draw to get them. Even as this thought flashed through Myers's mind, he knew the enemy soldier was about to shoot again before the Americans could shoot back. "[He] had one more chance. He had a choice of two targets. He chose Private Thorne." Thorne, the "old man," went down in a heap, dead before he hit the ground. "Fate is a funny thing," Myers opined. "Here was a man who never should have been in the army, let alone in combat." Moments later, Myers was a prisoner of war.

To the east, Sergeant Meller was crawling through the woods, trying to find his squad's lead foxhole. He slung his carbine and removed his Colt .45 pistol from its holster. The Germans could be anywhere in these dark woods. Meller's heart was thumping so wildly he was sure that any nearby enemy could hear it. He was breathing too loud, through his mouth. Adrenaline was coursing through his bloodstream. It was so dark in these woods that he felt as if he were blindfolded.

At last he found the foxhole, made out the familiar shape of one of his men, and carefully whispered so as not to startle him, "Bill, it's Sarge."

He got no response. "Leaning over the hole, I see him. He's dead, lying on his stomach at the bottom. He was my most trusted man. He had just returned from the hospital [the day before]. The back of his jacket is covered with those little black shrapnel pieces from a German grenade. His helmet is beside him, blown off. His face is clean. The concussion killed him instantly."

Tears streamed from Meller's eyes. How he hated the Germans who had done this to Bill! He vowed revenge. He propped Bill's body up so that it would look like he was still alive and covering this position. He took Bill's rifle, along with his remaining ammo, and headed for a nearby foxhole, where he warned two of his men of the close proximity of the

Germans. With amazing ease now, he made his way to the barn, where his mortar team and his assistant squad leader greeted him. Sergeant Meller told them about Bill's death.

"God, I'm sorry," the assistant squad leader replied. "I know you liked him."

"Yeah," Meller nodded, "we have to be very careful now. There are only eleven of us."

He decided to go back to the house and radio for help. He took a man named Slim with him and told him to call the company commander, First Lieutenant Douglas Paul, for help. Slim went into the house's kitchen, where the radio was stored, and called the company. As Meller listened, a voice at the other end told Slim that the lieutenant and everyone else were outside, fighting off the German attack. The voice said that two 81-millimeter mortar sections and an antitank platoon were firing at shapes in the distance. That did not sound good. Slim tried battalion, but with no luck. Meller noticed that the sound of German mortars and small-arms fire was picking up. This situation was getting worse by the minute.

"Open it up and use Mayday," Sergeant Meller told him. "We need tank support right now." The young NCO turned away and pondered what to do next. What the hell was happening out there, he wondered? When would the Germans attack this little position in greater strength? Outside, the explosions and shooting ebbed and flowed. Inside, in the kitchen, Slim kept up his monotonous cadence, "Mayday, Mayday, this is Fox Two, we need tank support right now. Come in." There was no answer. Sergeant Meller did not know it, but back in Weiler, I Company was fighting a company-sized force of Germans. More were on the way.[8]

"The woods are full of Jerries! The woods are full of Jerries!"

Private First Class Buck Bloomer awoke to the sound of this desperate, lonely cry. He and two buddies from K Company, 112th Infantry, were in the same bunker, near L Company's kitchen area, where they had holed up several hours earlier, after being relieved from OP duty at Sevenig. Bloomer and the two other men heard the warning voice again: "The woods are full of Jerries!" The voice belonged to one of the two guards that Lieutenant Larson, the platoon leader, had posted in the woods behind the platoon. The voice sounded panicked, almost hopeless.

A few yards away, in another bunker, Lieutenant Larson knew that the warning meant trouble: "It was a cry which I shall never forget." Larson was glad now that he had told his men to dig some reserve positions one hundred feet to their rear, "just in case," before getting some sleep. Since the Germans were obviously behind the platoon, Larson's people needed those positions to defend themselves against the Germans who would soon emerge from the woods. He ordered his men to leave their bunkers and occupy this ring of foxholes and slit trenches, closer to the woods where the guard was even now running for his life. "There was no time for reflection. Instinctively I grabbed my helmet and carbine, as did the other two platoon members who had been sleeping in that particular dugout." One of the men, a temporary platoon sergeant—Larson's regular guy was on leave in Paris—forgot something and went back to the dugout. Larson never saw him again.

When the platoon members were in their reserve positions, they peered into the pitch darkness, waiting tensely for the Germans. A few eerie moments of quiet passed. The voice had long since tapered off. Suddenly a flare shot up and illuminated the area, but only for a moment. In that instant, the Americans saw the distinct shapes of German soldiers, a couple of hundred yards away in the woods, moving toward them. Up and down the line, the Yanks opened fire with M1 Garands and BARs. PFC Bloomer spotted several figures, exhaled, and squeezed off several shots. "You could make 'em out with the flare . . . 'cause they were in the open and we were not. They were in and out of the woods."

Not far away, Lieutenant Larson was letting loose with his M1 carbine. He could just make out the tumbling shapes of German soldiers as they got hit. Then he heard the awful Bunsen-burner-like sound of a flamethrower. "A German flamethrower went into action, barely missing our positions. Rifle shots blared back and forth from both sides." The flamethrower found a victim somewhere in the distance. The man burned like a torch for a few minutes until he collapsed into a smoldering, charred heap.

More flares lit the area. The Americans kept up an accurate, disciplined volume of fire. The flamethrower notwithstanding, German return fire was not very accurate. "They couldn't spot us," Bloomer recalled. "They kept sending flares up that would light the whole area. But . . . evidently they couldn't spot . . . exactly where we were. We didn't fire unless we . . . were pretty sure that we could hit somebody or scare 'em off because we didn't have that much ammunition." Bloomer and the other riflemen had two bandoliers apiece. That translated roughly to sixteen clips—eight rounds per clip—for each man.

Fortunately the firefight did not last long, maybe twenty minutes at the most. When it was over, Lieutenant Larson took stock of the situation. He had lost his two sentries, and his temporary platoon sergeant was missing, as was another man who had elected to stay with the OP in Sevenig to be with a buddy. The man who had been scorched to death was from the 3rd Battalion. Larson did not know his name. The rest of

K Company was a few hundred yards away, scattered in and around captured Siegfried Line pillboxes. There were at least four dead Germans in the woods. Several others were wounded. Larson and the other Americans could hear them moaning somewhere out there in the renewed darkness. Lieutenant Larson thought he had defeated a German patrol. With no idea what was happening anywhere else, he settled his platoon down and waited for orders.

Larson had no clue that he had just encountered the leading assault troops of the 560th Volksgrenadiers Division. All night long, thousands of them had been working their way through no-man's-land and the wooded draws that honeycombed this area. Even now, they were bumping into forward positions all over the 112th Infantry front, getting between the 1st and 3rd Battalions, attempting to capture the two bridges at Ouren that would allow them to move vehicles across the Our.

Just beyond the woods from Larson's platoon, the Germans overran the kitchen trucks from L Company and captured several Americans. This was the same group of enemy soldiers who had been shooting it out with Larson. They helped themselves to some American food, which was a fatal mistake. Groups from L and M Companies were preparing an effective counterattack. Two sergeants, Bob Osborne and Don Gallagher, and another man spotted the feasting Germans and helped pour deadly 81-millimeter mortar fire on them. Shell after shell rained in on the enemy, spraying jagged shrapnel everywhere. The shrapnel peppered them, tearing off arms, slashing into torsos, and causing internal bleeding. The concussion of the exploding shells destroyed brains. "It must have been three hundred yards to the other side of the valley where we could see them," Private First Class Clarence Blakeslee, the thirty-year-old M Company mortar observer, recalled. "We were above them and we could see them scramble and try to crawl into a five-inch-deep mortar shell crater for protection. The wounded were screaming and calling, '*Kamerad!*'"

Blakeslee could not help but feel sorry for them: "Do we have to kill them all? Can't we go down and see if they will surrender?"

"When they want to surrender, they can send up a white flag," someone replied.

In a matter of a few minutes, one hundred dead Germans, in various stages of decomposition, were lying in L Company's kitchen area. "Some were lying dead with half of a hot dog in their mouths," an American soldier recalled.

The panicked enemy survivors either surrendered or got mowed down in droves by Americans with submachine guns. One mess sergeant alone captured twenty-five Germans.

But this was just one draw in one part of the line. Not far to the south, in another draw near Sevenig, more Germans were pouring through weak spots in the American defenses. Sergeant Murray Shapiro and his buddy Sergeant McGinnis were on the way to the frontline emplacements where their .30-caliber water-cooled machine guns were set up, covering a small gap between K and L Companies. Sergeant Shapiro had reported to his superiors that he had heard strange noises and seen the spotlights on the German side of the line a couple of hours before. Now he and McGinnis were determined to make sure that their men were ready for whatever might be on the way.

They plodded through a layer of snow that covered the pathway to the machine-gun nests. They passed an antitank gun position and saw that the entire crew was asleep, including the guard who was supposed to be looking out for his buddies.

"You think I should wake this guy up?" Shapiro asked McGinnis.

"You know if you do, he is going to get fucking mad at us," McGinnis replied.

Sergeant Shapiro silently agreed. These men were not under his command. They were someone else's problem. The two NCOs continued up a slight slope. Their machine guns were dug in at the top of this rise. Shapiro glanced up and saw ten "shadowy figures" approaching in the darkness. They were in a semicircle, and each one of them was bending under the weight of a heavy load. Shapiro could relate to that. He himself was loaded down with paperback books, K rations, a rifle, and ammo on his person, but that was not all. "In my left hand was a small sack of potatoes dug up from . . . no-man's-land. In my right hand was a canteen cup filled with butter, plus knife, fork, and spoon."

Both groups noticed one another at the same time and stopped walking. "Who are these jokers?" Shapiro asked his fellow sergeant.

"They must be K Company's carrying party," McGinnis offered. For the last several weeks, cooks from the rifle companies had carried food through there to the frontline soldiers.

A few uncomfortable seconds passed. Shapiro looked closer at the figures. These guys were weighted down with weapons, not food. Shapiro realized that he was looking straight at a German patrol. They had obviously overwhelmed the machine-gun positions at the top of the hill and were now advancing west. McGinnis seemed to divine the same thing at the same time. The enemy group soon tripled in size. They moved closer and began to spread out in an effort to get behind the two Americans.

Without exchanging a word, Shapiro and McGinnis turned around and began to descend the hill as nonchalantly as they could. "In some ways our descent . . . was humorous," Shapiro said. "We began to walk slowly, the Germans picked up the pace a little; we walked fast, they walked a little faster; we ran at breakneck speed, they ran, too."

Shapiro sprinted for his very life. McGinnis was running and firing his carbine at the same time. Shapiro made it to the antitank position, jumped into their dugout, and shook the sentry violently. "Wake up, you jerk! The krauts are coming down the hill in force!"

The sentry and his crewmen were drowsy and disoriented. They scrambled to put on their boots. McGinnis piled into the dugout. Shapiro unslung his rifle and began to take aim, when an enemy potato masher grenade landed on the dirt roof of the dugout. "Grenade!" he screamed, and hurled himself to the snow. "I lived out the burst although the blast momentarily stunned me, sending my helmet off of my head backwards," he said later. McGinnis was dead. The antitank gunners probably were, too. "The next thing I knew, the Germans were charging in with bayonets."

Terrified, Sergeant Shapiro put his helmet back on, grabbed his rifle, and ran. He wriggled through a thick hedgerow, in the process losing his rifle, parts of his clothing, and some skin. Behind him, he could hear German boots pounding through the snow, getting closer. He was going straight downhill, out in the open. If they saw him, they could pick him off with rifle fire. "I decided on a desperate strategy. I dived into a small depression partially filled with mountain sage, and quickly covered myself up with all the leaves and pine needles I could find."

The enemy soldiers ran right past him and almost over him. One German even stepped on Shapiro's fingers. "The pain was minimal considering what might have happened," he said.

Sergeant Shapiro lay completely still, listening to herds of enemy soldiers go by, moving west, closer to the Ouren bridges. He did not know it, but this kind of thing was happening in numerous draws outside of Sevenig and Harspelt. In Shapiro's little spot, most of the Germans were quiet, except for one man, apparently an officer, who kept hollering for his sergeant, *"Feldwebel Mueller! Feldwebel Mueller!"* For the moment, Shapiro could only remain silent and hope for an opening.[9]

The first rays of sunlight splashed across the Bastogne corridor, creating pinkish shadows that grew smaller with each passing minute. During the last minutes of night, the Germans had done their best to stay on the move, but they had trouble just finding their way through the darkness, much less avoiding American strong points. When the sun at last rose, around 0715, so too did the level of violence from the enemy attack.

East of Harspelt, Sergeant Olsen's embattled platoon was clustered together in the CP house, firing at anything that moved outside. "We had more men than windows or doors to shoot out, so some crawled up to the attic and poked holes in the straw roof to fire out of." The Germans were shooting back with small arms and a few mortars, but respecting the potency of Olsen's group, they did not attempt an assault. Outside the house, the snowy ground was dotted with the inert bodies of many Germans and a few Americans.

Several hundred yards to the west, in Harspelt itself, Corporal William Kelley was still asleep in the comfortable bed he had appropriated a few hours earlier when his forward observation team had entered the town. An American infantry soldier woke him with a whisper and told him to "make as little noise as possible. The house was surrounded by German infantrymen. I instinctively reached for my carbine and helmet." Kelley was on the second floor. He chanced a look out a window and saw the enemy soldiers just outside. "Through the window could be heard men sputtering in their sauerkraut language. I sensed fear, but there was a bit of thrill mingled. Their boldness suggested that there must be plenty more around."

There were. Enemy burp guns and machine guns shattered the calm. Kelley could hear mortar rounds exploding somewhere outside. The whole town seemed to be one big firefight. "Several bursts came through our window, and as we hugged the floor, I expected a potato masher at any second. Intense small arms fighting, broken by a few mortar bursts, continued."

A major enemy attack was hitting A Company of the 112th Infantry. In platoon-sized groups, the Germans attempted to rush the American positions in and around Harspelt. This made them vulnerable to U.S. mortar and machine-gun fire, which either slaughtered them in large numbers or forced them to retreat. One group of fifty enemy soldiers somehow pushed past Harspelt and approached Hill 539, a prominent clump of high ground that afforded clear observation of the area. One squad from C Company, plus a section of .30-caliber machine guns, defended the hill. As the Germans ascended the hill, these Americans opened up, but still the enemy kept coming.

The enemy did not know it, but they were in the kill zone of a .50-caliber machine gun located a few hundred yards from the hill. The 1st Battalion CO, Lieutenant Colonel William Allen, got on the gun and fired a burst of 150 rounds right into the vulnerable German soldiers. The effect was devastating. The .50-caliber bullets tore off arms and shattered heads and legs. "Immediately after the last burst, some forty of the enemy surrendered to [a] platoon of the Company," Allen said. "Others of the enemy were attempting to withdraw from the hill toward Lutzkampen. From the .50-cal gun position, our men shouted to them to surrender. When they started to comply, German artillery placed a barrage in front of them, boxing them off, and allowing them to make good their escape."

The pace of the barrage picked up. German rockets, known as screaming meemies, combined with 105-millimeter howitzer shells and pounded Allen's lines. The fire grew so intense that Allen moved his CP to a different building, farther to the rear. This house had once served as D Company's CP. Now it housed the battalion command group, plus twenty-five bewildered German prisoners.

Back in Harspelt, Corporal Kelley noticed the small arms fire dying down, even as the artillery fire picked up. A runner entered the building and told Kelley that the 1st Battalion had broken up an enemy attack and taken 120 prisoners. That was good, but Kelley's observation team had no wire or radio communication with their unit, Battery A, 229th Field Artillery Battalion. He and Corporal Peterson, a fellow member of his observation team, were debating whether to go out and repair the phone lines. "A heavy shell screamed into our house. Our observing room was laid wide open, all instruments mutilated. Now I was scared. Luckily we weren't in the room at the time. Everyone scampered down into the concrete basement." Six more rounds slammed into the house. Each explosion rocked the house, sending smoke and dust everywhere. With no communications, Kelley's little team could only sit in the dark and wait for the shelling to stop.

After a brief lull, the Germans made another push for Hill 539, right under their own barrage. Lieutenant Colonel Allen had anticipated this. He knew that one squad and some machine guns could not hold the hill against a determined enemy attack. He ordered C Company, his reserve, to secure the hill. Like many other outfits in the 28th Division, the company was under-strength, with a preponderance of new replacements.

Company C was dug in slightly behind the lines, closer to the Our River. Most of the men, like Sergeant Peter Friscan, a squad leader, had been awake for several hours, listening to the distant sound of combat, knowing something was up. "I thought at first it was some German patrol caught in our lines. My platoon lieutenant sent for me. I was instructed to get my men ready to move out." In the early morning light, they headed for Hill 539.

Company C, plus some supporting machine guns from D Company, clashed with the enemy at the foot of the hill. The Germans did not get up the hill, but the situation all around it was fluid and confusing. Sergeant Friscan's squad battled pockets of stubborn enemy troops hidden in draws, and captured more than a few.

In an adjacent sector, Private First Class Linford Lilly's squad, from the 3rd Platoon, got orders to go up the hill and clean out any Germans who might be there. Lilly was one of many new men. A draftee from Bethlehem, Pennsylvania, who had once worked in a steel mill, he had just joined the unit after Hurtgen. An officer told his squad, "If you see a German, shoot him." When the officer left, a couple of members of the squad refused to go up the hill. "We can see up the hill. Why do we want to go up there?"

Lilly, his sergeant, and several other men left them behind and ascended Hill 539, finding no resistance. They took cover while the sergeant scanned the area with a pair of binoculars. "The Germans are down there, and they've got our men," the sergeant said. As Lilly and the others watched in horror, the Germans captured the squad members who had refused to climb the hill. Artillery rounds then came in, and no one could see much of anything anymore.

The capture of these men notwithstanding, C Company's counterattack achieved its goal. For the moment, it kept the Germans from capturing Harspelt and Hill 539. Once again, the Germans pounded the area with artillery and regrouped.[10]

Half a mile to the north, at Lutzkampen, the Germans had captured the town, in the process killing or forcing out several B Company soldiers who had been on OP. Now the Germans were streaming north, right into a head-on collision with the company's positions just outside of town.

As previously noted, the company had two machine-gun nests perfectly situated on either side of the road that led out of Lutzkampen. The Germans were walking on the road "in a column of twos, talking, laughing, and joking," according to the recollection of one American soldier. Some of the enemy soldiers were even counting cadence, as if they were on a parade field. Still oblivious, they got within twenty-five yards of the machine guns before their world exploded.

The two machine guns, with the rhythmic, cyclic "budda budda" cadence so typical of these .30-caliber weapons, fired up and down the German column. Tracer rounds bounced crazily along the road. In a foxhole on the north side of the road, Private Cliff Hackett, a BAR man, was blazing away at the Germans with his powerful weapon. He could hardly miss. They were right in front of him, still walking on the road. They went down in twos and threes. Others kept coming. A new guy standing next to Hackett was firing his rifle at the enemy. In the next foxhole, no one was shooting. The two men in the hole were hugging the ground, cowering, totally unhinged by fear. Hackett and his buddy kept shooting clip after clip.

Close to Hackett, Lieutenant Hogzett told his platoon to open fire at the approaching Germans. "It was like shooting ducks in a gallery. You could see the tracer bullets as they struck the German troops." The slaughter went on for several long minutes. Dead and dying Germans were lying on the road and in ditches.

Now the surviving Volksgrenadiers began to take cover and maneuver. Four Germans managed to overrun one of the machine-gun positions. They killed everyone except for Private First Class Robert Vanderford, who acted wounded and then shot them from behind.

Other enemy groups, usually squad-sized, were fanning out from the road, attempting to close in on B Company's dug-in positions. Private Alexander Hadden, the former ASTPer, was several hundred yards from the road, near the company CP; he was scared and confused as he listened to the sounds of shooting—this was his first battle. Suddenly, from the cover of a hedgerow a couple of hundred yards away, a German MG42 machine gun opened up on him and the company command group. "It was firing tracers at a target to our right. I was horrified to see a number of GIs who were running for cover crumple and fall to the ground."

Hadden looked more closely at the hedgerow, searching for targets. He saw shadowy figures behind the hedgerow and then noticed one of them, adorned with a coal-scuttle helmet, straighten up and start barking orders. "The staccato German syllables came clearly across the snow to us. The man was outraged because his orders were not being obeyed. His voice was hoarse, guttural, and full of urgent purpose, and it struck terror into my heart." Hadden raised his rifle and squeezed the trigger. "The instant I fired, the man who had been shouting crumpled and fell to the ground."

Around Private Hadden, other Americans were directing their fire at the hedgerow, and this silenced the enemy MG42. The Germans either died or retreated, giving Hadden a moment to contemplate what he had just done: "I had taken out a German soldier! But it was as though I was at a movie and it was happening to someone else."

At nearly the same time, Lieutenant Hogzett sighted his weapon on an approaching German. "Without so much as a thought, I took my rifle, aimed, and fired. I saw his helmet fly up in the air and realized that this was the first of the enemy that I had shot and undoubtedly killed. I suddenly began to shake, and this spell lasted about 15 or 20 minutes before I could get my wits about me."

Stunned and bloodied though they were, the Germans were shooting back with everything they had. Their red tracers crisscrossed through and above the snow. Captain Dec was in his dugout, worrying about the increasing volume of the enemy fire and what he perceived as the slackening fire of his company. He left the relative safety of the dugout and ran in a low crouch toward the 1st Platoon positions. Private First Class Charles Haug, the runner, watched the captain and wondered if he had lost his sanity. Bullets were flying everywhere, but still Dec kept running. "The Germans spotted him. Just two shots and . . . [he] fell to the ground." Two medics rushed out to treat the captain. "They never made it. Both of them were shot down and killed before they had gone twenty yards." Dec and the medics lay dead, their blood draining into the snow.

The captain was dead, but the company kept fighting. The Americans were in prepared fighting holes; the Germans were either in the open or behind whatever cover they could find. Eventually that distinct advantage swayed the fight in B Company's favor. A group of forty-two Germans waved a white flag and surrendered. Most of them were boys between the ages of fourteen and eighteen. Other Germans were lying in the snow, too badly wounded to move. A few more retreated back to Lutzkampen. The shooting died down, and the only sound was the crying of the wounded. Private George Knaphus stood and surveyed the ghastly scene. "The killing and wounding were incredible. We did not count bodies, but a very conservative estimate would be 200 to 250 dead Germans." The German attack at Lutzkampen had been stymied.[11]

3

A mile and a half to the west, at Ouren, Colonel Gustin Nelson, commander of the 112th, was in an airy farmhouse that served as his CP. He had been up since 0530, when he had heard the artillery booming to the south in the 110th Infantry sector. For several hours, he had been working the phones, upward to division and downward to his battalions, in an attempt to clarify what was happening. The people at division did not seem to know much, only that the whole divisional front was under attack. Nelson's 1st and 3rd Battalions were being furiously attacked at such places as Lutzkampen, Harspelt, and Sevenig, but they were more or less holding.

The trouble, Nelson was beginning to realize, was that his regiment was taking on an entire German division. The enemy was not yet dislodging his frontline companies. Instead they were, through sheer numbers, bypassing them in spots. Even now, German infantrymen were pouring through the Sevenig gap and closing in on the vital Ouren bridges. If they succeeded in capturing the bridges, they could envelop and annihilate Nelson's entire regiment. Plus, they could move armor across the Our and advance deep into the division rear areas.

Colonel Nelson had actually planned for just this sort of crisis. Throughout December, he had prepared several counterattack plans with his battalion commanders. One of those blueprints, known as Plan B, called for the 2nd Battalion, his reserve unit, to attack and push the Germans back from the Our. Nelson knew that the time had come to set Plan B in motion. Now, at 0830, he picked up the phone, called the CO of the 2nd Battalion, Lieutenant Colonel Joseph Macsalka, and told him, "Execute Plan B."

At that moment, German patrols were nearing one of the Ouren bridges, specifically the stone bridge in the south, which was capable of supporting armored vehicles. The regimental Cannon Company, consisting of six towed, 105-millimeter howitzers, plus several .50-caliber machine guns, was dug into the hillsides that overlooked both of the bridges. Added to that was the 3rd Battalion Headquarters Company, along with a mixture of men returning from passes, or even the stockade. Phone lines were out, and even radio communication was spotty. These troops knew that the Germans were attacking the frontline companies, but they were aware of little else.

Captain William Cowan, a personnel officer, saw the approaching Germans and sounded the warning for Cannon Company and the 3rd Battalion headquarters group. "Get them when they cross the bridge!" he shouted as he entered Cannon Company's CP. Just then, Cannon's first sergeant, George Mortimer, was leaving the little kitchen room in the CP. "I was having a cup of coffee, and I seen these bastards, must have been about forty of them, coming across the . . . bridge."

Captain Cowan and the first sergeant of Headquarters Company, a twenty-six-year-old Pennsylvanian named Wayne Kugler, were rounding up anyone they could see, organizing them into fire teams amid the network of foxholes that overlooked the bridge. The enemy patrol, numbering between forty and sixty soldiers, was "almost marching in a column of twos," in the recollection of one soldier; "some of the men for a moment thought they might be prisoners coming to the rear."

They were not prisoners; they were just foolish. Since the Americans saw no white flags, they opened fire. First Sergeant Kugler was one of the first to do so. He "shot the first scout" at a distance of about two hundred yards. He was soon joined by the three .50-caliber guns along with plenty of rifle and BAR fire. The deadly fire swept through the enemy soldiers, tearing holes in their bodies, sending them careening for cover. They shouted and screamed in confusion. Kugler was pleased to see that many replacements were coolly aiming their weapons and firing. In just a few minutes, thirty enemy soldiers were dead or dying. The rest were running away or under cover around the bridge.

Captain Paul Troup, the CO of Headquarters Company, was, like so many other 28th Division soldiers, from Pennsylvania. He was also of German descent, and he knew the language. He made a personal reconnaissance to the bridge, under fire all the way from the surviving Germans. He took cover behind a wall near the bridge, within shouting distance of the Germans. As they fired their burp guns over his head, he hollered at them in German, urging them to give up. After several tense moments and some shooting back and forth, sixteen Germans surrendered. The first German push for the Ouren bridges had failed.[12]

Meanwhile, Counterattack Plan B was in full effect. Lieutenant Colonel Macsalka chose his F and G Companies to lead the way. They would be supported by the 229th Field Artillery, a fine unit whose batteries had stayed in action all morning, in spite of being harassed by German patrols. All of Macsalka's men had started the day in reserve. Indeed, the soldiers of F Company had been told the day before that they would be sent farther back to a bona fide rest area. "The morning of the sixteenth," one soldier recalled, "we had our bed rolls . . . stacked outside our huts awaiting trucks to transport them back. Everyone was eating and was excitedly waiting to go back when they got the attack order."

Grumbling but curious, the soldiers of F Company geared up and marched east. They moved across the northern footbridge, continued east, and then encountered the vanguard of the German advance. "Our forward platoons kept pushing forward," an F Company soldier wrote in his diary, "and the enemy kept falling back except for scattered resistance. We filed through the woods until we came to a draw. At the opposite side the Germans were busy digging in attempting to avoid our artillery fire and to set up a defense against us. Our company immediately fanned out and attacked. The men laid down a devastating . . . fire on the Germans. Sixty Germans were either killed or captured and five machine gun nests were destroyed." Company F dug into Sevenig Hill, not all that far from K Company.

The 2nd Battalion's counterattack stymied the German advance, inflicted hundreds of casualties on the enemy, and for the most part, restored the original defensive lines. Back in Ouren, at his CP, Colonel Nelson breathed a sigh of relief. For now, the 112th was holding.[13]

To the south, the entire 110th Infantry front was aflame with enemy attacks. At Marnach, as smoke billowed from crumbling homes, the Germans began to come out of the woods to the east and the north. These were the lead elements of the 2nd Panzer Division, an excellent formation whose mission was to lead Manteuffel's push for Bastogne. The smoke, morning fog, and low-hanging clouds all made it difficult for the Americans to see their attackers. Even so, they opened fire with mortars and small arms. Private First Class Whitey Schaller was shooting from a third-floor window of a house just east of the town church. He saw some Germans running in the distance, almost parallel to the house: "It was difficult to spot them even though they were only 150 yards distant."

Sergeant Stanley Showman, the Virginia farm boy, and his platoon had a better view of them from the vantage point of their fighting holes east of Marnach. Up and down the line of holes, Showman's men were blazing away with their rifles. Sergeant Showman himself had a BAR. Just ahead, a throng of enemy soldiers was moving right for the little hill mass that sheltered Showman's platoon. "I think a couple guys was counting 'em. They counted . . . about two hundred and ninety of 'em coming . . . after my little platoon. They come a hollering and a screaming and everything you could think of. None of 'em ever got up close to us."

The fog began to lift, allowing soldiers like Private First Class Schaller an excellent view of the enemy soldiers. "One could select from more than one hundred open targets." Schaller and his buddy Charles Larson took turns at a game they called "A nickel I get him." Larson proved to be more adept at the game. "With sights set at four hundred yards, Larson demolished a heavy mortar team trying to set up beside a straw pile."

Sergeant Kuhn, the salty Milwaukee native, was busy calling down whatever artillery he could get. Several guns from the 109th Field Artillery, which had an observer in town, and the regimental Cannon Company were saturating the approaches to Marnach. "The German infantry was coming toward us in waves, twenty, thirty men abreast. The artillery massacred the Germans. The few Germans that got through the artillery fire, we then picked off with our rifles. The German infantry kept coming out of the woods . . . and we kept killing them with our artillery. They just kept coming, one wave after the other. It was one of the saddest things I'd ever experienced in my life."

Half a mile east of Marnach, at Roder, the deadly artillery was the only thing that kept the Germans from overrunning Private Joe Norris's little OP squad. Since daybreak, Norris and his buddies had been in their fighting holes, firing at moving shapes in the distance. "They never got close to us. They were always about two hundred yards away. They weren't easy to see because it was . . . pretty foggy. So what we would do is simply fire in that direction." Artillery shells were landing among the shapes, keeping them dispersed and at bay.

Back at Marnach, German artillery was also coming in, mainly pounding the streets, making it dangerous to move around. Sergeant Kuhn and Lieutenant Carson were outside checking on their men when a shell exploded nearby. A piece of shrapnel took a chunk out of Carson's wrist, leaving an ugly, gaping wound. Kuhn helped him back to his hotel CP and supervised as a medic bandaged the wound. The medic made it clear that Lieutenant Carson needed surgery and would have to be evacuated. Kuhn put the lieutenant in a jeep and told the driver to go to the regimental aid station.

Kuhn gave the lieutenant a doll he had found in a destroyed house next to the town church. The doll had belonged to a young girl named Maria Eicher, and she would one day get it back. But for now, Kuhn gave it to Lieutenant Carson as a sort of going-away present. "I told the lieutenant that when he got to regimental he should wrap up the doll and send it to his daughter for Christmas. He laughed, wished me good luck, and away they went."

Even as the lieutenant's jeep left town, hundreds of German Panzergrenadiers were bypassing Marnach from the north and south, cutting the Skyline Drive, along with several other roads in and out of the town. The Germans had been stopped cold in their attempt to take Marnach, so they were simply surrounding it.[14]

Several miles to the south, the entire 3rd Battalion sector was aflame with crisis. The Germans were launching major attacks on Hosingen, Weiler, Holzthum, and Consthum. The enemy repeatedly hit the latter two towns, but the Americans were still holding out. At Consthum, for instance, a mixed group consisting of Major Milton's CP, his Headquarters Company, some artillerymen from the 687th, antiaircraft soldiers with quad .50-caliber machine guns, plus odds and ends repelled five separate attacks. The quad .50-calibers, designed to bring down airplanes, turned out to be especially devastating weapons against infantry. One burst could tear a man to pieces.

At Weiler, the soldiers of I Company were hanging on as best they could against an attacking force that outnumbered them at least five-to-one. At the edge of the town, Sergeant Jacob Welc, a squad leader who commanded two 57-millimeter guns that were attached to I Company, helped break up the enemy attack. He personally manned one of the guns, pumping round after round of high-explosive (antipersonnel) shells into German attackers whom he could clearly see on a nearby ridge. The Germans tried to rush his gun position, only to be torn apart by more fire. They keeled over, almost like bowling pins. They screamed in fury and desperation as fragments gashed through them. When Welc ran out of high-explosive rounds, he fired armor-piercing rounds and managed to score direct hits on at least four enemy soldiers.

Welc's heroics, combined with the furious resistance of several other infantry soldiers and accurate U.S. artillery, broke up this German attack.

Quiet settled over Weiler for a few minutes. In the distance, the Germans waved a Red Cross flag, hoping for a truce to recover their many wounded soldiers who were lying on the fringes of Weiler. The Americans agreed to the truce. German medics moved among the dead and dying, looking for people they could help. Moments before, this had been a kill zone. Now it was a place of mercy. "Friendly troops ceased firing for periods of twenty to thirty minutes," a U.S. officer later wrote. "Meanwhile, the Germans were maneuvering behind high ground in an effort to outflank the town." The Weiler garrison could do little to stop them.

To the east, nineteen-year-old Sergeant Thomas Meller's OP was behind enemy lines now. They had captured two Germans: a clean-cut, wounded captain and a haggard-looking medic. One of Meller's men, fresh out of a federal penitentiary, wanted to shoot the Germans, but Meller would have none of that. "You shoot them and I'll blow your fuckin' head off!" he bellowed. That ended all talk of shooting the POWs. Two soldiers put them in the CP.

Meller could hear sounds of fighting coming from the direction of Weiler. He planned to interrogate the two prisoners, but before he did, he went to a nearby wooded ridge in hopes of finding out what was going on. Around him the snow was melting in the light of day, dripping in soft patters onto the forest floor. He found a good spot under a tree and looked across a large valley, slightly to the southwest. What he saw nearly paralyzed his senses. He sat and stared for a moment, his mouth so dry he could not swallow: "The valley is filled with German troops. Everything imaginable that makes up an army is in front of me: armored infantry, personnel carriers, self-propelled artillery, jeeplike vehicles, antitank guns, and thousands of foot soldiers. They are spread out as far as I can see. They would run over us and not even hear us scream." Meller was looking at some of the first mechanized forces, probably from the 2nd Panzer Division, that the Germans now had across the Our.

He knew it was only a matter of time before they came for his squad at this little crossroads outside of Weiler. Feeling as if he had been kicked in the gut, he circulated among his men, telling them of their predicament, putting them on notice that they might have to fight their way out of here.

He went back to the farmhouse and sat down to speak with the German captain. He relieved the captain of a map case. In it was a map with the exact location and disposition of Meller's squad. Clearly the captain had been planning to lead an attack when he was captured.

A medic bandaged the enemy officer's wound. Blond and obviously intelligent, the German officer looked handsome and dignified in his gray uniform, adorned with combat decorations from the Battle of Stalingrad.

He had even earned the Iron Cross. He thanked Meller for not shooting him and also for dispensing medical care. "I wish to repay your kindness by saving your life and the lives of your men," he said in English. "You have done a commendable job here. There are three hundred companies of three hundred men each, coming down this road. They will take this position. Surrender now and save your life and the lives of your men."

Sergeant Meller politely declined, even as he wondered what in the world he should do now. A strange thought, something he had previously forgotten about, popped into his mind: I have orders to go on pass to Paris in two days, he recalled.[15]

Four miles to the north, at Hosingen, Private Edward Gasper was thinking about anything but Paris. He and two other K Company rifle-men were in a large foxhole, at the north end of town, just outside the barn where they had slept for several weeks. Gasper was pointing his M1 Garand rifle to the north, covering that side, while his two friends Privates Fox and Epstein covered the east: "This German . . . jumped up right in front of the foxhole. Epstein hit him with a BAR. He was dead before he hit the ground." Private Gasper spotted two other enemy soldiers "crawl-ing up toward the farmhouse. They weren't more than thirty or forty feet from me. I saw 'em and I shot 'em." To the left, two more Germans were walking down the main road that led into Hosingen. Before Gasper could shoot them, another rifleman, nicknamed Tennessee, shot them down. The five dead enemy soldiers lay in defeated heaps.

Gasper did not know it, but at that moment the Germans were con-verging on Hosingen from the north, east, and south. South of town, the Germans cut the Skyline Drive, overran an outpost on Steinmauer Hill, and cut off the 3rd Platoon of Company K, in addition to an antitank pla-toon. Some of these men retreated to the west. Others fought to the death or were captured.

Captain William Jarrett, the CO of B Company, 103rd Engineer Com-bat Battalion, was in the church tower and saw the whole thing. Jarrett's outfit of 125 engineers had been there for several days, with the mission of maintaining the Skyline Drive. Standing in the tower, Jarrett looked south and saw scores of Germans on foot, on bicycles, and on horse-drawn artillery caissons cutting across the Skyline Drive, some 500 meters south of Hosingen. Jarrett got in touch with Lieutenant Morse, an M Company officer who controlled a section of 81-millimeter mortars, and told him what he had seen. Morse's mortars pounded the Germans, temporarily halting their movement.

More enemy, from the 77th Grenadier Regiment, 26th Volksgrena-dier Division, were crossing the Skyline Drive north of town. Sergeant James Arbella, a 60-millimeter-mortar section leader, climbed into the water tower and called down fire on them. The two sides exchanged shots from a distance. The Americans inflicted a few casualties, but the Germans were still crossing the highway.

East of Hosingen, two enemy companies, contrary to Manteuffel's orders, were attempting a direct assault. Private Gasper and his buddies had killed the vanguard of these attackers. In their wake, more came. As they did, they blundered into a kill zone, on the gentle slope of a hill mass just beyond Hosingen's eastern edges. Arbella redirected his mortars. "We slaughtered the shit out of 'em." The mortar shells, combined with BAR, machine-gun, and rifle fire, shattered both enemy companies, stopping the attack. Scores of dead Germans were lying in grotesque heaps, all over the hill mass.

In the Hotel Schmitz, K Company's two-story command post in the middle of Hosingen, Captain Frederick Feiker, the CO, was calling for artillery fire, only to find that his supporting unit, Battery C, 109th Field Artillery Battalion, was under attack, firing their howitzers point-blank at enemy infantry. This kind of thing was happening to many other artillery units, too. Not one round of U.S. artillery fell at Hosingen, but Feiker's men stopped the German attack anyway.

The Germans now contented themselves with bypassing the town to the north and the south. The defenders of Hosingen were powerless to stop them. Moreover, Captain Feiker now had a clear sense of their objective—Bastogne. One of his men had captured a German officer who was carrying a map that revealed, in the memory of Captain Jarrett, "Battle Phase Lines extending all the way to Bastogne." Feiker fetched a runner and told him to get the map to Colonel Fuller in Clervaux, but the runner could not get past the swarms of Germans who were now west of Hosingen. He was lucky to get back to the Hotel Schmitz with the map.

Captain Jarrett came down from the church steeple and began organizing the evacuation of his company. He knew that Hosingen was slowly being cut off; he assumed that his engineers would be ordered out, and he wanted to be ready when the order came. The initial German artillery barrage had shredded the tires on many of his trucks (the company had about twenty). His men worked to replace the tires and loaded everything of value aboard the trucks, such as barbed wire, food, and packs. He had distributed his six .50-caliber and six .30-caliber machine guns throughout Hosingen to augment K Company's defenses. He planned to remount these guns at the last minute.

Corporal George Stevenson, one of Jarrett's engineers, was standing next to one of the trucks, helping load up and waiting for the word to get out. "[Jarrett] was going to put twenty men on each truck and we were going back to join our outfit in Wiltz." Stevenson noticed Captain Feiker talking to Jarrett. He heard the infantry captain ask Jarrett and his engineers to stay, saying that the infantry needed their help. At first Jarrett demurred. Major Milton, back in Consthum, settled the issue with a brief, fateful radio order: B Company, 103rd Engineers, was to stay in Hosingen and would be at the disposal of Captain Feiker. Milton signed off, promising that help was on the way.

With the issue settled, Jarrett dismounted his engineers and placed most of them on the western edge of town, where he and Feiker feared the Germans might soon attack. The two officers circulated around Hosingen, talking with their men and supervising the new defensive setup in and around the town.

Corporal Stevenson ended up in a barn at the western edge of town with an 81-millimeter mortar crew and his own .50-caliber gun. He and several other soldiers hauled shells for the mortar crew. Then they dragged sandbags from their trucks and placed them around the machine gun. With everything set up properly, they settled down to wait, for attack or relief, whichever came first. All around Hosingen, 270 other Americans did the same.[16]

4

Miles to the rear, at Bastogne, Major Malcolm Wilkey, the intelligence officer who had been so worried about the imminence of a German offensive, was sitting in the G2 office analyzing the confusing reports that were pouring in from the front. As Wilkey read, he realized that his worst fears were coming to fruition. Staff officers were scurrying back and forth along the narrow corridor of the crude building. A colonel and two majors from G3 found out about Wilkey's prognosis of the previous evening and came in to see him: "[They] tell me that you predicted this thing last night," the colonel said. "Now, how much do you know about it, and tell us all you know." Wilkey told him that this was a full-blown offensive and that VIII Corps would absorb the full brunt of it.

Just down the hallway in his private office, General Troy Middleton was realizing the same thing. The Germans were assaulting his entire eighty-eight-mile front. This was no "spoiling attack." His four and a half divisions were facing four times that number of enemy divisions. This was a genuine counteroffensive. The mission of VIII Corps was to defend in place. Middleton knew that his corps could not hope to stop the Germans. The enemy was too strong, and he was outnumbered badly. What's more, he had no air cover because of bad weather.

Slowly but surely, the reality of the situation coalesced in Middleton's mind. The crucial element here was time. The only thing VIII Corps could do, realistically, was cost the Germans valuable time while Eisenhower and Bradley rushed reinforcements to the Ardennes. That meant two things: First, Bastogne had to be held. If the Germans captured it within the next four days, the entire VIII Corps front would crumble before help could arrive. Second, in order to buy time, every VIII Corps unit had to stand fast and defend to the end. This applied particularly to the 28th Infantry Division, the only sizable force that stood between the Germans and Bastogne. For the time being, only the Bloody Bucket (the division's nickname) could buy the necessary time to save Bastogne. It must hold at all costs. It was a hell of a situation, Middleton knew, but then again, so was this war.[17]

This chilling "hold at all costs" order filtered downward from Middleton. At Wiltz, when General Norman "Dutch" Cota got the order, he had the awful feeling that his division would be sacrificed. All morning he had been receiving intermittent reports from his three regiments. The 112th was hard-pressed but holding. The Germans had surrounded two companies from the 109th, but Lieutenant Colonel James Earl Rudder was holding. The 110th was the only major unit directly between the Germans and Bastogne, and as such, it was in trouble. Its frontline companies at Hosingen, Weiler, Holzthum, and Marnach were surrounded or cut off. Clearly, Fuller's people were at the epicenter of this Nazi earthquake. Cota had only a small division reserve—the 707th Tank Battalion and Fuller's own 2nd Battalion. Fuller badly wanted the latter unit so that he could shore up his crumbling line, but Cota did not want to commit his key reserves so early in the battle.

The tanks were another matter. At 0700, Cota had alerted the 707th to be ready to counterattack. A couple of hours later, he called Major R. S. Garner, executive officer of the 707th, and ordered him to move out. Garner was temporarily filling in for the CO, Lieutenant Colonel R. W. Ripple, who was on leave but rushing back to the front. Company C would support the 109th, and Company D the 112th, while A and B Companies went to Clervaux in support of the 110th. For now, this was as much as Cota could do.

At nearly the same time, Colonel Fuller was pacing around his office at the Claravallis in Clervaux, trying in vain to get in touch with his battalion commanders. Ever since the initial artillery barrage, his phone and radio communications had been intermittent, and shells were still falling on Clervaux. At this point, he could not even communicate with Cota's division headquarters. Fuller sent Lieutenant Colonel Strickler downtown in hopes of communicating with division by commercial radio. "On the way, excited civilians milled around in the street and wanted to know what we were going to do," Strickler recalled. "You couldn't blame them for being worried." With no information and their town under fire, most of the civilians took refuge in their cellars.

Upon reaching the commercial radio facilities, Strickler saw that they, too, were not working. He went back to the Claravallis and reported this to Fuller. Exasperated, the colonel ordered Strickler to get in his jeep and go to the 3rd Battalion at Consthum by way of division headquarters at Wiltz, find out what was happening, and supervise the defense of the right flank.

Strickler and his jeep driver, Bob Martin, set off. They drove through shell fire but made it to Wiltz in short order. Strickler hopped out of the jeep and went straight to Cota's operations room. The general and his staff were all in there, thirsting for information. Strickler told them what little he knew and then prepared to go to Consthum. Cota took him aside and reported, "Strick . . . my orders are to hold at all costs." Strickler nodded his understanding and got into his jeep.

Martin stepped on the gas pedal, and in minutes, they were in Consthum. The town echoed with the sound of small arms and mortar fire. Major Milton's CP was in the east end of town, in a humble two-story house. Martin parked the jeep in a small courtyard behind a solid wall, dismounted, and went inside. The place looked like a beehive. Milton and his staff officers were frantically moving about, marking maps and talking to frontline units or supporting artillery batteries on scratchy radios.

"What's the story?" Strickler asked.

"The whole line is being battered," Milton shouted above the din. "The [Germans] are hauling men right up to within yards of our positions, and we are slaughtering them as fast as we can."

Milton had only one telephone line open, but after some persuasion, he let Strickler use it to call in his report to regiment and division. In his conversation with Fuller, Strickler relayed Cota's order to hold at all costs. Then, as ordered, Strickler stayed in Consthum, helping in any way he could. "Small forces were . . . sent out to block infiltrations by the enemy and to help battery positions repulse threats." Reports were coming in of Germans in American uniforms. This news spread like wildfire throughout the division.

Strickler went up to the attic, where a window afforded him a panoramic view of the whole area. He noticed a battery from the 687th Field Artillery dug in on a ridge some six hundred yards west of the CP. They were lowering the muzzles of their guns for point-blank fire. As Strickler watched in awe, Consthum came under direct attack: "The Germans came on in bunches, often coming close to our lines and unloading from trucks. They made pretty good targets, and the artillery laid direct fire on them, inflicting many casualties."

Back in Clervaux, Colonel Fuller was itching to relieve his besieged units. After the phone conversation with Strickler, the regimental communications were steadily coming back. Fuller was getting multiple reports from all over the regiment, most of them relaying bad news. His frontline companies were being cut off, yet his orders were to "hold at all costs." Fuller badly wanted to counterattack, link up with B Company at Marnach, then push on for Hosingen. To do that, he needed his 2nd Battalion, but much to Fuller's chagrin, General Cota still refused to release it from division reserve. However, at least two companies of tanks were on the way.

At 1030, they arrived. Fuller heard them before he saw them. They growled their way into Clervaux and waited for orders, engines idling loudly in the constricted streets. Major R. S. Garner, the tank commander, entered the Claravallis and met with Fuller. After some discussion of the multiple crises they were facing, they decided to parcel the tanks out in platoon increments. Two platoons from A Company would support C Company of the 110th Infantry in a push for Marnach. A Company's 3rd Platoon, under Lieutenant Richard Payne, would go to Hosingen. Company B would send one platoon to Holzthum and another to Consthum, while the third would remain in reserve at Pintsch. Garner left the Claravallis, and the Sherman tanks rolled out of town, heading east, into danger.

Even with help from the 707th, Fuller was so worried now about the security of his regiment that he ordered his officers to organize soldiers who were on leave in Clervaux into a provisional company. "They were armed only with rifles and carbines, but they constituted the only reserve available to me." MPs, sergeants, and officers rounded up anyone they happened to see. Private Harold Snedden, a jeep driver who was scheduled for a three-day leave in Paris, was "waiting for the truck to pick us up" when his first sergeant told him that his leave was canceled "because things were getting hot and heavy in the area." The first sergeant ordered Snedden to get a weapon and fall in for duty. Snedden and three hundred other soldiers were assigned to hasty defensive positions along the Clervaux-Marnach road east of Clervaux. There they waited, shivering from the cold, or perhaps from fear.[18]

Just east, over the ridge from Clervaux, at Urspelt, Lieutenant Colonel Donald Paul's 1st Battalion CP was in an old château belonging to the Bouvier family. The château overlooked rolling countryside that led to Grindhausen and Fischbach. A small, paved, tree-lined road slashed through the beautiful land, all the way into Urspelt.

Inside the château, Lieutenant Glen Vannatta, the executive officer of D Company, was standing among a small group of officers, discussing the battalion situation. Two miles to the south, Marnach and B Company were cut off. The company was holding firm, keeping the Germans at bay with effective fire, but cognizant that the enemy was streaming past the town on either side of the Skyline Drive.

A radioman came down from upstairs and informed the officers that B Company was running low on mortar ammunition. Vannatta exchanged a sharp look with Captain Andrew Carter, his CO. Both of them knew they could help B Company. Carter told Vannatta to go to Grindhausen, get some mortar ammo, and take it to Marnach. Lieutenant Vannatta ran out of the château, collared a driver, and took off. In three minutes, they were in Grindhausen. Vannatta and an ordnance sergeant loaded a trailer with all the ammo it could hold, hooked it to the jeep, and headed for Marnach, with a Corporal Crosby at the wheel. About three hundred yards west of the town, they stopped the jeep, hid behind a hill, and observed Marnach. Rifle and machine-gun fire was crackling all around town. A burst of enemy machine-gun fire stitched the road in front of their jeep. "Looks like we are going to have to run the gauntlet," Lieutenant Vannatta said.

Just then, Captain Jimmy Burns, the S3 of the 1st Battalion, rolled up in a jeep. Everyone in the battalion respected Burns. Some felt that he was the true brains of the outfit, not Lieutenant Colonel Paul. Burns's colleagues always seemed to have one question on their lips: "What do we do now, Jimmy?" Vannatta was no different. Burns told him to go ahead, and he would follow. Vannatta nodded at Corporal Crosby, and he gunned the engine. "Crosby drove expertly, not minding the crack of bullets. As we turned sharply to the left in the middle of town where mortar sections were located, the jeep skidded, hit something, and bent the right rear wheel." No one was hurt.

Vannatta's jeep was right in front of the local priest's home, across the street from the church and the crumbling remains of a house where the Eicher family had once lived. Soldiers materialized from the ruined buildings and began unloading the ammo. "German artillery shells exploded all around, and small-arms fire was continuous," Vannatta recalled. Someone told him that a whole company of Germans was pinned down in a draw south of town. The new mortar ammo would help keep them pinned down. Lieutenant Vannatta did not linger. With the ammo delivered and his jeep repaired, he and his men drove back to Urspelt, under small arms fire much of the way. Captain Burns stayed long enough to brief B Company on the counterattack, but he too left while it was still possible to do so.

A mile to the south, at Munshausen, the soldiers of C Company were moving north across rolling country, paralleling a small road that led north into Marnach. Lieutenant Colonel Paul had promised the company armor support from A Company of the 707th Tank Battalion, but now, at almost midday, the tanks still had not arrived. C Company attacked anyway. Back in Munshausen, artillery pieces from Cannon Company were lobbing shells into the woods ahead. The Germans were in there, everyone knew.

Lieutenant John Maher's platoon was at the point of C Company as it approached the woods. They were about halfway to Marnach now. All at once, the woods came to life with German fire. Several soldiers went down. Others spread out, found whatever cover they could, and returned fire. Maher knew immediately that there were way too many Germans up ahead for C Company to continue this attack. Somewhere behind him, the CO, Captain Carrol Copeland, got hit. He was badly wounded and needed immediate evacuation. More men were hit. Their cries echoed in the winter air. Everything was a mess. The new commander, Lieutenant Leo "Red" Seerey, ordered a withdrawal. Maher was fortunate to get out with most of his platoon intact. "The company returned to Munshausen," he recalled, "without contacting Company B."

They waited for the tanks, but again, they did not show up. Through a complete lack of coordination, the tanks—two platoons in all—missed connections with C Company and drove into Marnach, only to leave again amidst more confusion. In Marnach, Sergeant Charles Johnson, an artillery forward observer, had hoped that the arrival of the tanks might calm the situation in the town. Instead he watched in anger as the tanks left: "Abruptly the armor turned around and returned in the direction from which it had come. Some of us cursed about this. We felt deserted. That we had been let down by the tanks." Fair or not, this was the perception in Marnach. One tank platoon went back to Munshausen and eventually found C Company. The other, led by an inexperienced officer, made a confused retreat back to Clervaux (while Lieutenant Payne's platoon shot its way through to Hosingen). With every passing minute, more German soldiers from the 2nd Panzer Division were crossing the Our and streaming west, strangling Marnach ever so slowly but surely.[19]

All afternoon, the fighting ebbed and flowed along the 28th Division front. "Hosingen was completely surrounded," Colonel Fuller later wrote. "The same situation existed . . . at Weiler. A counterattack by Co. L at Holsthum was stopped at the crossroads east of Holsthum. The AT [antitank] platoon at Merscheid was surrounded." The same, of course, was true of Marnach. Further north, A Company at Heinerscheid was not surrounded, but the Germans were crossing the Skyline Drive north and south of town. A platoon-sized patrol from A Company, designed to push into Marnach, ran into swarms of Germans near Fischbach. They were fortunate to disengage and make it back to Heinerscheid. Fuller was doing the best he could to put up a fight, but his resources were limited. With the exception of his headquarters and his provisional reserve force in Clervaux, all of his frontline units were in action. As each minute passed, Fuller's situation was growing more desperate, and things were about to get even worse.

5

At 1600, German engineers finally finished construction on armor-capable bridges at Gemund (which Private Jackson and comrades had seen in its early stages on the evening of December 15) and Dasburg. The Germans finished the one at Dasburg at 1300 and started to move some armor across the bridge, but a tank slipped through the span and crashed into the river, drowning the driver. Repairs consumed the next three hours, but now they were done. The opening of these two bridges meant something very significant, and chilling: the Germans now had heavy armor across the Our.[20]

This impacted the fighting immediately. Dozens of Mark IV and Mark V (Panther) tanks from the 2nd Panzer Division and Panzer Lehr negotiated the hairpin turns that led to their new bridges, crossed the Our, and clanked up the winding, forest-encrusted roads that led west. Manteuffel had hoped they would be across the Our this morning, so that they could dart for Bastogne while the Americans were still in shock, but that had not happened. Instead, the tanks had joined up with their infantry friends and prepared to attack west on the roads to Bastogne, while reducing or destroying the stubborn American strong points along the way.

Three Mark IV's, plus elements of two Volksgrenadier regiments, attacked Hosingen at 1700 hours. Lieutenant Payne's five Shermans, from A Company, 707th Tank Battalion, had just arrived in town an hour earlier. They had come into the northern end of Hosingen on the Skyline Drive. Three of the Shermans deployed along the Steinmauer Hill. Payne placed his own tank in town, covering the south. Another Sherman was in a defilade position, not far from the water tower in northern Hosingen.

At the Steinmauer Hill, the German tanks quickly forced the three Shermans back into Hosingen. The Shermans took cover behind stone buildings and watched the southern approaches to town. The crews contented themselves with popping out of their positions, lobbing a few shells in the direction of the German positions, and racing back to cover.

At the same time, the main German attack was coming in the north, near the water tower. Enemy artillery chipped away at the tower, but still the American observation team stayed put, calling down fire from 81- and 60-millimeter mortars in the middle of town. Just west of the tower, there were about eight buildings on either side of the road. From the cover of these buildings, the Americans laid down devastating fire with well-sighted .30- and .50-caliber machine guns. Still the enemy kept coming. "The German infantry tried to enter the town but we were firing . . . point-blank with all our weapons plus some antitank guns we had placed on the road into town," Sergeant John Forsell recalled. "We did a lot of damage."

Not far away from Forsell, in a nearby barn, engineer Corporal George Stevenson and several other soldiers spotted a group of Germans about forty yards away. Stevenson was lying prone, pointing his rifle out of a window. He fired a full clip, trying to "aim at their stomach . . . all you're trying to do is stop them." Several Germans fell down. The rest retreated behind a haystack. Stevenson heard the thunk of an 81-millimeter mortar shell being placed down its tube. The shell arced over the barn and exploded "on that haystack and there wasn't many of them left. An 81 mortar is a big shell."

The Germans captured only a few houses on the outskirts of Hosingen. The fighting died down, although German patrols did maraud here and there. In the Hotel Schmitz, Captain Feiker took stock of the situation. Incredibly he had suffered only a few casualties in the course of this stressful day. He still controlled Hosingen; he was harassing German supply movements north and south of town. That was the good news. The bad news was that he was cut off, with a limited supply of food and ammo.[21]

At Lutzkampen, the enemy tanks arrived with the setting sun. In this sector, the enemy still had not crossed the Our. To do so, they needed the Ouren bridges. At around 1700, they began their push for the bridges.

Their path took them straight into B Company, 112th Infantry. The soldiers of this company had fought hard all day and had held off the Germans. For an hour or two, the Americans had heard German tank engines idling while enemy soldiers cleaned out Lutzkampen. Now, as B Company watched in horror, the tanks, accompanied by hundreds of infantry soldiers, emerged from the northern end of town. Officers were frantically calling for artillery, but none was available. The company had little, if anything, with which to fight tanks.

In a foxhole on a hillside overlooking Lutzkampen, Private First Class Charles Haug reflexively ducked in anticipation of the tank fire he knew was coming. "The tanks seemed to crawl along about two or three miles an hour. We bit our lips and prayed." In another foxhole, Private Alexander Hadden watched through wide eyes "the huge, black, obscene shapes" of the tanks. There were seven in all. "They approached up the road from the middle of Lutzkampen toward one of the farmhouses used by the company. All of a sudden there was a horrendous detonation from the cannon of the lead tank and the house collapsed and fell inward on itself in a shower of sparks."

Small-arms fire erupted. Tracers whizzed back and forth. The Americans were mowing down columns of German troops, but the tanks kept coming. At least one of them was a flamethrower. Jets of flame stabbed through the air. The sound of the flamethrower was eerie, unearthly, a tenor of hydraulic immolation. Haug and his fellow runners heard screams from somewhere up ahead. "We witnessed the most horrible thing any GI dreams of," he said. A flamethrower tank stopped fifty feet from an occupied hole. "As the two kids sat there helplessly, a gigantic stream of roaring fire shot in on them. They had been burned to a crisp." It was hard to envision a more horrible death.

Fingers of flame continued to seek out more victims. This was too much for several men around Haug. "Many of them jumped up from their holes and ran back over the hill and into the thick woods in back of us." Haug wanted to run with every fiber of his being, but he couldn't. He was too scared of the tanks to risk running away from them and drawing their attention, and he knew the first sergeant might need him to carry a message. The tanks were getting closer by the second. Two hundred yards and closing. Haug and many others were shaking uncontrollably, crying in their holes and praying for deliverance.

Half a mile to the north, several American soldiers were clustered around a 76-millimeter antitank gun. They were from the 820th Tank Destroyer Battalion, attached to the neighboring 106th Infantry Division. Now, in the distance, the antitank crew could see the German tanks silhouetted in the early evening darkness. Working together as a team, they loaded their gun and sighted on the lead tank. Led by their gunner, Paul Rosenthal, they snapped off a shot that missed. In a matter of seconds, they reloaded and fired again.

Haug watched in giddy amazement as the shell streaked past him, scored a direct hit on the front of the lead tank, and turned it into a flaming pyre. There was another shot, and the last tank blew up. In an impossibly short period of time another one brewed up. Concussion waves rippled from the blast area. Flames shot into the air. Haug could not help but smile at the carnage. "Did we ever have fireworks. Shells exploding in every direction. It was only a matter of seconds and the fourth and fifth tanks were also hit. Their tracks were knocked off and they weren't able to move." The burning crewmen were screaming in desperation as they died.

Enemy tanks and soldiers turned around and headed back into Lutzkampen. The carcasses of the destroyed German tanks continued to burn furiously. The Americans still firmly held the Ouren bridges. Manteuffel's careful timetable was in shambles here. One of the B Company lieutenants, obviously high on adrenaline, jumped from his hole and screamed, "We licked 'em!"

In their fury at being stopped, the Germans unleashed a massive artillery and screaming meemie barrage that caused many casualties, both physical and psychological, in B Company. Still, enough of the Americans remained to deter another German attack. The company's survivors stayed in their holes and kept watch. The very air around them stank of burned flesh—sickly sweet, distinctly crispy, like a strange mixture of spoiled meat and charcoal.

A couple thousand yards to the west, a lonely figure trudged into Colonel Nelson's command post at Ouren. He was cold, wet, hungry, and tired. Nelson's staff welcomed him, fed him, and gave him dry clothes. Sergeant Murray Shapiro, the machine gunner, had had a hell of a day. His entire squad was dead or captured. He himself had hidden among the Germans most of the day until they moved on. He had wandered for several hours, finally finding his way to Ouren. Like so many other men in the 112th, he had lived through the most harrowing day of his life, but he was still alive and willing to fight some more. He, like many others in the 112th, settled into an exhausted, grateful sleep.[22]

Several miles to the south, at Weiler, the end was near. The Germans were closing in on every side. Ammo was low. Company I could not hold out much longer. Sergeant Fred Pruett's machine-gun section was out of ammunition. He and his guys, about a dozen soldiers, destroyed their machine guns and hid in some haystacks. In a short time, the Germans found them. "I really expected them to fire into the haystacks. I did a lot of praying. One of the Germans could speak some English, and he directed us to come out from under the haystacks." Pruett was scared to death, and he hated the idea of giving up, but he knew that he must. He and the others came out with their hands over their heads. The Germans searched them for weapons, stripped them of valuables, and lined them up.

At the same time, Sergeant Meller's little OP was still holding out, waiting for help. Slim was still on the radio calling for tank support. Meller heard the distinctive rumble of armor, saw a tank in the distance, and practically jumped for joy. "Our tanks are coming. They're here," he said to Slim.

Slim emerged from the kitchen and looked out the window. "That's not ours. See the cross on the side?"

Meller's heart sank. Slim was right. The tank was German, and it was sitting right where one of his machine-gun nests had been. Another tank was approaching, as were multitudes of enemy soldiers. Transfixed, Meller watched them as if he were only a spectator: "I am petrified. I can't move my feet. I watch the nose of the cannon [on the tank] as it slowly turns and is now pointed right at me. He is going to shoot me. I'll be killed." The enemy tank fired.

In the nick of time, Meller dived to the floor. The shell whooshed through the house and went outside, hitting the barn where the mortar crew had set up. Meller and Slim crawled upstairs and took up firing positions at a window. Outside, there was shooting, tracers flying in the darkness. They fought until their ammo ran out. In a bizarre juxtaposition, they tried to kill the Germans outside and safeguard the lives of their two German prisoners inside. Finally, they had nothing more left to fight with. The shooting outside had died down. Sergeant Meller saw several of his men lined up, surrendering. "The Germans have lighted the barnyard with lights much like a night baseball park."

Meller went down to the kitchen, destroyed the radio, and prepared to surrender. He was filled with despair. "God help me, I tried," he thought. "In the movies the good guys are rescued at the last minute." This was not the movies. No one was coming. They were doomed. He stepped outside, holding his hands high, blinded by the lights.

There were eleven Americans, all standing in a row. Enemy soldiers stood stoically, pointing their burp guns at them. A high-ranking German officer, monocle in his eye, baton in his hand, looked the Americans over and began yelling at his men. Slim understood German. The officer was apparently dressing down his guys for allowing Meller's little squad to hold them off for the entire day. At least there was some satisfaction in that.

The blond German captain whom Meller had captured that morning spoke to the senior officer and vouched for how well Meller had treated him. Another officer stepped forward: "You will walk in single file with the German guards. You will not talk or make any sound. When you reach your destination, you will be counted. If anyone is missing, you will all be shot immediately." For Sergeant Meller and his men, these first few moments of captivity were only the beginning of months of privation, hunger, and misery.

Back in Weiler itself, the American defenses were on the verge of collapse by 1900. Captain Floyd McCutchan, the CO of I Company, and Lieutenant Edward Jenkins, an officer from the antitank company, decided to split their survivors into two groups and fight their way out of Weiler. Many of them did make it out. One of them was Private First Class Chester Kuzminski, who that morning had first alerted his unit to the German attack on Weiler. His little group made it all the way to Clervaux, where they reported to a major at Fuller's headquarters. "What do you want?" the major asked.

"I Company reporting."

"I Company is captured," the major replied.

"Sir, there are six of us left here."

Kuzminski and his five buddies found foxholes and augmented Colonel Fuller's scratch defense force in Clervaux. McCutchan and twenty-five others eventually made it to Consthum. Jenkins and much of his group also got away.

Meanwhile, back in Weiler, the Germans were finishing off any Americans who had not been able to get out. Half the town was burning. Sergeant Pruett, the machine gunner who was now a POW, was outside of town with a few other men, waiting under guard. A firefight was going on inside Weiler. On one of the streets, a German soldier was badly wounded, "screaming and crying," in a prone, fetal position. The guard told Pruett and another man to go get the wounded German. Pruett was afraid they would be caught in the crossfire, but he went anyway. "At that moment when we started out in that street, the firing . . . ceased. We got out to the soldier and he'd been shot in the stomach."

Pruett remembered hearing that if a man had a belly wound, he should not drink water, as it could kill him. For a brief moment, he thought of giving this German some water, just to finish him off. But he could not do it. He and the other man half-carried, half-dragged, the wounded German to safety. Behind them, Weiler burned fiercely. The shooting had stopped for good. There were no more live Americans to resist.[23]

Several miles to the north, at Marnach, the Germans were attacking with tanks and half-tracks. The town lay astride the main Clervaux-Bastogne highway. With the Our River bridges in service, scores of vehicles were crossing the river, winding their way up the narrow road, and dashing west along the Marnach plateau. As they did so, they poured fire into the already smoldering buildings of Marnach.

With the exception of a few bazookas, the Americans had nothing with which to fight tanks. The tanks were rapidly approaching Sergeant Morris Pettit's foxhole just east of town. He felt helpless, knowing that he could not stop them. "We did not have a single tank in support. I decided the best thing to do was to get my men in the woods north of Marnach. Every man had to get to the woods as best he could. Only four of my eleven men made it out of Marnach." Pettit made it all the way to Clervaux.

Back in town, Sergeant Charles Johnson, the artillery forward observer, got a radio call from his captain: "[He] . . . ordered us to return to Reuler." Johnson and his two team members scrambled into their jeep, under small-arms fire all the way. The driver smashed his knee against the jeep, injuring himself in the process. The radioman took the wheel and drove, while Johnson and the other man "faced backward in the jeep firing our rifles." They made it safely to Reuler. Johnson never found the other observer he had been sent into town to retrieve.

The observer, a corporal, was still somewhere in Marnach, radioing fire missions to the battery. The Germans were so close to him that he was trying to call down fire on his own building. In his last transmission he whispered, "Hurry. Fire. They're coming up the steps." No one ever heard from him again.

Private Whitey Schaller and a small group of his buddies were in a different spot now than earlier in the day. They had vacated the building east of the church because the Germans had seemed to be zeroing in on it throughout the course of the day. Now they were on the second floor of a house that overlooked the little intersection that led to Roder. "The room was a hayloft entered from the top of the stairway and situated over a single car garage." They had a bazooka, but no rockets for it. German armor was cruising just below, back and forth, into and out of Marnach. Schaller and his terrified comrades held their fire for fear of revealing their position to the enemy tankers. Then, as Schaller and the others watched in horror, a German tank parked in the garage right below them, so close that they hardly dared to move. Outside, more tanks were finding bivouac spots. Schaller and company were right in the middle of a German encampment.

At the same time, Sergeant Stanley Showman, the Virginian, and three of his men were in a stone house in Marnach, peeking through windows, watching as German half-tracks rolled into town. Around them several buildings burned, but not theirs. "It was almost like daylight." Several Germans hopped off the half-tracks and began walking around. Showman and the others opened fire on them. Scores of the enemy went down. Some were dead; others were flopping around, wounded, screaming for help. The half-tracks backed up and left. "Then they came in with a tank. It had a long barrel." Showman's group was face-to-face with a Mark V Panther. The steel monster could not have been more than twenty or thirty feet away.

For a few minutes, only the crackling of the fires and the muffled sobs of the wounded could be heard. "Come out or we're going to blow the building down!" a German shouted in accented English. Showman knew there was a rear door in this house, away from the tank. "Come on!" he ordered.

They ran as fast as they could. "We came out of there and down over [a] hill and through the snow. We went there along the woods and the four of us . . . got up underneath a pine tree. Some of them old pine limbs came right down to the ground. We raised 'em up and crawled out of there." Behind them, they heard no shooting, and there was no sign that any German infantry were trying to apprehend them. Sergeant Showman and the three others huddled together, shivered in the snow, and waited for the night to pass.

The same was true of the rest of the doomed garrison at Marnach. The Germans were not organized enough to occupy the town yet. They contented themselves with shooting at American-occupied buildings, and then they either bivouacked or kept moving west. The surviving members of B Company could only hide, hold out, and hope to be rescued in the morning.

Ten miles to the southwest, at the division headquarters in Wiltz, General Cota was on the phone with Colonel Fuller in Clervaux. In his brusque way, Fuller was still lobbying Cota to release his 2nd Battalion. Up to now, the general had resisted doing so, but he was reconsidering. For the last few hours, the general had been piecing together his division's situation. This had been a rough day, but it could have been worse. The 109th Infantry was under pressure but holding. The same was true for the 112th. Fuller's 110th Infantry, though, was in serious trouble. Company A at Heinerscheid was still holding the town but had been bypassed by strong enemy formations to the north and south. Company B at Marnach was, of course, surrounded and on the verge of annihilation. There were even reports that the Germans were closing in on Reuler, where Captain Andy Carter's D Company had set up hasty positions. The Germans had taken Weiler. They had cut Hosingen off and were on the verge of overrunning Holzthum and Consthum. Cota knew that German armor and reinforcements were pouring across the Our. They would make tomorrow a living hell for the survivors of the 110th.

Cota knew that his mission had not changed. His 28th Division must sacrifice itself to save Bastogne. The 110th Infantry would pay the highest price. They deserved what little help he could give them. The time had come to release his last reserves. "If I give you the 2nd Battalion," he asked Colonel Fuller, "what will you do with it?"

On the other end of the line, Fuller perked up. "I'll use it to counter-attack with the object of relieving Marnach and then Hosingen."

Cota gave his assent. He would send E and F Companies of the 2nd Battalion to Fuller. For the moment, Company G would remain in Wiltz to guard the division headquarters. When Fuller hung up the phone, he felt good for the first time that day. At last he could strike back at the enemy, maybe even restore his shattered front. He immediately set to work with his staff, planning his counterattack. As they worked, the final hours of December 16 ticked away.[24]

4

SUNDAY, DECEMBER 17

1

At Eselborn, a little town two kilometers west of Clervaux, Corporal Frank Stepnick was inside a warm farmhouse, snoring inside a GI sleeping bag. A twenty-three-year-old native of Claridge, Pennsylvania, he was part of a light mortar crew that belonged to F Company, 110th Infantry. At 0200 the farmhouse door swung open. A whoosh of chilly night air engulfed the room. A sergeant told everyone to get up immediately. Company F was moving out. Orders had come down—something about attacking east to relieve B Company in Marnach.

Corporal Stepnick shook the cobwebs of sleep from his brain, got up, rolled up his sleeping bag, collected his weapons and his equipment, and got ready to move out. So did the rest of F Company. They stood outside, waiting for word to leave, shivering a bit in the moist, dewy winter night. The residents of Eselborn noticed that their American guests of the last few weeks were leaving, and they knew exactly why. The Germans were obviously making a big push. The idea of a second occupation was repugnant to these Luxembourgers. A woman came up to Corporal Stepnick. "Don't let them come!" she pleaded earnestly. He nodded awkwardly, not quite sure what to say.

Company F moved off into the darkness, heading uncertainly to the east. A little to the north, at Boxhorn, so did E Company. The men of these two companies formed the backbone of Colonel Hurley Fuller's counterattack. Stumbling and cursing in the night, they made their way along the little road that led to Clervaux. Somewhere up ahead loomed the spire of the Abbaye St. Maurice. They marched past the Abbaye, many of them gawking at the spire, just visible to the right. On and on they went, descending the steep hill into Clervaux.

At Clervaux's medieval castle, Sergeant Charles Johnson, the Battery B, 109th Field Artillery, observer who had just vacated Marnach, was standing outside the main gate when he caught sight of the two companies "silhouetted against the night skyline . . . in ranks, prepared to enter the battle against the Germans. I recall thinking how magnificent . . . they appeared, but suddenly my heart saddened with the thought that death was near for many of these men. Bullets, mortar shells, tank shells and artillery shells would take a heavy toll on these infantrymen."

Sergeant Johnson also felt a bit guilty. They were advancing while he was retreating. Since leaving Marnach last night, he had made it to Reuler, only to find out that the battery was retreating to Clervaux. Now the Germans were so close to Clervaux that if Battery B did not get out of Clervaux, it might lose its guns. The situation was so hectic that Johnson's lieutenant would not even let him go back into the castle to fetch a duffel bag full of Christmas presents from his family.

In a bizarre juxtaposition that could happen only in a combat situation, Private Jack Chavez, another artilleryman, was a couple of blocks away, in the basement of the Hotel Commerce, having a good time. Chavez was in Clervaux on leave. Since the advent of the offensive yesterday, he had stood guard and dodged shells. With his guard shift over, he and his friend Private Waites were now back in vacation mode: "There were five or six gals taking shelter in the hotel cellar. We had a couple of the gals lined up." They were getting to know the girls, planning to open a bottle of wine, when they found out that the two soldiers who had replaced them on guard duty had left their post. "They thought that we were surrounded, the yellow b . . . ds," Chavez wrote in his diary.

With enormous reluctance and resentment, Chavez and Waites rose, dusted themselves off, said good-bye to the girls, and went back on duty. As they did so, they noticed that the hotel was taking some enemy small arms fire. That meant the Germans were close! In fact, they were in the Parc Hotel, a stately building carved into a hillside, which the Clervaux villagers called the "new" castle. Chavez and Waites set up in ambush positions, covering the door of the Commerce. "We can blast anyone coming in the main door," Chavez wrote.

If the Germans were now in Clervaux, they were also in Reuler, just over the ridge to the east. In the humble little house that served as D Company's CP, Lieutenant Glen Vannatta heard the fitful crackling of small arms fire outside. Enemy machine guns emitted short, tearing bursts, occasionally answered by American machine guns or rifles. The lieutenant stationed himself at an upstairs window that overlooked the ridge, toward Clervaux. "As I watched, I could see vague shadows moving in the ravine behind the house. By cracking the window, I was able to hear crunching snow accompanying the shadows. We were being surrounded by German infantrymen." The shadows vanished as the German soldiers moved west into Clervaux. Lieutenant Vannatta left the window and told Captain Andrew Carter what he had seen. Not wanting to give away their position, they decided to hold their fire for now.

The same kind of enemy movement westward was going on all over the 28th Division front. Most of the division's soldiers had slept only sparingly during the night. Some had eaten only one K ration meal. Everyone knew that as bad as things were yesterday, they would be even worse today.

German General Hasso von Manteuffel knew he was already falling behind his original timetable. For instance, he had thought he would have Bastogne by noon on December 17, at the latest. But as dawn approached on the seventeenth, he did not even have Clervaux yet. "When we hadn't captured Clervaux or crossed the river down there . . . I got worried that things were not turning out like they should," he later said.[1]

Thus he knew he had much ground to cover on this day. As ever, speed was of utmost importance. Now, just before dawn, the second day of his offensive began with a vengeance. Searchlights stabbed through the misty winter darkness. An artillery barrage, similar to the one the day before, battered American-held towns or known concentrations of U.S. troops.

As the shells rained down on Marnach, Private James Smith, a rifleman in B Company, was running for the shelter of his foxhole. "I caught the seat of my pants on some barbed wire. I was hung up there." All around him, German shells were exploding. He frantically tried to work himself free. All at once, a "shell hit not more than ten yards nearby and blew me off [the barbed wire], minus the seat of my pants." Badly shaken, he hopped into his foxhole. "I lit a cigarette, then another." He found out later that he had three small fragments lodged in his body.

By the time the sun rose, ushering in yet another cloudy, chilly, sodden day, the shelling had petered out. As before, it damaged communications and infrastructure but did not inflict many casualties on the Americans. The greatest danger lay in the overwhelming force that Manteuffel had at his disposal. Against the 112th and 110th Infantry sectors, he was attacking with the better part of the 560th Volksgrenadier Division, the 116th Panzer Division, the 2nd Panzer Division, the 26th Volksgrenadier Division, and Panzer Lehr.

At Lutzkampen, armor and infantry from the 116th Panzer (the Greyhounds) were massing for a renewed attack on beleaguered B Company of the 112th Infantry. The whole area stank of the burned flesh of German tank crewmen who had been immolated the night before.

In their holes overlooking Lutzkampen, the Americans could see the 116th Panzer getting ready to make trouble. First Sergeant Ralph McGeoch wanted badly to call down artillery on them, but communications with the 229th Field Artillery Battalion were out. McGeoch chose Private First Class Charles Haug and another man to go back and make contact with the artillery.

Upon receiving this order, Haug felt like he was being condemned to death. The Germans were shooting at anything that moved. He made his peace with God and set out, dodging shells and running to the rear. Try as they might, Haug and his buddy could not find the artillerymen. The two men emerged from a clump of trees into an open field. "Just as we started across the field, we heard a roaring sound to our left. We took one look and our hearts jumped to our throats. What we saw was a huge black German tank." Haug did not know it, but this tank was one of many that were making a renewed push for the Ouren bridges. The two American soldiers took off running. "As we ran, we heard a machine gun open up from the tank. As the bullets hit the ground, we could see the snow jumping about thirty feet from us." They made it to the woods and kept running "until we were so tired we couldn't hardly breathe." They caught their collective breath and continued their search for the artillery.

Not far away, Sergeant Peter Friscan, whose squad had fought so hard the day before, was distributing fresh ammo to his men. Friscan had caught some shrapnel from the morning's artillery barrage, but he was okay. He figured that he and his men would stay there, mixed in with D Company, and wait for orders, but those plans soon changed. "German tanks suddenly appeared in the area firing point-blank at us. The infantry followed." They could not even begin to stop this powerful force. The battle was over in minutes. "We were picked up by some of the Germans and taken to the rear about one thousand yards. From that point, I could see the Germans rolling on with nothing to stop them."

Indeed, three whole enemy regiments, the 156th Panzer Grenadier, the 1130th Volksgrenadier, and the 60th Panzer, including eighteen Mark V Panthers, were on the attack, working their way through the considerable gaps in the American defenses.

Corporal William Kelley, the artilleryman from Battery A, 229th Field Artillery, had the misfortune of running right into many of them. He and his buddy Pete were all that remained from their forward observation team. They had spent the night in Harspelt and had endured the morning's artillery barrage. Rather than sit idle, they wanted to do something, anything. In hopes of finding a battery for their useless radio, they left Harspelt and walked along a little road that led to Ouren. "The grind of heavy armor filled the air. The hope that it must be American renewed our energy." It was not American. "They were unmistakably [enemy] Tanks with their broad treads . . . and huge muzzle breaks [*sic*]."

Kelley and Pete took shelter ninety yards from the road in an old dugout. Two of the enemy monsters rolled by just below them. "There were several running, shouting Panzergrenadiers scurrying to keep up. As the tanks approached us along the road, we were literally looking down their muzzles." Kelley thought that any minute now they would spot the dugout and put some shots in there. He noticed a stand of pines just along the drop of the road and felt it might make a good hiding place. He told Pete that he was going to make a dash for the pines. "I'm right behind you," Pete replied.

Kelley made it to the pines, but Pete did not. Kelley had no idea what had happened to his friend. He lay there wondering if he had been seen. Were the Germans coming for him? "I was as scared as it is humanly possible to be." He was actually closer to the road in this hiding place. "I thought the rumble of the tanks would drive me mad. I heard the men's voices . . . and their cocking of rifle bolts. I counted eleven tanks in all roll by." He kept as still and quiet as possible, and waited and prayed, not necessarily in that order. Out there beyond Corporal Kelley's little hiding place, the race for the Ouren bridges was on.[2]

Miles to the west, at the Claravallis Hotel in Clervaux, Colonel Fuller was putting the finishing touches on his counterattack plan. During the night, he had ordered a few ill-fated jabs for Marnach. Now, in the daylight, his plan called for a three-pronged assault on the Germans besieging the town. Companies E and F, safely out of Clervaux now, would attack east along the Marnach road. To the south, a platoon from C Company, supported by a platoon of Shermans from A Company, 707th Tank Battalion, would push north from Munshausen. In the north, D Company of the 707th, consisting of M5 Stuart light tanks, would attack south on the Skyline Drive. General Norman "Dutch" Cota had just given Fuller these light tanks, and the colonel was only too happy to make use of them. They had spent the previous day waiting uselessly in reserve, near Ouren, in the 112th Infantry sector.

With his counterattack plan set, Fuller paused and puffed on his pipe. He was fighting exhaustion. He had been on his feet for nearly twenty-four hours now. Around him, the Claravallis was a beehive of activity as staff officers absorbed reports and carried out myriad tasks. For the moment, Fuller knew he had done all he could do. He was throwing his last bit of strength into the fight. He hoped to hell it would be enough.

A mile and a half to the east, the men of E and F Companies were patrolling warily through the trees that lined either side of the Marnach road. To their immense horror, they saw German tanks and infantry in the distance, heading right for them. The two attacking forces met head-on. It was like a Mack truck colliding with an economy car (with E and F Companies being decidedly the latter). The Americans tried to call down artillery on the enemy, but there was little to be had. Two batteries of the supporting 109th Field Artillery, B and C, were displacing under duress. The other, Battery A, was in the process of disintegrating under German attack. The soldiers of F Company inflicted some serious casualties on a group of German infantry moving southwest in a draw, but overall the Germans were simply too powerful. In a close-quarters brawl, the enemy steadily pushed the two companies back in disorganized pieces.

Corporal Frank Stepnick, the mortarman, was peering through a pair of binoculars, watching the Germans close on his position from a quarter mile away. He could see "tanks, trucks, and soldiers." Stepnick and his crew found a snow drift by the side of the road and hid. The German column passed by and disappeared in the direction of Reuler. "We got out of there and went up to this . . . little farmhouse where [a] hay mound was" and hid again. A few minutes later, the Germans found the hiding place and cornered them, forcing Stepnick and the others to surrender. "The Germans took my rings, my wallet and money and a new pair of boots I had just received."

Because the 2nd Battalion had run right into this large enemy formation, the main thrust of Fuller's counterattack was shattered before it even had much of a chance to unfold. Gradually the American survivors retreated back to Reuler, where the intensity of the fighting was growing.

Somewhere near that town, Private Bob Phillips, a young medic, was helping evacuate the wounded, who were drifting back after the failed counterattack. A twenty-year-old native of South Dakota, Phillips had fought with the 110th in Normandy, only to be wounded in the chest early in the fall. The only good thing about his wound was that it had kept him from experiencing the Hurtgen Forest.

On December 15, barely forty-eight hours earlier, Phillips had returned to his unit. Casualties had been so bad at Hurtgen that most of the faces were new. Now he was back in the vulgar world of combat. "It was hard to face. I hadn't adjusted to this way of life. Coming back, it's grim." Streams of wounded men were coming back—gashed by shrapnel, and with bones broken by bullets. Phillips helped put them on litters and carry them to safety on vehicles and on foot. He ended up in Clervaux, among a cluster of wounded soldiers, doing whatever he could for them.

Four miles to the northeast, Captain Herbert Ellison's D Company, 707th Tank Battalion, was on the Skyline Drive, rolling south out of Heinerscheid. Behind Ellison's force of eighteen tanks, Heinerscheid was still under the control of A Company, 110th Infantry. In front of him was no-man's-land. Lieutenant Thomas Byerly's 2nd Platoon led D Company's column. The terrain on either side of this stretch of the Skyline Drive sloped upward, forcing Captain Ellison to keep all of his M5 Stuarts on the road, in a linear formation.

On the outskirts of Fischbach, Byerly's platoon was descending a hill. Marnach was a mere two miles away. Crack! The bullwhip sound of a German antitank gun knifed through the crisp morning air. A millisecond later, Byerly's lead tank exploded into a fireball. "The Germans then proceeded to, methodically, pick off each tank in the stalled column which was unable to maneuver because of the steep shoulders of the road," an officer of the 707th later wrote. Company D was in an absolute kill sack. They were trapped, under direct observation from German tanks, antitank guns, and even Panzerfaust-toting infantrymen. The light armor of these little Stuart tanks could not ward off the enemy ordnance. One by one, the tanks got hit; their turrets were smashed; their treads were shot off; their hulls were penetrated by high-velocity shells that ricocheted around inside, shredding crewmen into dismembered pieces; their gas tanks or engines caught fire, singeing skin, burning hair, asphyxiating the men, and consuming flesh and bones in avaricious flames.

Surviving crewmen bailed out and found themselves under intense small-arms and antitank fire. They scattered about, looking for cover. Lieutenant Orville Nicholas's tank took a direct hit in the tread. He and his crew evacuated the tank, grabbed the .50-caliber machine gun from the turret, and took shelter in a nearby house, only to find it occupied by the Germans. They quickly surrendered. As the enemy herded them east, Lieutenant Nicholas saw the smoldering remains of one of his platoon members lying in a ditch. Hoping to extinguish the flames, Nicholas took a step toward the body, only to be sharply prodded back into line by his captors.

In a matter of ten awful minutes, D Company was virtually destroyed. Two tanks managed to take cover behind a church and then escape back to Heinerscheid. Five more made it to Urspelt, and even got some payback against an exposed company of Panzergrenadiers along the way, killing or wounding fifty of them. These five refugee tanks made common cause with Lieutenant Colonel Donald Paul's 1st Battalion, 110th Infantry, headquarters near his château in Urspelt.

Company D, totally unsupported by any infantry, artillery, or heavier armor, had blundered into a much stronger enemy force and had paid a terrible price. "It was criminal that they should have been sent on such a mission," Major R. S. Garner, the battalion executive officer, later commented.

To the south, the lone platoon of tanks and infantry (2nd Platoon, A Company, 707th Tank Battalion, with a platoon from C Company, 110th

Infantry, riding on its decks) sallied forth from Munshausen and made it to the edges of Marnach, but with little effect. Instead of turning around and going back to Munshausen, Fuller ordered them to Clervaux. His counterattack had failed. Marnach was on its own.

Inside that little town, the situation was growing increasingly desperate as B Company died a slow death. Private First Class Ed Uzemack, a bespectacled, twenty-nine-year-old native of Chicago's south side, was running ammo to the remaining company positions. His glasses were cracked, so he had trouble seeing more than a few feet away. He had once attended the Northwestern University school of journalism and had even worked as a reporter. Now he was loaded down with bandoliers of .30-caliber machine-gun ammo, zigzagging his way along an icy sidewalk. "A German machine gun opened fire to my right as I slipped and fell on my back, sliding toward an open door. A couple of GIs grabbed my legs and dragged me inside."

These men were manning a machine gun in a shattered house. In an adjacent room, the freshly killed body of an American, still warm, was lying in a grotesque heap. Outside, a wounded German soldier was crying for help, imploring his buddies to come get him. The cries would "fade and then return, louder than ever."

For several minutes, Uzemack and the others sat and listened to the pitiful moaning of the wounded man, until they could stand it no longer. "Why don't we put the bastard out of his misery?" one of the men blurted. He and a couple of others went outside. Uzemack heard several bursts of fire and then "no more cries from the wounded man." Scared, numb, and fatigued, Uzemack's group held on and waited for help.

In the small house that overlooked the Roder intersection, Private Whitey Schaller's group of five men had spent a hellish night hiding in the hayloft while thirty-four German vehicles bivouacked outside and enemy soldiers walked around downstairs. Now a new group of enemy soldiers entered the house, scavenging for food or valuables. One of the Germans walked right up on Schaller's group and saw them trying to hide. "Why, good morning, gentlemen," he said to the Americans. Schaller and the others glumly raised their hands over their heads. They were POWs.

A half mile to the east, at Roder, Private Joe Norris, still in the same fighting position where he'd been since the battle began, heard the sound of a tank engine behind him. He turned around and saw a German tank no more than thirty feet away. The sight of this armored monster, a "damned metal garage" as Norris called it, was overwhelming. The tank clanked to a halt and loomed over Norris and the men of his squad. Rifles and burp guns at the ready, German soldiers cautiously moved next to the tank, approaching the Americans. "These guys looked like they were fifteen or sixteen years old," Norris said.

The Americans dropped their weapons and reached for the sky. The teenage Germans descended on them and "just grabbed everything in sight, strip-searched us, took watches, money, cigarettes, anything they could get their hands on." When they finished, they marched Norris and his friends east toward the Our River. Bit by bit, the Germans were cleaning out Marnach and its environs.[3]

<h1 style="text-align:center">2</h1>

Back at Clervaux, T/Sergeant James Pelletier, a wire man with Headquarters Company, 110th Infantry, was at a .50-caliber machine gun, in the shadow of the old castle. Since the previous evening, he and three other men had been at this gun, blocking the main road through Clervaux. Now, in the morning light, Sergeant Pelletier looked to the east, toward the hairpin turn of the road that led into town from Reuler and Marnach. Not more than a quarter mile away he saw several Mark IV's, followed by half-tracks that were packed with Panzergrenadiers. Pelletier estimated that there were at least thirty half-tracks and maybe two platoons of tanks. The enemy vehicles were near the sanatorium and the town cemetery, gingerly attempting to negotiate the sharp turns of the road into the southern part of town. "We went back into the castle and set up the .50-caliber machine gun to help defend the castle." As they did, they stopped to warn two American tanks that they encountered on the other side of the castle, out of the Germans' line of sight.

These were the first two tanks of the 2nd Platoon, A Company, 707th Tank Battalion, Colonel Fuller's armored reserve. He had heard about the presence of the German armor. He knew that the enemy tanks and half-tracks on the Marnach road had just overrun the scratch force of GI vacationers he had emplaced there the previous day. Now he was sending the tanks to intercept the intruding enemy armor.

The American tanks carefully edged past the castle and drove along the southern edge of town, paralleling the Clerf River. Tanks were not designed to fight in this kind of terrain: lots of buildings, narrow streets, hairpin turns, and very little room to maneuver. One or two feet in the wrong direction could put a tank directly in the sights of an adversary. The Shermans made it around three hairpin turns on the Marnach road, at a higher elevation than the town now, rather close to the cemetery, and screeched to a halt. There, not more than seventy yards distant, were the Mark IVs. This was point-blank, the armored equivalent of hand-to-hand combat.

Main guns boomed on both sides. High-velocity shells tore through turrets and treads. Tanks exploded. "When the smoke of battle cleared," a 707th historian wrote, "the wrecks of four German and three American tanks littered the roadway battlefield. The remaining tanks of each side withdrew." The two surviving American tanks retreated from Clervaux to Drauffelt, ostensibly to replenish their ammo and medical supplies, but perhaps they had had enough of armored close combat for today.

Down in beautiful little Clervaux, near the Parc Hotel, German soldiers were peppering the medieval castle with small-arms fire and heavier munitions, too. They set up an antitank gun behind the Parc and lobbed shells at the castle watch towers, where they suspected that American snipers were holed up. The shells bounced off the thick walls of the venerable castle. "Every time there was an impact, lots of stones and dust came down, but the building stood firm," one Clervaux resident recalled.

A mile away, at the Claravallis Hotel, Colonel Fuller was pacing around the second floor, wondering if he could hold off the German armor. He knew that the two surviving tanks of the 2nd Platoon, A Company, 707th Tank Battalion, had left town, so he ordered another platoon of the company, the 1st, into Clervaux. This was the same one he had earlier ordered to support his counterattack at Marnach. This abrupt change of mission was a prime example of just how overextended the 110th Infantry was at this point. Right now, the 1st Platoon, plus a platoon from C Company, 110th Infantry, riding on the tanks, were out there roaming around the Ardennes roads, looking for a safe route into Clervaux. Obviously, they would not be there for a while.

In the meantime, Fuller needed more armor to deal with the German tanks around Clervaux. Earlier that morning, General Troy Middleton had ordered Combat Command Reserve (CCR) of the 9th Armored Division to set up roadblock positions west of Clervaux. CCR was a regiment-sized blend of tanks, self-propelled guns, tank destroyers, and armored infantry (riding in half-tracks). It consisted of portions of the 2nd Tank Battalion, the 73rd Armored Field Artillery, the 811th Tank Destroyer Battalion, and almost all of the 52nd Armored Infantry Battalion.

For several days now, CCR had been at Trois Vierges, backing up the 28th Division front. In fact, just the day before, CCR's commander, Colonel Joseph "Duke" Gilbreth, had offered to help Colonel Gustin Nelson's 112th Infantry, but Nelson had been able to stabilize his front without Gilbreth's assistance. Now, the increasing intensity of the German offensive created plenty of jobs for CCR. Realizing this, General Middleton, in consultation with General Cota, placed CCR in the center of the 28th Division front, right behind the hard-pressed 110th Infantry Regiment.

Colonel Fuller had been in communication with Cota for much of the morning, asking for help. In response, Cota now sent him B Company of the 2nd Tank Battalion (CCR). The company consisted of seventeen Sherman tanks, most or all of which were equipped with 76-millimeter guns. For several hours, they had been at Donnange, manning a road-block with C Company of the 52nd Armored Infantry. Now they rolled into Clervaux just when Fuller needed them. Inside the Claravallis, the colonel met with B Company's commander, Captain Robert Lybarger. Fuller, with crises to deal with all over his front, ordered Lybarger to send his 1st Platoon to Heinerscheid, his 2nd Platoon to Reuler, and his 3rd Platoon into Clervaux. Captain Lybarger left, disseminated the orders, and sent his Shermans on their way.

Minutes later, the five Shermans that made up the 3rd Platoon were creeping along a narrow street, near the castle. In the fourth tank, Ser-geant Donald Fink was standing in the turret, warily scanning ahead for signs of the German armor he knew was nearby. The gassy exhaust fumes of the tanks ahead of him were blowing in his face, but he was used to them. They even warmed this raw winter day a bit.

Just ahead, the lead tank stopped and took up position adjacent to the castle's main entrance. Fink glanced at the building next to his own tank and noticed a sign advertising the town post office. In the next instant he heard the supersonic sound of a high-velocity shell whizzing just past his tank. Then there was another shot. "The last [fifth] tank was hit. Of the five men in that tank, one was killed." Almost immediately, the tank burst into flames. Four men got out and took cover in a nearby building. The body of the dead man, the bow gunner, cooked inside.

Soon the Germans drew a bead on the lead tank and blasted it. The second tank bravely dashed forward, exposing itself, and pumped several rounds into the German antitank gun behind the Parc Hotel. "A couple of well-aimed shots crashed into the Parc, and the German cannon got quiet," an observer related.

The American tank was frantically trying to maneuver west of the castle, closer to Fink's tank, but it got hit and started burning. Another shell hit the third tank in line, just in front of Fink's. The shell bounced off the armor, but the crew had had enough. They bailed out of the tank and left it in the middle of the street. An artillery round whistled in and exploded in a building to the right of Fink's Sherman, collapsing the building into jumbled rubble, much of it cascading onto the Sherman.

Fink swung his head back and forth. Behind him the fifth tank was burning in the narrow street. In front of him, two more were destroyed, and the third was abandoned. Rubble was hemmed against his Sherman, making it difficult to move the tank without damaging the treads. The Germans, shooting from heights at the crest of the Marnach road over-looking Clervaux, obviously had this street zeroed in. "With the tank in the middle of the street and on fire, we could not get back out." Nor could they go forward. If they stayed in the tank, Fink knew they would eventually die inside it. He ordered his crew to abandon the tank. They ran into a nearby stone building "and only came out to fire on what a member of the infantry asked us to." Someone got on the radio to Colonel Gilbreth and told him, "We're surrounded and can't get out. They're closing in, and we're fighting like hell. Guess this is it."

Fink's platoon had sacrificed itself to buy more time for the garrison of Clervaux. The Germans, wary of more American armor, were content for the moment to keep their tanks perched on the heights above the town and shoot at anything that moved, while their infantry slowly infiltrated the buildings around the castle.[4]

Several miles to the northeast, German tanks from the 116th Panzer Division were racing for the Ouren bridges. They had overrun many frontline positions (crushing men in their foxholes or blowing them to bits) and were moving steadily along the Ouren road. "We saw eighteen tanks in column coming down the road," Captain Guy Piercey, the commander of M Company, reported. "Behind the tanks were deployed infantry. There were four personnel carriers in with the infantry. There were also three or four motorcycles amongst them. We dropped mortar and artillery fire on this column and the infantry dispersed into the woods . . . and the personnel carriers pulled into the woods." Even without their infantry support, the tanks kept going west, getting closer to the bridges by the minute.

The irony of this situation was that the day before, Colonel Nelson had had Colonel Gilbreth's CCR available, but the Germans had employed very little armor. Now, when the enemy was attacking with multiple tanks, CCR was no longer available to Nelson. To counter the attack, Nelson had a platoon of self-propelled guns from the 811th Tank Destroyer Battalion; some towed three-inch guns from C Company, 630th Tank Destroyer Battalion; and more towed 105-millimeter guns from his Cannon Company. The platoon from the 811th was east of the Our, right in the path of the Germans. Nelson's other guns were deployed west of the river, on the heights overlooking the bridges. He also had bazooka men. These brave men generally operated in two-man teams: one to load the ponderous, five-foot-long antitank weapon and another to fire it. In order to have any real chance of destroying a tank, they had to be within fifty yards of their target, way too close for comfort.

Now, as rays of late-morning sunshine attempted to penetrate leaden clouds, the enemy tanks shredded three of the tank destroyers from the 811th with absurd ease. The fourth one fled west out of danger. The German tanks kept moving, over the last ridge before Ouren, within sight of the bridges.

On a hillside overlooking the river, Sergeant Murray Shapiro, the M Company machine gunner who had made such a harrowing escape the day before, was now in command of a small rearguard section. He and this group were ensconced in foxholes. Only a few minutes earlier, they had gorged themselves on French toast and bacon that the cooks had left behind when they retreated that morning. They had also found several Christmas packages, cracked them open, and enjoyed fruitcakes, candy, soda, and beer. For a brief moment, everyone actually felt good.

But now they looked down into the valley and saw the enemy tanks. "We more or less froze, not knowing what to do with the tanks. At this point, the men I was given to command suddenly broke out of their holes and hightailed it down the slope to the valley floor." Sergeant Shapiro believed that they were running away, and he was outraged. He yelled at them, called them cowards, and told them to come back, but to no avail. "I was quickly to regret those harsh words of condemnation. These were antitank men and they were running to a concealed [three-inch] antitank gun camouflaged on the valley floor." Shapiro could only support them with ineffectual rifle fire.

Shapiro's antitank crew and several others fired at the lead enemy tanks. The German tanks, road-bound at the moment, fired back. As Shapiro watched in horror, an enemy tank fired a shell that tore through the camouflage netting of his antitank crew, ripping through them. To the sergeant, it looked like they had all been killed. The tank's turret turned in Shapiro's direction. He froze like a deer in headlights. Then, out of his peripheral vision, he saw one antitank man back on the gun. "He was mounting the gun and turning the barrel toward the tank. The German tank noticed it too" and began turning its turret back in the direction of the American gun.

By now, Sergeant Shapiro was shouting at the top of his lungs, urging the antitank man to fire. "He got off one shot, hitting a gas can on the side of the tank. The tank exploded in flame. Quickly the crew began to exit." Shapiro howled in delight and shot at the retreating crew, but it was hard to see them through all the smoke and flame. The next tank in line backed up, out of range of the antitank gun. Shapiro had just witnessed an incredible act of bravery from the surviving antitank crewman, and he did not even know his name.

As this was happening, the self-propelled guns of Cannon Company hurled their 105-millimeter shells at the German tanks. Cannon Company's guns were actually howitzers, designed to fire their shells in a parabola at distant targets, not at visible tanks at such short range. But the crews were resourceful. They depressed their barrels almost as low as they could go and bore-sighted on the tanks (in other words, they looked down the bore, sighted on the target, and fired, just like a man would do with a rifle). In order to achieve maximum muzzle velocity and a flat trajectory to the tanks, they loaded their shells with "charge five" powder, usually reserved for long-range targets. This created a slingshot effect. In the memory of one soldier, "At eight hundred yards, charge five gave the shells a terrific muzzle velocity and a very flat trajectory."

The result was devastating. Two shots took out the leading German tank. It exploded, sending flames licking into the air. Several more enemy tanks were hit. Captain Charles Crain, the CO of H Company, was watching from somewhere east of the Our and called this "the prettiest sight I had ever seen!" The burning lead tank blocked any further advance for the enemy. They maneuvered their tanks off the road, dispersed as best they could, and returned fire. Private First Class Clarence Blakeslee, the M Company mortar man, was in a shallow foxhole so close to the tanks that spent howitzer shells "were bouncing off" them. "The ricochets snarled by us and cut down large trees." Blakeslee, having little else to do, was gawking at nearby bazooka teams, watching them snap off shots and displace. He was so transfixed that he stood up. "I saw a tank turret revolving toward me. The muzzle flashed and there was a big explosion behind me. The turret revolved and flashed again." Once more he escaped injury, but the same could not be said for his lieutenant, who was disemboweled.

On the other side of the river, one of the Cannon Company guns took a direct hit, killing and wounding the whole crew. A shell exploded near another gun, wounding or driving away most of the crew. Corporal Howard Minier, the gunner, stayed at the gun all by himself. "He 'bore-sighted,' loaded, and fired along for eight or ten rounds," another soldier recalled.

Other fully crewed guns were firing with everything they had. One of them damaged a German tank on the road, close to Blakeslee's foxhole. He saw the tank commander, clad in shiny black boots, an officer's cap, and a black uniform, dismount the tank. "He started to walk back to a tank waiting for him. He walked straight, almost arrogantly, until the bullets began kicking up dust around him. He then started on a dead run, but too late. He went down and began dragging himself with his elbows." The tank that was waiting for the German officer now shielded him from the American fire, saving his life. All around them, the firing died down as the Germans began to withdraw out of range and into the woods. Cannon Company and the surviving guns of the 630th fired at their retreating shapes. Some crews even shot smoke shells when they ran out of armor-piercing ammo. Four enemy tanks were now little more than burning metal. Many more were damaged.

Colonel Nelson's 112th Infantry was chopped up and bloodied, but for the second straight day, it had stopped the Germans short of the Ouren bridges. This was important for several reasons: First, it bought time for Nelson to withdraw his artillery support, the 229th Field Artillery Battalion, west of the Our. Second, it saved his regiment from being cut off east of the Our. Third, and most important, it denied a vital river crossing to the Germans. They were now forced to reroute the bulk of the 116th Panzer Division south to the Dasburg River crossing. This was no mere inconvenience. The failure to capture the Ouren bridges during these first two days deprived Manteuffel of one of his key northern approaches to Bastogne and the Meuse River.[5]

In the south, at the opposite end of the 28th Division sector, the Germans were launching a brand-new series of attacks on Colonel James Earl Rudder's 109th Infantry. At Walsdorf, Private Robert Jackson and the remnants of F Company were still in their holes, hoping to survive the day. A day and a half earlier, Private Jackson and his comrades had discovered the secret German bridge-building project at Gemund. That now seemed like ages ago.

Fog blanketed the entire area around F Company. Jackson was clutching his Browning automatic rife (BAR) and peering into the fog. He and his foxhole buddy, Roger, heard unnatural swishing noises out there somewhere. Slowly the fog rose a few feet, fully exposing eight German soldiers right in front of their hole. "They had been creeping up on our position and soon would have been in our foxholes." Two GIs in a neighboring foxhole hurled grenades at the crawling Germans. "Two of them are hit and now the air is filled with their screams." One of the unwounded enemy soldiers threw a concussion grenade at Private Jackson's foxhole. It exploded, momentarily stunning him. The enemy soldiers used this to get away, under the dip of a sunken road.

The two sides now waited at a wary distance as a German medic appeared with a white flag. Company F held its fire as the Germans removed their shrieking wounded. When they were done, the battle resumed. A German tank was idling its engines, preparing to close in on F Company. As the enemy infantry soldiers fired from the cover of the road, the tank churned past them, "throwing chunks of dirt into the air behind it." An American rifle grenade team fired at the tank and scored a lucky hit. The grenade penetrated the side armor and ricocheted around inside, killing the crew. The tank skidded to a halt and sat there, an eerie relic with its engine still running as it spat diesel fumes into the fog.

Even without tank support, the enemy attacked again. They poured machine-gun and rifle fire at Jackson's positions. They ducked and covered, zigzagged, and flanked the Americans. Jackson had only a few clips left for his BAR. Captain Ronnet, the company commander, was dead. So was Lieutenant Cummings, the only other officer. For some reason, though, the Germans were reluctant to home in for the kill. They surrounded the Americans and waited. Exhausted, Private Jackson slumped into his hole and wondered what would become of him and the twenty others who were still alive. "What is left but death, retreat, or surrender?" he wondered. There were no other options. Not long after this bleak thought flashed through Jackson's mind, the Germans came and captured them. For him, the fighting was over, but the ordeal of captivity was beginning. Thousands of other soldiers from the 109th Infantry were more fortunate. They were fighting a steady withdrawal. Rudder's regiment was paying a heavy price, but it was holding the Germans in place, bleeding them steadily, giving ground only grudgingly.[6]

3

By early afternoon, the real crisis was developing to the north, for Fuller and the 110th. The Germans had Heinerscheid and A Company surrounded. Now the enemy brought up seven tanks, six 75-millimeter anti-tank (PAK) guns, plus plenty of supporting infantry, and went in for the kill. These Germans were from the 116th Panzer Division and had just crossed the Our at Dasburg rather than Ouren as they originally planned. Presently, they were rumbling north on the Skyline Drive.

Just outside of town, at a foxhole near the Skyline Drive, Private First Class Walter "Willie" Dayhuff heard the menacing sound of the German armor. Dayhuff came from Beecher City, Illinois, and had once worked for the Pevely Dairy in St. Louis. He was in his midthirties, an unlikely age for a rifleman. "I was on lookout. It was raining by that time. I heard the tanks coming down the road. I could hear the cleats." Dayhuff scrambled back into Heinerscheid to warn his company commander, Captain LeVoe Rinehart.

At almost the same time, the leading Shermans of the 1st Platoon, B Company, 2nd Tank Battalion (the CCR tanks recently dispatched by Colonel Fuller), arrived in Heinerscheid. Immediately, the Germans opened up on them, destroying the lead tank and wounding the platoon leader. For several minutes, the shots flew back and forth. A German Mark IV got hit and blew up. So did another Sherman. German PAK gunners battered American foxholes beneath the town water tower.

Captain Rinehart knew that he was hopelessly outnumbered and outgunned. He ordered the surviving tanks to join their 2nd Platoon comrades at Reuler. He also told his men to break into small groups and infiltrate west. At Heinerscheid the Germans captured thirty-eight Americans and claimed to have destroyed three tanks, but they did not eliminate all of A Company.

A mile to the east, at the Kalborn crossroads, Corporal Cecil Hannaford was listening as the firefight at Heinerscheid petered out. Amazingly, since coming to this OP almost forty-eight hours earlier, Hannaford and the 3rd Platoon of A Company had been unmolested. When he and the others had arrived on the evening of December 15, they had cursed their bad fortune. But now it seemed they were the lucky ones from A Company.

From the vantage point of his foxhole, Hannaford could observe the Skyline Drive and did not like what he saw. German vehicles, "dozens of them," were rolling north and south. "We just sat there and watched 'em go by. We had no idea of the significance of what was going on, none whatsoever." Hannaford and the other 3rd Platoon soldiers only knew that for them, everything was still quiet. They resolved to stay there, out of sight, and wait.

Twenty miles to the south, at Holzthum, Lieutenant Bert Saymon's L Company was clinging to the western edge of town. Saymon's company had been so badly shot up that it was down to platoon size (roughly forty men). This morning two Mark V Panthers had closed in on his schoolhouse CP. A bazooka team had driven them back with near misses. Later two Shermans from B Company, 707th Tank Battalion, had appeared as if out of nowhere. Reluctantly, they had engaged the Panthers. One of the Panthers fired a flanking shot at the leading Sherman and destroyed it.

Now Saymon was getting civilian reports that the Germans were massing their forces for a major assault on the remnants of L Company. As if on cue, the volume of enemy mortar and small-arms fire increased. Lieutenant Saymon knew it was time to get out. Earlier, Major Harold Milton had told him to defend Holzthum as long as possible and then fall back to Consthum, a mile and a half to the west. Saymon and his soldiers destroyed anything of value, left the schoolhouse, and retreated to Consthum, where Lieutenant Colonel Daniel Strickler, Major Milton, and a hodgepodge force were still holding out against repeated attacks. Holzthum was gone. Consthum was hanging in the balance.[7]

So was Hosingen. The Americans were still holding the town, and the Germans could not allow this to continue. As long as the Americans controlled Hosingen, Manteuffel's mobility and supply lines were in jeopardy. Without Hosingen, the 26th Volksgrenadier, Panzer Lehr, and the 2nd Panzer Divisions would have difficulty massing their formations and moving freely on the west side of the Our. Frustrated at the stubbornness of the American garrison at Hosingen, the Germans planned a major attack with elements of all three of those divisions. Early this morning, the enemy had pummeled the whole town with artillery, including 150-millimeter shells that turned several buildings into dusty rubble and wounded Captain William Jarrett, the engineer commander, in the foot. They followed up the barrage with a furious attack that failed.

Now, at 1300, they came again. Two Panthers took up position north of Hosingen and hurled high-explosive shells at the water tower. German officers had offered the tank crews some sort of reward if they could destroy the tower and, more important, the American observers inside it. Several times the tankers scored direct hits, only to see the tower remain intact. "The outside walls were of thick concrete and a steel shaft enclosing a circular steel stairway supported in the center," an American soldier recalled. "The steelwork deflected shrapnel from shells which penetrated the concrete walls."

Six more German tanks—from the 2nd Panzer—joined in the shooting, but to no avail. As they fired away, waves of German soldiers moved in on Hosingen from the north and the west. American machine gunners and riflemen opened fire from the cover of buildings, rubble, or foxholes. Mortar shells, still directed by observers in the tower, exploded among the Germans. Flying rocks and masonry added to the killing power of the mortars. The Wehrmacht soldiers were taking terrible casualties, but they kept attacking.

The battle was a slow, cumbersome slugging match. Enemy Panzerschreck teams or tanks blasted holes in the walls of buildings. Riflemen, snipers, and burp gunners then assaulted the buildings. "Our troops remained in firing positions in the houses as long as possible and then left the back doors to set ambushes for the Germans advancing in front of the buildings," Lieutenant Thomas Flynn remembered. Often they left booby traps behind. In this costly manner, the Germans took some of the northern buildings of Hosingen and began to put serious pressure on Jarrett's engineers along the western perimeter.

This put the opposing forces in close proximity to one another. Not far from the water tower, in one farmhouse, Private Edward Gasper, the nineteen-year-old rifleman, cornered an attacking German with the help of a couple of his buddies. "He didn't have his helmet on. He had a pistol. I think he was an officer or noncommissioned officer. We all had our rifles on him." Fingers on triggers, Gasper's group tensely stared at the enemy soldier. With wide eyes, he put one hand in the air and reached for his pistol with the other hand. "Now that was the dumbest thing I ever saw in my life. I guess he was gonna give us the pistol." But no one could be sure if he wanted to do that or to shoot at them. Gasper stood frozen in horrified fascination as the German's hand moved for his pistol. The whole incident took no more than a few seconds. When the man's hand was about halfway to the pistol, one of the other Americans "shot him right in the chest." As blood spurted from his chest, the German soldier fell backward into a hedge. No one even bothered to search his lifeless body for valuables.

In the wake of this incident, Gasper's squad, for fear of being cut off, withdrew into the interior of Hosingen under small-arms fire. Their fears were valid because even now, some of the engineers and a few soldiers from the 1st and 2nd Platoons of K Company were isolated in various sections of town. Like Gasper's squad, much of the American garrison was steadily being forced into a shrinking perimeter in the middle of Hosingen. This included Lieutenant Richard Payne's tanks, which were largely restricted to Hosingen's main street, around Captain Frederick Feiker's command post.

Feiker now took stock of his situation. His ammo was running low. Three of his machine-gun nests were gone, as was one of his 60-millimeter mortars. The cooks were running out of food. The power was out in Hosingen, and there was no running water. His thirsty soldiers had taken to melting snow for drinking or cooking water. He had no artillery support. No relief force was on the way. He suspected that he and his men would die together in this little Luxembourg town. Yet for now, his surrounded force was hanging on to battered Hosingen, costing the Germans precious time and manpower. As ordered, they were holding at all costs.[8]

Five miles to the northwest, at Munshausen, Lieutenant John Maher was looking to his left, gaping in amazement at what he saw. Maher's C Company rifle platoon was deployed at the northeastern edges of this little town. To his left, howitzer crewmen from Cannon Company were at their 105-millimeter guns, warding off a close-range enemy attack, something they were not trained to do. Munshausen was little more than a few blocks of stone barns and farmhouses with a small church in the middle.

As Maher watched, the howitzer crewmen loaded their pieces and fired high-explosive rounds at charging waves of German infantrymen. The shells exploded and tore gaps in the German host, but still they kept coming. Maher and his men opened up with their rifles and machine guns. In the distance, several German vehicles, probably tanks and scout cars, were raking over Munshausen. "Despite their superiority in arms and personnel . . . the Germans failed to make maximum use of their advantages. Enemy casualties seem to have been high against the stubborn defenses."

Stubborn was the right word. Munshausen was under attack from the north, south, and east. The Germans were throwing the better part of 2nd

Panzer's Abteilung 2—a mixed reconnaissance-oriented force of infantry, tanks, scout cars, antitank guns, and half-tracks—at the town. The American defenders, mindful of their sobering orders to fight to the end, did just that. In one howitzer position, the Germans overran the gun, killing some crewmen and capturing others. Near the gun, Captain Irving Warden, Cannon Company's CO, lay motionless, feigning death. He heard the German soldiers talking and moving around him. One of them stopped, bent over, and took his pistol. Leveling his weapon at Warden's head, he kicked the captain's body. Warden's heart was racing, but somehow he remained completely still. The Germans moved on. When they were gone, Warden slowly got up and made his way back to the American-held section of Munshausen. All around him, buildings were burning.

As the German infantry approached the houses of Munshausen, they came under intense sniper fire. American riflemen were concealed expertly at windows, in attics, in the church steeple, or anywhere else that afforded a nice field of fire. One after the other, M1s barked single-kill shots. Seemingly each time an M1 fired, a German soldier went down in a heap, dead by the time he hit the ground, blood spurting from head or throat wounds. One enemy assault group tried to sneak into town from the north. "All of them perished or were soon found dead with fatal head wounds," a German officer recalled. The dead included "their commander, Lieutenant Gelinek, who was a reservist and professor at the University of Vienna."

Close by, two Mark Vs edged carefully through an open farmyard, scanning for targets. One of them fired several shells into the church steeple, sending it crashing down in a mix of cobbled masonry. It was hard for the German tank commanders to see through the smoke from all the fires, so they had their hatches open and were standing in their turrets. In a house somewhere nearby, an American sniper was looking down the sights of his M1, zeroing in on one of the tank commanders, waiting for the right moment to take the shot. He exhaled and squeezed the trigger. An instant later, the .3006-caliber bullet smashed into the tank commander's head, spraying pink and gray shards of skull in a halo around what remained of his head. The commander slumped back a bit and then went straight down. The Mark Vs backed up and contented themselves with firing from a safe distance.

The German commander at Munshausen, Captain Heinz Novak, was impatient for more progress. Novak was popular with his men but perhaps a bit impulsive. He foolishly decided to dismount from his vehicle and recon the town by himself. He walked along a seemingly deserted street, within sight of the damaged church. A few feet away from Novak, an American soldier was hiding behind the town water basin, bayonet in hand, waiting to strike. In civilian life, the American soldier had been a butcher in Chicago. He knew knives and he knew how to kill the old-fashioned way. He had sharpened his bayonet to a fine edge. When Novak reached the water basin, the American leaped from cover, grabbed him, cut his throat from ear to ear, and plunged the bayonet into his chest. Warm, bright red arterial blood gushed from Novak's throat all over his chest. He fell to the ground. The butcher finished him off with blows to the head and then left quickly. Novak lay dead in the street, the bayonet stuck in his chest. Not long after, Lieutenant Rudolph Siebert, one of Novak's platoon leaders, found the captain's body. "His throat was cut, his jaw and skull were smashed," and his binoculars were gone. Civilians had taken them. Later, when German soldiers found Novak's body, they wanted to exact reprisals on some Americans whom they had captured. Their first sergeant put an end to any such thoughts.[9]

A few miles to the north, the American defenders of Clervaux were also holding on as best they could. At the southern end of town, there was a tense standoff. Scores of German tanks and half-tracks were on the Marnach road, overlooking Clervaux, firing at American-held buildings, especially the castle. By the hour, the German armored strength grew as more of the 2nd Panzer Division arrived. As yet, though, they had no orders to push down the road, past the cemetery, and into the town. Plus, the hulks of several Mark IVs that had been destroyed during the morning battle were blocking parts of the road.

One German tank did make a dash into Clervaux, though. It rumbled across the Clerf River bridge and past the Parc Hotel, stopped at a curve near one of the castle's watchtowers, and hid below the gable roof of a nearby house. One hundred meters away, there was a Sherman tank, possibly from Sergeant Fink's platoon, adjacent to the post office. Inside the Sherman, the crewmen could hear, but not see, the enemy tank. They snapped off several shots that hit in and around the roof, wounding a civilian inside the house but missing the German tank. When the American crew paused to reload, the German edged from cover, aimed at the Sherman, and fired. The 75-millimeter armor-piercing shell smashed into the U.S. tank, destroying it at once. The main road through town was now free of functioning American tanks, but the Germans were not yet ready to exploit this.

Their other tanks were still on the ridge overlooking Clervaux, and the crewmen were in rest mode. They hopped out of their vehicles, brewed coffee, and relaxed. Inside the castle, the small American garrison, consisting of 102 soldiers from Headquarters Company, 110th Infantry, enjoyed an excellent view of the enemy tankers. The castle had multiple stories, with several watchtowers and a solid stone facade that curved around the whole structure. The facade was honeycombed with apertures that made ideal firing slits. At one aperture, Staff Sergeant Frank Kusnir, the experienced intelligence and reconnaissance man who had several days earlier sensed that the Germans were planning something big, could hardly believe the enemy Panzertruppen were this foolish. "What the hell's going on?" he wondered.

He poked his rifle through the aperture. "These German . . . tankers . . . started smoking cigarettes and drinking coffee." He fired a clip and hit several enemy soldiers. Others around him did the same. "We started picking 'em off one by one. It was like ducks on a pond. After several of 'em got hit, then they all scampered back into their . . . tanks." They shot at the castle, but with little effect, except to chip away at the stone walls.

There were still plenty of targets for the Americans. At another aperture not far from Sergeant Kusnir, an American sniper calmly took aim and fired. Somewhere out there a German soldier went down. The American had a sniper scope on his rifle and a cigarette dangling from his lips. As calmly as if he were at a shooting range, he aimed and fired several more times, scoring hit after hit. Jean Serve, a sixteen-year-old local kid, was standing next to the sniper, picking up empty casings as they ejected from the sniper's rifle. As Serve watched, the sniper's bullets ripped into at least four Germans. One of them got hit and rolled down the hill behind the Parc Hotel, coming to a lifeless stop at the bottom.

The boy was squatting up and down—one minute gawking at the dead quarry, another minute bending over to pick up the hot casings that jangled on the floor at the sniper's feet. Sedately, almost clinically, the GI scanned for targets, all the while absentmindedly sucking on the cigarette that dangled out of his mouth.

Serve left the sniper and walked around the castle. He was one of seventy-five civilians who had taken refuge there. This was a town tradition. Since the twelfth century, the residents of Clervaux had come to the castle in times of danger. Serve had come to the castle with his parents the day before, soon after the German attack began. His parents and most of the other civilians were in the basement, waiting apprehensively, some of them crying, and hoping that the Germans would not take the town again. There were also eighteen German prisoners down there. Most of them were quiet but smug, as if they knew their comrades would soon liberate them. A deep gloom settled over the civilians, some of whom were elderly or sick.

For teenaged Jean, though, this experience was an adventure, a lark. He wandered around the castle, taking in the sights, watching the Americans and helping them any way he could. In one room, he saw an American soldier at a piano. As shells exploded outside, the soldier played the

piano, banging out popular American tunes, seemingly oblivious to anything but his music. Jean stood and listened for a time, then continued his
impromptu tour of the castle.

Beyond the castle walls, small groups of German infantry soldiers
were steadily capturing houses or shops that lined the streets of Clervaux.
Ever so slowly, they were cutting off the castle and the southwestern part
of town.

A mile away from the castle, at the Claravallis, Colonel Fuller was in
full crisis mode. His regiment needed help, and it needed it now. He knew
that the Germans were steadily overwhelming the 110th. A few minutes
ago, German soldiers had come within two hundred yards of the Claravallis, only to be driven back by some of the colonel's headquarters troops.

Fuller was working the phone to division, begging for reinforcements.
"Our situation in Clervaux was growing more desperate by the hour," he
wrote. "I asked for more artillery support, more tanks, and a battalion of
armored infantry." He was hoping that Cota would send him elements of
CCR, parts of which were even now setting up roadblocks west of Clervaux astride the Bastogne road. But CCR was not Cota's to give. It was
under the control of General Middleton, and the situation was so critical
now that Middleton needed CCR's tanks, half-tracks, and self-propelled
artillery to defend the approaches to Bastogne. General Cota told Fuller
that all he could send him right now from CCR was a platoon of M18
Hellcats from C Company, 811th Tank Destroyer Battalion, in Drauffelt.
Cota signed off with what had now become a monotonous, grim mantra
for the 28th Division: "Hold at all cost. Give up no ground."

Fuller hung up the phone and strode out of his office into the hallway. This headquarters was like a recently disturbed anthill. Officers and
NCOs were scrambling back and forth. Confused reports were streaming
in from what was left of the frontline companies.

Fuller looked in the direction of the lobby where the S2 desk was situated. "Captain Rensmeyer! Report to me immediately!"

Edwin Rensmeyer hustled up the stairs and into Fuller's office. On
the evening of December 15, the young captain had returned to the 110th
and settled into his new job in the S2 section. Things were so quiet that
night that he had spent most of his time writing letters home. Now he had
no time for such things. As Rensmeyer listened, Fuller asked him if he
knew where Drauffelt was. "I replied I did not know where it was but that
I was certain my driver would know it," the captain said. Fuller ordered
him to take his driver, go to Drauffelt, find the tank destroyers (TDs)
and guide them into Reuler, where the American defenders were "in
real trouble." Rensmeyer grabbed his weapon and left. He and his driver

easily found Drauffelt and the TDs. They then drove north through Clervaux and over the ridge into the northern part of Reuler.[10]

Just ahead, the Americans at Reuler were engulfed in the desperation of a house-to-house fight. Powerful armor and infantry formations of the 2nd Panzer Division were pushing north, into the town. The southern part of Reuler was at the junction of the Marnach road. A vehicle continuing west on that road would end up at the hairpin turns that led downward into Clervaux. If the vehicle turned right at the junction, it would go north into the heart of Reuler. The 2nd Panzer was doing both. Some of its tanks and half-tracks were going west to Clervaux (chipping away at the castle, pushing for the Claravallis), while others turned right into Reuler.

The Germans took the southern houses of Reuler against little resistance. Now they were moving deeper into the village—which lay on a gradually sloping hill—straight into the heart of the American defenses of the town. The GI defenders were a mixed collection of troops. There were machine gunners and mortar men from D Company, riflemen from E and F Companies who had retreated into Reuler that morning, and some officers from both the 1st and 2nd Battalions. For armor support, they had the TDs, five tanks from the 2nd Platoon, B Company, 2nd Tank Battalion, plus a few more B Company tanks that had retreated from Heinerscheid.

Some of the infantrymen were lying behind hedges or in ditches. Others were in houses. German soldiers, clad in the distinctive field gray uniform of their army, were on either side of the road that bisected the town. Many were on their bellies, crawling while others covered them. Hollering back and forth, they went into a couple of farmhouses, rounded up the owners, herded them into cellars, and told them that they would be shot.

The Germans approached a house that almost hung over the road, with windows facing right down on their advancing troops. In that house, an American soldier was crouched against a wall, listening to the Germans but unable to see them just yet. The window was open just enough for him to poke his rifle muzzle through it. Across the street was a ditch. Figuring that it would be a good hiding place for the enemy, the GI fixed his attention on it. He was right to do so. He saw a German helmet pop up. He aimed and squeezed the trigger. The bullet knifed through the helmet and struck home with an odd sound, like a mixture of a bell's quick ring with the clank of a hammer on a steel girder. The helmeted head disappeared, but the sniper kept aiming at the ditch. Another helmet popped up. The sniper squeezed the trigger again. *Crack! Clank!* Another German soldier was dead. Two more chanced a look but did not live to tell of the experience. The rest clung to the ground. They had no idea of the sniper's whereabouts, and they did not wish to find out the hard way. The sniper leaned back and waited. From the foggy shrouds of the road, he heard the sound of tank engines.

Several German Mark IVs were driving right up the main road, blasting suspicious buildings, setting them afire. At that same moment, American tanks were on the same road, approaching from the other direction. The two tank columns were face-to-face in the street, like gunfighters in a spaghetti western. "In the narrow street neither party could escape," one witness recalled. "Whoever was quickest by a fraction of a second remained the victor." Both sides lost two tanks. Their remnants burned within a few meters of one another. Somehow the surviving American tanks backed into the northern end of the village. German soldiers, worried about American snipers and Luxembourg partisans, raided the houses around the burning tanks, forcing more civilians outside. They lined up one group of men against a wall and threatened to shoot them if they moved.

At almost the same time, Captain Rensmeyer and the Hellcats came into town from the north. Rensmeyer told the tank destroyer commander which direction he was supposed to take and watched as they rolled over the dip of a small hill. "A heavy firefight and tank battle was in progress. One of the German tanks put a round squarely in one of the TDs. It appeared to be a case of almost outright slaughter, they were so clearly out-gunned."

Rensmeyer did not linger. His orders were to go back to Clervaux and report to Fuller, and he did so, even capturing a German prisoner on the way. The TDs did not stay in Reuler much longer, either. Under intense artillery fire, they bugged out of Reuler and back into Clervaux, and then points beyond. "I saw them withdrawing from Clervaux at a high rate of speed," Fuller related. "In fact, so great was their haste to withdraw that one gun was overturned and abandoned on a curve while coming down the ridge."

In the meantime, German tanks kept rolling through Reuler. Lieutenant Vannatta, the D Company officer who had seen German soldiers infiltrating the town that morning, was still in the company CP, observing the action. From his vantage point, he saw dozens of German half-tracks, trucks, vans, and tanks lined up in the distance, on the Marnach road. Now as he watched in awestruck horror, two German tanks were approaching the CP, blasting any buildings in their way. He, Captain Carter, and their radioman, Corporal Ameluxen, fled the house and took shelter in a nearby pigsty. While Captain Carter worked the radio, trying to get information, Lieutenant Vannatta kept a sharp watch on what was happening around them. Fifty or sixty meters away, at the edge of a courtyard, a shell scored a direct hit on Company D's kitchen truck, setting it on fire. Carter looked at Vannatta and said in his New Orleans accent, "There goes our bed and chow." Vannatta nodded absently.

The din of battle was deafening. "The sound of machine-gun fire was almost continuous," Vannatta said, "both American and German, easily distinguishable." Vannatta saw a German tank about a block away. "The panzer rolled on, knocking out buildings. German infantry with machine pistols followed on each side spraying everything in sight. The street was a steady stream of bullets and flying shrapnel."

The tank was getting closer. Captain Carter peeked around the corner of their pigsty, right into the ugly barrel of the tank's main gun. "Let's get out of here, Van!" he shouted. Carter, Vannatta, and Ameluxen rose as one and dashed for safety. They ran across the courtyard and made it to the temporary shelter of a little schoolhouse that the medics had turned into an aid station. They smiled at Captain Lawrence Woodley, the 1st Battalion surgeon, and "with a wan smile" he looked up from the wounded man he was working on. The moment passed quickly. Woodley turned his attention to the wounded soldier. Vannatta, Carter, and Ameluxen exited through a rear window and kept retreating north.

Not far away, T/Sergeant Stanley Showman, the Virginia farm boy, and three other men were fifty feet away from another German tank, preparing to fire a bazooka. Showman and these other men from B Company had gotten away from Marnach the previous evening. They had spent the night in the woods, huddled together for warmth in the snow. They nearly froze, but managed to make it through the night. This morning, they had worked their way west into Reuler. Among them, they had about a dozen shells and one bazooka.

Now one of the other men loaded the shell into the rear of the bazooka and wired it up. Sergeant Showman stepped out from the cover of a house, aimed at the tank, and fired. The rocket streaked from the front end of the bazooka and hit the tank but did no damage. Showman ducked back behind the building. Again and again, they loaded and fired. "We just jumped back, put one in, jumped out and hit her again." Each time, the shell glanced harmlessly off the tank's frontal armor.

Frustrated and frightened, Sergeant Showman and his three men ducked back behind the building and tried to decide what to do. They had no small-arms ammo and no more bazooka shells. There was no way to get out of there. The German tank had them cornered. For some reason it did not shoot at them (perhaps they were too close for the main gun, and its machine gun was jammed). Instead the enemy tank commander yelled, "Come out of there, or we are going to blow the building down." Showman knew that he had no choice but to comply. He walked into the street, his hands held high. Behind him, the three others did the same. Many grim months of captivity lay ahead for all of them.

Inside the schoolhouse aid station, Captain Woodley was still trying to save lives, even as the Germans edged closer by the minute. He was working on wounded men from both sides. Some of them had shrapnel wounds from grenades, mortars, and tank shells. Others had bullet wounds, usually from close-range, high-velocity shots.

Elsewhere in the aid station, Corporal Carl Montgomery, a chaplain's assistant from Washington, Pennsylvania, was taking care of a wounded German officer. Montgomery's boss, Captain Rowland Koskamp, a Dutch Reformed minister, was circulating around the schoolhouse, doing what he could for the wounded men. Montgomery functioned as Koskamp's jeep driver and personal assistant. Montgomery was a thoughtful, literate twenty-three-year-old. He was an amateur photographer and an inveterate letter writer and record keeper who had been with the 110th since 1940. He tagged along with Koskamp wherever he went, and today the minister wanted to be here, right on the front lines, in the middle of the enemy attack. They dispensed water, gave out cigarettes, and generally did whatever they could to make the wounded soldiers comfortable.

Corporal Montgomery, like so many other men in Reuler, had seen the armada of German vehicles in the distance, cruising along the Marnach road. At first he had been unconcerned. He figured that American tanks, planes, and artillery would stop them in their tracks. "They always had before, and I had no reason to think they wouldn't this time, too."

As the hours in Reuler wore on, and the situation grew more desperate, Montgomery's attitude changed. He knew now that they were in trouble, and for at least two hours, he had been trying to convince Captain Koskamp to leave. Koskamp would not hear of it. These days he was a little impatient with Montgomery anyway. Several weeks before, Koskamp had chastised his assistant for stealing bedsheets from a German home. Since then, their relationship had been a bit strained. Even so, Montgomery could not abandon his chaplain. He had already spent part of the day arguing with another buddy who wanted to leave. Montgomery wanted to get out, but he could not bring himself to leave Koskamp's side.

Now Corporal Montgomery moved away from the wounded German officer and stood by a blown-out window. A Sherman tank was parked right outside, so close he could have "reached out . . . and touched the thing." As Montgomery blinked in horrified surprise, the Sherman took a direct hit, caught fire, and blew apart. The concussion waves nearly overwhelmed him. The ammo from the tank scattered into the room and "proceeded to explode."

Montgomery and everyone else skittered away and took cover. To make matters worse, a German tank "was firing direct fire into the building too." The tank pumped round after round into the schoolhouse. Each shell ricocheted around the building and exploded, adding to the swelling number of casualties. A strange calmness came over Corporal Montgomery. He was too disgusted to care much about what happened next. He was very angry at Koskamp for not heeding his warnings. "I just sat there disgustedly not giving a damn."

Montgomery and his buddy could still, at that point, have made a run for it, probably in the same direction that Lieutenant Vannatta's group had gone. But Corporal Montgomery could not do it. "Somehow I couldn't summon up enough energy to do anything." He sat complacently as Koskamp left the building, waving a Red Cross flag. In a few minutes, German soldiers poured into the schoolhouse and took them prisoner.

By now, the Americans controlled only the northern edges of Reuler. Since leaving the aid station, Lieutenant Vannatta, Captain Carter, and Corporal Ameluxen had made it to the 2nd Battalion's CP. The entire way, machine-gun bullets stalked them. They had even "kicked up dirt" at Vannatta's heels as he ran for the CP. The situation inside the house was hardly relaxed. "It seemed like bedlam," Vannatta wrote. "The officers were trying to issue orders, but no one was functioning very well, it seemed to me. Stragglers from every unit in the area were collecting in the house or the adjacent barn." An excited bazooka team burst inside and said that they had just bounced two shells off a "Tiger tank" without destroying it. Like almost all American soldiers in Europe, they thought of every German tank as a Tiger. In fact, the 110th Infantry did not face any bona fide Mark VI Tigers, the sixty-ton monsters with 88-millimeter cannons. They did face plenty of Mark IV and Mark V tanks, which were dangerous enough. The bazooka team went upstairs and tried to line up another shot at the enemy tank.

Outside, the panzer pointed its turret at the house and fired. Luckily the round was armor-piercing so it sailed right through the CP and did little damage. Tired of being stalked by tanks, Captain Carter told Vannatta to take a few men, go over the next hill to Urspelt, and make contact with Lieutenant Colonel Paul. "I'll follow you with the others as soon as I can," Carter promised.

Vannatta hated to leave his captain, but orders were orders. He and two other men took off running across an open area of about two hundred yards. This was not the place to be. Vannatta quickly realized that they were right between a Sherman and an enemy tank. "I dashed between the Sherman and the panzer just before the latter fired. The shell was high and passed over my left shoulder and over the Sherman turret. My heart stopped momentarily, but I kept running. The American tank then fired and an exchange of tank fire at close range ensued." Lieutenant Vannatta and the other soldiers made it over the hill, encountered some American soldiers digging in, and paused to talk with them. As they did so, Vannatta cast an apprehensive glance back over the hill at Reuler. Plumes of smoke were rising from the burning town. What a pity it was to see this beautiful, peaceful little farm town reduced to a smoking ruin. He wondered if Captain Carter was on his way.[11]

4

If Lieutenant Vannatta had known what was happening in Urspelt at that moment, he would not have been in much of a hurry to get there. For much of the day the Germans had been launching probing infantry attacks, but with no success. Lieutenant Colonel Paul's 1st Battalion headquarters personnel fended off these attacks with small-arms fire and artillery support. The eastward approach to his château CP was mostly open, rolling terrain, some of which was soggy from melted snow.

At 1600, just before sunset, the Germans brought up tanks and self-propelled guns. Lieutenant Colonel Paul had little with which to fight them, other than a few three-inch guns from the 630th Tank Destroyer Battalion that were deployed on a hill west of the château. Outside the château, in the yard, an M5 Stuart was standing watch. A couple more were scattered around the area.

The Germans deployed their guns and tanks about 1,400 meters away on the leeward side of a hill, and carefully scouted the American positions. Then they unleashed a hellish barrage, pounding the tank destroyer positions. The crews responded with several shots, scoring five hits on German tanks, before their guns were obliterated (not to mention many of the crewmen, too). A 75-millimeter round from a Mark IV zipped through the turret of the Stuart that was posted outside the château. A crewman was standing in the turret. The shell sliced him into two pieces before exiting through the rear of the turret and going into the stone barn adjacent to the château. Another quick shot hit the tank's engine, immediately setting it on fire. The severed remains of the crewman burned into a melted lump.

With this favorable exchange of fire, the Germans now went into motion. Their tanks and self-propelled guns rolled across the field, closing in on the château. Infantry soldiers scuttled forward, all around the tanks and along the road leading into town. The Americans shot at them with whatever they had. The tanks reached a mined creek crossing two hundred meters to the east of town. A German officer, First Lieutenant Knoth, dismounted and blew the roadblock up, all under fire.

Inside the château, Lieutenant Frank Richwine, the battalion communications officer, was standing near Lieutenant Colonel Paul. Outside, the volume of small-arms fire was reaching a crescendo. Richwine could hear the distinctive tearing sound of German MG42 machine guns. "They sprayed everything with machine guns as well as a few seventy-five rounds. One of the machine-gun bursts broke some windows out in our place."

Lieutenant Colonel Paul was holding a coffee mug in his hand, gesturing with it. A machine-gun round crashed through a nearby window and hit Paul's mug. For one shocked moment he stared at it. Then he looked at the headquarters men around him and hollered, "Let's get the hell out of here!" Paul ordered all of them to get to Clervaux as best they could. He left the CP, jumped into his jeep, and took off. "That's the last I saw or heard of him," Richwine said.

Paul had actually anticipated the vulnerability of his command post and had worked out an evacuation plan with his officers. Half of the headquarters men were to go with Lieutenant Raymond Beaucar, and the other half with Richwine. Beaucar's group left at once, and some of them did make it to Clervaux. Richwine's left a bit later: "I was supposed to lead the . . . procession, which would be through a barn behind us . . . and up over a hill." Richwine had even reconnoitered this route, as had his friend Beaucar.

Lieutenant Richwine ordered the message center and switchboard soldiers to burn or destroy everything. They set off on foot with only their personal weapons. The little group, including crewmen from the tanks, made their way west, across the frigid Clerf River, and kept moving. At an intersection, they met up with Beaucar, who still had most of his group together. Behind them, to the east, the Germans were moving into Urspelt. The 1st Battalion of the 110th Infantry had ceased to function as an organized combat unit.

Throughout the chilly Ardennes, shadows lengthened into darkness. At Reuler, Lieutenant Vannatta and a small group of soldiers were still a couple of hundred yards outside of town, next to the Urspelt road, contemplating what to do next. Crackling fires were consuming many farmhouses in Reuler. The fires lit up the night and shot eerie, flickering shadows in every direction. There were about a dozen jeeps and a few trucks on the road. The lieutenant was considering whether or not to drive these vehicles to Lieutenant Colonel Paul at Urspelt.

Now Vannatta heard a jeep approaching from the north. The jeep braked to a halt and out jumped Lieutenant Colonel Paul. Lieutenant Vannatta filled him in on the serious situation in Reuler and ventured the opinion that Captain Carter and the rest of D Company had all been killed or taken prisoner. "[Paul] said that Urspelt had been captured and that only a few of the HQ staff had escaped." With a short farewell, Paul got back in his jeep and continued to the 2nd Battalion CP, at the northern end of Reuler, the only part of town still under American control.

Vannatta decided to take a small group and go back into Reuler in hopes of finding more D Company survivors. As they approached the town, they came under fire from German machine guns to their left (east). "We could see about a squad of Germans bearing down on us from the left flank. A soldier next to me was hit through the stomach, and two of his buddies tried to carry him a few yards down to a jeep." The volume of fire grew more intense. Bullets were snapping through tree branches around them. "The wounded soldier vomited blood as he was lifted to the jeep trailer."

All thoughts of going back into Reuler were gone now. Vannatta's men scrambled for the jeeps, under fire all the way. The lieutenant got up and dashed for a jeep trailer and dived aboard just as the driver of the jeep gunned the engine. Groggy from the concussion of being under close-range shell fire all day, and exhausted in general, Lieutenant Vannatta passed out. The small convoy pressed on, into the night, west and south, all the way to Wiltz.

At the 2nd Battalion CP in Reuler, Lieutenant Colonel Paul placed a harried phone call to Colonel Fuller. He reported what had happened to his headquarters at Urspelt and said he had only a few men with him. Fuller knew that if the remnants of his 1st and 2nd Battalions could not hold on to the crucial northern road junction at Reuler, German armor would come charging into the northern reaches of Clervaux, just opposite the Claravallis. He told Paul and the 2nd Battalion officers to hold fast.

This was easier said than done. Only the survivors of E and F Companies, a few leaderless D Company soldiers, a 57-millimeter antitank gun, a .50-caliber machine gun, and some bazooka teams were available to defend the junction.

The Germans had been staggered by the bitter fight in Reuler today, but now they had regrouped. A freshly organized combined force of tanks, half-tracks, and dismounted infantry pushed past the 2nd Battalion CP and approached the road junction. In a foxhole just off the road, Sergeant Bob Bradicich heard them. Just two nights before, he had spent a pleasant evening dancing with several Clervaux residents. A young girl had given him a card with a soldier's prayer printed on it. The card was still tucked into one of Bradicich's pockets, but it offered small comfort now. An American guard shouted for the lead tank to halt. The tank's commander, in a muffled voice, said: "The Krauts came through and we're going back to get more gas." Satisfied with this explanation, the guard let it pass.

The tank kept coming, closer to Bradicich's foxhole. It was very dark, but he could see infantry riding on the tanks. In a neighboring foxhole, Bradicich's commanding officer, Captain William Dobbs, was suspicious. When the tank was no more than fifty feet away, he halted it again and asked for the password. This time the response was not as benign as before. The infantry jumped off the tank and opened fire. The tank's machine gun chattered. Sergeant Bradicich tried to shoot at the enemy infantry soldiers, but the German fire was devastating. "We were no match against the infantry and the tank blasting away at us from point-blank range." Rather than be killed in his hole, Bradicich retreated. He managed to link up with Captain Dobbs and a few other men, and they headed for Clervaux.

Having smashed through the forward American positions at the road junction, the enemy force picked up momentum. Private Bob Pocklington, a soldier from Headquarters Company of the 2nd Battalion, peeked over the edge of his foxhole and saw them coming. He actually thought the tanks might be American. He saw soldiers on the tank decks. "They were laughing and joking. Some were smoking cigarettes." Pocklington sat down in his hole. A tank stopped five yards away. Infantry soldiers jumped off and began running from hole to hole in the area where Pocklington's buddies were taking refuge. "They went down the row and machine- gunned those guys. They had hand-to-hand combat. I heard a lot of moanings and groanings."

Pocklington was frozen with fear. A couple of foxholes away, one of his NCOs, Sergeant Walker, crawled to the .50-caliber machine gun and unloosed a volley point-blank against the tank. The tank responded with a shot that blew up somewhere near Walker, and he fell to the ground. Scared into action now, Pocklington left his hole and crawled alongside the tank, all the way to some bushes just behind the 57-millimeter gun position. As far as he could tell, no one was on the gun. He paused to gather himself. "I tried to get myself calmed down; my heart was pounding so hard all I could hear was the pounding in my ears."

He nearly jumped out of his skin when something, or someone, fell heavily beside him. He was relieved to see that it was Lieutenant Dana Speer, one of the company officers. They talked in low whispers, trying to decide what to do. As Speer covered, Pocklington crawled up to the foxholes behind the 57-millimeter, looking for anyone who might still be there. He found First Sergeant Bill Korte, but no one else. "There was still some small-arms fire going on. The Germans were hollering like they were high, gung ho." Enemy tanks and other vehicles were slowly moving west beyond the gun, toward Clervaux. Pocklington and Korte made their way back to Lieutenant Speer. The three men, plus some other survivors, retreated west down a hill, across the freezing cold Clerf River, and into Clervaux.

Back at the Reuler CP, Lieutenant Colonel James Hughes, the executive officer of the 2nd Battalion, placed a quick call to Colonel Fuller and reported that six tanks had just passed the CP and the road junction and were on their way to Clervaux. Hughes, Lieutenant Colonel Paul, and the others in the CP then made their escape as best they could. Organized resistance at Reuler was at an end.[12]

5

In Clervaux, the Germans were in control of most of the town. They had surged past the castle, cutting it off, and were steadily fighting their way from house to house. Their vehicles were moving with impunity around the town.

Private Jack Chavez, the artilleryman who was technically still on R & R, had been guarding or fighting most of the day. Now he and a scratch group of soldiers were fighting north of the castle, from the cover of a building that overlooked Clervaux's main street. Chavez had only his M1 carbine and three clips left to fight with. German tanks and infantry were plowing down the street outside. A tank turned its turret in the direction of the building and fired. The shell crashed into the facade of the building, and a piece of hot shrapnel gashed Chavez's right leg. Alongside him, his buddy Waites blazed away with his carbine and saw a German go down. "He was so proud he put a notch on the stock of his carbine."

Enemy machine guns hosed the street, sending shards and splinters flying through the air. Chavez and Waites ducked. Chavez felt warm blood trickling down his leg. The wound, more than anything else, made him angry. He was really hoping to see "a Jerry poke his head up" so he could shoot it off. It was the first time that he really wanted to kill the enemy. A white phosphorous shell burst twenty yards away but did no damage. The Germans were attempting to set fire to the roofs of Clervaux, and they were having some success, judging by the smoke that was hanging over the whole area. Chavez, Waites, and several others got out of the building and retreated north, in the direction of the Claravallis Hotel. They found a vehicle and hitched a ride to Wiltz.

Just across from the hotel were the railroad station and a bridge over the Clerf River. This bridge was the entryway for anyone coming into Clervaux from Reuler. Now a long column of German armor descended the ridge and closed in on the bridge. Ahead of the armor, enemy reconnaissance troops were crawling or running for the bridge. At the bridge, a lone 57-millimeter gun stood in their way. Lieutenant Kenneth Maddox, an officer from Headquarters Company, 2nd Battalion, was pointing out targets to the gun crew. Out of the corner of his eye he spotted an enemy soldier drawing a bead on the gun crew with his burp gun. Maddox tried to shout a warning, but loading and firing as they were, they could not hear him. Maddox ran between the crew and the German, whose name was Sergeant Schulz, and shot the enemy soldier. At the same moment, Sergeant Schulz unleashed a burst from his submachine gun into Maddox's chest. Both men were mortally wounded. Moments later, the Germans blasted the 57-millimeter position, knocking out the gun and killing or wounding the crewmen. Enemy vehicles now rolled unopposed across the bridge, past the railroad station, and onto the street outside the Claravallis.

Inside the hotel, Captain Rensmeyer, the S2 officer, was on the second floor, trying to decide whether he should destroy a trash can full of sensitive intelligence documents. The trash can was outside, just below the fire escape. When he heard the tanks outside, he had his answer. Captain Rensmeyer hopped out of a second-floor window and dropped to the ground next to the trash can. He tossed an incendiary grenade into it and saw the papers catch fire. As he watched, they burned and crackled for a few furious seconds before disintegrating into little more than black embers. Then Captain Rensmeyer began an arduous climb, straight up the cliff behind the Claravallis, into a little forest and to the west, toward freedom.

Elsewhere in the hotel, on the first floor, Sergeant Clarence Johnson, a Galesburg, Illinois, native who worked in the regimental S1 section, was standing at a window, gazing into the street. There were at least six German tanks out there, gradually rolling along the street, guns oriented in several directions. "Some guys down the street were surrendering and they'd shoot 'em." Enemy infantrymen were running back and forth like chickens with their heads cut off. "We figured the Germans had been pretty well doped up or were under the influence of drugs, because they were hollering and screaming and carrying on." Sergeant Johnson backed away from the window before they could see him. His heart was racing. He knew that he had to either escape or die. "It was the scariest thing in my life."

Upstairs in his office, Colonel Fuller knew the game was up. He was on the phone, arguing with Colonel Jesse Gibney. Soon after, a German tank pumped several shells into the first floor. Fuller left his office and circulated a withdrawal order. Everyone was supposed to go to Eselborn, where Fuller hoped they could hook up with G Company and set up a new defensive line.

Downstairs, Chief Warrant Officer Ralph Johnson (no relation to Clarence) had just settled into his bedroll for some much-needed rest when the shells exploded. To Johnson it seemed as though the entire hotel was about to collapse. He scrambled out of his bedroll and heard someone say, "There's a Kraut tank out there!" Captain Gerald Harwell, the regimental adjutant, stepped outside of the hotel and fired several carbine shots at the tank. He had no sooner ducked back inside when the tank unleashed a new volley of main-gun and machine-gun fire. The power went out in the hotel. Outside, enemy soldiers were driving around in captured U.S. jeeps, shooting flares, illuminating the area and parts of the Claravallis.

Shortly after this, German infantry entered the building. Johnson heard them somewhere down the hall. "The enemy soldiers seemed to be drunk as they were yelling and screaming like mad." In the half-light, they played a deadly cat-and-mouse game with the American headquarters troops.

Throughout the Claravallis, the GIs were doing anything they could to get out. Colonel Fuller went back to his room to get his carbine and his overcoat. With the power out, the room was quite dark, but he could see ten men in there. "I found my carbine and trench coat and was asking questions to learn who was in the room when a projectile of some kind . . . came through a window and exploded, wounding five of those in the room." The projectile was either a Panzerfaust or a bazooka shell misfired by a nearby American.

One of the wounded men was Lieutenant Jack Haisley, a C Company platoon leader who had hours earlier fought his way into Clervaux with part of his platoon and a couple of Shermans from the 707th Tank Battalion. Since then, he and his men had functioned as an impromptu CP guard. Now he was lying on the floor, his lifeblood draining into the carpet. Fuller covered him with blankets and tried to stop the bleeding, but there was little more he could do. Someone took Haisley down to the cellar, where other wounded men had gathered. Fuller turned his attention to another wounded man who had been blinded by the explosion, either because of tiny fragments or flash burns. "It was too dark to see his wounds, but I bandaged his eyes with my first aid bandage. Others in the room . . . gave first aid to the rest of the wounded."

A military policeman came into the room and indicated that he had found a way out of the hotel if Colonel Fuller wanted to "take a chance." Fuller and the others had no choice. They followed the MP to the fire escape on the third floor. All the while, Fuller led the blind man by the hand. The hotel was built against the solid rock facade of a cliff, and the fire escape was nothing more than an iron ladder that spanned from the third floor, across a fifteen-foot gap, to the cliff. Fuller waited for an enemy flare to die down, held the man's hand, and climbed across the ladder. "Reaching the cliff, we found that steps had been cut in the earth, and we climbed to the top. I was very tired when I got to the top of the cliff, so I lay down there to rest." Several others from his group soon joined him. Fuller wandered the woods with this small group, hoping to reach Eselborn. He had effectively lost control of his shattered regiment.

Back at the hotel, Chief Warrant Officer Ralph Johnson and other soldiers soon learned of the fire escape and ventured out onto the ladder. "It was straight down 50 feet. It was pitch black, except when the flares went off and then the entire building . . . was lit up like day." Behind Johnson, others were waiting their turn. One of them was Sergeant Clarence Johnson. He was at the window, watching others cross. He glanced down and saw "jeeps parked" three stories below. Clarence Johnson's friend, Staff Sergeant Bob Miller, was on the ladder. Suddenly Miller lost his grip: "I fell and knew I wouldn't get far with my side hurting as it did, so I went down to the cellar" with the other wounded. Meanwhile, Sergeant Johnson crossed the ladder and began climbing the cliff. "You had to grab ahold of tree roots and everything you could hang on to and get up the steep part." He and dozens of others got to the top, dodged German flares, and made their way west to Eselborn.

By that time, the Germans had finally secured the Claravallis. "A Mark IV tank, from directly outside on the sidewalk, was raking the 1st floor," Sergeant Miller wrote. "Finally it stopped firing and the Krauts came in from all doors, even the third floor exit. They searched us and stripped us of our weapons and valuables. Then we were marched up the street a few doors to their CP."

Sergeant Jerry Demaria, a communications specialist, was wandering around outside, trying to find a safe exit route. He went into the hotel and somehow got to the regimental switchboard unmolested. He placed a call to division and got Colonel Gibney: "I'm Sergeant Demaria from the 28th Signal Company," he said. "This town's all kaput. There's Tiger [sic] tanks outside the door ready to blow us apart, so I gotta get the hell out of here."

"All right, try to get back to me," Gibney replied. "Report to me."

"I'll try," Demaria said. He signed off, dragged the switchboard upstairs to the third floor, and escaped across the ladder.

Throughout Clervaux, the Germans were on a rampage. Only the castle remained in American hands. Before bugging out of the Claravallis, Fuller had told the castle defenders to retreat to Eselborn, but this was not possible. The castle was an American island in a German sea. All over town, the enemy soldiers looted everything they could carry. Dressed in long leather coats, they smashed in doors with their rifle butts or shot through locks. They stole from private homes, loaded their booty aboard trucks, and sent them east across the Our, back to Germany.

Some of the Germans were dressed in American uniforms (a common enemy tactic during the Battle of the Bulge). In one instance a group of Germans clad in American uniforms entered the rectory of the local priest. "Are you really Germans?" the priest asked them three times.

"Yes, we are Germans!" they answered proudly in perfect German.

Armored vehicles poured into and through Clervaux. The main avenue through town was packed with them. "Two columns were rolling side by side along the road, bruising stairways, balustrades, gables and ornament," an eyewitness later wrote. "All troops were very excited. All had the order to use every hour, every minute, every second, moving forward."

Three miles to the east, at Marnach, Sergeant JJ Kuhn knew the end was near. He and a few others were still holed up in the hotel that had served as B Company's CP, back when it was an intact combat unit. Now it was shattered, on the brink of annihilation. Kuhn was on the second floor with a box of grenades, watching enemy half-tracks pass by in the street below. He tossed grenades into four different half-tracks, heard explosions, and then went downstairs to the basement, where eight wounded men were suffering in varying degrees of pain. Kuhn checked on them, explained that they could not be evacuated, and went back to the first floor. As he stood there, a German tank smashed through the front door, sending masonry and wood crashing all over the place. German soldiers charged in, pointing their weapons at Kuhn and shouting, "Raus! Raus! [Get out!]" Kuhn grimaced and put his hands up. Marnach had fallen at last.

To the south, at Munshausen, Cannon Company and C Company had fought house-to-house all day. Having battled like demons, the survivors prepared to escape west out of the town. They left their wounded in the priest's house, organized themselves, and set off. "The remnants of two companies, over two hundred men, moved out of a surrounded town single file in a southwesterly direction," Lieutenant Maher, the C Company rifle platoon leader, wrote. "Visibility was zero in the darkness and each man kept one hand on the rifle belt of the man ahead."

Now only Hosingen and Consthum remained under the control of the 110th. Ever so surely, the regiment was dying. But the Germans were paying a heavy price for destroying the 110th. That price was time.[13]

6

Over the course of the evening, Colonel Nelson of the 112th began to withdraw his regiment to a new defensive line west of the Our. His outfit had fought brilliantly and had denied the Germans the use of the Ouren bridges for two full days when they badly needed them. Finally, at 1800, orders came from division to withdraw if necessary. Nelson skillfully coordinated a plan with his staff and ordered what was left of his companies to withdraw to Weiswampach.

Communications were sketchy, but by and large his battered formations got the word and slipped west in the dark night. West of Sevenig, Lieutenant Ralph Larson and K Company moved "single file through the heavily wooded Ardennes. We were tired, even at the outset." As the march wore on, Larson divested himself of three heavy blankets he was carrying. On and on they went, basically asleep on their feet. For a few hours, Lieutenant Larson's platoon got lost, but they eventually hooked up with the company near Weiswampach. They also welcomed back one of their own, Private First Class Buck Bloomer, who had been missing since going out on a contact patrol the previous evening.

Somewhere west of Harspelt, along the Ouren road, Corporal William Kelley, the wayward artillery observer, decided to emerge from his hiding place. He had been lying motionless all day, even as German soldiers and vehicles moved west on the road. Now, in the inky darkness, he got up and slipped past an enemy tank and truck. He made it into a stand of nearby woods. "I heard German voices on my left, then on my right, and miraculously I didn't encounter any head-on. Eventually I sensed that it was no-man's-land. I crossed streams [the Our River] and went up and down cliffs heading directly for artillery flashes." By following the flashes, he found his battery.

In groups small and large, the 112th withdrew. Along the way, they destroyed the Ouren bridges, further hindering the German advance. At Weiswampach, Colonel Nelson went about the formidable task of organizing a new defensive line.

The temptation among the exhausted soldiers who had made it this far was to relax. Nelson was miffed that he had not been challenged by any sentries during his own retreat to Weiswampach. "This alarmed me greatly for . . . there was nothing between ourselves and the enemy." He circulated around, kicking butts, disseminating orders, motivating people to get back into combat mode. "I went to a nearby bistro where I saw a light and found about thirty soldiers drinking free beer passed out by the Luxembourgers. In ten seconds I had the place cleared and the soldiers moving out to man the outposts." As midnight approached, Colonel Nelson, along with many of his officers and NCOs, succeeded in setting up a makeshift defensive line in and around Weiswampach. The 112th was bent but not broken. In the process, Nelson's soldiers had done a superb job. They denied the Germans a valuable northern route to Bastogne.[14]

As Nelson and his people experienced a sleepless night of crisis management, another regiment-sized unit was many miles away, driving north through western Luxembourg. Combat Command B (CCB) of the 10th Armored Division was a mechanized strike force, consisting of Sherman tanks, half-tracks, self-propelled guns, and myriad other vehicles. The commander of CCB, Colonel William Roberts, was an experienced armor officer who had seen combat in World War I.

Roberts's command was split into three battalion-sized teams: Team Cherry, under Lieutenant Colonel Henry Cherry, was in the lead; Team O'Hara, under Lieutenant Colonel Jim O'Hara, was right behind Cherry; and Team Desobry, under twenty-six-year-old Major William Desobry, brought up the rear. Each team had three to five hundred men and at least a company of tanks. The night before, at their billet in Remeling, France, CCB had received a movement order from division. Roberts and his troops had been on the road since this afternoon. The convoy snaked along for miles, passing beautiful old trees that engineers were wiring up for demolition as roadblocks, in case the Germans got that far. There were dozens of vehicles of every type: deuce-and-a-half-ton trucks, three-quarter-ton trucks, jeeps, half-tracks full of infantry, half-tracks towing antitank guns, half-tracks mounting antiaircraft guns or radios or machine guns, Sherman tanks, armored recovery vehicles, trailers, and self-propelled guns.

At this point, no one, not even the commanders, knew where they were going. Some of the men were hoping that this was the beginning of an R & R stint or maybe even the end of the war. Others had heard about the German offensive and assumed, correctly, that they were going north to counterattack. Many of them had noticed that blackout restrictions had been lifted. Drivers were allowed to use their headlights, something the 10th Armored Division had not done since leaving the States several months before. Clearly, someone wanted them somewhere as quickly as possible.

Onward they drove in the night, bantering and bickering among themselves, speculating and spreading rumors. In the accordion manner so typical of large convoys, the vehicles stopped and started, averaging about ten or fifteen miles per hour. At one brief stop somewhere in Luxembourg, Private First Class Spurgeon Van Hoose, a nineteen-year-old half-track radioman, noticed a few civilians lining the road. A woman walked up to the half-track and dispensed coffee and trinkets to the soldiers. "She gave us a little red, white, and blue ribbon, a little piece of ribbon about four inches long. She said it'd bring us good luck." Figuring he had nothing to lose, Van Hoose opened his wallet and put the ribbon inside. The vehicles started rolling again, and the woman faded into the distance. Van Hoose settled back into his uncomfortable little seat behind the driver and wondered again just where in hell they were going. Not long after, the clock struck midnight.[15]

Major General Norman "Dutch" Cota, commanding officer, 28th Infantry Division. Cota's division bore the brunt of the German offensive in the Bastogne corridor.

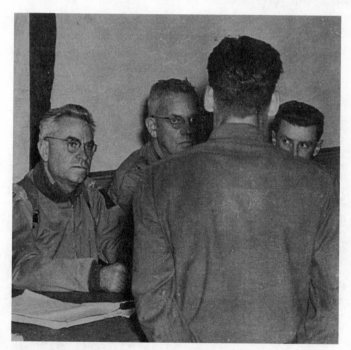

Testy and cantankerous as ever, Colonel Hurley Fuller (far left) glowers at a defendant in a military court proceeding. Fuller took command of the 110th Infantry Regiment just three weeks before the German offensive. Outnumbered ten to one, the 110th was annihilated but fought a courageous delaying action that cost the Germans valuable time. The pain of his regiment's annihilation stayed with Fuller until his dying day.

Clervaux castle, burning fiercely on December 18, 1944. One hundred men from Headquarters Company, 110th Infantry, held off the Germans here for three days.

The aftermath at Marnach. B Company of the 110th Infantry held out in this little village for two days, impeding the German advance to Bastogne. American soldiers recaptured the town in January 1945, when these photos were taken.

A famous image of two 28th Division soldiers in Bastogne after several days of hard fighting. These men were probably part of Task Force Snafu, the scratch force that helped the 101st Airborne Division hold Bastogne. Notice the mud on the trousers of the soldier on the right. Hundreds of 28th Division soldiers trudged through mud and snow to escape captivity and keep fighting the Germans.

A lieutenant munches on a C ration biscuit after making it back into American lines. Thousands of 28th Division soldiers wandered the Ardennes and fought in small groups. Many were captured or never heard from again.

Weary members of the 28th Division band who were pressed into combat service to defend the division command post at Wiltz.

The outskirts of Heinerscheid, where A Company, 110th Infantry, and tankers from the 707th Tank Battalion fought waves of German attackers. Weeks after the battle, two GIs are inspecting destroyed German vehicles. German corpses, barely visible, are strewn around the field.

The Bouvier Château in Urspelt as it looks today. This was the command post of Lieutenant Colonel Donald Paul, commanding officer of the 1st Battalion, 110th Infantry.

The little town of Clervaux today. This view is from Reuler, to the east, over the prominent ridge that separates the two towns. Many German soldiers saw Clervaux from this vantage point before they attacked. Notice the restored castle in the middle of this image.

The courtyard of Clervaux castle today. This area was under intense fire on December 17 and 18, 1944.

The Claravallis Hotel today. On the evening of December 17, 1944, Colonel Fuller and his headquarters soldiers came under close-range attack here. They fled from the fire escape of the hotel rather than surrender.

128

A present-day photo of Colonel Ted Seely's ill-fated command post at Allerborn. On the evening of December 18, 1944, German attackers overran the house, capturing Seely and scattering many others west toward Bastogne.

After the battle, a little girl kisses a 9th Armored Division soldier on the cheek, while several other soldiers and a pet dog watch. Notice the censor mark obscuring the unit identification on the left sleeve of the soldier sitting next to the dog. The 9th Armored Division was on the "secret list" for the first few weeks of the Bulge and never got the credit it deserved for its part in keeping the Germans out of Bastogne.

Combat Command (CCB) of the 10th Armored Division arrives in Bastogne.
The commander of CCB, Colonel William Roberts, spread his troops out among
three key roadblocks around the city.

Troopers from the 101st Airborne Division arriving in Bastogne, where they fanned
out into defensive positions around the town.

A makeshift 101st Airborne Division aid station in Bastogne. Although short on medicine, surgical instruments, and other necessities, the medics did the best they could for the growing number of wounded men they had to treat.

The American cost: dead soldiers of the 28th Division, possibly executed in cold blood by the Germans, lie in the snow. Notice that the Germans have taken their boots and gone through their pockets for valuables. The 28th was shattered in the Bastogne corridor. The 110th Infantry alone suffered 2,750 casualties out of an original complement of 3,250 soldiers.

The German cost: the frozen body of a dead German soldier lies in the snow near Neffe. There were many others around the Ardennes. The Germans lost approximately 100,000 soldiers in the Battle of the Bulge.

General Dwight D. Eisenhower presents troopers of the 101st Airborne Division with a unit citation for their successful defense of Bastogne. The 101st received most of the postbattle citations and historical plaudits for holding Bastogne.

5

MONDAY, DECEMBER 18

1

Ninety miles west of Bastogne, inside an old French Army barracks building at Mourmelon, Corporal Arlo Butcher was in his bunk, sleeping soundly. He and thousands of other men of the 101st Airborne Division were enjoying a well-earned rest after seventy-two days of continuous combat in Holland. They slept on straw-filled mattresses, in crude buildings with stucco walls and concrete floors, but for the first time in many months, the men were enjoying indoor plumbing and power. The division was drawing new equipment, welcoming replacements, and training for future airborne operations. The paratroopers and glider soldiers of this outfit knew little or nothing about the intense drama unfolding to their east, but that was about to change.

Corporal Butcher was a member of Battery F, 81st Airborne Antiaircraft Artillery Battalion. He had been through combat in Holland, and he was still decompressing. Now, in the darkness of early morning, he was awakened "by a lot of noise in the building next door. Jeeps and trucks were running all over the place." He exchanged knowing glances with his buddies in adjacent bunks. "We all knew something was in the wind."

They were right. The phone call had come from the XVIII Airborne Corps at 2030 the evening before. The division was being alerted for movement to Belgium. The "Screamin' Eagles" of the 101st Airborne Division were to pack up and be ready to go by 1400 that afternoon.

Throughout the barracks complex, officers, NCOs, and guards were busy waking their soldiers. Private Cleto Leone was on charge-of-quarters duty—similar to night watch—for his squad. He got the order to wake his comrades, and he breathlessly dashed inside the barracks: "Everybody up! Everybody up! We're moving out!"

The reaction from his squad mates was decidedly negative: "I was deluged with a barrage of boots—mess kits—everything imaginable. I was lucky to get out of there alive."

In another barracks that housed a squad from A Company, 506th Parachute Infantry, the door flew open, the lights came on, and a sergeant strode into the room: "Awright, you guys, let's hit it! Let's go, hubba-hubba one time. Off your ass and on your feet! We're moving out—now!" A swirl of damp, cold December air followed the sergeant into the room, chilling everyone to the bone.

In a nearby bunk, Private Donald Burgett could hardly believe his ears. He rolled over and peered at his sergeant, wondering if he had lost his mind. Unfortunately he was all too serious. "The Germans have broken through our lines someplace," he said. "It's up to us to stop them before they go all the way to the Channel."

Private Burgett cursed and swung his feet onto the cold concrete floor. He could actually see his breath in this frigid barracks. He was bitter and he was angry, at whom or what, exactly, he did not know. Maybe it was just the idea of going back into combat with so little mental preparation. He had jumped at Normandy and Holland. He had been wounded in Normandy. Before and since then, he had had too many close calls to count. Somehow he was still alive. He was only nineteen years old, yet he was intimately familiar with death.

Still bitter, but resigned, Burgett got up, dressed, and started packing for combat. All around him, in this barracks and in dozens of others throughout Mourmelon, the rest of the 101st Airborne did the same.[1]

As the darkness of night gave way to a rain-soaked, foggy dawn, this was the situation in the Bastogne corridor: In the north, the 112th Infantry was in a makeshift defensive line around Weiswampach, but its southern flank was wide open. In the south, Lieutenant Colonel James Earl Rudder's 109th Infantry was holding off, under intense pressure, the 352nd Volksgrenadier and 5th Parachute Divisions east of Diekirch. Rudder's E and F Companies were surrounded and on the verge of annihilation. In the center of the 28th Division, a serious crisis was brewing. The 116th and 2nd Panzer Divisions, along with Panzer Lehr and the 26th Volksgrenadier Divisions, had mauled Colonel Hurley Fuller's 110th Infantry. He was now a fugitive. His valorous regiment was shattered, largely reduced to small, wandering groups. The Germans now controlled Heinerscheid, Urspelt, Reuler, Marnach, Munshausen, Holzthum, Weiler, Hoscheid, and Clervaux. Only Hosingen and Consthum were still under some sort of American command and control.

The middle of the 28th Division front—the direct route to Bastogne—had been ripped open, and the Germans were pouring through this gaping hole. The 28th Division still controlled Wiltz, but the Germans were getting closer to the town by the hour. The 9th Armored Division's Combat Command Reserve (CCR) was busily setting up roadblocks at Antoniushaff and Feitsch, two vital crossroads about twelve miles east of Bastogne. Another CCR task force was in place two miles to the west at Moinet.

Some help was on the way. Colonel William Roberts and Combat Command B (CCB) were making their way north, although Roberts was still not entirely sure where he and his men were going. Finally, to the west, the 101st Airborne Division was gearing up, getting ready to enter the battle. The race for Bastogne was on.

2

Hosingen was now a field of ruins. German artillery had battered the town into rubble. House-to-house fighting had brought even more destruction. All night long, the fight had raged in uneven spurts. The American defenders were slowly being constricted into an ever-tighter perimeter, mostly in the southern and western portions of town. Two of the Shermans had been destroyed, probably by Panzerfausts. Among the Americans, ammo and food were low, while exhaustion was high.

Major Harold Milton, the 3rd Battalion commander, had radioed Captain Frederick Feiker during the night and told him to infiltrate out of Hosingen, but the captain told him that that would be impossible. The Germans simply had "too much stuff" around Hosingen. No group of any size could make it out. Milton, who was fighting for his own survival a few miles away at Consthum, told Feiker to hang on as best he could. At one point during this ordeal, the major had actually promised to send a relief force to Hosingen, but both officers knew that was not possible now. Hosingen was miles behind enemy lines. Only Feiker and Captain William Jarrett, the engineer commander, could decide how much longer they could hold out.

In a barn in western Hosingen, Corporal George Stevenson and several other engineers were huddled around a .50-caliber machine gun peering into the morning mist. In the distance, they could see several German horse-drawn supply wagons. Stevenson's squad did not have much ammo left, but they knew that this was a perfect target. The gunner opened fire. The gun bucked around but poured out several hundred rounds, right into the wagons, setting them afire. "I heard them Germans cussing and cutting them horses loose from the wagons," Stevenson recalled. Captain Jarrett, watching from elsewhere in town, called it "a grand sight."

Unfortunately, the Americans could not follow up with anything heavier or more effective. They were down to a couple of smoke shells and little else for their mortars. They had no artillery. Their tanks were cornered. They had little left to fight with other than their own personal weapons, and most soldiers were down to their last clip or two.

At the Hotel Schmitz, Captain Feiker was meeting with his officers, trying to decide whether resistance could continue. They sadly and reluctantly concluded that they must surrender. They radioed Captain Jarrett, and he reluctantly agreed. Together they decided that before surrendering, they would destroy everything of use to the Germans. The engineers would provide TNT for demolition. "All engineer trucks and road equipment was burned, jeep tires were shot and cut," Lieutenant Thomas Flynn recalled. "The vehicles and garage were set on fire. Bulk rations, mail, and other paper were soaked with gasoline and burned. Field ranges and supplies were destroyed. The men demolished their own weapons, and the weapons in the tanks were rendered useless."

In the meantime, Captains Feiker and Jarrett raised a white flag and ventured into the German lines. Once the Germans saw the white flag, they immediately stopped shooting. Inside the command post, someone got on the radio and told Major Milton of the surrender: "We've blown up everything there is except the radio. It goes next. I don't mind dying— I don't mind taking a beating—but we'll never give up."

Just outside of town, Feiker and Jarrett spent about an hour parleying with the enemy. The Germans searched them. Captain Jarrett had wrapped his dentures in a handkerchief that he kept in his pocket. For some reason, the Germans took the teeth from him. "We were then marched into town at gunpoint and given orders to have the men come out of the bldgs [buildings] in a column of threes with hands on helmets."

During the parley, word of the surrender had spread among the garrison. Now German soldiers were all over the place, rounding up their American prisoners. Private Edward Gasper, the young rifleman, heard them and prepared to give up. "I slammed my rifle, broke the stock, threw the parts away." He came out of his building with his hands up. "They took the watch off my hand and a pack of cigarettes and K rations."

Elsewhere, on a hill overlooking much of Hosingen, Sergeant James Arbella, the 60-millimeter mortar section leader, was just now learning of the surrender. He could see men emerging from buildings, with hands on heads, being lined up. He and his soldiers went into town to find out what was up. He saw an old buddy from another platoon and asked him, "What the hell's going on?"

"The old man's giving the word to surrender."

"How come I didn't get the word?" Arbella asked.

"You know how the ball bounces? Some people never see it bounce," his old friend replied.

Sergeant Arbella nodded his head in agreement. From the start of this debacle, he had had very little communication with Captain Feiker, nor much in the way of orders, so this was fitting. Arbella went to the garage where he kept his jeeps and tried to burn them, but failed. He gathered his mortar soldiers and prepared to surrender. As he did so, he ran into a small group of eight Army Rangers. These men had been there for several days, even before the battle. They were either genuine Rangers from a Ranger battalion or they were 28th Division soldiers who were engaging in a special training program to become Rangers. No one was ever sure. Arbella had struck up a friendship with their leader. Now the Ranger leader asked the sergeant if the surrender order was true. Arbella told him that it was. "We ain't giving up," the Ranger declared.

The little group of Rangers followed their leader out of western Hosingen, to unknown points beyond. Sergeant Arbella watched them with admiration. "He took his men and went the other way [away from the Germans]. I never heard nor seen them after that." When the Rangers were out of sight, Arbella gathered his men and joined the swelling ranks of American soldiers who were lined up on Hosingen's main street.

The mood was very tense. The Germans had suffered badly in taking Hosingen, and they were in no mood to be charitable to the Americans. "They were slapping the shit out of us," Lieutenant Bernie Porter remembered. Porter was very worried about something he had done during the battle. A German medic had shot at him, and he had fired back, hitting the medic. Now Porter was very worried that the Germans would want to find the man responsible for shooting the medic. One German officer even asked, "Who shot my medic?" Lieutenant Porter and everyone else kept quiet.

Even as the German soldiers hollered, slapped, and lined their American captives up, two enemy machine-gun teams were setting up MG42s, pointing them ominously at the American POWs. One machine gun was atop a trailer and the other on the ground. "It was about twenty-five yards away from us," Private Gasper recalled. Gasper could not keep his eyes off the guns. He figured that all of them were about to be mowed down, killed in cold blood on this rubble-strewn street. Sure enough, one of the machine gunners opened fire.

The burst killed two Americans and wounded two others. But this was an accident, not a massacre. "The German captain cursed the man and made a move to strike him with his pistol," Captain Jarrett later wrote.

If not for the enemy officer, "there would have been a pile of dead GIs there," Gasper opined. Instead, the Germans separated the eight American officers from their three hundred enlisted men and marched all of them to a church near the Our River. All along the way, German soldiers gaped in surprise at the small group that had held elements of three divisions at bay for more than two days. A German staff officer expressed shock that this motley force had held for so long. The German corps commander, General der Panzertruppen Freiherr von Luttwitz, later wrote, "A special mention must be made of the defenders of Hosingen. We were able to break the resistance in Hosingen only after the Seventy-eighth Grenadier Regt. of the Twenty-Sixth VGD had arrived on 17 December." This was a regiment badly needed elsewhere. For Luttwitz, the resistance at Hosingen "was altogether more stubborn than I had expected."

The Americans suffered seven killed and twelve wounded at Hosingen. The Germans lost over three hundred killed. The Americans knew this because, after they were captured, they were put to work burying the broken, lifeless bodies of their adversaries. The soldiers of K Company, 110th Infantry; B Company, 103rd Engineers; B Company, 707th Tank Battalion; as well as the mysterious Rangers; had collectively made a stubborn, gallant stand. As instructed, they held out as long as possible and bought precious time for Bastogne.[2]

Miles to the north, east of Harspelt, Sergeant Frank Olsen was at his wit's end. For nearly three days now, his platoon-sized force from A Company, 112th Infantry, had been in an abandoned house holding out against ten times their number.

Now Olsen knew that he could not hang on much longer. He was hoping to hold on until nightfall, split his men into groups of two, and escape. He knew that his platoon had been sacrificed (or perhaps abandoned), but he had no idea of how isolated he and his men truly were. The rest of the 112th Infantry was all the way on the other side of the Our River, more than ten miles away at Weiswampach. Sergeant Olsen did not know it, but the regiment was even now in the middle of a fighting retreat to Huldange (and soon to be attached to the 106th Division, effectively out of the fight for the Bastogne corridor). He just knew that he was on his own.

Presently, the Germans brought up three tanks, with plenty of infantry, and unleashed yet another attack. Olsen and his men shot at the infantry until they had no ammo left. The tanks kept coming until they were within fifty yards of the house. They stopped and lowered their guns at the American-held building. Instead of shooting, they remained in place. An uncanny quiet descended over the area. Sergeant Olsen was peering out of a window, watching the tanks. A staff car drove up and stopped, and a German officer stepped out. "It looked like he'd come out of the movies—shined boots" and a crisp, clean uniform. In English, the German officer asked to speak to the American commander.

Sergeant Olsen was a mess. He had a beard, and his clothes were filthy. As he left the house, his legs felt like rubber. They were actually shaking beneath him. He walked up to the enemy officer and saluted. The German returned the salute: "Ten minutes. I'll give you ten minutes. Put your guns down, come out like good boys, we'll give you a home . . . until the war ends." Olsen said that he would think it over and went back to the house.

Inside, he looked around at each of his men. "They were looking at the floor." Olsen pondered his hopeless situation. He had tried hard to live up to his orders. Now he had nothing left to fight with. Should he order his men to fix bayonets and make one last suicidal stand? Outside, the German officer was counting down the minutes. Olsen could feel tears—bitter tears—streaming down his cheeks. In frustration, he picked up several glasses and threw them against an oven. The glasses broke with a shattering sound. There was nothing left to do but surrender, and Olsen knew it. A bayonet charge would accomplish nothing other than to end the lives of his remaining soldiers. By surrendering, at least some of his men would make it home. The German officer was still counting. Time was running out. Olsen looked around the room and said, finally, "Put your hands on your heads and get out."

Slowly they filed out of the house. The Germans stripped them of their watches and rings and tried to line them up in two columns. Fifty feet away, Sergeant Olsen noticed an enemy machine gun pointing right at them. "All of a sudden, the machine gun started firing and the three men on my right dropped dead." They had been shot "in cold blood." Olsen and a German officer narrowly missed being killed. The shooting stopped. "The German officer was furious, not because of the dead men, but because the shooting was so close to him. I thought he was about to shoot one of his own men."

Everyone settled down, and the Germans marched their GI captives east, deeper into Germany. As Sergeant Olsen trudged along, he felt a piece of paper in his pocket. What's this? he wondered. When the Germans were not looking, he reached into the pocket and looked at the paper. It was Corporal Green's telegram, the one that Olsen had received on the evening of December 15. Olsen read it. The telegram announced the birth of a son. Olsen studied it for a few moments and then put it back in his pocket. With all the excitement of the last couple of days, he had never had time to give Green his telegram, nor could he do so now. Green was dead. He never knew that he had a son.[3]

3

At Consthum, the Germans were getting ready for a new attack. The day before they had come in waves, only to be driven off. For hours now, they had been throwing artillery and mortars at the town. Lieutenant Colonel Daniel Strickler, Fuller's erstwhile second-in-command, had been there, mostly at the two-story home that served as Milton's CP, for two days. He and Major Milton did not have much left to defend the town and 3rd Battalion headquarters. There were about eighty headquarters troops, twenty men from M Company, Lieutenant Bert Saymon and a platoon's worth of escapees from L Company, a quad-.50 antiaircraft gun, a 40-millimeter Bofors gun, three M8 armored cars, and a few Shermans.

Somehow, this ragtag force had held on through the evening. "All night the enemy pounded us incessantly with heavy fire," Strickler said. "Tanks came against us; screaming meemies shrieked through the air; flares and rockets of all colors were seen constantly as the Germans signalled [sic] each other." German searchlights only added to the spectacle. A block away from the CP, an American tank was burning, right at the spot where a German tank shell had destroyed it. The ammo inside the Sherman kept cooking off, leading to an unnerving series of explosions.

The owners of the home were constantly in and out. "Some would go to the cellar. Others would disappear to seemingly safe corners. Sometimes, with dejected and inquiring looks, [they] would slink near our operations room." Worried about their safety, Strickler had issued an order, telling these folks and anyone else remaining in Consthum to leave. Most had resisted or ignored the order.

Lieutenant Colonel Strickler knew General Hasso von Manteuffel's whole battle plan now. He had obtained it from a captured German officer. He knew how badly they needed Bastogne. Strickler also knew that the 110th Infantry had been effectively destroyed. He understood that his fledgling Consthum force was the only serious obstacle between the Germans and division headquarters at Wiltz. "Knowing the strength of the enemy forces against us now, we could not be hopeful of holding out for very long. But we were determined to make them pay for every foot of ground we gave up, and hoped that other American units would come to our aid."

Now, in the daylight, the volume of enemy artillery fire grew to a crescendo. "The very air seemed to be compressed by shot and shell."

Strickler watched as German shells rained in and around the CP. The out-house in the courtyard took a direct hit from something big. Another shell slammed into the CP itself, shattering windows and sending plaster fly-ing. Artillery rounds peppered the surrounding buildings, setting some of them on fire. Somewhere in the distance, Strickler could hear the rum-bling of tanks. From the perspective of his attic window, he could see that the Germans were attacking from the same direction as before. "Attack after attack was repulsed, but on and on they came." Many of these attack-ers had recently been at Hosingen, but that town's surrender had freed them to fight here in Consthum.

Strickler went downstairs and called General Norman "Dutch" Cota at Wiltz. "I informed [him] of the situation, asking that the main road from Consthum to Wiltz be kept open." Cota had no such power. The Germans had already cut the road several times. Wiltz itself was under attack. Cota was surprised that Strickler's force was still holding out at Consthum. The general authorized a withdrawal, told Strickler to use his best judgment, wished him luck, and hung up. Strickler lowered the phone from his ear, gently placing it back in its cradle. He pondered his next move. Outside, the shooting was louder and closer. A bitter house-to-house fight was unfolding. The 3rd Battalion had fought a very good fight here. It was clearly time to get out. But how?[4]

At nearly the same moment, Sergeant Charles Johnson from Battery B, 109th Field Artillery, was about ten miles to the north, a few miles west of Clervaux, outside of a little town called Donnange, shaking himself awake. He had spent the night in a foxhole. He and Battery B, like so many artillery units in the Bastogne corridor, had been frantically displac-ing, setting up, firing, and displacing again, rather than be overrun by the onrushing Germans. Sergeant Johnson had picked up a new lieutenant as his forward observer, and a new radioman too. They were working with G Company, 110th Infantry, the only intact company left in the regiment.

Now Johnson got up, stretched, and wondered what the situation was. They were in a little pasture. He walked over to Captain George Pre-stridge, the G Company CO, and offered his observation services. "I wish you would find out for me what is out there," the captain said, as he sipped a cup of coffee. "It would be a big help."

Johnson took his radioman and jeep and drove into Donnange. "We decided that the steeple of a church was the best observation post in the vicinity." They parked their jeep nearby and set out on foot for the church. They found that the church was surrounded by a solid stone wall. Inside the walls were numerous gravestones. Johnson went into the grave-yard and looked for an entrance to the church. As he did so, he almost bumped into a woman who was walking among the gravestones. "She was an attractive brunette of about thirty-five, neatly dressed in what I would call a traveling suit." To Johnson, she was out of context in a combat zone. She looked like she should be in an English garden or some other pleasant place. She asked him if he needed help. When he told her that he wanted to go up into the church steeple, she "unhesitatingly led me through the yard, through the church door, sanctuary," and up some narrow steps to the top of the steeple. Sergeant Johnson thanked her and told her that a German attack was imminent. "She hurried off with a worried expression."

Johnson opened the steeple window, raised his binoculars to his eyes, and studied the ridgeline just east of Donnange. There, plain as day, were several large German tanks, engines idling, clearly preparing to attack. Johnson sent the radioman back to G Company and tried to call down artillery fire on the tanks. A few minutes later, he looked at the G Company foxholes and saw the company bugging out. In response to the radioman's warning, Captain Prestridge was ordering a withdrawal. "As the tanks opened fire with machine guns," Sergeant Johnson wrote, "our infantry began to hustle for the next village [Lullange] and the cover it would provide. Seeing the speed of the advancing enemy, I began thinking of my plight and decided to abandon the church steeple hoping to join my own troops."

Johnson destroyed the radio by chucking it out of the church steeple. It hit the ground with a metallic crash. He hotfooted down the narrow steps and out into the yard, and was pleased to see that the radioman was there, waiting in the jeep. They made it into Lullange with G Company. At Lullange, Johnson found another good observation spot in a two-story house and with another radio called down effective fire on the advancing Germans. "I could hear some of the shells hitting armor and some Germans yelling [as] smoke and dirt, and other debris, rose skyward." The momentum of the German attack waned. Sergeant Johnson did not know it, but the enemy had little interest in Lullange. Instead, they were flanking to the north on the two-lane N18 highway, pushing for a roundabout crossroads called Antoniushaff.

On the N18, 2nd Panzer Division vehicles snaked in a column over the eastern horizon, all the way to Clervaux. The streets of that town were still choked with German vehicle traffic, rolling west as fast as possible. At the castle, the Americans were still holding out. All night long, they had heard German tanks driving past them. Early that morning a lone American tank (probably from Sergeant Donald Fink's platoon) had taken up position next to the castle. With lightning speed, the Germans battered the tank, knocking off its main gun. The crew escaped and melted away, somewhere into Clervaux.

In the meantime, the GIs in the castle were making life miserable for German soldiers in Clervaux. Anyone who moved under the all-seeing gaze of the castle's apertures risked getting shot. Even as Mark IV's and Panthers rolled past the castle, German infantry launched an all-out assault on the little fortress. Standing in windows and apertures, the Americans blazed away with everything they had left. "They sent in swarms of infantrymen," Sergeant Frank Kusnir recalled. "We killed quite a few of 'em, and then they would withdraw." German bodies lay in the streets and near the castle walls.

Still the enemy kept coming. Staff Sergeant Bob Kalish was in his room on the top floor of the castle, firing his carbine at the many targets some forty yards below. "We killed a bunch of 'em that tried to storm the castle. I don't know how many there was. It was a hopeless situation," because the Americans were surrounded and had no hope of relief. In addition, their ammo was running out.

At last the Germans wheeled up several self-propelled guns. Instead of wasting their ammo on the sturdy castle walls, they fired their 88-millimeter shells into the vulnerable roof, setting numerous fires. As the fires spread throughout the castle, plumes of smoke belched into the air and through the castle hallways. A burning communications half-track—destroyed in the courtyard by the Americans lest it fall into enemy hands—only added to the conflagration. A German tank rammed the large doors at the entrance to the courtyard and started pummeling the castle from close range. In the basement, the civilians could hear the ruckus above them. They groaned and cried. Some of them begged the Americans to surrender before everyone got killed.

Upstairs, Captain John Aiken, the commander, was contemplating that very possibility. The baby-faced captain was the regimental communications officer. Now he found himself pondering the fate of more than one hundred people. Aiken huddled with Captain Lloyd Mackey, his second-in-command, and many of the NCOs, including Sergeant Kusnir. Kusnir could see how frightened the two young captains were. "They were scared to death. They didn't know what to do."

Together they discussed the grim situation. Mackey said, "We can't afford to surrender. We've just gotta fight to the last man, until we're all gone." There was a rumble of disagreement from the NCOs. Captain Aiken clearly did not like that idea either. His last communication with division had been at 1000, a few hours earlier. He knew that he was authorized to withdraw, but at this point, that was not an option.

He had two choices: surrender or annihilation. He could not throw the lives of his men away on a futile last stand. They deserved a chance to survive this war, and surrender would give them that. Moreover, Aiken knew that if he fought to the end, the civilians in the basement would probably die. He could not live with that. Ever so reluctantly, he gave the order to surrender. Mackey seemed to agree (perhaps his statement had been just false bravado). At 1300, someone poked a white flag through a window.

Aiken and the other Americans stood tensely behind the door, waiting to go out. All of them were worried that the Germans would exact reprisals for their many dead.

"Who's gonna go out first?" someone asked. In an act of true bravery, Sergeant Kusnir volunteered. "Well, if nobody'll go out, I'll go out first," he said.

He took a German prisoner, with the idea of using him as a shield of sorts. "I'll go out behind him," he told the other Americans, "and if he steps aside and you hear . . . them fire, then you know they're gonna shoot us all."

He nodded at the German and off they went out the door, right into the waiting enemy muzzles. At that moment, Sergeant Kusnir was thinking of his family back home, especially his girlfriend. He wondered if he would ever see any of them again. The German soldier stepped off to the right and several armed enemy soldiers converged on Kusnir: "Raus! [Get out!]" They stood him against the castle wall but did not shoot. The rest poured into the castle. They herded the American soldiers outside and lined them up. In the basement they liberated their comrades and rousted the civilians: "Everyone out! The house is on fire!" they screamed.

Jean Serve, the sixteen-year-old local boy, was helping a wounded American radioman. The soldier had been hit in the cheek and had lost a lot of blood. Serve put his arm around him and led him out of the castle. At the courtyard gate, they stepped over the body of a German soldier. Others in front of them and behind them did the same.

With much hollering and screaming, the Germans were lining the Americans up and searching them. "They went through and . . . took . . . whatever they had . . . cigarettes, watches, and everything," Kusnir remembered. "Boots, overcoats and whatever else." He lost a watch, a ring, and some money. The German soldiers looked like teenagers. With a fanatical look about them, they stood motionless a couple of feet away, covering the Americans with their burp guns. Sergeant Kusnir glanced at the German who was guarding him and thought, "Boy, I hope this kid don't have a twitching finger."

He noticed his former prisoner having a conversation with the colonel who seemed to be in charge. Kusnir wondered what they were talking about. He knew that the man standing next to him, Sergeant Kalish, spoke some German: "Bob, can you understand what they're saying?" he asked.

Kalish listened as closely as he could, but caught only snippets. "I think that he's saying . . . that we befriended him and his patrol and kept 'em segregated and also protected 'em while we were being bombarded by their shells."

Both of them let out a sigh of relief. They were glad that they had treated their enemy prisoners well. If they hadn't, who knows what would have happened? Kalish also heard several other Germans asking their sergeants, "What are we gonna do with these guys? How are we gonna feed 'em? Where do we take 'em?"

The German colonel quieted everyone down and addressed his American prisoners in English: "You men now are prisoners of the Third Reich. Originally my intent was to shoot you for . . . all my dead soldiers. But this sergeant tells me that his treatment in your captivity was good." He ordered the guards to move everyone out. The Germans put the civilians in the nearby Hotel Koener, interrogated them, and let most of them go. Jean Serve helped clean up the town and slipped away when no one was looking (although the Gestapo arrested him two weeks later). The Germans marched their American prisoners out of town, eastward, on the long road to incarceration. American resistance in Clervaux was finally over.[5]

Eight miles to the southwest, at Eschweiler, the soldiers of the 28th Division Mechanized Reconnaissance Troop were dealing with a major German attack. Private George Mergenthaler, the wealthy Princeton graduate, and his fellow GIs were close friends with the civilians here. They had lived with them, eaten with them, gone to church with them, and generally become part of the community.

All morning the Germans had thrown shells at Eschweiler even as they probed it with infantry patrols and armor. Several buildings were now on fire, including the barn where the troop kept all of its maintenance equipment. The Americans could see the Germans in the distance, flanking the town, surrounding it. Now, at 1300, Captain Lewis Meisenhelter, the troop commander, could sense that the Germans were about to overrun the town. He had only sixty men to oppose them. He knew that if he did not get his people out of there immediately, the Germans would sweep them away like dust beneath a broom. He ordered his men to board the six remaining reconnaissance jeeps and leave town via a small road that led to Wiltz.

Private Mergenthaler shook hands with his many local friends and climbed into his customary machine-gun position in the back of a jeep. Father Bodson, the town priest, and many other people were weeping as they watched Mergenthaler and their other American friends leave town.

Cautiously, the six vehicles moved out in a column, down a hill, around a slight bend in the road, and right into a German ambush. "All of the road around the curve was completely zeroed in," Private Cletus LaFond recalled. "They hit us with everything they had, including small-arms, mortar, rifle, machine-gun, and tank fire. A mortar shell fell on the hood of the jeep ahead of us and the assistant driver fell out." The Germans were in the woods, on either side of the road. Spent bullets were bouncing along the road and ricocheting off the jeeps. Private LaFond took off and made it to the shelter of the woods.

The driver of the lead jeep stepped on the gas in an attempt to run the gauntlet. Staff Sergeant Richard Sheesley, riding in the back, fell off the jeep and into a ditch. As quickly as he could, he got up, ran after the jeep, and jumped aboard. "[We] headed down a hill to the crossroads at the bottom. Here we were faced with a large column of German tanks." They had little choice but to give up.

Meanwhile, the other jeeps were back at the bend, halted and under fire. A German soldier crawled close enough to unleash a burst of burp-gun fire. The Americans bent over in their seats, ducking their heads. In the middle of the column, Private Mergenthaler ("Merg" to his buddies) stood up, got on the machine gun that was mounted in the back of his jeep, and began looking for the German soldier.

In an adjacent jeep, Private Joe Vocasek heard someone yell, "There's the son of a bitch down in the ditch! Get him!"

Vocasek spotted him and squeezed the trigger of his M1 Garand. The bullet smashed into the German soldier's hand. He ducked down and crawled closer to Private Mergenthaler's jeep. Mergenthaler's machine gun was jammed, and he was frantically working the bolt. "Make a run for it!" he yelled at Vocasek. Mergenthaler squeezed off a quick burst, but the gun jammed again. Vocasek and several others ran for the woods.

The German soldier was very close to Private Mergenthaler now. With the burp gun cradled in the crook of his injured arm, the German aimed at Mergenthaler and fired. The bullets tore into Mergenthaler's torso. His lifeless body slumped over the jammed machine gun.

By now the other Americans had scattered into the woods. A few made it to American lines. Most were captured. The Germans buried Mergenthaler's body in a shallow grave just outside of town. The people of Eschweiler never forgot him.[6]

Even as Mergenthaler lived his last moments, Lieutenant Colonel Strickler was still in Consthum, coordinating a withdrawal. A fog was descending over the troubled town, shielding the German attackers. They had captured much of Consthum. The clanking sound of German armor filled the air. For Strickler, there really was no time to lose now. "We would be gobbled up unless we left to fight again somewhere else." He and Major Milton crawled out of their embattled CP. "Our next move is to Kautenbach . . . two miles to the rear," Strickler told the major. "Break contact, withdraw the troops cross country, and meet me there."

Milton nodded his understanding. He and several of his staff officers were huddling behind the cover of a stone wall, finalizing the withdrawal plans. Strickler took the battalion intelligence officer, a rifleman, and his driver with him. They got into his jeep and left Consthum, under fire all the way.

Strickler did not even know if the Germans were in Kautenbach, but he had little choice but to find out firsthand. "When we arrived in Kautenbach, no one was in sight. It was an eerie feeling to ride through a ghost town." Worried that a tank might poke its muzzle from a corner somewhere, they dismounted and searched through an abandoned American aid station. The medics had clearly left in a hurry. Food was still on plates. Unmarked maps lined the walls. Blood-spattered litters were lying in random rows. Pens, pencils, and papers were strewn atop a couple of desks. Someone had even left his spectacles.

A few minutes later, Major Milton and the remnants of his 3rd Battalion arrived in Kautenbach. Strickler placed them on a hillside defensive position west of Kautenbach and drove on to Wiltz—again under fire—in hopes of getting information from the division staff.

Wiltz was a beautiful town that was bisected by a river of the same name. Part of the town was on the heights above the river and part below it. Initially General Cota had his headquarters in a stately building in the upper portion of Wiltz, but with the town under constant artillery fire (and now some ground attacks, too), he had moved his CP into a cellar in the lower section of town. Strickler's jeep had no sooner skidded to a halt when he jumped off and strode into the cellar. "I found consternation. Division was preparing for an attack from three directions. General Cota wanted us [3rd Battalion] to try to hold out until morning in the vicinity of Nocher, a small town about three miles from Kautenbach." Strickler left the CP and went to Nocher, where he prepared to spend yet another sleepless, stressful night dealing with recurring German attacks.

General Cota was scrambling to defend Wiltz. For the past twenty-four hours, he had commandeered every man he could. His headquarters commandant, Lieutenant Colonel Thomas Hoban, had gathered most of the division rear-echelon personnel and organized them into a provisional battalion. These men were the division's last line of defense. There were finance people, signalmen, cooks, drivers, cartographers, medics, quartermasters, and even the division band. These were specialists, not combat soldiers. Some of them did not even know how to load their rifles. One trombone player watched as a bandmate received a carbine and several clips of ammo from an armorer. The musician looked at the clips and asked the armorer, "What are they for?"

Fortunately, these rear-echelon types had been augmented with some reinforcements. Six Shermans and five assault guns from the 707th Tank Battalion had managed to find Wiltz. There were six antitank guns from the 630th Tank Destroyer Battalion deployed in roadblock positions outside of Wiltz. There were several quad-.50s and 40-millimeter Bofors guns from the 447th Antiaircraft Artillery Battalion, plus a few M8 armored cars from the remnants of the division reconnaissance troop. Most of the 687th Field Artillery Battalion had managed to displace from Bourscheid the previous evening and were now dug in at Roullingen, south of Wiltz. Their howitzers could cover the whole Wiltz perimeter. The bulwark of Cota's defense was the 44th Engineer Combat Battalion, under the command of Lieutenant Colonel Clarion Kjeldseth. This unit belonged to General Middleton's VIII Corps engineers. Knowing how badly Cota needed troops, Middleton had sent him the 44th the day before. Companies A and C of the 44th were now in place, prepared to fight as infantry at roadblock positions east of Wiltz. In addition to these organized units, Cota had some 110th Infantry stragglers who had been steadily trickling into the perimeter.

By now, at 1400, the general had deployed most of these hodgepodge forces into a semicircular perimeter, blocking the roads into Wiltz. He knew that CCB of the 10th Armored Division was on the move. At this point, General Cota thought that CCB was coming to Wiltz. Colonel Roberts, after all, was an old friend. Surely he would come to the rescue, so it was just a matter of holding on at Wiltz until CCB arrived.

A natural combat leader, General Cota circulated among the men, talking with them, explaining their mission, bucking up morale, even teaching them how to use their weapons. He came across one weary-looking soldier whom everyone called Panama.

Cota was concerned that Panama might not be aware of the gravity of the situation. "Look, son," he said to him "the Germans will appear any minute. You want to be alert."

"I'm alert, General," Panama replied. "I wanna live as long as anybody." Panama turned to his buddies. "Hear that, you guys? My pal, the general, says be alert." Cota and everyone else enjoyed a good chuckle.

Soon after this, grenadiers, tanks, and self-propelled guns from Panzer Lehr unleashed an attack on the forward positions northeast of Wiltz. In a farmhouse at the edge of the American perimeter, Sergeant Bob Bradicich heard them coming. He and several other soldiers (probably engineers) were watching the road. They had their rifles and a couple of bazookas. Bradicich had experienced quite a bit in the last twenty-four hours. The day before, he had fought German tanks at Reuler. He had begun this day in Clervaux, clashing with German soldiers before making his way to Wiltz. He was so tired and hungry he could hardly think, but now the sound of the enemy tanks prompted a surge of adrenaline through his veins. He peered into the fog, trying to catch a glimpse of the tanks: "The waiting and the listening to the tanks got everyone on edge. The waiting was driving me out of my mind, for I knew they would mount a frontal assault. Then we spotted them coming down the road out of the fog."

There were three Mark IVs and some accompanying infantry. Bradicich and the other GIs opened fire "with everything we had. The bazookas fired, but the shells bounced off the armor on the tanks. We were firing at the infantry and we were getting an awful lot of them." The tanks were blasting the farmhouse with their main guns. Each time, the house shook, but it did not crumble. Sergeant Bradicich took to firing at the Mark IV muzzles in hopes of exploding their shells in their breeches before the tank gunners could fire. This was ingenious, but unlikely to work.

A bazooka shell smashed into one German tank, disabling it. The crew abandoned the tank and escaped into the fog. For a few minutes there was a lull, but then the Germans came back with more tanks and infantry. The tanks came at the Americans full speed, shooting as they went, blowing soldiers into pieces. They rolled down the road, past the farmhouse, outflanking Sergeant Bradicich's little group. "This started a mass retreat. They were butchering us and we had no defense against these tanks. It was a terrible sight to see. This was not an orderly withdrawal."

Running as fast as they could, American soldiers streamed west down the road, past the tanks. The Mark IVs sprayed them with machine guns, sawing some men in half. The German grenadiers tried to catch up and join in on the spoils. Sergeant Bradicich spotted a retreating American truck and ran for it. He made it to the truck and tried to climb aboard. Someone in the back reached down, grabbed him, and hoisted him inside. The truck escaped to the west, far to the rear. Mentally and physically exhausted, Bradicich slumped down and cried. For him, the Bastogne corridor fight was mercifully over.

For a few hours, the Germans tore a gaping hole through the lines of A Company, 44th Engineers. Captain Thomas Johnson's B Company was at Wiltz in reserve in case such a crisis developed. Johnson rounded up his men and marched them northeast, right into the path of the advancing Panzer Lehr troops. "Members of Co. A were straggling back, wounded, shocked and frightened. Total confusion existed . . . and it took a little time to reorganize what remained of Co. A with Co. B. We were about two or three miles from Wiltz." Johnson found a couple of tanks and two three-inch antitank guns. He set up his defenses at the edge of a little cluster of houses, with a wooded hill to his right. He expected a major attack at any moment, but it did not happen. The Germans did not yet have enough troops in place (or a coordinated plan) for a full push on Wiltz. Instead they battered the town with artillery and put pressure on the perimeter with small attacks and patrols.[7]

4

Antoniushaff was a lot like Chancellorsville. It was little more than a lonely crossroads with an adjacent three-story structure that, frankly, looked out of place. Antoniushaff was not a destination. It was a place that people traversed on the way to somewhere else. That was never more true than on this day. The main road from Clervaux ended (in perpendicular fashion) at this crossroads. In order to turn south and roll on to Bastogne, the Germans had to have Antoniushaff.

General Middleton understood this quite well. The night before, when he learned that the Germans had captured Clervaux, he immediately ordered CCR to set up one roadblock at Antoniushaff and another one three miles to the south, near Allerborn. The general knew that Clervaux's fall amounted to the destruction of the 110th Infantry. This meant that there was a large hole in the middle of the 28th Division front, along the direct route to Bastogne. Middleton knew that until the paratroopers and 10th Armored Division teams arrived in Bastogne, CCR would be all that stood between the Germans and the vital town. The road junctions at Antoniushaff and Allerborn had to be held long enough for the reinforcements to set up in and around Bastogne. Thus, CCR represented Middleton's last hope of hanging on to these road junctions long enough to save Bastogne.

With such a daunting task in front of him, Colonel Duke Gilbreth, CCR's commander, had little choice but to split up his command. He had already lost B Company, 2nd Tank Battalion, in the fighting at Clervaux, Reuler, and Heinerscheid, so his resources were somewhat limited. He ordered Task Force Rose, under Captain Lyle Rose, to defend Antoniushaff. The task force consisted of A Company, 2nd Tank Battalion; Rose's own C Company, 52nd Armored Infantry Battalion; plus a platoon of engineers from C Company, 9th Armored Engineers. At the Feitsch crossroads, half a mile east of Allerborn, Gilbreth placed Task Force Harper (under Lieutenant Colonel Ralph Harper), consisting of the remnants of Harper's 2nd Tank Battalion, and B Company, 52nd Armored Infantry Battalion.

At Antoniushaff, Rose fanned his tanks out into the fields surrounding the roundabout crossroads. There was very little cover there. The terrain was mostly flat, with intermittent patches of woods. Rose's infantrymen dismounted from their half-tracks and dug in three hundred yards in front of the tanks. That morning, three German tanks had emerged from the woods just north of the Clervaux road and exchanged shots with Rose's tanks. The Americans had destroyed one of the enemy tanks, and the other two retreated back into the woods. These Germans belonged to the 2nd Panzer's reconnaissance battalion and were probably the same enemy tanks that Sergeant Charles Johnson, the artillery observer, had seen from his perch in the church steeple at Donnange.

By midday, German columns were forming on the road from Clervaux, but they were still out of range for Task Force Rose. The Germans then laid a smoke screen directly across Rose's front, obscuring their movements as they closed to within eight hundred yards of the crossroads. As the smoke lifted, the volume of enemy artillery fire increased. The shells buffeted the American infantrymen in their holes and menaced the tankers inside their Shermans. American artillery fire, from the self-propelled guns of the 73rd Armored Field Artillery Battalion south of Allerborn, answered in kind.

The Germans were massing the better part of two tank battalions to throw at Antoniushaff. These Mark IVs and Mark Vs had rolled through Clervaux the night before. Now they were eight hundred yards away from the crossroads, spreading out all over the plain, opening fire. The shells slammed into the infantry positions with devastating accuracy. Rather than be blown to pieces, the infantry soldiers left their holes and took cover behind the Shermans.

But the tankers had problems of their own. They were trading shots with the German tanks. High-velocity shells from both sides whizzed through the crisp winter air. Most of the shots missed, but a few struck home. Three Mark IVs got hit and stopped shooting. An American tank got knocked out and had to be abandoned. Another Sherman had its main gun destroyed. Still another Sherman was maneuvering around, looking for a good shot, when it threw a track (the treads came loose from the bogey wheels). The crew had to abandon the tank.

The Americans were holding their own, but the German strength was overwhelming. The Germans soon pushed large numbers of tanks and troops across the road, north of Task Force Rose, and attacked. This meant that the task force was now surrounded on three sides. Slowly but surely, the noose was closing.

Colonel Gilbreth, from his command post six miles away in Longvilly, was listening to radio reports from Task Force Rose, so Gilbreth understood the gravity of the situation at Antoniushaff. He picked up the phone and called Middleton's headquarters at the Belgian barracks in Bastogne and dictated a message to the operator: "Task Force Rose . . . is as good as surrounded," Gilbreth said. "Have counted sixteen German tanks there [in actuality, the Germans probably had more than twice that number]. TF is being hit from three sides. Recommend that they fight their way out" to the Allerborn roadblock.

Minutes later someone handed the message to General Middleton. He read it with a heavy heart because he knew that he could not authorize a withdrawal from Antoniushaff. Time was simply too short now. The Germans would have to pay, in time and in blood, for every gain they made. Task Force Rose had to remain in place.

The Germans overran the task force and seized the Antoniushaff crossroads. Seven American tanks were destroyed or abandoned. Captain Rose managed to escape cross-country to Houffalize with five tanks and the assault-gun platoon. They ran into an ambush, but some made it into Bastogne.

Other task force survivors drifted south or west, away from the advancing 2nd Panzer Division. Everyone else was either dead or taken prisoner. The Germans reorganized their assault columns and headed south in the direction of Allerborn. Task Force Rose had delayed the Germans for seven crucial daylight hours. Nothing more could have been asked of them.[8]

Amazingly, there were still small pockets of American soldiers operating miles behind the German lines. For instance, Corporal Cecil Hannaford's 3rd Platoon of A Company, 110th Infantry, was still in its original roadblock position at Kalborn. For three full days now, Hannaford and the others had heard sounds of fighting all around them. But here in this spot, everything had remained peaceful. The commanding officer was a brand-new, youthful lieutenant who would do nothing without orders from higher headquarters. The problem now was that higher headquarters no longer existed. So here the 3rd Platoon still sat, a tiny island in the eye of a large hurricane.

Corporal Hannaford looked to the west and saw, through a layer of clouds, slivers of the sun setting. He was amazed at how short the days were in the Ardennes this time of year. Then he heard engine sounds coming from the east. His heartbeat quickened. The vehicles had to be German. Were they finally going to destroy 3rd Platoon?

The Americans had placed mines on the road. The soldiers, spread out in fighting holes on either side of the road, pointed their weapons east, in the direction of the engine noise. Sure enough, in the distance, they saw a command car, with three trucks trailing behind it. Hannaford and the others prepared to open fire: "When they got in range . . . the sergeant said, 'Fire.' Everybody fired on this convoy. They stopped and the Germans jumped out of the truck, and over the hill they went. They left all those vehicles there. We knew that they'd found us and that they'd probably be back."

The platoon was fortunate in two respects: First, it had an experienced platoon sergeant who was not shy about telling the lieutenant what must be done. Second, they were in contact with the 2nd Battalion, 112th Infantry, which had outposts just over the next hill. The sergeant made it very clear to the lieutenant that the time had finally come to leave Kalborn. They hooked up with the 112th, waited for darkness, and then retreated to the northwest. In so doing, they joined Colonel Gustin Nelson's fighting retreat. He successfully extracted his regiment from Weiswampach and gradually fell back to Huldange and then farther west. The 112th Infantry had done its part in defending Bastogne. It was now part of the fight for the northern shoulder of the Bulge.[9]

Many miles to the west, on the road north of Martelange, Private First Class Don Addor was riding in a communications half-track, feeling apprehensive, cold, and dirty. All day long, his unit, Headquarters Company, 20th Armored Infantry Battalion, Team Desobry, had been on this road. A light rain was falling now, but it seemed like a heavy rain because the weather was so chilly. Addor was a communications specialist who hailed from Washington, D.C. Like so many others throughout the column that stretched for miles ahead, he wondered where they were going. "Mud was everywhere. It had fallen off the tires and tracks of the vehicles in front of us so that there was at least a foot of it on top of the road's hard surface. All of these vehicles plowing through this mud sent up a fine spray until every part of us was covered with mud." The mud was speckled all over his helmet, his fatigue jacket, and his face, too. Addor heaved a sigh of resignation and hoped that wherever they were going, it would be warm and dry.

A couple of miles ahead, Staff Sergeant Rufus Lewis felt the same way. He was a "computer" in the fire direction center of the 420th Armored Field Artillery Battalion. His job was to calculate the distance from the battalion's M7 "Priest" 105-millimeter self-propelled guns to their targets.

The son of a jeweler in Spartanburg, South Carolina, he had attended Clemson University for a year and a half before leaving school in 1942 at age twenty to join the army. Now he was sitting in the passenger seat of a half-track, feeling chilled to the bone. The half-track afforded precious little protection from the whipping rain and mud. "At times it was . . . sleeting. It was right miserable." Sergeant Lewis shivered and scrunched lower in his seat in a vain attempt to get warm. He sat still and wished they would hurry up and get to wherever they were going.

Actually, they were only about ten miles from their destination—Bastogne. Roberts had originally thought he was going to Wiltz to help his old friend Dutch Cota. But by this time, Colonel Roberts and many of his officers had been in touch with liaison officers from VIII Corps who gave them orders for Bastogne.

Now Colonel Roberts knew that CCB would reach Bastogne within the hour. He wanted to be sure that he knew what to tell his team commanders when they arrived in Bastogne, so he decided to go to VIII Corps headquarters before CCB reached the town.

He arrived at the Belgian barracks at 1600 and immediately met with General Middleton. He told the general that CCB would soon arrive. Middleton was clearly tired, but he briefed Roberts in his usual calm manner: "The 28th Infantry Division and the 9th Armored Division [CCR] are ahead of us—but badly cut up. The situation is fluid. How many teams can you make up, Robby?"

"Three," Roberts replied.

Middleton nodded and turned to a map that was hanging on the wall: "Okay. CCB will move without delay in three teams to the following positions to counter enemy threats: one team to the southeast of Wardin, one team to the vicinity of Longvilly, and one team to the vicinity of Noville. Move with the utmost speed. Hold these positions at all costs."

The gravity of the situation was sinking in to Roberts. "Sir, there will be stragglers. I want authority to use these men." Middleton readily assented and then sent Colonel Roberts on his way. Roberts left the barracks, got in his jeep, and drove a mile south of Bastogne to meet his columns. As he waited for them, he was wrestling with some serious misgivings. Like most armor officers, he believed that tanks were most effective when used as one concentrated force. That, of course, was more appropriate for an offensive mission, not a defensive one that this situation called for. Roberts understood that, but he was worried that his teams were too spread out: "I did not think it was a good employment of my force because they were dispersed over a great many miles, but I knew the General knew the situation better than I."

Indeed, Middleton did have a better grasp of the situation. He knew that CCB had to be split up to guard each of the major road networks that led into Bastogne from the east, the north, and the south. This was the only way that CCB could stop the potent German mechanized forces that were nearing town by the hour. S. L. A. Marshall later correctly wrote, "Middleton's decision was the initial tactical step which led finally to the saving of Bastogne." In time, Roberts also agreed with Middleton.

Not long after Roberts left the Belgian barracks, another welcome visitor soon arrived. Brigadier General Anthony McAuliffe was the acting commander of the 101st Airborne Division. The actual CO, Major General Maxwell Taylor, was back in Washington, D.C., for official meetings (and to spend Christmas with his family, his critics unfairly claimed). The diminutive McAuliffe was the division artillery commander, and in Taylor's absence, he had seniority.

The 101st Airborne Division was still several hours away from Bastogne, but like Roberts, McAuliffe forged ahead of his unit's column. All day long, he had been under the assumption that the 101st would be deployed to the north, at Werbomont. But at a crossroads west of Bastogne, he and his operations officer, Lieutenant Colonel Harry Kinnard, decided, by sheer good instincts, to pay a visit to Middleton. They hoped that he could give them more information on what was at this point a murky situation.

As they entered Bastogne, their driver had trouble negotiating their command car through streets jammed with retreating vehicles, soldiers, and bewildered, frightened civilians. "Sir, unless these people are having a premature case of jitters, I'd say the Germans must be barreling this way fast," Kinnard remarked.

"We'll soon find out," McAuliffe replied.

At last they made it to the Belgian barracks. Middleton welcomed them, briefed them on the situation, and told them that the 101st was earmarked for Bastogne. By now, Middleton had consulted with his immediate superiors, Lieutenant General Courtney Hodges at First Army and General Omar Bradley at Twelfth Army Group, and they told him that the 101st Airborne was to be attached to VIII Corps at Bastogne. Hearing this news, McAuliffe and Kinnard were relieved that they had detoured for this visit with Middleton. The conference lasted about half an hour, and then Middleton dismissed them.

The two Airborne officers left VIII Corps headquarters and began a hasty reconnaissance of Bastogne. At that point, they were basically doing the job of the entire division staff. They were not even in communication with the division convoy. Lieutenant Colonel Kinnard briefly thought of the panic-stricken scenes he had witnessed an hour earlier in the streets of Bastogne. It all made more sense now—too much sense.[10]

On a wooded hill somewhere west of Eselborn, Colonel Hurley Fuller was holding out, cornered with forty other men. Since escaping from the Claravallis the night before, Fuller had wandered all over the area. At first he had tried to reorganize the remnants of his regiment, to no avail. Then he had attempted to make a stand with fifty men from the 630th Tank Destroyer Battalion, only to be encircled by German infantrymen, prompting another perilous escape. Since organizing this new group of fugitives, Fuller had been looking for any way to avoid the swarms of German troops that were overrunning the area. A few hours earlier, he had ordered these men to dig in atop this hill.

Now, after darkness, German Panzergrenadiers, supported by tanks, were attempting to take the hill. The Americans were inflicting casualties on the German attackers, but they were running low on ammunition, and they were trapped. "We lost twelve or fifteen men, mostly from tank fire," Fuller wrote. He ordered an ammo check: "A check of ammunition . . . revealed that it was virtually exhausted. I ordered the group to break up into five-man patrols and attempt to infiltrate west."

Fuller and four others started walking west. They covered about a mile and were moving through some woods when they heard German voices. Silently they took cover. The fifty-year-old Fuller was in the throes of complete exhaustion. For more than three days he had hardly slept. In the last twenty-four hours he had had little to eat. He was cold. His bones ached. He wondered how much more of this he could take.

The Germans were all around them now and getting closer by the second. An enemy soldier spotted one of the Americans and leveled his rifle at him. "Kamerad!" the American screamed. Fuller and the other three Yanks tried to run away, but the Germans caught them. The colonel felt a terrific blow to the head and fell unconscious. "When I came to, I felt a burning sensation in my stomach, where I had been bayoneted slightly. The wound . . . was not deep but that, coupled with the blow I had received to my head, made me quite weak and nauseated."

Fuller looked around and saw German soldiers standing guard over him and the four other soldiers. "Tell the SOBs nothing but name, rank, and serial number," the colonel whispered. A German officer who was standing behind him smashed his pistol into Fuller's head and told him to shut up. Fuller now felt even more nauseous. A German guard yanked him to his feet, kicked him several times, and told him to march.

By now it had dawned on the enemy that Fuller was the CO of the 110th Infantry. They took him to 2nd Panzer Division headquarters at Bockholz and interrogated him. True to form, Fuller told them nothing. The contentious Texan had done everything he could to fulfill his hopeless mission in the Ardennes. Now the agony of captivity lay ahead of him. He scowled at his captors. Inside, he felt almost like weeping. In his heart, he knew he would never command troops again. His regiment was shattered.

Even as Fuller became a prisoner, the Germans were about to attack Task Force Harper at the Feitsch crossroads. Since overwhelming Task Force Rose at Antoniushaff, the 2nd Panzer Division had been moving south, carefully preparing to take this section of road that was only ten miles from Bastogne. The crossroads was basically a T junction. Anyone turning right at Feitsch would drive half a mile to the west, past Allerborn, and then on to Bastogne. The Germans aimed to do exactly that.

Task Force Harper's tanks and half-tracks were deployed on either side of the junction and east of it, too. Many of the crews were dismounted, keeping watch near their tanks in the darkness. West of the junction, Harper got some unexpected help. A couple of days earlier, Colonel Theodore Seely, the man who had commanded the 110th Infantry before Fuller, had left the hospital and returned. With Fuller on the run, Cota had placed Seely back in command of whatever remained of the outfit. Seely and several staff officers had spent the day at Allerborn, salvaging remnants of the regiment. In all, they had about 260 men. Some were in Allerborn. Others were in foxholes west of the Feitsch crossroads. Colonel Seely placed his CP in a sturdy, two-story stone house adjacent to the Bastogne road.

One of Seely's castaways was none other than the resilient Lieutenant Glen Vannatta, the executive officer of D Company. He had made it to Wiltz the night before and spent the evening there. This morning, he had made it to Allerborn and, much to his delight, had found himself reunited with Captain Andrew Carter, his CO, plus several other D Company men.

Now Vannatta and the others were outside of Seely's CP, listening to the rumble of armor in the distance: "Occasional flares punctuated the darkness. Then, as if by signal, bedlam broke loose when one of the jeeps at the crossroads was hit and set afire. The Germans started shelling our positions at the crossroads and also where we were around Allerborn." American artillery (probably from the 73rd and 58th Armored Field Artillery Battalions at Longvilly) answered in kind. "Machine gun fire opened up from the direction of the crossroads and many tracers" streaked through the air.

Under cover of this fire, the Germans closed in for an intimate attack. "The enemy began infiltrating and there was no warning to the battalion," an eyewitness later wrote. "Enemy tanks fired into several . . . vehicles, setting them afire. The burning vehicles lighted the area, revealing the positions of other vehicles. The CP received a direct hit." German tanks picked off Shermans, trucks, and half-tracks at will. Harper's jeep driver jumped aboard one tank, only to discover that it was German. He quickly jumped off. A gunner in one American tank spotted a Panther fifty yards away and drew a bead on it. The only trouble was that so many retreating soldiers were clinging to his Sherman that the gunner could not get a shot off. The tank commander pushed several of them off the tank, allowing the gunner to snap off a shot and destroy the Panther.

Such successes were few, though. The Germans were annihilating Task Force Harper. Some American vehicles got away, but most were not so fortunate. Harper himself was killed while trying to escape with a small cluster of half-tracks. Dismounted tank crewmen and armored infantry-men retreated west from Feitsch into the night, avoiding the Germans any way they could. As with Task Force Rose earlier today, Task Force Harper had sacrificed itself to buy time to allow others to get in place at Bastogne.

Now the enemy began a steady advance west from the T junction, in the direction of Allerborn. Sergeant Charles Johnson, the artillery observer, was standing outside Colonel Seely's headquarters building. Since re-treating from Donnange to Lullange this morning, Johnson had experi-enced a frustrating day of more withdrawals. His lieutenant had proven himself to be a coward. The man had actually sabotaged their radio in order to have an excuse to flee. Johnson was angry at him, but he also felt a little sorry for him. Finally, they had ended up at Allerborn. The lieu-tenant was now inside the CP, and Johnson was waiting out here for him. Johnson had heard the tank battle, but the shooting was getting closer. "Small-arms fire was coming down the road."

Sergeant Johnson was standing next to a tree, wondering what was going on, when a man emerged from the CP and approached him. The ser-geant immediately recognized that it was Colonel Seely. "I was elated at being so near a man of such rank." For a few minutes, the two men stood together wordlessly, listening to the shooting. Seely was trying to get a feel for the situation. Johnson was wondering what was on the colonel's mind.

A tracer round zipped over their heads. Seely turned to Sergeant Johnson: "He really laid that one in there, didn't he?"

"Pretty close," Sergeant Johnson agreed.

Colonel Seely nodded, turned away, and went back inside his CP. Johnson found out from a sentry that Seely had placed his lieutenant under arrest for dereliction of duty. For the life of him, Johnson could not figure out how the colonel knew of his lieutenant's cowardice, but he was glad that the man was getting what he deserved. Thus unencumbered, Johnson started walking west on the road, looking for his battery. He made it to Longvilly, and from there, he hooked up with some American troops. His Bastogne battle was over.

As Johnson left Allerborn, the Germans arrived. Their tanks were rolling west along the Bastogne highway, heading straight for Colonel Seely's CP. Someone burst inside the house and said, "There's a Kraut tank on the highway!"

Colonel Seely had a cigarette dangling from his mouth. He squinted at the man (much like Humphrey Bogart, in the memory of one officer) and said, "Are you sure it's a Jerry?"

"It must be," the man replied. "It's shootin' at our men and it came from out in front, Colonel."

Seely left the CP, went out to the road, put his ear to the ground, and listened carefully. He could tell that the approaching tank was a Sherman, "but it was coming very slowly and I figured it was driven by a Boche" who was not familiar with how to drive a Sherman. The Germans had apparently captured this American tank and were using it as their lead tank. Behind the Sherman, there were several Mark IVs.

Colonel Seely hurried inside the house and told everyone to scatter and go to Mageret, if possible. For a few moments, there was silence as everyone got ready to leave and listened to the tanks outside. The colonel was putting on his coat and folding his maps. The only light inside the house came from candles. The Sherman stopped outside the front door, turned its turret toward the house, and fired. "The . . . round went through the left side of the house and did little damage except for . . . plaster dust and debris as the gunner was using AP [armor piercing]," Chief Warrant Officer Ralph Johnson later wrote. For Johnson this was déjà vu. The night before, he had escaped from the Claravallis under similar circumstances. Tonight he was dealing with the exact same scenario at this makeshift regimental headquarters. "We all made a mad scramble down the hall toward the back of the house."

It was a chaotic free-for-all as the soldiers stumbled over one another trying to make it to the rear of the house. Some were crawling. Some were running. The enemy-controlled Sherman unleashed a volley of machine-gun bullets. A Mark IV took up station somewhere beyond the back door and added its own machine-gun fire.

Colonel Seely, Lieutenant Colonel Robert Ewing, the CO of the 109th Field Artillery Battalion, and Sergeant James Hanna were at the tail of the retreating mob. Worried that the Sherman was about to snap off a shot, they went down in the cellar. "To our dismay, when we got there, we found that the only exit was a front door," Seely said. They went to the door and saw the Sherman right outside. There was also an abandoned Task Force Harper jeep. "The tank fired into the building above us." They ducked against a wall for cover. It was very foggy now, so they hoped that perhaps they could make a break for it, past the tank and into the night. They crouched in the doorway, waiting for their chance.

The Sherman did move on, but it was followed by eleven Mark IVs. Each pumped a round into the house. Behind the tanks there were half-tracks loaded with infantrymen. Two Germans dismounted and inspected the jeep. One of the Germans happened to shine his flashlight at the doorway, catching the three Americans. "We were immediately separated and put into different half-tracks."

In a matter of a few hours, the Germans had captured two commanders of the 110th Infantry. Ironically, this created some confusion for them.

With Fuller in custody, they figured they already had the CO of the 110th, so they decided that Seely must be the CO of the 111th, a regiment that was once part of the 28th Division but not anymore. Seely did nothing to disabuse them of this mistaken notion.

Even as Seely and the two other soldiers got captured, the rest of the command group was scrambling out the rear of the house. Chief Warrant Officer Johnson "ran to the kitchen window and jumped out into a manure pile. Feeling my way around in the dark, I found Captain [Gerald] Harwell and one or two others, and we ran directly back of the house to safety in the night."

Lieutenant Vannatta slithered on his belly out the back door of the house, dodging machine-gun bullets all the way. Just ahead of him, Lieutenant Harry Mason, a platoon leader in D Company, "took off on the run, down along the road. The tank firing along the back of the house paused momentarily." Lieutenant Vannatta took advantage of the moment, running as fast as he could in the same direction as Mason. Both of them made it out—Mason to Longvilly and Vannatta all the way to Bastogne.

In the big picture, that was small consolation, though. When the Germans overran Allerborn, they effectively destroyed whatever remained of the 110th Infantry, not to mention Task Force Harper. Both of these valiant units had fulfilled suicide missions so that other American units might live. Nonetheless, the 2nd Panzer Division was inexorably rolling west toward Longvilly, a mere six miles from Bastogne.[11]

5

At Longvilly, Colonel Gilbreth, commander of CCR, was in a gloomy mood. With the routing of Task Forces Rose and Harper, he had lost two-thirds of his command. He still had one more combat team, Task Force Booth, deployed a mile to the north on high ground east of Moinet, but he had no communications with them. For all Gilbreth knew, Task Force Booth was also gone. Longvilly was teeming with straggling men and vehicles from CCR and the 28th Division. Some were wandering aimlessly past the town church, with its unique onionlike dome, more characteristic of Russia than Belgium. Others were setting up new fighting positions in houses or in vehicles at the edges of town. The rest were just relaxing, glad to be out of the line of fire for the moment. On either side of Longvilly, self-propelled guns from the 73rd and 58th Armored Field Artillery Battalions were firing at unseen targets miles away. As far as Gilbreth was concerned, these shattered remnants were all that remained between the Germans and Bastogne. For now, he resolved to stay in place and hold off the enemy as long as he could.

Actually, the situation was not as grim as Gilbreth thought. At Moinet, Task Force Booth was still intact, in roadblock positions. The task force consisted of the Headquarters Company of the 52nd Armored Infantry Battalion; two platoons from A Company, 52nd Armored Infantry; a platoon of tank destroyers from the 811th Tank Destroyer Battalion; and a platoon of light tanks from D Company, 2nd Tank Battalion. The commander, Lieutenant Colonel Robert Booth, was the CO of the 52nd Armored Infantry Battalion. He was a 1935 graduate of West Point. A fine soldier, Booth was liked and respected by the men under his command.

Now Booth's infantrymen were dug in east of little Moinet, on either side of the road. Behind them were the tanks and tank destroyers, also flanking the road. In the recollection of Major Eugene Watts, Booth's operations officer, they were under "moderate artillery and small-arms fire," but otherwise the situation was stable there. Watts was a twenty-six-year-old Citadel graduate from Union, South Carolina. As a youth, he had been interested in attending Furman University, but his Southern Baptist family was so conservative that when his grandmother found out that Furman students were allowed to dance, the family forbade him from attending the school. Instead, he went to Citadel and became a soldier. With no way to communicate by radio or phone with Colonel Gilbreth, Major Watts had been sending out runners for several hours, but none of them ever came back (nor did any of them reach Longvilly).

Some stragglers from the 2nd Tank Battalion started coming through Task Force Booth's lines. They were "real shook up," in the memory of one soldier. They spoke of legions of German tanks and told tales of what had happened to them at Antoniushaff and Feitsch. In the distance, there were faint sounds of enemy armor, some of which seemed to come from behind them, but little else was happening. Clearly the Germans were out there somewhere, but at least that night they were not coming through Moinet. Task Force Booth remained in place, waiting and watching.[12]

Instead of smashing straight into Longvilly from the east, the Germans chose to flank it. The 2nd Panzer Division, fresh from its triumph at Allerborn, turned off the Bastogne highway at Chifontaine and rumbled northwest, toward Bourcy and Noville. These were the tanks that Task Force Booth heard to their rear. The division commander, Colonel Meinrad von Lauchert, did not want his tanks involved in a close-quarters fight in a big town like Bastogne. His primary orders, from army and corps, were to reach the Meuse. Lauchert, then, was taking a shortcut to Noville. If he could capture that little town, he could pivot north to the Meuse, or even south into Bastogne, as circumstances dictated.

At the same time, Panzer Lehr was also in position to strike Longvilly. The division had spent the day fighting on the fringes of Wiltz before ascending the high ground west of that town. Along the way, they had gotten mixed up with two advancing regiments of the 26th Volksgrenadier Division. This slowed them down but did not stop them. Now the lead companies of Panzer Lehr's 902nd Panzergrenadier regiment, plus fifteen tanks, were in Neiderwampach, a hamlet half a mile south of Longvilly. The commander of Panzer Lehr, Lieutenant General Fritz Bayerlein, was an old campaigner who had been in charge of this outfit since Normandy. He had seen his division annihilated at Normandy, only to be reconstituted in preparation for this offensive.

Here at Niederwampach, Bayerlein stopped his half-track to pore over his maps and consider his best route of advance to Bastogne. Essentially he had two choices: He could push south to the N34, a paved highway that led through Marvie and into Bastogne. Or he could go due west, on a muddy, unpaved country road, through Benonchamps, past Longvilly, and into Mageret, where he could then get on the paved N12 road three miles from Bastogne. Bayerlein had spoken with local farmers who assured him that the dirt road was usable. Armed with this knowledge, he chose to take the dirt road, because it was the most direct route to Bastogne, and he figured that the Americans would not defend such a minor route. He folded up his maps and ordered his companies forward into the foggy night.

By the time that Bayerlein made this decision, Team Cherry (CCB) was in the process of arriving in Bastogne and driving east to Longvilly. Colonel Roberts met with Lieutenant Colonel Henry Cherry and gave him his orders. Now the lead vehicles of Team Cherry were driving east on the N12 road. First Lieutenant Edward Hyduke was in command of this advance guard. Hyduke's column drove through Neffe and Mageret. At any minute, he expected to run into CCR. At 1920, when Hyduke's convoy approached Longvilly, he noticed the presence of stragglers and saw a line of vehicles packing the road into town. In fact, the streets of Longvilly were "filled with vehicles of CCR."

Rather than get his vehicles mixed up with those of CCR, Hyduke ordered a halt just west of Longvilly. He contacted CCR by radio, and they requested that Lieutenant Colonel Cherry come to see them. An hour later, Cherry and his S3 officer strode into Colonel Gilbreth's CP. Gilbreth, who had felt so gloomy and hopeless only minutes before, snapped out of his funk. He greeted them like long-lost brothers, slapped the S3 officer on the back, and said, "You couldn't look any better to me if you were Jesus Christ himself!" Gilbreth's staff laughed. Cherry and his officer chuckled self-consciously.

The merriment soon faded as neither group got what they wanted from the other. Gilbreth and his people were hoping that Team Cherry would relieve them and set up a new defensive line east of Longvilly, but Cherry, of course, had no such orders. Cherry was hoping that Gilbreth could provide much-needed information on the situation there, but the CCR commander had little to offer beyond an assurance that his unit would try to hold "at all costs."

After a short meeting, Cherry left and returned to his column. Tank crews and armored infantrymen were topping off their fuel tanks with five-gallon jerry cans. Cherry told Lieutenant Hyduke to recon the area and occupy an advance position. In the meantime, the main body of Team Cherry would set up one thousand yards west of Longvilly. Cherry was out of communication with Colonel Roberts, who had set up headquarters in the Hotel LeBrun, a solid wood and stone two-story building in Bastogne's main square. Cherry decided to visit Roberts and brief him on the Longvilly situation. He set out in his jeep and drove west on the Bastogne road.

Up and down the expanse of that road, his men waited in their vehicles. This was typical army stuff. They had driven here as fast as possible, with little pause for sleep or sustenance. Now that they were finally here, they were sitting around and waiting. Most took advantage of the lull to catch some sleep. One of the few who did not was Lieutenant Carl Moot, a forward observer from the 420th Armored Field Artillery Battalion. Moot was attached to one of Team Cherry's tank platoons. He functioned as a Sherman tank commander and had a three-man crew. Now Moot was inside the turret of his Sherman looking at his maps under the beam of a flashlight. He was surprised and dismayed to discover that his maps did not include Longvilly or, indeed, much of the area where he would have to call down fire.

He called battalion headquarters, which was now in place just east of Bastogne, and told them of his problem. "They already knew about it and told me that the Battalion had gotten the wrong maps." Moot cursed inwardly. The voice on the other end of the radio promised to send him some new maps by jeep as soon as possible. Lieutenant Moot, like the other men around him, settled in and waited.

Five miles to the west, at a little crossroads just south of Bastogne, Corporal Mike Heyman, a reconnaissance section leader in Team Cherry, was riding shotgun in his jeep. As a section leader, he was in charge of two jeeps. For several hours now, they had been functioning in a role like that of herding dogs—policing up vehicles, pointing people in the right direction, retrieving strays, and generally getting Team Cherry where it needed to be.

Now at this crossroads, Heyman could see a long line of stationary American vehicles, apparently waiting for some guidance. He made contact with them and realized that he was looking at an important segment of Team Cherry under the charge of Captain William Ryerson, the CO of C Company, 20th Armored Infantry Battalion. Ryerson was not sure which way led to Longvilly, and Corporal Heyman was only too happy to show him. "After a happy exchange of greetings and welcomes," Heyman wrote, "the column moved out behind our jeep." Heyman's section guided them through Bastogne and onto the correct route to Longvilly. With his job done, Heyman returned to Bastogne. Ryerson's column drove through Neffe and Mageret, and kept going east, in the direction of Longvilly.[13]

Colonel Roberts's other two teams were also entering Bastogne and moving toward their objectives. As they proceeded, they ran into a growing number of soldiers fleeing from the east. Some were from CCR, but the majority seemed to come from the 28th Division. These men had been through three days of absolute hell. Their overarching thoughts were of food, warmth, and safety (not necessarily in that order). Many of them streamed through the forward elements of Team O'Hara southwest of Wardin. "They rode in vehicles," one soldier remembered, "but their columns and knowledge of the enemy were wildly confused."

Bastogne itself was crowded with retreating men and vehicles. Trucks, jeeps, and trailers jammed the streets, making it difficult for CCB to move. Team Desobry was attempting to negotiate its way through the crowds. The column halted while commanders sorted out the situation or spoke to their men. Staff Sergeant Bill Kerby, the acting leader of his 81-millimeter mortar platoon, dismounted and participated in a leaders' meeting by the side of the road. Captain Gordon Geiger, his CO, pulled out a map and told them everything he knew: "We're gonna set up our defenses here," he said, jabbing a finger into the map, "at Noville. We'll try and stop the Germans cold right there." This was the first time that Kerby had heard of the German offensive.

Kerby returned to his half-track and told his mortar people where they were going. Before the war, the Detroit native had hoped to become a professional golfer. He had actually worked as an assistant club pro, giving lessons and refining his game, but the draft call had come in 1942.

Now he was in charge of twenty other soldiers because his immediate superior, the platoon sergeant, was back in Metz receiving a battlefield commission. Sergeant Kerby gaped at the scores of retreating men and vehicles he saw all over Bastogne. He wondered who they were and where they were going. With plenty of time to kill, he hopped off his half-track and struck up a conversation with one man who was riding on a tank. "What's going on?" he asked.

"I don't know what's going on, but we're just getting out of here," the soldier replied. Away went the tank. Sergeant Kerby returned to his half-track, shaking his head in bewilderment. Whatever was up there, it must be bad, he thought.

As Kerby and the other members of Team Desobry waited in the streets of Bastogne, their commander was in the Hotel LeBrun receiving his orders from Colonel Roberts. "Roberts told me to go to Noville, seize the town, and defend it," Major William Desobry recalled. "He did not know if there were Germans or Americans there." The two officers stood in front of a map. Roberts was showing Desobry which road led to Noville and explaining why he was sending Desobry's team to that little town seven miles north of Bastogne.

At twenty-six, Desobry was younger than some of his men. Rail thin at six feet four and 160 pounds, he was the son of a career soldier. He qualified as something of a family rebel because he had elected to go to Georgetown University instead of West Point. He graduated in 1941 with an ROTC commission. Although he had been in the army for only four years, he had ascended the ranks quickly by proving himself to be a fine combat leader. He enjoyed serving under Colonel Roberts, a man for whom he had great respect, to the point where he was like a second father.

As Major Desobry studied Noville on the map, he understood at once that his team was about to go into a vulnerable spot. He turned away from the map and looked at Colonel Roberts: "If this situation gets to the point where I think it's necessary to withdraw, can I do that on my own or will I need permission from you, sir?"

Roberts temporized a moment but then said firmly, "You know, Des, you will probably get nervous tomorrow morning and want to withdraw, so you had better wait for any withdrawal order from me."

"Yes, sir," Major Desobry replied. The two men shook hands, and the major left Hotel LeBrun. He found an VIII Corps military policeman to guide him to Noville. Then Team Desobry mounted up and moved slowly north.[14]

Fifteen miles to the west, Colonel Thomas Sherburne, the new artillery commander of the 101st Airborne Division—thanks to General McAuliffe's ascension to division commander—was in his command car at a crossroads, contemplating the quickest way to Werbomont. He had not been in communication with McAuliffe, so as far as he knew, the division was headed for Werbomont.

Straight ahead, Colonel Sherburne could see the rear of the 82nd Airborne Division's column at a dead stop. It was 2000 now, and Sherburne knew that the 101st had to keep moving as rapidly as possible. He had no desire to stack up the entire 101st Airborne Division in a traffic jam behind the 82nd. He wondered if it might be best to veer east, through Bastogne. He got out of the car and asked a military police sergeant if any previous 101st Airborne vehicles had gone into Bastogne. The sergeant told him that a few hours before, General McAuliffe's party had gone that way. This information clinched Colonel Sherburne's course of action. He told the MP to route all 101st traffic east, through Bastogne. On the sheer chance of Sherburne's decision, and McAuliffe's a few hours earlier, the 101st Airborne was heading for Bastogne.

For many miles west of Sherburne, 380 vehicles carrying the entire division were stretched, with their lights on, along the road, moving in stops and starts. Most of the men were traveling in open flatbed trailers that were pulled by trucks of every description. These trailers reminded the men of cattle cars. The Airborne soldiers were accustomed to jumping into combat, not riding there. They had been on the road for more than six hours now, most of them exposed to whipping winds and an intermittent, chilly rain.

In one trailer, Private Ewell Martin, a rifleman in the 506th Parachute Infantry, felt the telltale call of nature. He and his buddies had enjoyed a bottle of champagne during this drive. Now Martin was paying the price for imbibing. He and the others were "packed into this cattle trailer so tightly that there was no way to move to the back of the truck," where they were keeping the five-gallon can that served as a latrine. By the time it was passed to Martin, "it was full."

Farther along in the column, Corporal Arlo Butcher, the antiaircraft man, was fighting exhaustion: "I was so tired I couldn't stand any longer, so . . . I crawled out of the trailer and . . . sat on the back of the semi-truck." His buddy, Private First Class Wayne McCaffrey, held him against the truck's spare tire. "I slept one and a half hours while we were moving."

About two hours after Sherburne's decision, the head of the column arrived at Mande-St-Etienne, a small town three miles west of Bastogne. To their dismay, the drivers saw that fifty large trucks were blocking the road. A heavy-maintenance company from the 28th Division was parked on both sides of the narrow two-lane road, preventing anyone from passing. The captain in charge of this company refused to move his trucks. Lieutenant Colonel Kinnard had actually dealt with this man a few hours earlier. The captain had told Kinnard that this was his area, and he could not leave. Kinnard had gone into Bastogne to get a movement order from General Middleton himself, but he had yet to return.

Now the entire 101st Airborne convoy was halted along the road, prompting a massive traffic jam at Mande-St-Etienne. The troopers hopped off their trailers and stretched, getting the circulation in their legs and arms going again. They waited by the side of the road and eyed the 28th Division trucks curiously. Officers were trying to reason with the 28th Division captain, but with no luck. Brigadier General Gerald Higgins, McAuliffe's second-in-command, arrived on the scene and went to work on the captain. Higgins was a no-nonsense thirty-five-year-old Irish American man from Idaho. He did not suffer fools with much equanimity: "Our division is coming up here to fight, Captain, and we must use this road to bring them in."

Private Donald Burgett, the veteran rifleman in A Company, 506th Parachute Infantry, was standing nearby, listening to the conversation. "Get the goddamn things out of the road," Higgins roared. "That's an order."

Still the stubborn captain refused. "He claimed he was missing some men and thought the best way to intercept them would be to block the entire road and not allow anyone to pass in either direction until he had located them," Burgett related. He and the other paratroopers had no patience for this argument. Higgins was getting angrier by the minute, and according to Burgett, the general was "formidable when angered."

Private Burgett noticed that all around him, troopers were reaching for their fighting knives, edging closer to the captain, preparing to kill him if necessary. "If he had died on the spot, no one would have missed him— although I'm sure the men in his command would have been greatly relieved." The paratroopers were some of the best soldiers in the U.S. Army. They were trained to kill face-to-face if necessary. They knew they were needed in Bastogne, and they were eager to get there. They had little time for this captain. To them, he was insignificant, a bug to be crushed.

By now, General Higgins had exhausted his own patience. He drew his pistol and threatened to blow the captain's head off. "This time he saw the wisdom of prompt obedience," Captain Francis Sampson, a chaplain, recalled. The general immediately started walking up and down the line of trucks, ordering the drivers to move them off the road. Amazingly, the 28th Division captain could not resist walking alongside Higgins, loudly protesting his orders, "yapping like a mongrel dog," in the memory of Burgett.

Fortunately for everyone, the road was cleared, the troopers got back into their trailers, and the 101st resumed its drive into Bastogne. Only now they started running into the stragglers that had so plagued CCB. Private Burgett eyed them with a mixture of sympathy and revulsion: "They shambled along in shock and fear, blocking the road completely, eyes staring straight ahead, mumbling to themselves. I had never before— or since—seen such absolute terror in men."

The men in Burgett's trailer called to them and asked questions: "What's going on up there? How many Krauts are there? How close are they? Do they have tanks?"

Most shuffled past without replying. The few who did respond said, "You're going up. We're going back. You'll all be killed! You'll all be killed!"

Nearby, Private First Class Bob Dunning, another 506th trooper, watched one young soldier "jogging along and slogging along . . . no weapons or anything, and he was actually crying."

Dunning, Burgett, and the other 101st Airborne soldiers were witnessing the results of the three-day stand that the 28th Division and CCR had made east of Bastogne. Many of those who were now streaming past their trailers had bought them just enough time to get here. To do this, they had paid a heavy price: for example, the 110th Infantry suffered 2,750 casualties out of an original complement of approximately 3,200 soldiers. In that context, these stragglers were the lucky ones. Most of their comrades were miles to the east, lying dead where they had fought to the end, or being marched into Germany as prisoners of war.[15]

Although the 101st had reached Bastogne, it would still need most of the night to get in place around the town. Most of the men bivouacked outside of Bastogne for the night. In the meantime, CCB was the first line of defense. At 2200, Team Desobry was on the paved N15 highway, carefully approaching Noville. Major Desobry had placed his reconnaissance elements, mostly jeeps, in the lead. They made it into Noville without incident. "There were no Germans there. The town was deserted."

A thick fog had descended over the town. Desobry's staff hastily set up in a little schoolhouse that was located catty-corner from the town church. The church was astride the main crossroads that made Noville valuable. Three roads converged here. One led south into Bastogne and north to Houffalize; one east to Bourcy; another one northwest to Vaux. Desobry immediately ordered Captain Omar "Bud" Billet, commander of B Company, 20th Armored Infantry, to place outpost roadblocks eight hundred yards outside of Noville, astride the three roads. Each roadblock consisted of two Sherman tanks and two infantry squads. "They were to stop any advance in our direction," Desobry wrote, "report contact, and withdraw to prepared defenses in the main position" in Noville. Engineers went to each roadblock, dug holes, and waited for the word to plant their mines. As yet, Desobry did not want them to do so, because he knew that American stragglers would probably be walking on these roads. As Desobry indicated, he placed the rest of his command in a perimeter defense around the town, "with tanks covering all avenues of approach suitable for enemy armor. Infantry protected the armor and filled in the gaps."

At the southwestern edge of Noville, Sergeant Kerby's mortar platoon, for the first time in the war, removed their mortars from their half-tracks and dug them in. Closer to the CP, Private Addor's communications squad parked their half-track a few houses down from Desobry's headquarters in case the major needed it. Addor was exhausted from the trip up here. He went inside an adjacent house, into the cellar, and curled up to sleep atop a pile of turnips. "I was so tired that the lumps didn't keep me from going to sleep."

In the schoolhouse CP, Sergeant Larry Stein was exploring the building. The staff was setting up radios, maps, and telephones on the first floor, in a small room where Belgian children had once learned arithmetic and reading.

Years ago, Stein had actually been a schoolkid on this side of the Atlantic. He was born and raised in Eschwege, Germany, the son of a prosperous middle-class Jewish businessman. When the Nazis came to power, life had gotten very difficult for the Stein family. They had faced terrible discrimination. In Larry's case, Nazi youths harassed him each day as he made his way to and from school. After years passed and things got worse, the Steins decided to leave Germany. They jumped the border into Holland, but German guards caught Stein's sister. The German government allowed her to purchase a passport, but only in exchange for all the family's assets. Even then, they made sure to stamp a large, red J (for Jew) on the passport. Eventually, the Steins made their way to New York City, where Larry got drafted after the onset of the war.

The army had transformed Stein from an alienated immigrant youth to a bona fide American soldier. In fact, he felt that the army had taught him much about American life and culture, even the American sense of humor. He had, in his view, become a true American in the army. At twenty years of age, he was now a naturalized American citizen. The 20th Armored Infantry was, in a sense, his new home. He had made himself valuable as an intelligence specialist, interrogating prisoners, gathering information from locals, and routinely risking his neck on patrols.

Now he was amazed to find evidence of a previous American military presence here in Noville. "The whole upstairs had been occupied apparently by Air Force people who had left all their stuff there—beautiful flight jackets, lots of chocolate . . . bars. I didn't take any. I was okay the way I was." He took a last look around and went back downstairs. As was his usual practice, he hovered close to Desobry, waiting to be sent out on a mission. For now, the major was too busy setting up his defenses.

Outside, the fog was getting even thicker. It was very difficult to see more than ten or twenty yards ahead. In houses, barns, and freshly dug foxholes around Noville, the soldiers of Team Desobry waited and watched as best they could. All of them knew now that the Germans were out there somewhere—beyond the fog, in the dark, forbidding night. Would they come here to Noville? None of them knew yet.[16]

By the final minutes of this Monday evening, the fate of Bastogne hung in the balance. The Germans were in position to take the town.

In the north, reconnaissance elements from the 116th Panzer Division were on the verge of cutting the Houffalize road. The vanguard of the 2nd Panzer Division was crawling northeast through Bourcy, bearing down on Team Desobry at Noville. To the south, General Bayerlein and the lead battalion of Panzer Lehr were just entering Mageret, a mere three miles from Bastogne. He was about to find himself in good position for a thrust into the city. These formidable mechanized forces were augmented by the 26th Volksgrenadier Division and a slew of supporting artillery, supply, and transportation units.

To oppose them, the Americans had one and a half divisions. The 101st Airborne was here, but not yet in position east of town. The 705th Tank Destroyer Battalion, Middleton's last corps reserve, had just begun a road march from Kohlscheid. They would not be there for many hours. Team O'Hara was in place south of Wardin, blocking the N34 highway that led to Marvie and Bastogne. A couple of miles to the north, Team Cherry was strung out on the N12, east of Mageret, all the way to Longvilly. Cherry himself was at the Hotel LeBrun, reporting the Longvilly situation to Roberts.

In and around Longvilly, Colonel Gilbreth and the remnants of CCR were in a holding pattern, waiting for a withdrawal order or a German onslaught, whichever came first. Gilbreth's one intact element, Task Force Booth, was a mile to the north, vaguely aware of German movements but completely out of touch with Gilbreth's headquarters. At the northern edge of the fledgling American perimeter, Team Desobry was firmly in place at Noville. The stragglers who proliferated in the area were, at this point, more of a hindrance than a help.

The Germans had planned to take Bastogne a day or two sooner than tonight. The bravery of the 28th Division and CCR had kept them from succeeding. Bastogne could still be valuable to the Germans, however. If they could take it in the next twenty-four to thirty-six hours, they would be in a position to drive north and west with large, mobile formations. Bastogne would then function as a vital road net and supply hub for them. This would significantly strengthen the northern shoulder of their offensive, where even now a diverse array of American units (including the 112th Infantry) were fighting ferociously. The stronger the German advance in the north, the better their chances of breaching the Meuse and fulfilling the strategic purpose of this offensive—Antwerp and the strangling of two Allied armies.

Thus, the stakes were high as December 18 came to a close. The Americans could not rely on air power to save them. The weather was too cloudy, rainy, and foggy for that. This clash of wills would be decided by individual soldiers amid adverse, even desperate, circumstances.

6

TUESDAY, DECEMBER 19

1

As the clock struck midnight, General Fritz Bayerlein and the lead elements of the Panzer Lehr Division were in Mageret. The route from Neiderwampach to Mageret had been anything but ideal. What started out as a small paved road had degenerated into little more than a muddy farm track. Some tanks and half-tracks had gotten bogged down, forcing the general to leave them behind. Even now, some of the crews were still back in the mud, cursing, trying to extract their vehicles, and getting filthy in the process.

Most of Bayerlein's force of fifteen Mark Vs and a battalion of Panzergrenadiers were intact, though. Once in Mageret, they brushed aside a small roadblock maintained by the 158th Engineer Combat Battalion and overwhelmed some artillerymen from the 73rd Armored Field Artillery Battalion to establish control of the town. The question for Bayerlein was what to do next. Should he push west into Bastogne, or consolidate here and wait for the rest of his division? Before making such a decision, he wanted all the information he could get on the area and its American defenders. During the move up there, he and his men had heard the telltale sound of American armor, but they could not pinpoint the location of the enemy tanks.

General Bayerlein struck up a conversation with a local man, Emile Frere, and mentioned the tank sounds he had heard. Frere nodded knowingly and told the German general that a couple of hours earlier he had seen fifty American tanks plus forty other vehicles rolling east toward Longvilly. According to Frere, a general had been in command of this column. Frere was, of course, unknowingly referring to Team Cherry, although he was greatly overestimating its strength (whether intentionally or not is still unclear). Nonetheless, Frere's observations made perfect sense to

171

Bayerlein. He knew that American armor was operating on the Longvilly road, and he fully expected a counterattack from a U.S. armored division. Bayerlein felt that he could not afford to have such a powerful enemy strike force to his rear so for now he decided to sit tight in Mageret. In so doing, he forfeited a major opportunity to get into Bastogne because at that moment there was very little to stop him from getting there. Of course, if he had pressed on to Bastogne, his battalion-sized force might well have been cut off and destroyed by the 101st Airborne Division as it arrived in town.

East of Mageret, on the N12, his men set up a roadblock consisting of a minefield, three tanks, and some supporting infantry. To the west, they fanned out in defensive positions on either side of the highway.

Two miles west of Mageret, at that same time, Lieutenant Colonel Henry Cherry was in his jeep, driving on the N12, intending to link up with Captain William Ryerson's column. A few minutes before, Cherry had met with Colonel William Roberts in Bastogne. Cherry had briefed the colonel on the situation his team was facing. He had told him that Combat Command Reserve (CCR) would probably retreat at any minute. Roberts and Cherry both felt that it was pointless to hold Longvilly if CCR left. Roberts told Cherry to cover CCR's expected retreat and keep the Germans out of Bastogne.

Now Cherry rejoined his headquarters team at Neffe and spoke to a wounded reconnaissance soldier, who told him that his vehicle had been shot up near Mageret. An artilleryman from the 73rd Armored Field Artillery Battalion chimed in—a German patrol in Mageret had destroyed his schoolhouse fire direction center. Someone else had apparently spotted tanks in the town. An hour or two earlier, Cherry himself had been shot at in Mageret while he was on the way to meet with Colonel Roberts. At the time, Cherry had thought the fire came from trigger-happy Americans. After hearing these reports, an unsettling possibility was becoming apparent: the Germans were probably in Mageret. If so, they were about to cut off most of Team Cherry. The only other possibility was that the tanks were Captain Ryerson's. Cherry decided to radio the captain and find out.

A mile east of Mageret, Private First Class Spurgeon Van Hoose, a teenage radioman in Ryerson's company, was dozing in his half-track, half-listening to the steady buzz of chatter that emanated from his radio set. He had long since learned to tune out everything that was not important. Van Hoose's half-track was in the middle of Ryerson's column, moving slowly east. The night was foggy and dark, raw and cold, with the slightest hint of a drizzle. As usual, Private First Class Van Hoose had no idea where they were going.

Now he heard Cherry's voice on the radio, and that was unusual. Ordinarily he heard only the company radio traffic, not the whole battalion. Cherry was talking to Captain Ryerson, asking him if he had left tanks back in Mageret. "Negative," Ryerson replied.

"Well, there's probably three or four German tanks back there," Cherry said. "Send a patrol in there to check it out."

Captain Ryerson said he would, and the conversation ended. The column came to a stop. Van Hoose remained at his radio set, more alert now, but still wondering what would happen next.

Back at Neffe, Cherry now knew that the Germans were in Mageret. His team was cut off on the Longvilly (N12) road. On that very road, in a Sherman tank, Lieutenant Carl Moot, the forward observer from the 420th Armored Field Artillery Battalion, was also listening to the radio chatter. For most of the night, he had been stewing about the inability of headquarters to get him some decent maps. Now when he heard that the Germans were in Mageret, he understood why no one had brought him the maps. "I drew in some coordinate lines past the edge of . . . one map and located the approximate location for Longvilly on them, so that I would have some kind of . . . coordinates to call in if and when I wanted to adjust some artillery fire." Lieutenant Moot finished this task, turned off his little flashlight, and peered outside his tank. There on the road were several American vehicles moving west, sideslipping the stationary Team Cherry tanks and half-tracks.

Moot did not know it, but these vehicles belonged to CCR. Just before midnight, Colonel Gilbreth had decided to retreat from Longvilly to Bastogne. The colonel planned to move his headquarters troops first, while his infantry and tanks covered their withdrawal. The lead half-tracks—which Moot saw—contained the message center, the executive officer, and other headquarters types. The trouble for Gilbreth was that in the darkness, the confusion, and the desperation of the moment, he could not coordinate his withdrawal. Anyone who could hop into a vehicle was trying to get out of Longvilly. Thus, there was no semblance of order to the retreat. Some vehicles made it as far as Mageret, where the Germans picked them off. Others took small roads to Bastogne and then on to Neufchateau. However, with the Germans in control of Mageret, most could not get very far. They were soon enmeshed in a dangerous traffic snarl with Team Cherry on the narrow N12. Vehicles of both units were bottled up on the road. Colonel Gilbreth knew that he could not allow this to continue. One of his artillery officers, who had been in North Africa and had seen his share of retreats, advised him that this could quickly turn into a disaster. The colonel agreed. He ordered a halt until daylight. The order did not solve the traffic problem, but it kept it from getting worse.

At the eastern approaches to Mageret, a lone U.S. half-track, packed with two squads of infantry soldiers, was warily rolling west on the N12 highway. These were the brave men whom Captain Ryerson had tapped to check out the situation in Mageret. They knew that there had been numerous reports of German tanks and troops in and around the town. Several hundred yards east of Mageret, the half-track driver braked to a halt and edged his vehicle off the road. The infantry soldiers dismounted, spread into patrol formation, and moved out. At the edge of town, they saw the three German tanks that Bayerlein had deployed in a roadblock position an hour or two before.

Now they heard what sounded like a tank coming from behind them. Terrified that they were about to be cornered by a Mark V, the men hugged the ground and kept the road under observation. For a few moments, they "sweated it out" as the engine noises grew closer. To their immense relief, the vehicle was a CCR tank destroyer. They halted the vehicle, discussed the situation with the crewmen, and decided that they had fulfilled their mission. Fortified with the firepower of the tank destroyer, they returned to Captain Ryerson, who was waiting in his own half-track a mile to the east, and told him what they had seen in Mageret. The captain knew that where there were three enemy tanks, there were sure to be more. Sure enough, he understood, the enemy was in Mageret in strength. He was cut off, and he would have to fight his way through them.[1]

Back at Bastogne, in the Belgian barracks, General Troy Middleton and his VIII Corps staff were preparing to leave town while they still could. Many of the supporting units—signals, cooks, quartermasters, and the like—had already left the day before for the new command post at Neufchateau, seventeen miles to the southwest. Tonight it was time for everyone else to go. Middleton hated to leave, but General Courtney Hodges, his immediate superior, had issued him a direct order, and he knew Hodges was right. The VIII Corps staff had stayed long enough to brief the incoming Combat Command B (CCB) and airborne reinforcements the previous evening. They all knew that Bastogne was now their fight.

Right now, a group of staff officers was gathered in an office, making plans for an exodus. Among them was Major Malcolm Wilkey of the G2 section. Exactly three nights earlier he had predicted, albeit belatedly, the very offensive that was now underway. Since then, he had spent most of his time in the G2 office, working around the clock. Wilkey, like everyone else, was battling exhaustion. Just an hour before, he had been napping, only to be awakened with the news that they were leaving.

Now Wilkey listened as Lieutenant Colonel Hauge, the assistant G2, outlined the plan: "We'll go out in a column on the road to Neufchateau. Colonel [Andrew] Reeves [the G2] will stay with the General until he leaves. Major Wilkey will lead the column in a command car. I will bring up the rear in a jeep. If we run into any enemy patrols, the first two vehicles will have no choice but to barrel ahead as hard as they can for Neufchateau. The rest of us may have a chance to turn around and get back to Bastogne."

There was nothing more to say. They loaded up and took off. Major Wilkey, with pistol in hand, sat in the passenger seat of the lead car. "There was no snow on the ground at this time, but it was . . . so foggy that we could hardly see six feet ahead. We crept forward at the very slowest pace." They made it to Neufchateau, unloaded their map boards and other equipment, and settled in. Wilkey flopped down on an old straw mattress for some much-needed sleep. His participation in the Bastogne battle was over.

Fittingly, General Middleton was the last VIII Corps headquarters soldier to leave Bastogne. Even as Wilkey and the staff were en route to Neufchateau, Middleton was still at the Belgian barracks—soon to be the headquarters of the 101st Airborne Division—dispensing some last-minute advice to General Anthony McAuliffe: "Now Tony, you're going to be surrounded here before long. But don't worry; help is on the way from Patton. You've got fine men. There's a lot of artillery backing you up. It can put plenty of fire on any point around Bastogne. I'd prefer not to leave this place, but Hodges told me I have to go. We'll be in contact with you all the time." With that, the general climbed into his command car and drove to Neufchateau as part of a two-vehicle convoy. As Middleton left Bastogne, he was probably no more than two miles away from Bayerlein and the Germans.[2]

2

Lieutenant Colonel Julian Ewell was only twenty-nine years old, not all that far removed from his cadet days at West Point, yet he was in command of the 501st Parachute Infantry Regiment. He had once studied at Duke University to be a chemical engineer but had opted for the soldier's life instead. Perhaps, as the son of a soldier, the army was in his blood. He had started as a battalion commander in Normandy before being promoted into the regimental commander's slot. He was emblematic of a rising generation of young military professionals who had proven themselves in combat command. Cool, dry-humored, and ramrod straight in his bearing, he oozed confidence.

Now, two hours after midnight, he, his staff, and his battalion commanders were packed into a small Belgian house that was temporarily serving as the regimental command post. Ewell, in his distinctive twang, was telling them what little he knew about the situation. A few hours earlier, Lieutenant Colonel Ewell had arrived in Bastogne amid the mass confusion of many retreating soldiers. When Ewell had tried to talk to them, most had said simply, "We've been wiped out," and walked away. After enough of this, he figured it was useless to waste any more time on them. He then met with General McAuliffe and pressed him for some kind of specific mission. Working from limited information, McAuliffe told him to take and hold the road junction east of Longvilly.

Presently, in the shadows of this Belgian house, Ewell passed the word of this mission along to his officers and watched their facial expressions tighten. The jaws of some of them, agape with unwelcome surprise, were practically on the ground. They knew very little about what kinds of enemy forces might be in front of them. Some of their men were not even properly armed or equipped yet. Lieutenant Colonel Ewell knew the terrain a little bit because he had walked it several weeks before, but most of them had not seen it in daylight. They had all been in tight spots in Normandy and Holland, but this figured to be even worse.

Youthful though he was, Ewell sensed the tension. He looked around the room, let out a rueful chuckle, and said, "Cripes, what a mess, huh?"

Just that quickly, the tension dissipated. Some of the officers laughed. Others nodded their heads in agreement. Ewell finished his briefing: "The situation is bound to clarify some in the morning [daylight]. In the meantime, the enemy are sure to be just about as confused as we are."

The meeting broke up, and Ewell checked his watch. They were to move out in less than four hours, at 0600. He spotted the regimental chaplain, Captain Francis Sampson, and said, "How about putting a petition in to your boss for clear weather? We're going to need some air support." The two men shared a chuckle and a cup of tea. Prayers or not, there would be no good weather and no air cover, only a clash of wills.[3]

An inky blackness, augmented by fog, hung over little Noville. It was hard to see more than ten or fifteen feet in the distance. Out there in the dark void beyond town, Major William Desobry's OP soldiers were experiencing terror and uncertainty in fits and starts. They sensed that the Germans were out there somewhere and that they would soon want Noville. The question was when, not if. Every few minutes, it seemed, a vehicle would rumble toward one of the OPs. Some brave soul would halt the vehicle—usually a half-track or a jeep—and find himself looking at retreating U.S. soldiers from CCR, the engineer battalions, or the 28th Division. Invariably they said that the Germans were close behind. The Team Desobry sentinels would tell them to go back into town and find a defensive position. Some of the stragglers came in on foot. These haggard-looking men shuffled past the roadblocks and, generally, into the cellars of Noville. By 0430, the parade of stragglers trickled into nothing, ratcheting up the tension even more. Everyone understood that the next OP visitors would probably be speaking German, not English.

Back in Noville, Private First Class Jack Garrity was feeling a bit disoriented. He actually thought he was in Germany. He did not know the name of this town, but it looked about the same as any other that he had seen in Europe. It had a church, a school building, some houses, some barns, and a road junction.

Garrity was a young Irish Catholic from Philadelphia. He had attended the University of Pennsylvania as part of the Army Specialized Training Program (ASTP) before ending up as a rifleman in the 20th Armored Infantry Battalion. A week from tonight, he would turn twenty-two—if he lived that long. Right now, Private First Class Garrity was trying to get into an old stone farmhouse. He pounded on the house's wooden door. A man upstairs poked his head through the window. Garrity saw the man and shouted: "*Raus!* [Get out!]"

The man came downstairs and opened the door. Garrity and a couple of his buddies brushed past him, into the dark house. They lit candles and warmed themselves next to a stove. When they had sufficiently warmed up, they stationed themselves at various points in the house, looking north and east, into the night. Garrity looked in the direction of the Bourcy road. He could swear he heard the sounds of vehicles and voices.

Eight hundred yards away from Garrity, at the Bourcy road OP, Sergeant Leon Gantt and his squad of infantry soldiers were crouched behind a small embankment that overlooked the road. Several half-tracks were on the road, driving straight toward them. Were these more stragglers, or were they Germans? The night was so dark that no one could tell. A sentry yelled, "Halt!" Still the half-tracks kept coming. The man yelled three more times, until finally the lead half-track slid to a halt a few yards away. "The driver was heard to mutter an exclamation in German," a soldier recalled.

The Americans pitched several grenades into the vehicle. One after the other, the grenades exploded, tearing into the German soldiers, riddling them with fragments. Their screams pierced the night air. Behind them, the other enemy personnel carriers disgorged their soldiers. They took cover in ditches on either side of the road and opened fire at the American-held embankment. Gantt's people shot back and threw their remaining grenades at the Germans. The firefight crackled for about twenty minutes.

Gantt glanced behind his position. He was hoping and expecting that the two Sherman tanks that were assigned to cover his roadblock would open fire. They were back there about one hundred yards away. To Gantt's great disappointment, their guns remained silent. Knowing he was badly outnumbered and that the Germans would soon overwhelm him, Gantt gave the word to withdraw. His job, after all, was to spot the enemy and fall back to Noville. At some point during the retreat, a round smashed into his mouth.

He and his men made it back to the tanks. The Germans climbed back into their half-tracks and drove away. They were members of a 2nd Panzer Division reconnaissance element who had fulfilled their mission of finding the Americans. Sergeant Gantt was having a difficult time talking, but he was so enraged at the tankers for not firing that he confronted their commander, a Lieutenant Johnson. The lieutenant was apologetic. He claimed that his crews could not see any targets in the darkness, and rather than risk hitting Gantt's men, they decided to hold their fire. Gantt, dripping blood from his wounded mouth, understood, but he was still not pleased. Perhaps to placate him, Johnson fired two shots in the direction of the retreating Germans, but he did not hit anything. The Germans answered with a few inaccurate rounds. Having done their job, Gantt and Johnson decided to pull back into Noville and report to Major Desobry.

At almost that same moment, the major was standing next to the church, right at the main crossroads, listening to the distant sound of Gantt's firefight to the east. The major was peering helplessly down the Bourcy road, wondering what was happening. When the shooting died down, he correctly surmised that his OP was on the way back.

Now Desobry heard the foreboding sound of vehicles out there in the darkness, moving north. "Sounds at night are much louder and seem much nearer" than they are. "This was obviously a big outfit with lots of tanks, because the German tanks [had] a way of clinking with their suspension system. We didn't know whether they were going to go around us, attack us, or what." As Desobry listened, one thought kept flashing through his mind: "Oh brother! There is really something out there!"

On the Houffalize road, several hundred yards to the north of where the major was standing, Sergeant Major Jones (Major was his first name, not his rank) was crouched along the road, in the forwardmost position on this OP, clutching a Browning automatic rifle (BAR), listening to the engine noises grow louder by the second. He knew that these sounds could only come from tanks. He and his men had heard the noise of Gantt's battle and figured that they would be next on the firing line. But an hour before that, a couple of American tanks had come through, so Jones wondered if perhaps these tanks could be American.

Now Sergeant Jones could just make out the silhouette of a tank some seventy-five yards away. He yelled, "Halt!" and fired a burst from his BAR. Still the tank kept coming until it was about fifty yards away. Jones heard the tank crewmen speaking English, yet one of them opened up on him with a .50-caliber machine gun. The sergeant flattened himself in his foxhole. The .50-caliber bullets snapped inches above his back. Someone yelled, "Cease fire, they're friendly troops!" For a minute or two everything was quiet. Sergeant Jones did not know what was going on. He still did not know whether the tank was American or German. He did not even know who ordered a cease-fire.

One hundred yards behind Jones, an American Sherman tank crew identified the tank on the road as German and opened fire. Instead of hitting the tank, the shell exploded about fifteen yards from Sergeant Jones, jostling him but otherwise not wounding him. Jones saw the road-bound tank fire six times, destroying both American tanks on his roadblock. He heard the screams of the American tank crewmen. In the tanks, one of the Americans was dead and many others were severely wounded. One soldier had his leg blown off; the leg of another one was shattered, perhaps beyond repair.

Now the first enemy tank was joined by others. They poured machine-gun fire on Sergeant Jones's foxhole and those of his men along the road. From somewhere closer to Noville, American half-track crewmen blazed away with their own .50-calibers. A bazooka team tried to sneak up on the Germans but could not get in position for a shot. The two sides contented themselves with firing at each other from a distance. The two burning Sherman tanks were blocking the road, making it difficult for the German tanks to get past them and into Noville. The Americans were buying time for a withdrawal back into Noville, similar to what Sergeant Gantt's team was doing at that same time. Chastened and filled with foreboding, Sergeant Jones gathered up his men and slipped back into town. Behind them, the German tanks remained on the road, shrouded in the foggy darkness, looking for targets. To the north and the east, the better part of the 2nd Panzer Division was massing for an attack on Noville.[4]

At almost the same moment, twelve tanks and two companies of Panzer-grenadiers were moving west on the N12, approaching Neffe. This was the vanguard of Bayerlein's Panzer Lehr. After sitting tight in Mageret for several hours, the general had, at last, ordered this push for Bastogne.

Right now they were taking some fire from the north side of the road, but still they kept moving. The infantrymen advanced alongside the tanks, taking cover when necessary. The tanks gingerly rolled along the paved road. The Germans could see the first houses of Neffe, hugging the south side of the road.

Just east of these buildings, near a junction that bordered the eastern edge of Neffe, Private Bernard Michin was crouching in a ditch, holding a bazooka over his right shoulder. He belonged to a small roadblock detachment from the 35th Engineer Combat Battalion. Private Michin could not see very far in the darkness and fog, but he heard the lead tank. Suddenly it was right there, ten yards in front of him. Michin aimed and fired.

The bazooka shell penetrated the armor of the German tank and produced a devastating explosion. Flames shot in every direction. Michin was so close to the fire that it burned him badly. His eyebrows were singed, and his clothes were smoldering. A machine gun opened up, searching for him against the flicker of the flames. He hurled a couple of grenades in the direction of the machine gun. His grenades seemed to silence this gun, but there were many others spewing bullets in every direction.

Somehow medics got to Private Michin and took him, along with several other wounded GIs, back to Bastogne. The Germans were pouring so much firepower on the road that they were on the verge of overrunning the junction. Corporal Mike Heyman, the Team Cherry reconnaissance section leader, was pinned down in a farmyard adjacent to the junction. The Germans were spraying the whole area with main gun rounds from their tanks, small arms, and much to Heyman's horror, plenty of rounds from captured American .50-caliber machine guns. Heyman was absolutely terrified of being hit by a .50-caliber bullet: "I dreaded the thought of ever facing it. It wouldn't leave a wound, in the simple sense; it would carry away whatever part of the anatomy it encountered." Corporal Heyman worried, in particular, that a .50-caliber slug would smash into his knee, destroying it beyond any hope of repair. He tried to snap off a few rifle shots, but there was simply too much enemy fire. A German tank blasted his jeep, wrecking it and angering Heyman because there were photographs of his girlfriend in the jeep. He could do little besides lie there and stew about it.

Up on the road, German soldiers were on their hands and knees, disarming American mines. Slowly but surely, enemy vehicles edged around them and into Neffe, but their advance was slow because crews were quite wary of encountering more bazooka men like Private Michin. Bayerlein was as cautious as his men. He could have continued driving west, ever closer to Bastogne, but as before, he elected to pause.

To the south of the N12 road, a company of Panzergrenadiers moved west across open ground toward the château where Lieutenant Colonel Cherry had set up his headquarters. This beautiful, solidly built three-story building was about three hundred yards south of Neffe. The château itself was surrounded by mature trees, some of which stretched taller than the building. To the north, there were open fields and a pond.

The château had once housed an VIII Corps signals outfit. The day before, when they left, they had scrawled a message on a wall for the Germans: "We'll be back—The YANKS." A few hours earlier, when Cherry and his headquarters group had taken control of the deserted building, a couple of them read the message and said: "We'll be back—hell, we're here to stay." Now they were forced to make good on their promise. The Germans were a couple hundred yards away, shooting at the little castle, waiting for the order to assault it. Cherry and his people prepared to fight for their lives.

To the west, on the N12, Corporal Heyman and a few other reconnaissance men were escaping from the Germans. Heyman and the others were heading for Bastogne, planning to brief Colonel Roberts on the perilous situation at Neffe. "Along the way, we encountered a column of angels—the forward elements of the 501st Parachute [Infantry] Regiment." At precisely 0600 Lieutenant Colonel Ewell's 1st Battalion had begun its eastward movement. At first they had gone the wrong way and were bound for Marvie, but Ewell had caught the mistake and now had them going in the right direction, on the N12, a mile outside of Neffe. Corporal Heyman and his buddies told the paratroopers everything they knew about the situation and then made their way back to Bastogne.

Meanwhile, General Bayerlein, after an hour's sojourn, ordered his tanks to resume their westward advance at 0800. They sprang to life and rumbled west on the N12, out of Neffe. They were now less than two miles from Bastogne.

The sun was beginning to peek over the eastern horizon. The temperature was rising steadily; it was already in the upper forties. The air was moist with precipitation and mist. Clumps of fog clung to low ground and hills alike.

One thousand yards west of Bayerlein's lead tanks, the first of the airborne troopers were spread out along the road, marching east. Private First Class Robert Wickham, a member of the 1st Battalion, 501st Parachute Infantry intelligence section, was near the front of the column. "It was so foggy you couldn't see 100 feet," he later wrote. He was amazed to see two jeeps from the division reconnaissance platoon whiz past him and roar ahead into the fog. "Hell, if those guys are going out like that," Private First Class Wickham thought, "the Germans can't be as close as we were led to believe."

Up ahead, the jeeps rounded a bend in the road and ran right into General Bayerlein's first tank. The enemy panzer shattered the first jeep with a well-placed shot. The other jeep turned around and sped back around the curve, past Wickham and the other dismounted soldiers "faster than it had passed us just a moment before."

Wickham was carrying a bazooka that he had bummed from a retreating 28th Division soldier who told him that he had destroyed at least one tank with it. Now Private First Class Wickham saw the lead German tank cautiously edging forward, rounding the curve. Wickham was lying prone, aiming at the tank. He realized that he had never even fired a bazooka before, and he mentioned his inexperience to his loader. As it turned out, the loader had much more experience, so he took the bazooka and fired. "There was no question at all who should give it a try," Wickham said. "Wham! The damn shell hit about two feet in front of the tank." The tank was undamaged, but Wickham and the other man were relieved to see it stop. Grateful to be alive, they displaced and dug in at a safer distance.

Having found the enemy, the 1st Battalion, 501st, now spread out, mostly on sloping hills north of the road. Both sides probed around, firing back and forth, looking for a weakness. In the parlance of military professionals, it was a classic meeting engagement.

Both sides were taking casualties. Father Sampson, the chaplain, heard that a wounded man needed a priest. The man was lying just off the road near the lead German tank. Sampson, T/5 Leon Jedziniak (a medic), and another soldier tried to make it to the wounded soldier. Father Sampson saw a German soldier atop the tank, pointing a machine gun in his direction. "He let go at us. The soldier leading us had the upper bone in his arm shattered by a bullet. We all three took a dive to the ditch by the railroad track." The paratrooper with the shattered arm crawled away. Sampson and Jedziniak managed to crawl to the stricken man who had asked for a priest. "We were pinned down by crossfire. I lay down beside the wounded man, heard his confession, and anointed him. He uttered no word of complaint but expressed his thanks."

Jedziniak, who was examining the man's wounds, looked at Sampson and shook his head. The man was apparently not going to make it. Even so, Father Sampson and the medic dragged him out of there, under intense machine-gun fire all the way, and got him to the rear. "I never heard whether he lived or not," Father Sampson said later.

Ninety yards behind the spot where Sampson anointed the wounded soldier, Private First Class John Trowbridge, a machine gunner from Valparaiso, Indiana, was squatting in a ditch when he noticed Lieutenant Colonel Ewell's jeep brake to a halt ten feet away. Trowbridge had no idea what was going on. He knew only that there were plenty of bullets flying back and forth, sweeping up and down the road. Trowbridge had never been this close to Ewell before, and he was impressed. "His calm, cool composure had a reassuring effect on those near him." Ewell was talking into his radio, telling someone on the other end to "hold right where you are and develop the situation."

That person was Major Ray Bottomly, the CO of the 1st Battalion. Bottomly did exactly what Ewell told him to do. His battalion was in the process of fighting the Germans to a stalemate west of Neffe, almost within sight of Bastogne. The 501st had arrived at exactly the right time in exactly the right place.[5]

3

Several miles over the eastern horizon, at Moinet, a small group of American officers was standing in a circle, discussing their grim situation. Their commander, Lieutenant Colonel Robert Booth, was trying to decide what to do next. All night long his task force had remained in place at Moinet. They had heard scores of German vehicles moving behind them. Booth's patrols confirmed that large numbers of enemy troops and vehicles were to the rear, headed northwest. They belonged to Meinrad von Lauchert's 2nd Panzer, which had spent the night pushing for Noville (where they were now in position to launch a major attack on Team Desobry).

Lieutenant Colonel Booth faced two unpalatable options: He could stay here, fight any Germans he encountered, and hope to be relieved by counterattacking U.S. forces. Or he could retreat into Bastogne. If he stayed, he risked being surrounded and annihilated. If he retreated to Bastogne, he would almost certainly run into the 2nd Panzer Division somewhere along the way. Major Eugene Watts, the Citadel graduate who was serving as Booth's operations officer, firmly believed that they should remain in place. "We had Germans everywhere. We didn't know where we were going. We had plenty of ammunition and food and we had tanks and artillery. To go out behind us not knowing what was between us and Bastogne, it was almost inevitable we were going to get ambushed. I tried to point it out, but Colonel Booth was itchy, and he didn't like it there."

Much to Watts's chagrin, Booth decided to retreat to Bastogne. He ordered everyone to mount up and get ready to move out. Booth circulated up and down the column, talking to his soldiers, getting them ready for the ordeal ahead. At the very front of the convoy, he approached Private First Class Carlton Willey, a jeep driver in his intelligence and reconnaissance platoon. Willey was from Bangor, Maine, and he had the New England accent to prove it.

He was sitting in the driver's seat of his jeep when Booth appeared at his side: "Hey, Private Willey, do you think you can lead us out of here?"

Willey nodded. "I'll do my best, sir."

Booth nodded, smiled, and moved on. A few minutes later, he gave the word to move out. Led by Willey's jeep, the column snaked its way east out of Moinet and then north onto a narrow, muddy country road that led to Bourcy. Here and there, they came under fire as enemy machine gunners spotted them. Tank destroyers from the 811th Tank Destroyer Battalion, along with some light tanks, shot back and protected the flanks of the more vulnerable half-tracks and jeeps.

When they reached Bourcy, they clashed with three German armored cars and a platoon or two of infantry soldiers. The tanks quickly blew up two of the armored cars, while everyone else dealt with the infantry. During the firefight, Corporal Elmer Oakes, a twenty-year-old rifleman from Saltville, Virginia, spotted a German soldier. Oakes raised his rifle and fired. "It went off and the guy fell. The bullet went right through his eye and tore the back of his head off when it came out." Oakes was so frightened he was shaking. He felt completely nauseated at what he had just done. When the shooting died down, Oakes went over and looked at the dead German he had shot. The young Virginian turned away, bent over, and threw up.

As Oakes vomited up his breakfast, Lieutenant Colonel Booth now decided to move the column northwest toward Boeur. He walked up and down the line, passing along the information. He saw a moving half-track that belonged to one of his commanders and attempted to hop on the running board but slipped. The wheels of the half-track rolled right over one of his legs, breaking it. His soldiers helped him into a jeep while medics gave him first aid.

The convoy moved out and wound its way into Hardigny, a little hamlet located about a mile and a half northeast of Noville. They made a left turn and began heading west, down a steep hill. They saw about a dozen German half-tracks in the distance. Task Force Booth had plenty of firepower to deal with them. Tank fire and .50-caliber machine guns tore into the German vehicles and their accompanying infantry. "I think we probably got fifteen or twenty of 'em, maybe more," Major Watts recalled.

At that moment, Watts felt elated, but the feeling soon passed. All of a sudden, they were taking heavy fire from every direction. German tanks and self-propelled guns, firing from flanking positions around Hardigny, had them cornered. Enemy shells laced into the light tanks and half-tracks, setting them ablaze, tearing people apart inside. For the enemy, it was like a shooting gallery. Their tank crews simply shot one target after the other, usually scoring hits. Machine-gun and mortar fire added to the horror. Task Force Booth had blundered into one of the 2nd Panzer Division's assembly areas.

The Americans, desperate for survival, fled their vehicles and fought back as best they could. Corporal Oakes grabbed a bazooka and saw a German tank about fifty yards away. These damned enemy tanks scared the hell out of him: "Just the tracks would put the chills in you."

Now he was fighting for his life, and he had no time to dwell on his fear. The road had high banks on either side, so Oakes took cover behind a bank and made sure the bazooka was loaded. Back in the States, he had learned how to use this weapon, but he had never fired one in combat. A soldier sitting next to him said, "Put it on your shoulder. Pull the trigger when you're ready."

Oakes rose up slowly, aimed at the tank, and fired. "The bazooka shell hit the tank, and it looked like it bounced off. I dropped the bazooka and took off."

Many others were doing the same, trying to make it to a patch of woods just beyond Hardigny. Private First Class Willey drove his jeep off the road and into the woods, under intense fire all the way. Not far away from Willey, Corporal Ray Stoker, another New Englander, abandoned the half-track he had been driving only a few minutes earlier. His job was to haul ammunition for self-propelled artillery pieces, and he had no desire to be in his half-track if the Germans sent all that ammo sky high. He and his buddy, a man from Chicago, found a pile of hay and hid underneath it. They lay there watching their abandoned half-track.

Stoker kept thinking about the German flag he had captured as a souvenir a few weeks ago. He sure hated to lose the thing. He turned to his buddy and said, "I left my flag in there."

The other soldier was a large, beefy man inevitably nicknamed Tiny. He looked at Stoker: "I don't give a damn. We're not going back for it."

An instant later, a German shell tore into the half-track, blowing it up, sending flames licking into the air, ending any debate about the flag. Stoker and Tiny got up and ran out of there. They hooked up with a group of Task Force Booth soldiers and looked for an escape route. In the process, they saw Lieutenant Colonel Booth in his jeep. They offered to help him, but he refused, telling them to get out as best they could and not worry about him.

Many of the Americans made it into the woods only to be trapped by the enemy. "The Germans would run machine guns across the top of the pine trees and then yell for us to come out," Lieutenant Frank Richwine recalled. He realized that there was no way to escape. Richwine was actually from the 1st Battalion, 110th Infantry. Two days earlier, he had barely escaped from Urspelt and had, in the meantime, joined up with Task Force Booth. Lieutenant Richwine and another officer from his outfit, Lieutenant Raymond Beaucar, conferred with a major from Task Force Booth about whether to surrender. The major wanted to surrender. Richwine and Beaucar reluctantly assented. Beaucar dropped his rifle, waved a white handkerchief, emerged from the woods, "met a German half-track, and then turned around and signaled for us to come out."

Private First Class Willey destroyed his jeep and then his personal weapon. "I knocked hell out of my tommy gun . . . busted it all up and buried it so they didn't get that." With his hands on his head, he too emerged from the woods. Like many others, he was angry at the officers for surrendering.

Task Force Booth had ceased to exist. "Practically our entire column was wiped out, and casualty rates were terrifically high," Major Watts said. "We lost all the tanks. We lost everything except me and my men." Watts and 225 other men, including Stoker, Tiny, and Oakes, eventually made it to Bastogne, where they participated bravely in the siege. Booth, hobbled by his broken leg, could not get away. He hid in a Belgian barn, but the Germans found him and captured him.[6]

Southeast of Bastogne, Team O'Hara had enjoyed a relatively quiet night and morning. Lieutenant Colonel Jim O'Hara's troops, tanks, and self-propelled guns were deployed astride and abreast of the N34 highway, not far from Marvie. The tranquillity notwithstanding, Lieutenant Colonel O'Hara was worried. The area was very foggy and he knew so little about the proximity of enemy forces that he almost felt blind.

Right now he summoned T/Sergeant Tom Holmes, the leader of his Intelligence and Reconnaissance platoon, to his little farmhouse CP outside of Marvie. Holmes was from Detroit. Before the war, he had worked for Plymouth as a tool and die maker. At age twenty-six, and with a wife waiting back home, he was a little older and more mature than most of the soldiers under his command. O'Hara was only thirty-two, so the two men, agewise, were almost like peers.

Now in the CP, Lieutenant Colonel O'Hara told T/Sergeant Holmes to take his five reconnaissance jeeps, plus one M8 armored car, and drive east on the N34 to Bras and beyond, in an effort to find out what was out there. O'Hara was sorry to admit that he could not tell Holmes much about what to expect. He did not even have a map for him. "Hey, just go out and find 'em," O'Hara said. "See where they're at but, whatever you do, don't become engaged."

As O'Hara spoke, he was smiling, and that was typical. For some reason, he grinned at everything, whether it was funny or serious, earning him the nickname "Smiling Jim." Some of his men found this habit disquieting, others amusing. Sergeant Holmes was too focused on the dangers of this mission to care all that much about the colonel's predilections.

He left the CP and got his jeeps on the road. On and on they drove, into the mist, their tires sliding a bit on the wet road. They reached Bras, found nothing, and kept going, all the way to a spot somewhere west of Wiltz. Holmes halted his jeeps, took out his binoculars, and looked around. He blinked in surprise as the image of German soldiers filled his lenses. There were so many Germans that Holmes thought they had taken over Wiltz (they had not). "They were crossing [a] bridge . . . very rapidly. We figured we'd report that back."

Sergeant Holmes attempted to radio O'Hara but could not get through. "So I had to send one jeep back, and I guess he made it . . . with the information." The other four jeeps quickly turned around and leapfrogged west, with one jeep covering the next while it advanced. After what he had seen, Holmes was surprised that the Germans were not on this road yet. He sensed their presence though. "[They] were probably not more than a mile and a half in from that road on secondary roads."

Holmes's reconnaissance platoon made it back to Bras. He told his men to set up a roadblock position just north of the N34. They were in the process of doing this when they noticed a Volkswagen reconnaissance car come out from the fog on the main road. "Because we had been busy, it surprised all of us," Holmes said. "We're looking at them. They're looking at us. Nobody's doing a thing."

The Volkswagen got as close as seventy-five yards before someone yelled, "Krauts!" The German vehicle braked to a stop. An American machine gunner tried to open fire, but his gun jammed. Other soldiers dismounted and fired at the Volkswagen with their small arms. The bullets riddled the German jeep, shredding the three occupants.

Then the Americans saw two Mark IV tanks and an armored personnel carrier trailing behind the destroyed Volkswagen. Behind them, but shrouded in fog, were many other vehicles. This was the leading element of a Panzer Lehr formation. Holmes, knowing they could not hope to stop this powerful force and mindful of his orders to avoid an engagement, ordered his platoon to retreat. They made it safely back to Marvie and set up about a quarter mile east of O'Hara's command post. As they did so, Lieutenant Ted Hamer, a forward observer from the 420th Armored Field Artillery Battalion, called down devastating fire on the Panzer Lehr column, slowing it for now.

A mile and a half to the west, at nearly the exact same moment, two of O'Hara's officers, Captain Edward Carrigo, his S2, and Captain John Devereaux, his B Company CO, were riding in a jeep, entering Wardin. Devereaux was driving. Carrigo was in the passenger seat. The two men were reconning the area for O'Hara. Captain Carrigo had plenty of reconnaissance experience. Back in the States, he had assembled the Intelligence and Reconnaissance platoon, handpicking men like Sergeant Holmes and training them. For a time he had led the platoon, before being promoted to S2.

As the two officers entered Wardin from the west, the fog was so thick that they could see only fifty yards in the distance. Many frightened-looking residents of Wardin emerged from cellars and doorways and clustered around the jeep. All morning, people had been coming into Wardin, telling them that the Germans were very close. Some had even claimed that they were as close as Benonchamps, a mile away (they were right). Speaking in a gaggle of voices, many of the civilians said, "The Germans are all around here!"

Captain Devereaux was a member of the famous Barrymore family. Before the war, he had been a Broadway actor, so drama was in his blood. He climbed onto the hood of the jeep and addressed the civilians in French: "Do not be afraid. We Americans are here to stay. Go to your cellars and stay there, but do not be afraid." In response he got "a big reception." Many of the people actually cheered.

Satisfied that he had calmed these folks down, he wedged back into the driver's seat and drove off. He and Carrigo drove through Wardin and to the east. The fog lifted. Two hundred yards in the distance, they saw a vehicle of some sort. For a few seconds, the two captains peered at it, trying to determine whether it was an American half-track or a German scout car. Carrigo figured it out first: "My God, those are Krauts!"

Devereaux threw the jeep into reverse. There was a flash from the enemy scout car. Something hit the jeep and bounced off it, right where the wire catcher met the front bumper. Devereaux stepped on the gas pedal and drove back through Wardin to the same spot where moments before he had addressed the townspeople. Many of them were still milling around, talking about the confident young American officer they had just seen. Captain Devereaux slowed his jeep long enough to warn them, in a much less reassuring tone than before, "The Germans are coming! Get back to your cellars!" Devereaux gunned the engine and left town. The civilians scattered for cover, no doubt disillusioned by Devereaux's mixed messages.

Devereaux and Carrigo made it back to O'Hara's CP and told him what had happened in Wardin. Smiling Jim was not happy with Devereaux for attempting to reassure the civilians without knowing more about the situation. "You've got no business doing things like that," he said. Captain Devereaux bit his tongue. He had never much liked O'Hara, mainly because his persistent smile made it hard to know if he was serious or joking. This time, though, he knew O'Hara was serious.

Beneath the veneer of anger, O'Hara was not that displeased. To be sure, Devereaux's dramatic streak was annoying. But thanks to him, Carrigo, and Sergeant Holmes, the colonel now knew that "the Team . . . was being moved on from two directions" by Panzer Lehr. The whole team was in place to oppose them. The next move belonged to the Germans.[7]

West of Longvilly, Colonel Gilbreth and the remnants of CCR were retreating, hoping to make it to Bastogne. Gilbreth had tried the night before, only to see his command plunge into chaos. This morning the retreat was more orderly, at least for a while. "There were all kinds of vehicles, from jeeps and R & R cars to half-tracks and medium tanks," Lieutenant Carl Moot, the forward observer from the 420th Armored Field Artillery, recalled. Moot watched them with detached interest. "This column toward the rear was jammed up, bumper to bumper, moving very slowly. Some of the soldiers going by asked us what we were going to do, and we told them we had come up to help stop the Germans. They said we were crazy, that there were thousands of Germans behind them."

Most of these CCR soldiers had no idea that the Germans were in Mageret and Neffe. The head of the column ran into enemy roadblocks at Mageret and were stopped cold. To make matters worse, the CCR vehicles were getting mixed up with the vehicles of Team Cherry, which were languishing on the same road. The result was a massive traffic jam, and a juicy target. By sheer happenstance, self-propelled guns, tanks, and infantry from three German divisions—2nd Panzer to the north; Panzer Lehr in the north, east, and south; plus 26th Volksgrenadier to the south—appeared on either side of the N12 road. The enemy tank and gun crews could not have asked for a more advantageous situation. They were deployed on high ground, most of them about a half mile off the road, to the north and the south. Plain as day, on the road, hundreds of American vehicles were bunched up.

The Germans opened up with mortars, artillery, rockets, and machine-gun fire. Then came the antitank and tank fire. Up and down the column vehicles exploded, sending flames and steel shards into the air. Ammo trailers got hit, cooking off their deadly cargo. German shells punctured the thin skins of trucks and half-tracks, creating strange, high-velocity metallic sounds of trauma from the destroyed vehicles. The Americans shot back as best they could, but they were outgunned and outflanked.

One of the deadliest spots in this awful kill sack was just west of Longvilly at St. Michael's grotto. The grotto was a Catholic shrine, literally cut into the side of a rocky span that dominated the southern side of the road. The grotto consisted of a cross, an altar, various candles, and numerous statues. A metal gate restricted access to this shrine. There was also a dominant rocky ridge on the other side of the road, and it was honeycombed with religious statues and the stations of the cross. American vehicles were down on the road, caught in this stone canyon.

In one of those vehicles, Captain Edwin Rensmeyer was cringing as each German shell found a target. Just a few days before, the young intelligence officer had been sitting quietly in the Claravallis, writing letters to his family. After being forced out of the hotel on the evening of December 17, he had been on the run with other soldiers from the 110th Infantry. This morning, in hopes of getting into Bastogne, he had hitched a ride with CCR, feeling elated at his apparent luck. Now he felt anything but lucky: "Every time there was a shot it did one of two things—it knocked out another vehicle of some sort, or—if it were a bit high—it caromed off the high rock cliffs on our left. The screetch [sic] those shells made when they hit the white rock cliffs was enough to curdle your blood."

Not far away from Rensmeyer, Chief Warrant Officer Ralph Johnson was sitting in the back of a CCR half-track, hoping with all his might that no enemy shells would hit this vehicle. The night before, he had escaped Allerborn when the Germans overran Colonel Ted Seely's CP, only to end up in this terrifying situation. "No matter how great a faith one might have, nothing was going to stop the carnage." As Johnson watched in horror, the Germans picked off vehicles in front and behind his. "The lead vehicle and the last vehicle . . . were hit and set on fire, thus blocking the road. Then systematically the German gunners knocked out most of the other armored vehicles. Some of the drivers jackknifed their self-propelled mounts over their ammunition caissons in an attempt to get into firing positions. Trucks were burning and ammunition was exploding, dying and wounded were strewn all over the road. It was utter chaos." The stench of burning hair and flesh wafted through the winter air, mixing with the smell of burning cordite and diesel fuel. The noise of the guns, the explosions, and the screaming of men defied belief. Johnson, Rensmeyer, and dozens of others abandoned their vehicles and headed for Bastogne on foot. They made it. Many others did not.

West of the grotto, Sergeant Wayne Wichert was in a truck that for the moment was protected by a patch of fog. Wichert was a squad leader in C Company, 55th Armored Engineer Battalion, a unit that was attached to CCR. He and his men could hear the shooting up and down the N12, but they had no idea what was happening. The night before, an officer had told Sergeant Wichert to be prepared to blow up a bridge half a mile away. Since then he and his men had heard nothing.

Now, in hopes of finding out some information, he dismounted from his truck and took up station under an evergreen tree. For a few minutes, he examined the road and a stand of woods in the distance, but the fog was too thick to see much. Now he heard the crack of a self-propelled gun and, a nanosecond later, an explosion in the tree a few feet above him. Then the world went black.

Sometime later, he regained consciousness when he felt something tickling his neck. Wichert thought that perhaps he had fallen asleep "and that some German Soldier had slipped up on me and was tickling the back of my neck to wake me up . . . and stick me with a bayonette [*sic*]. I kept my eyes closed for quite awhile afraid to open them." Finally he chanced a look. The tickling was not coming from a German soldier. Instead his left arm was broken, twisted around behind him, tickling his neck with clammy, shaking fingers. The tree had been completely blown from its base. The sound of small-arms and artillery fire enveloped the whole area.

A medic came to Wichert and gave him some sulfa pills and morphine. A few minutes later, two of his men found him and dragged him back to the road. "The distal end of my fractured humerus [bone] was sticking out of my jacket. As my men ran between two trees the bone hooked on to a tree." His useless left hand flopped up and slapped him in the face. The pain was immense, but it snapped him out of his stupor.

When they made it to the road, his men told him to get medical attention and then left. Sergeant Wichert stood up and tried to stand on the running board of a half-track as it drove west, trying to escape the pervasive enemy fire. For obvious reasons, he could not hold on, and he fell into the mud. He wandered up and down the column, hoping to find a medic or a stationary vehicle, under fire all the time. At last, he found a radio half-track. "I opened the back door of the half-track and asked if I could get in because I was exhausted. [The radio operator] said sure, so I crawled in and laid down on the floor." Gobs of blood ran from his shredded arm onto the floor of the half-track. The radio operator took one look at the arm and gagged.

It was to the Germans' advantage to fire from a distance. After all, they held good ground and had plenty of targets to shoot at. The closer they got to the column, the more vulnerable they would be to American machine guns, quad-.50's, M7 Priests, and riflemen. Thus, they contented themselves with picking off CCR at a distance. This, in addition to the heroic efforts of small groups of tenacious fighters—such as self-propelled artillery crewmen from the 58th Armored Field Artillery and quad-.50 gunners from the 482nd Antiaircraft Artillery Battalion—kept the Germans at bay and staved off annihilation for CCR.

Lieutenant Moot contributed much in that regard. By sheer luck, the Team Cherry tanks he was riding with were positioned in a defiladed spot just left of the road that shielded them from German fire. The Germans were hitting vehicles fifty yards away, but they apparently did not have a clear field of fire at Moot's tank or the others in this platoon from the 2nd Tank Battalion. Now Moot noticed German soldiers coming over a hilltop just outside of Longvilly. As the American tanks began shooting at them, Lieutenant Moot called back for artillery fire.

Four and a half miles to the west, atop a hill located on the outskirts of Bastogne, several M7 self-propelled guns responded to Moot's order. They pumped shell after shell on the Germans at Longvilly. "The shooting was constant," one officer remembered, "and the ammo trains were busy resupplying us to keep up with the demand."

In spite of the fact that Lieutenant Moot did not have good maps of Longvilly, his shelling was accurate. He watched as the projectiles exploded, sending up little clouds of smoke and dust. Then he detected movement to the right. "A wave of German soldiers came over a hill . . . to the east and slightly south. The hill top was not too close to us, possibly two hundred yards or more. About ten or twelve Germans came running as fast as they could toward us. They were carrying only Panzerfausts . . . and were apparently trying to get close enough to knock our tanks out with them. This was a disastrous mistake for them." Those who were fortunate enough to make it through Moot's barrage fell prey to machine-gun fire from the American tanks. They fell heavily to the wet ground and lay motionless or writhed in pain. Not one of them made it within one hundred yards of the tank platoon.

To the west of Moot, Colonel Gilbreth and his headquarters managed to find their way into Bastogne on back roads. They took some of the 58th Armored Field Artillery with them, along with various stragglers from CCR. Dozens, if not hundreds, of his men straggled into Bastogne on foot. Their vehicles were still back on the N12, burning or sitting useless in an endless traffic jam. Other men were still in their vehicles, taking shelter, fighting back, or just cowering. The colonel himself was thoroughly exhausted, as were his battered survivors. Gilbreth's command had basically ceased to exist.

As CCR died a slow, terrifying death, Captain William Ryerson of Team Cherry was attempting to recapture Mageret. When his lead tank was within three hundred yards of the town, it rounded a curve and took a direct hit, right through its frontal armor, from a German antitank gun. The platoon leader, a Lieutenant Bolton, was killed instantly. Several other crewmen were badly wounded. The burning tank came to a dead stop, blocking the road in a narrow choke point, with embankments on either side.

Captain Ryerson ordered his infantrymen to dismount, move forward, and see if the antitank gun was alone or if the German defenses were stronger. "They were protected by a rise in the ground thru which the highway . . . was made," an officer later wrote, "but beyond this point they could not go because of heavy automatic and mortar fire." Two M7 "Priests" came up and shot at likely targets, slackening the enemy fire.

From the east, two CCR antiaircraft half-tracks drove right past Ryerson's vehicles, heedless of any warnings, and rounded the bend into Mageret. The men inside the half-tracks took one look at the burning tank and abandoned their vehicles, adding to the jam. This drew German artillery and mortar fire. The angry shells exploded up and down the road. With the road into Mageret completely blocked and evidence of strong enemy defenses in front of him, Ryerson knew that he was stymied for now. He heard that friendly infantry forces were coming from Bastogne. He did not know which units or in what strength; he only knew that they were supposed to be on the way. Perhaps when they arrived, he could coordinate some kind of attack into Mageret with them. Most of his men dismounted, dodged shells, and probed around, looking for a different way into town.

In one communications half-track, Corporal Spurgeon Van Hoose was still sitting at his radio, but now he was alone. His squad mates were out there somewhere, fighting around Mageret. Van Hoose's job was to stay with the radio, all alone, while shells exploded outside. Part of him would rather have been out there with his buddies, but he did the best he could to concentrate on his job.

Now the back door of the half-track opened, and his sergeant sat down heavily on one of the benches. The NCO had a strange look on his face, and Van Hoose asked him what was wrong. "He was in a state of shock. He had been standing by a guy, one of the stragglers. The guy got hit directly by an artillery shell and it blew him all over." The sergeant sat there, trying to pull himself together, staring vacantly—at nothing and everything.[8]

4

At Noville, Major Desobry had spent the last couple of hours moving around his unit's perimeter, checking his defenses, and talking with his men. This town was a real challenge to defend because it was situated on low ground with distinct ridges to the north and east, plus wooded draws to the west, southwest, and east. There was something good about the terrain, though. Noville was surrounded on every side by large swaths of open ground, creating beautiful fields of fire for Desobry's machine gunners and tankers. This meant that anyone wishing to take Noville had to approach from the open ground or on the roads.

Since Team Desobry's initial contact with the enemy a couple of hours earlier, the roadblock OPs had pulled back into town. The Germans had been probing around for an hour or two (skirmishing here and there with the Americans), but the fog was still so thick that it was difficult for the Germans to see where they were going. Desobry's soldiers kept watch, waited for the inevitable attack, and listened to the ominous rumble of tanks and the Teutonic shouts of infantry soldiers outside of Noville, deep inside the mantle of fog. Some houses, barns, and vehicles were on fire, reducing visibility that much more. The flames flickered in weird shadows off the fog, as if it were dusk or early evening.

Right now, at 1010, Major Desobry was standing on the main N15 road at the north end of town, right next to the town cemetery. He was with the crew of a 57-millimeter antitank gun and some infantry soldiers, listening to the growing noise of enemy vehicles. At that moment the fog rose like a curtain in front of a stage. Straight up the road, about fifteen yards away, Desobry and the others "could see the shapes of these huge German tanks . . . coming down the road. Their Panzergrenadiers were all around them." On the second floor of the schoolhouse CP, Captain Bud Billet, the B Company commander, glanced out a window and saw, in the distance, more than thirty tanks. They were spread into a skirmish line along a ridge that saddled the Vaux road.

At the Bourcy (northern) crossroads, mere yards away from Billet and Desobry, there was an M18 Hellcat tank destroyer on post. As the fog lifted, the crew spotted two Mark IVs to the left. Inside the M18, Corporal Colby Ricker, the gunner, traversed the turret in that direction. The Mark IVs were incredibly close, certainly within shouting distance. Ricker lined up a broadside shot: "The tanks were very nearly the same color as our own, which caused me some concern in making sure they were not our own, being at such close range." When Ricker was certain that these were enemy tanks, he opened fire. "Two shots were fired. When I saw the crew bail out of the first tank, I immediately traversed to the second one and fired."

Not knowing whether Ricker had hit the second one, Ricker's tank commander ordered the driver to displace. They turned around and sped through the little town to a southerly position. "I doubt that this entire episode consumed more than one minute in time." This was standard operating procedure for tank destroyer crews. Their Hellcats were offensive, not defensive, weapons. They were thinly armored, very fast, very maneuverable, and very deadly to enemy tanks. It made good sense to snap off a few shots, displace, and then do it again.

As Ricker's crew destroyed at least one Mark IV, the rest of the Americans in northern Noville opened up on the now visible enemy attackers with everything in their arsenal. "Everybody on the northern perimeter of the town, the tanks . . . the assault guns, the 57 MM guns, bazookas, pistols, rifles, you name it, everybody opened fire," Desobry recalled.

The tanks on the Vaux ridge stayed in place and spat shell after shell at the American defenders. Other tanks, like the ones Corporal Ricker shot at, edged all the way to the northern buildings of Noville. German artillery crashed all over town, tearing into roofs or doorways, exploding on the streets, battering the church steeple that served as an obvious observation post.

Immediately west of the CP, right where the Vaux and Houffalize roads came together, Private First Class Jerry Goolkasian, a loader and radioman on a Sherman tank crew, was feeding an armor-piercing shell into the breech of his tank's main gun. He was a native of Dorchester, Massachusetts, who had once been in the ASTP program. Now, in Noville, Goolkasian was crouched on the right side of the turret. The gunner, Private First Class Delmer Hildoer, was on the left side. This tank belonged to Captain William Schultz, the commander of B Company, 3rd Tank Battalion. But the captain was not in the tank right now, and that was typical. He was usually on the ground, reconnoitering, giving orders, and taking orders. That made Hildoer the nominal commander, but the other three crewmen would overrule him if they did not like his orders. For instance, the night before when they arrived in Noville, Hildoer had wanted to position their tank beside a haystack, but Goolkasian and the others had thought that this spot, next to a little brick wall that surrounded the CP, was better, so there they were.

As Goolkasian and Hildoer peered into the distance, they saw three enemy tanks on the Vaux ridge, well within range of the main gun. The two men did not really like each other. Goolkasian felt that Hildoer had a hero complex, and Hildoer wished that Goolkasian would simply do as he ordered. Nevertheless, they worked well together. Moving quickly and smoothly, Goolkasian loaded while Hildoer fired four rounds at one of the enemy tanks. On the fourth shot, Goolkasian saw their armor-piercing shell ram into the turret of the tank. "With that it stopped [moving]. Then we just traversed only a little bit. In the meantime, the other two tanks turned sideways and gave us their whole broad sides which, of course, you never do with a tank. With one shot we got the second one." They fired three times before hitting the other one. "We saw the blast and then stuff go all over the tank." Unseen American machine gunners slaughtered the fleeing enemy tank crewmen. Both of the tanks that had turned sideways were stuck in the mud, a real problem for the Germans at Noville, since their wide treads were not designed to negotiate wet ground.

Now Goolkasian and Hildoer spotted an enemy half-track on the Houffalize road. Goolkasian loaded a high-explosive round into the breech while Hildoer lined up the shot and fired. Goolkasian saw the shell smash right into the half-track. "We opened up on them something fierce. They got blasted to smithereens." Through the smoke that boiled up from the enemy personnel carrier, he could see enemy soldiers bailing out or falling out, badly wounded.

Not far from Goolkasian's tank, two German tanks charged down the N15 at well over twenty miles per hour, somehow slipped past the destroyed tanks just north of the Bourcy crossroads, and were driving straight at the American positions around the CP. From the veritable spitting distance of thirty yards, a self-propelled gun opened up on the first German tank and destroyed it with two shots. A Sherman took care of the other one. The burning, wasting hulks served as an ideal barrier. "The road was relatively narrow and they made a heck of a good roadblock," Major Desobry explained.

The Germans were mainly attacking with armor, but some of their infantrymen made it into Noville under the cover of the fog or their tanks. A sniper found his way onto the second floor of a house and shot at anyone walking around the streets near the church. Not far from there, Private First Class Jack Garrity, the Irish American rifleman from Philadelphia, was holed up in a chicken coop, just outside the house where he had spent much of the night. In spite of the shooting all over town, Garrity could hear a creek babbling somewhere in the woods just east of Noville. He also heard the shuffling sounds of enemy soldiers on the move. Garrity's buddy was several yards over on the right flank. He had told the man to yell over every few minutes so that Garrity would know he was still there. Garrity heard shots on the right and then nothing from his buddy. He called to the man and still got nothing in response; he crawled over to him. "He was unconscious. He was very bloody." He had been hit by rifle fire. "I pulled him in the stable." This made no difference. Garrity's buddy died.

Elsewhere, a large group of enemy soldiers got caught out in the open ground to the northeast of town. Lieutenant Pete Greene, a forward observer from the 420th Armored Field Artillery, saw them and called down withering fire. Machine-gun, rifle, and tank fire only added to the carnage. Some were lucky enough to make it over the ridge and out of sight. Others never made it that far. Their dead, traumatized bodies were scattered randomly, like leaves.

The German attack was fading out, and as if in frustration, the enemy let loose with an angry barrage of artillery, tank, and machine-gun fire. With the possible exception of cellars—where civilians and GI stragglers hid in sheer terror—there was no safe place to be in Noville. Shells were exploding all over the place. Machine-gun bullets zipped up and down the streets, through windows and doors.

Across the street from Desobry's CP, First Lieutenant Jack Prior, the battalion surgeon, was dealing with a growing number of patients in a makeshift aid station. Just a few days earlier, this place had been a tavern. In fact, Dr. Prior had chosen this building because the barroom afforded plenty of open space for stretchers. He and his platoon-sized unit of some thirty-five medics cleared out the tables and chairs and arranged their growing number of patients in rows. "I had probably half a dozen seriously wounded in this little bar. They were on the floor. We didn't have enough litters. I had a belly wound. I had a chest wound. I can remember a head wound."

There was little that Prior, a young doctor fresh out of medical school at the University of Vermont, could do besides bandage them, stabilize them, and prepare them to be evacuated to a real hospital. He himself was new to this unit. The regular battalion surgeon had come down with a case of pneumonia, and Prior had replaced him a couple of days before the German offensive. Almost immediately, Prior had run into a problem. The medical detachment had one remaining officer, Dr. Lee Naftulin, and he believed he should take command. But Naftulin was a dentist, not a physician. "He'd been there longer than I had and he was a captain," Prior explained. "He resented my coming in as a first lieutenant, taking over the detachment."

Prior knew that according to regulations, dentists had no command functions. Physicians were supposed to be in charge, regardless of rank, but he had trouble convincing Naftulin of this. Finally, Prior decided to take the issue to Major Desobry. He had done so immediately before the unit left for Bastogne a couple of days earlier. Much to Prior's delight, Desobry knew the medical regulations. He had turned to Naftulin and said, "The lieutenant's right. You can't command." That settled the issue. Since then, Prior and Naftulin had worked well together, and they were actually becoming friends.

Now the two of them were doing the best they could for the wounded men who were sprawled all over the barroom floor. Outside there was a terrible racket of constant explosions combined with the zipping, buzzing-bee sound of bullets. Prior recognized the distinctive ripping sound of German machine guns. Bullets shattered the tavern's front window, spraying glass shards everywhere. Anyone who was standing risked getting hit. Prior stayed as low as possible. "Naftulin . . . and I were crawling around on the floor to take care of the wounded 'cause you couldn't stand up. There was small arms fire coming into the room. Someone had selected our backyard as the 'ammo' dump and this did not boost our equanimity." Downstairs in the basement, the elderly couple who owned this tavern were huddled together, crying and saying the rosary. Upstairs in the barroom, the small arms fire was so steady that Dr. Prior did not dare raise his head more than a couple of feet at a time. "What a hell of a way to practice medicine," he thought.

Just across the street, in the schoolhouse, Major Desobry was taking stock of his situation. The German attack was slowing down, although Noville was still under persistent fire from enemy artillery and machine guns. Minute by minute, his casualty numbers were growing. He had sent out reconnaissance patrols that never returned. Moreover, in the daylight and with the lifting of the fog, Desobry now understood the true nature of the ground that surrounded Noville. He knew that the Germans could lie back and pound him from the ridges, even as they cut the roads that led into town from the north and south. At this point, Desobry's guys had destroyed at least ten tanks and had damaged several others. The young major expected that as long as his team had enough ammo and food, it could hold out in Noville. But he knew that with control of the high ground and the roads outside of Noville, the Germans could strangle Team Desobry. "We were out on a limb," he later said.

Now Desobry wondered if it might be best to withdraw south to more defensible ground around Foy. At this stage, such a withdrawal was still possible via the southerly route out of Noville. In a few hours, that could change, though. As the idea of withdrawal occurred to him, he could not help but flash back to his conversation with Colonel Roberts the previous day. "You know, Des," the wise old colonel had prophetically said, "you will probably get nervous tomorrow morning and want to withdraw, so you had better wait for any withdrawal order from me." Then again, Major Desobry was not sure if Colonel Roberts had a full appreciation of the situation here at Noville. This morning, CCB had actually sent him an order to reconnoiter as far north as Houffalize, an absolute impossibility under the circumstances.

Desobry decided to get in touch with Colonel Roberts, apprise him of the situation, and request permission to withdraw. At CCB headquarters, in the Hotel LeBrun at Bastogne, Roberts received Desobry's message, but he was not sure what to do. Noville was vitally important, but Desobry was looking at the real possibility of being surrounded and destroyed. Roberts trusted the major and knew he would not request to withdraw unless the situation was truly serious. But in order to fulfill its mission, Team Desobry should probably remain in Noville at least until the 101st Airborne Division got in position around Bastogne, and the paratroopers were still in the middle of that process.

The colonel decided to discuss this Noville situation with General McAuliffe. Roberts left the Hotel LeBrun and began walking to the Belgian barracks. On the way, he ran into General Gerald Higgins and told him about his dilemma. As the two officers were talking, the 1st Battalion, 506th Parachute Infantry Regiment, was marching past them. Colonel Robert Sink, CO of the 506th, and Lieutenant Colonel James LaPrade, commander of the 1st Battalion, were at the head of the column. General Higgins waved them over and ordered Sink to send LaPrade's 1st Battalion into Noville.

Satisfied with these arrangements, Colonel Roberts shook hands with his airborne colleagues and returned to the Hotel LeBrun. Major Desobry was once again requesting permission to withdraw. Roberts got on the telephone with the major and asked the size of the enemy force he was fighting. "I told him a reinforced tank battalion because that [was] all I could imagine," Desobry recalled. In truth, he was facing most of the 2nd Panzer Division, but he did not know that at the time.

Roberts was reluctant to give any sort of "stay or else" type of order. Instead he said: "You can use your own judgment about withdrawing, but I'm sending a battalion of paratroopers to reinforce you."

At Noville, on the other end of the line, Desobry's intentions changed completely. Instead of withdrawing, he figured he could stay in Noville awhile longer. But if he did that, he absolutely had to control the ridges outside of town. "Well, if this battalion will come up," he told Roberts, "and if the battalion commander would agree, we would counterattack and drive the Germans off the ridgeline and set up our defense up there."

Roberts thought this sounded good. He told Desobry that Lieutenant Colonel LaPrade and the 1st Battalion were moving on foot, so it would still be several hours before they arrived. They said good-bye and hung up. Major Desobry was still worried about his situation, but he felt better than before. At least help was on the way. The colonel would make sure of it. "Perhaps the biggest factor in deciding to stick it out," Desobry later said, "was complete faith in Colonel Roberts. He had been a very close friend and advisor during training days and I respected him as being a much better judge than myself."

After his conversation with Roberts, Major Desobry found himself dealing with a crisis of sorts. In passing along the major's original request to withdraw, his operator spoke in a loud voice that everyone in the little schoolhouse CP could easily hear. The withdrawal request spread like wildfire around Team Desobry. Hoping that the request was equivalent to an order, soldiers began drifting back from their foxholes into Noville. Officers and NCOs disavowed the retreat and assured the soldiers that no one was going anywhere. The leaders went around, bullying, cajoling, threatening, and in some cases, begging the men to go back to their positions.

In the meantime, Major Desobry sent his intelligence officer, Captain Kalgren, into Bastogne to fetch Lieutenant Colonel LaPrade. Kalgren drove there in a jeep, quickly found LaPrade, and zipped back to Noville within half an hour. They entered the CP at 1125. Neither Desobry nor

LaPrade was certain at this point who was supposed to be in overall command, but they took to each other immediately. "He was a wonderful guy," Desobry said. "A big, tall guy, very confident. He brought with him a couple of officers and I went over the situation with him and showed him the German positions." LaPrade agreed with Desobry on the necessity of taking the ridgeline. "So we dreamed up a scheme to put his paratroopers with some tanks and armored infantry and one outfit would go out to the northeast and get that ridgeline, and two other companies would go out to the north and northwest and secure [that] ridgeline." LaPrade's men were just now leaving Bastogne, walking north up the N15, so they would not be there for a while. Also, many of them did not have adequate weapons and ammunition. Desobry dispatched Lieutenant George Rice, his supply officer, to Foy with the mission of scrounging up some weapons and ammunition for the paratroopers. Major Desobry and Lieutenant Colonel LaPrade agreed to launch their attack at 1400. With the plans finalized, Desobry took a moment to exhale and relax a little bit. Help was on the way. For now, all his men could do was wait—and try to survive.[9]

5

West of Bras, on a patch of high ground that overlooked the Wiltz–Bastogne N34 highway, five American tanks were in place. In one light tank, Lieutenant Ted Hamer, a forward observer from the 420th Armored Field Artillery Battalion, was looking through binoculars, hoping to catch a glimpse of the Panzer Lehr vehicles he knew were in and around Bras. All at once, two armor-piercing shells tore into the light tank, setting it on fire and wounding Hamer. He and three other badly wounded men escaped; the other man did not make it out. Behind Hamer's tank, a Sherman took a direct hit in the left side of its turret, turning the gunner into little more than bloody pulp. Crazed with fear, the driver threw the tank into reverse. The wounded tank bucked and jostled its way down the hill before bogging down hopelessly in the mud. The crew abandoned the tank, even as enemy artillery shells rained down around them.

Just ahead on the road, a German Kubelwagen reconnaissance vehicle from Panzer Lehr stopped at the cusp of a small minefield that Team O'Hara engineers had sown. Several enemy soldiers got out of the vehicle and set about the task of disarming the mines. Two hundred yards to the west, several Team O'Hara half-tracks and tanks opened up on them. Somehow they missed, and the Germans got into the Kubelwagen and escaped. The point elements of the 901st Panzergrenadier Regiment

(Panzer Lehr) had been pushing west, right at Team O'Hara, but this little incident prompted them to turn north toward Wardin.

A few minutes later, the Team O'Hara soldiers noticed groups of infantrymen approaching from the west. These men were clad in unfamiliar green uniforms, and their trousers were bloused in their boots. Some of the armor soldiers almost opened fire, but they soon realized that these infantrymen were friendly paratroopers. They were from I Company, 501st Parachute Infantry Regiment, and they were headed to Wardin. One of Lieutenant Colonel O'Hara's advance patrols was just west of that town. Like their comrades to the south, these men at Wardin did not know the airborne was on the way and they came close to shooting them, but fortunately they did not. The patrol returned to O'Hara's perimeter, but three of his tanks took up station west of Wardin, covering the town's exits. Apparently no one told the paratroopers what Captains Devereaux and Carrigo had experienced near Wardin only a couple of hours earlier. In fact, there was probably no communication at all between the troopers and O'Hara's men.

Company I and the rest of the 3rd Battalion, 501st Parachute Infantry Regiment, had spent the morning snarled in Bastogne traffic. Thus they were the last of Colonel Ewell's troops to enter the fight. The rest of the battalion was heading for Mont. Company I's purpose was to secure the southern flank and hold Wardin. The company entered the town without incident. The village was the usual collection of stone houses and barns. A stream ran straight through Wardin, and there was a small bridge on the west end of town.

Captain Claude Wallace, the CO, set up his CP in a house in western Wardin. Lieutenant Howard Gielow's First Platoon went east on the main road and headed for the eastern edge of town, almost half a mile away. The 2nd Platoon, under Lieutenant Bob Harrison, went to the south, where a church dominated the southern approaches to Wardin. "Both of them were to go out a few hundred yards and dig in," Staff Sergeant Robert Houston recalled. He was a veteran platoon sergeant who had earned a Distinguished Service Cross in Normandy. "Our platoon, the 3rd, set up at the crossroads, with a deserted house at the northwest corner for our CP. The company CP was directly across the road that we had come in on." Sergeant Houston spread his squads throughout positions that covered the crossroads. "Everyone was told to dig in and be prepared for whatever the 1st and 2nd platoons found."

Many of the town's residents had fled after Captain Devereaux's escapade that morning, but a few were still there, hiding in their cellars.

Captain Wallace sent Private First Class Marvin Wolfe and two other men on a scouting mission near the church. They reached the town square, not far from the church, took cover, and paused to look around. Just ahead, outside the church, there were swarms of German soldiers and a couple of tanks too. Wolfe turned his little reconnaissance force around and started back to warn the captain, but it was too late.

An entire battalion of infantry from the 901st Panzergrenadier Regiment, supported by seven tanks, was entering Wardin from every side. Seventy-five yards away from the company command post, Lieutenant Leonard Witkin was on the way to one of his machine-gun nests. He had just retrieved some shovels and was about to distribute them throughout his platoon. As he was walking, he saw several enemy tanks emerge from a tree line and level their main guns at the CP. A second later, one of the tanks snapped off a shot. It smashed into the stone facade of the command post and buzzed through the house. Private First Class Frank Guzy, a radioman, was standing inside with the company command group when the shell went "right through the living room, wounding several and penetrating a second wall, a barn . . . killing the first sergeant [Carl Sargis] and a cow."

It was the first shot in a violent, brutal battle. Company I was cornered, fighting a close-quarters battle with a force many times its size. German tanks continued blasting away. Paratroopers ran in and out of the CP "with reports and requests for more weapons and ammunition," Guzy remembered. Radios were crackling with frantic calls from the platoons, asking for information and fire support.

Not far from the embattled CP, Staff Sergeant Erminio Calderan, the ranking NCO in the Second Platoon, was in the street with a squad-sized group, totally exposed to the enemy tank fire. Everyone scrambled for cover on the right side of the street, but Calderan headed for a house. A tank shell zipped over his head and exploded somewhere not far away. He looked around and saw a tank muzzle pointing right at him: "That SOB had me zeroed in! I did a fast turn and got behind a small outhouse. A shell struck the front." The concussion was immense, like being jostled around the inside of a bass drum. "I was badly shaken. I went to another house with a barn attached and the doors were open." Lieutenant Ray Mulligan and a radioman were in there. He asked them if artillery support was on the way, but they were noncommittal. As Calderan conversed with them, he saw a man outside running zigzag away from the same enemy tank. The Germans fired three shots at him, missing each time.

There was no artillery support of any kind. The troopers fought back with the only antitank weapons they had—bazookas. Sergeant Houston was running from a pursuing German tank. He briefly took shelter in a house where several frightened civilians were hiding, and continued into a garden where he had previously placed one of his squads. Still the tank was on the prowl. "We fired a bazooka shell, which hit the front of the tank where its armor was heavy, so it wasn't knocked out." The bazooka team maneuvered to the side of the tank, only five yards away, and poked their tube through some bushes. "The explosion put a hole in the lower part of the tank and we picked off the crew as they scrambled out. Another tank came up and pushed the one we had knocked out off the road."

Across the street, a bazooka man from the 2nd Platoon was crawling toward another tank. "He got almost beside the tank before he fired his bazooka," Staff Sergeant Calderan recalled. "The explosion was so great he came tumbling down [a] hill. He got up and yelled, 'I got it! I got it!'"

Not far away, Private Richard Hahlbohm was crouched behind a log pile, listening to the ominous clanking sound of another German tank on an adjacent street. Before long, the tank came into view. In its turret, a machine gunner was standing exposed at his gun, looking around for targets. Private Hahlbohm saw a bazooka man a few yards away, squatting by the corner of a house. He yelled "Tank!" and pointed at the street. A few seconds later, he glanced in the direction of the bazooka man. He was gone, but the weapon was still there.

Hahlbohm took aim with his rifle and shot the enemy machine gunner. In response, the turret swung in his direction. "I got up on my haunches to make a dash behind the house after he let the first [shot] fly." At nearly the same second, the tank's main gunner fired a shot while a new machine gunner let loose a deadly burst. "I started my 10- to 12-foot leap. The bullets imbedded in the house. The . . . concussion caught me halfways there. It made me like a rag doll flying through the air. My overcoat was hit in a few places by shrapnel, but luckily, I wasn't hit." Someone pulled him inside the house. "My ears were ringing like two dozen phones. We were trapped in the house. As I looked out the window, I saw wall-to-wall Krauts." German infantrymen were everywhere, running around, screaming, and shooting. They were overrunning Wardin house by house.

To Hahlbohm, it seemed like there was an entire regiment out there. He and the seven other men who were in the house with him debated what to do next. As they did so, the Germans overran their house and took them prisoner. They took them outside, lined them up against a hedgerow, and covered them with a .50-caliber machine gun that was mounted on a captured U.S. half-track.

Elsewhere, enemy soldiers were on the verge of taking Captain Wallace's CP. The captain got on the company radio net and said: "Every man for himself!" He and the small command group tried to escape through an adjoining barn. They hoped to make it across the stream and then south, out of town. They took off at a dead run. Private First Class Guzy still had a forty-two-pound radio strapped to his back, so he lagged behind. Up ahead, he could hear small-arms fire. He saw the dead body of Private Gullo, a man who had been in the CP only moments before.

Guzy had been trying unsuccessfully to call battalion on his radio for nearly an hour. Indeed, the failure of communications equipment was a major reason why I Company was in such serious trouble. They had no way to call for artillery support or any other help from higher headquarters. With his life at stake, Private First Class Guzy ditched the useless radio. "I dropped it on the ground and double-timed it out of there."

Just ahead, Sergeant Richard "Buck" Ketsdever was running with Captain Wallace and his executive officer, Lieutenant William Schumaker. Schumaker was first, then Ketsdever, then Wallace. "As the lieutenant turned into [a] gate, I thought he tripped because he fell to the ground," Ketsdever recalled. "I was so close to him by then, I fell over him and Captain Wallace fell on top of me. They had both been hit, either by rifle or machine-gun fire, and both were dead. I crawled into the creek and started moving up the hill toward Bastogne."

Back in Wardin, close to where the CP had been, Private First Class Wolfe was fleeing in confusion. He watched one of his buddies, Private Wilbrod Gauthier, stand right in the middle of the street and fire a bazooka round. The rocket hit one tank—to Wolfe it looked destroyed—but another tank opened up with a machine gun. The bullets stitched Gauthier, and he went down in a heap, probably dead before he hit the ground. Wolfe made it to the creek and hid. He decided to wait until darkness and then escape to Bastogne.

Staff Sergeant Calderan retreated to the doorway of a house across the street from what had been the company headquarters building. He found out the hard way that the Germans now controlled the CP. "I saw a German stick his head out of the company CP window. I saw that Kraut put his machine pistol to his shoulder and fire. I saw five bullet holes in the door starting from where my belly button would be and going up to my head. I was half in and half out of the door. I know he was aiming at me. I stood there—frozen." Fortunately for Calderan, a nearby group of Americans saw the German and shot him. From there, Calderan made it out of the town and saw a group of civilians. He borrowed an overcoat from one of them and tried to blend in with them as they walked west. "The Krauts spotted our boots and opened up. I don't know if any of the civilians were hit, but there was a road with high banks." Sergeant Calderan hid there and waited for darkness.

Just outside of Wardin, Private First Class William McMahon and a machine-gun crew were on a little hill that overlooked the town. When the shooting started, someone had ordered them to come up there and keep the Germans from flanking I Company. They heard the crackle of small-arms fire and high-velocity shells down in Wardin. They could hear the distinctive squeaking sound of tank bogey wheels. "That's our tanks!" one man wishfully asserted. McMahon knew better: "Our tanks wouldn't be coming down the street blowing the hell out of buildings where our guys are hiding."

They argued about whether to go down and help or not. Lieutenant Witkin, who had been fetching shovels for them, appeared and settled the debate. "Anybody that wants to live—follow me," he said. Under cover of the smoke that was pouring from burning buildings, they made it across the main road and out of Wardin. Along the way, McMahon tore his trousers on some barbed wire and then had to cross the stream. "That was the coldest goddamn water I . . . ever felt in my life." McMahon's group made it to a ridge and dug in. There were only ten of them, and the young machine gunner wondered if that was all that was left of I Company.

There were others. Escaping and evading any way they could, 83 out of an original 140 soldiers from I Company made it out of Wardin and back to Bastogne. Sergeants Houston and Calderan made it out, as did Lieutenant Witkin. Privates Wolfe, McMahon, and Guzy also escaped. The rest of I Company—57 men in all—were killed or captured. The company destroyed at least three enemy tanks and killed untold numbers of German soldiers. Throughout the short, bitter battle for Wardin, the Team O'Hara tanks did not fire a shot or do anything to help the paratroopers. No one was ever sure why.[10]

Colonel Ewell's 501st Parachute Infantry Regiment was fully deployed now. His 2nd Battalion took Bizory against little resistance and pushed for Mageret in hopes of joining forces with Captain Ryerson. But the 2nd Battalion ran into dug-in positions manned by the 26th Volksgrenadier Division and Panzer Lehr. Major Sammie Homan, the battalion CO, told Ewell he could not think about taking Mageret. He needed everyone he had just to defend his front line. The same was true for the 3rd Battalion at Mont. Lieutenant Colonel George Griswold, the CO, hoped to push for Neffe, but he soon found out that German opposition was too strong for that.

One platoon from G Company of the 501st did manage to make it to Lieutenant Colonel Henry Cherry's besieged château CP, just south of Neffe. All morning long, Cherry and his headquarters soldiers had been fighting a substantial enemy force of four tanks, an armored car, and the better part of two companies. "The enemy destroyed one of the headquarters tanks and encircled the Château on three sides," Cherry said, "covering the fourth [west] side by 20mm and mg fire. Some enemy infantrymen worked their way to within five yards of the building itself before they were killed. None of the enemy succeeded in entering the

Château." Cherry's men had dismounted several machine guns from vehicles and had placed them in various windows throughout the château. They ran from gun to gun, meeting threats wherever they arose.

The paratroopers added whatever firepower they could, and they began to take casualties. "Our machine gunner was hit just as he set up his gun," Private Walter Davis, a radioman, recalled. "He had a bullet in the right shoulder and back." During a lull in the fighting, Davis saw two Americans get into a jeep and attempt to make a dash for Bastogne. "They didn't get fifty yards before both were hit by heavy machine-gun fire. They groaned and fell off the jeep. We tried to get to them but could not, due to heavy fire." In any case, they were both dead. Cherry and his stalwarts kept fighting and waited for relief or darkness, whichever came first.

Two miles to the east, at Mageret, General Bayerlein was in a gloomy mood. His troops were holding the town against American pressure coming from the east (this was Ryerson's group). To the German commander, it seemed as though every time his Panzer Lehr made any progress toward Bastogne, it ran into tough resistance. He knew now that Ewell's regiment was in the fight, and he had never, in his mind, resolved the issue of the supposed enemy "armored division" at Longvilly. To Bayerlein, it seemed his flanks were wide open, menaced by multiple U.S. formations, with plenty of firepower. "I felt that resistance on my flanks would have to be annihilated before I could attack. The movement of the infantry regiment [the 501st] which had come out of Bastogne to attack me had reacted decisively on my thinking." As far as the general was concerned, his main focus now should be extricating his division, not hurling it at Bastogne. Any attack on Bastogne, Bayerlein felt, would require the efforts of multiple divisions, not just his own.

Now he noticed a group of American prisoners who came from a medical unit. They had apparently been captured in the woods outside of Mageret. Hoping that they might help take care of his own wounded, Bayerlein spoke to them. He was amazed to see that one of the American prisoners was a female nurse. She was a stunning, gorgeous woman. Bayerlein described her as "young, blond and beautiful." Absorbed in the pursuit of this attractive woman, the general lost whatever remained of his aggressiveness and initiative. She held him "spellbound" for much of the rest of the day.

At Wiltz, another general had no time for such distractions. General Norman "Dutch" Cota knew that the 28th Division could not hold this town for much longer. His hodgepodge forces had managed to hang on through the night, but only because the Germans had not mounted an all-out attack. Cota knew it was only a matter of time until they did so. This morning he had designated Lieutenant Colonel Daniel Strickler as the commander of all forces in Wiltz. This included the tattered remains of the 110th Infantry Regiment—Strickler was now the third regimental commander in as many days. His orders were to hold out as long as possible while the division headquarters group and rear echelons withdrew to Sibret. The longer the 28th Division could hold out here, the fewer Germans would be available to fight around Bastogne.

Cota was a courageous man who had proven his mettle many times in combat. With the evacuation of his division headquarters, he knew that the time had come for him to leave Wiltz. Personally, he preferred to stay with his men, but that was neither practical nor wise. No purpose would be served if Cota got killed or captured. He could do far more good escaping to lead other fights on another day. He knew that, but he did not like it.

Now, in Wiltz, with all his arrangements made, Cota jumped in his jeep, nicknamed "Fire and Movement," and ordered his driver, Sergeant Robert Milbier, to take off. A couple of miles to the west, at the Café Schuman crossroads, where they were about to turn onto the N15 that led into Bastogne, they saw droves of German soldiers. General Cota ordered Milbier to step on the gas. The jeep sped past the Germans, so close that the Americans could clearly see the surprise on the faces of their adversaries. Several more times on the N15, they ran into small groups of enemy soldiers. Each time the Germans opened fire, but Milbier skillfully maneuvered past them and kept driving at top speed.

When they were about three miles from Bastogne, they saw two American jeeps on either side of the road. Men were standing in the back of each jeep, pointing .30-caliber machine guns at "Fire and Movement." Sergeant Milbier slowed down. Cota was relieved to see that the men in the jeeps were indeed Americans.

As it happened, T/Sergeant Tom Holmes, the Detroit native who commanded Team O'Hara's Intelligence and Reconnaissance Platoon, was in charge of this roadblock. Holmes eyed Cota and his jeep suspiciously. He and his men knew that Germans were masquerading as Americans, and they wished to take no chances with this old man. "General Cota was unknown to me. I didn't know him from a bale of hay at that time. He was looking very worried and concerned."

Sergeant Holmes and one of his gunners questioned Cota intensely on American culture. "Who won the pennant last year?" "What team plays in Brooklyn?" "Who's dating Rita Hayworth these days?"

Cota patiently answered and then posed a question of his own: "I'm looking for any of my 28th Division. Can you tell me where any of them are?" Sergeant Holmes had no idea. He hardly knew what was happening with his own Team O'Hara, much less the 28th Division. Cota looked anxious. Holmes figured that the poor man had been through hell, and he felt badly for him. "We . . . decided that he was genuine. He went on through." Cota met with O'Hara and then drove into Bastogne, where he was reunited with his old friend Colonel Roberts. After talking with Roberts and General McAuliffe, and thus learning much more about the battle raging around Bastogne, Cota returned to his jeep and went to his new, fledgling headquarters at Sibret. Back in Wiltz, his battered survivors prepared for the final assault.[11]

Two and a half miles northwest of Bastogne, one U.S. jeep and two armored cars were driving north on a small paved road. They had just passed Longchamps and were approaching Bertogne. The command vehicle was known as an M20. It was stubby-looking, with a skin of light armor. The vehicle had no turret, nor did it have tracks; instead it had three tires on either side. Its main weapon was a .50-caliber machine gun in a ring mount near the main hatch.

Inside the M20, Lieutenant Colonel Clifford Templeton was concentrating on making it to his objective, and it was not all that far away—four, maybe five, miles at the most. He was the commander of the 705th Tank Destroyer Battalion, a powerful unit that was equipped with maneuverable M18 Hellcats, exactly the kind of weapons the Americans badly needed to counter German armor at Bastogne.

The last sixteen hours had been quite a whirlwind for Templeton and his 705th Tank Destroyer Battalion. The night before, VIII Corps had alerted them for movement to Bastogne. They had left their base at Kohlscheid, Germany—some sixty or seventy miles from Bastogne—at 2240 hours and had spent a confusing night trying to find a good route into Bastogne. Along the way, they had seen and heard many buzz bombs in the vicinity of Liège. This morning Templeton's 705th had attempted to go into Bastogne via Houffalize and the N15 road (the same one that went through Noville), only to find out from a military policeman that the road was in enemy hands. Templeton had successfully rerouted his battalion west to La Roche, although one of his reconnaissance platoons had mistakenly strayed into Houffalize, mainly because the MPs failed to divert them. There they engaged in a bitter, close-quarters fight with the Germans.

That morning in La Roche, Templeton had seen firsthand the backwash of the chaotic American retreat: "Various units were sprawled on both sides of the road. These outfits did not seem to have any plans for their own defense, and the uncertainty of the true situation only added to their bewilderment." With the gravity of the situation dawning on him, the colonel had ordered his battalion into defensive positions in and around La Roche while he tried to find the best way into Bastogne. His men set up a roadblock in the northern part of town, while the bulk of the battalion deployed to the south of La Roche.

Templeton had learned from a "reliable source" that VIII Corps headquarters had moved to Neufchateau, so he decided to go there and see General Middleton. For the journey, he brought along a reconnaissance jeep and an armored car. In Neufchateau, General Middleton had reiterated his previous order—Templeton was to get his battalion into Bastogne. The colonel had sent Lieutenant Morris Klampert, one of his operations officers, in a jeep to La Roche to convey this order to the battalion and get them moving.

About an hour earlier, Templeton and his little group had gone to Bastogne, where General McAuliffe told the colonel to "bring your battalion up as quickly as possible." Templeton planned to do so along the very road he was on right now. He half-expected to meet his battalion just ahead at Bertogne, or perhaps a little beyond. He peered through a slit in his armored car, looking for them, but he saw nothing. The whole area was quiet. Nothing and no one was stirring.

In the other armored car, an M8 with a turret and a 37-millimeter gun, T/5 Larry Tanber was sitting in the gunner's seat. Like Templeton, he too was scanning the area, looking for threats. "It was an eerie silence, with no guns being fired and no artillery shells falling around us." Just ahead, the jeep was rounding a crook in the road. In the jeep one soldier was driving, one was in the passenger seat, and another was standing in the back, manning a .50-caliber machine gun. Just as the jeep rounded the bend, Tanber heard the industrial ripping sound of German machine guns, combined with the bark of a 75-millimeter gun. Bullets shredded the jeep. The driver slumped over the wheel, and Tanber could tell he was dead. The other two men ran from the jeep and took cover. Just behind Tanber's M8, Lieutenant Colonel Templeton's M20 absorbed several hits from a quacking 40-millimeter antiaircraft gun. The colonel ordered his crew to destroy their M20, dismount, and take cover. Templeton made it out and took cover in a ditch, as did a couple of other men. One of the assistant gunners, Private Bennie Chambliss, went a different way and got captured.

Meanwhile, Tanber's driver was frantically maneuvering his vehicle off the road, into a defiladed firing position. Bullets were ricocheting off the pavement, and Tanber could hear them hitting the tires of his armored car. Tanber spotted the enemy machine gun that was responsible for this fire. "I fired two rounds from the 37-mm cannon, destroying the machine gun emplacement, and our vehicle turned around while taking heavy fire from other enemy gun emplacements." At this moment, it might have been easier and safer to abandon the M8 and run away, but Tanber and the other crewmen stayed right where they were. Tanber fired round after round at the Germans, allowing Templeton and the other dismounted men to retreat to a safer spot. "All you do in that situation is react," Tanber later said. "Survival is utmost in your mind. All the training you had to prepare yourself for combat comes to the forefront."

The M8 driver managed to get the vehicle back on the road and retreat south. They picked up Templeton and the other survivors and went back to Bastogne, where they began searching for a good place to set up a command post. Along the way, the colonel radioed the battalion, warned them of the enemy roadblock at Bertogne, but told them to "come any way possible" to Bastogne.

Templeton's S3, Major Worth Curtiss, was in charge of the battalion convoy in the colonel's absence. To avoid the Bertogne roadblock and whatever other enemy forces might be nearby, he decided to employ a circuitous westerly route via Champlon and Ortheuville and into Bastogne. Lieutenant Colonel Templeton could do little now but settle in and wait for them. He knew how badly General McAuliffe needed his Hellcats. He only hoped they would make it to Bastogne before it was too late.[12]

6

A few miles to the north, just outside of Foy, Private Donald Burgett was walking on the wet N15 highway, putting one foot in front of the other, fighting off the queasy feeling that accompanied his return to combat. He was one small part of a long, staggered line of Lieutenant Colonel LaPrade's paratroopers, all of them ambling north to Noville. Here and there artillery shells exploded inaccurately. Small patches of snow clung to adjacent fields. Everyone could see his breath, but the day was not that cold, really. Burgett figured the temperatures were probably in the upper thirties or lower forties. Up ahead, in the middle of the road, he saw a jeep. A lieutenant with a 10th Armored Division patch on his sleeve was standing in the back of the jeep, talking to a couple of airborne officers. Much to the delight of Burgett and the other troopers, "the jeep was piled high with ammo of all kinds." The 101st Airborne's journey to Bastogne had been so frantic that many of the troopers did not have proper weapons and ammunition.

The 10th Armored Division officer was Lieutenant George Rice, Desobry's S4, and he had spent the last couple of hours scrounging for ammo and weapons anywhere and everywhere. Rice had brought up several jeeploads and one truckload of ammo, all of which was now organized in neat piles. There were bandoliers of eight-round clips for riflemen, .45-caliber slugs for men with Thompson submachine guns, .30-caliber belts for machine guns, rockets for bazooka men, 60-millimeter mortar shells, hand grenades, and the like. Burgett walked past the jeep and, like so many others, grabbed what he needed. "I reached out and accepted two bandoliers of M1 cartridges, which I slung around my neck over my left and right shoulders as did the rest of our riflemen." He also got some .45-caliber bullets. Nearby, Private Donald Straith, a new man in Burgett's squad and a fellow Michigan native, noticed a crate of grenades. "These were distributed, one to a man, until the supply was exhausted." Straith hooked a grenade to his cartridge belt and kept moving. Everyone thanked Lieutenant Rice for his efforts. "It was nice to feel . . . that at least we had something to fight with," one paratrooper said.

Thus replenished, LaPrade's battalion kept marching all the way to Noville. Once again a shroud of fog had descended over the little town, and it was under intense artillery and small-arms fire, making movement very dangerous. Houses, jeeps, and half-tracks were on fire.

Private First Class Jerry Goolkasian, the tanker, looked to the south and saw the paratroopers appearing out of the fog and thought they might be Germans. Like nearly every Team Desobry soldier, Goolkasian had no idea that the 101st Airborne was joining them in Noville. "We turned our turret around. We were gonna fire on 'em. We never expected 'em." Fortunately, Goolkasian and the other tank crews had served at Fort Benning, so they knew what paratroopers looked like. "We noticed the jump boots . . . and we noticed they were walking in column." The troopers waved and shouted to the tankers and took cover in doorways or demolished houses. Standing next to Goolkasian in the turret, Private First Class Hildoer asked an airborne officer what was going on and learned for the first time of the counterattack that Desobry and LaPrade were planning to launch in mere minutes.

The plan was to send four tanks north on the Houffalize road and another three east on the Bourcy road. Each tank group would be accompanied by a platoon and a half of armored infantry in half-tracks. LaPrade's battalion would then fan out and capture the ridges—C Company directly to the east on either side of the Bourcy road, A and B Companies to the north of Noville, with the former on the east side of the Houffalize road and the latter on the west side. Basically, the tanks and half-tracks would provide fire support for the paratroopers who were supposed to take the ridges on foot. Even now, howitzers from the 420th Armored Field Artillery Battalion were pounding those ridges.

This attack would be a difficult proposition under ideal circumstances, and these were far from ideal circumstances. The enveloping fog made it tough to see any farther than fifty yards in the distance. The open ground around Noville was a death trap. The Americans were badly outnumbered and outgunned—a reinforced battalion was about to attack the equivalent of a division. To cap it all off, the attack was not well organized. Most of the paratroopers had been told next to nothing about this assault. They were used to receiving extensive briefings before jumping into combat. Instead, right now in Noville, officers or NCOs pointed in the distance and said things like: "Hey, we're attacking. Go there!" or "Follow me. We gotta take some ridges outside of town!"

At 1430, the courageous paratroopers began the attack. They sprinted into the fog, fired their weapons, took cover anywhere they could, then got up and ran again. Some of them got as far as the ridges. "As we proceeded to do this," Lieutenant Joe Reed of C Company recalled, "we came upon a bunch of Krauts sleeping in their holes. We started to pop them as we ran along the ridge. Immediately we heard a bunch of tank motors start up just over the hill in a wooded area."

At this exact moment, the Germans were launching an attack of their own. Their Mark IVs and Mark Vs emerged out of the fog, seemingly everywhere. The tanks rolled straight for the very ridges the paratroopers were trying to take. At the same time, the volume of enemy artillery and screaming meemie fire in Noville increased to a violent crescendo. Some of the paratroopers were caught out in the open and slaughtered in hordes. "The tanks came over the hill[s] and poured heavy fire from machine gun and cannons into our infantry," one paratrooper later wrote.

Team Desobry's tank, half-track, and tank destroyer crews could see that the American attack was shattered, so they hung back and tried to give covering fire to the stricken paratroopers. They picked off a couple of enemy tanks, but most of the troopers were on their own in this kill zone.

At the town cemetery, Private Straith and much of A Company were pinned down under the barrage of furious tank and artillery fire. "I immediately dove between two gravestones and lay there waiting." He could hear intense fire just beyond the wall of the graveyard. "An occasional shell would pass overhead, one striking the side of a small mausoleum nearby. From various shouts I heard around me, I soon found out that those men who had crossed the wall were pinned down in the fields beyond and that forward movement had come to a standstill."

Not far away from Straith, Private First Class Steven Polander was lying against the graveyard wall, cringing under the enormous weight of enemy fire. Round after round of German artillery or tank shells exploded uncomfortably close. Suddenly a shell hit the top of the wall. The concussion "knocks me senseless," he wrote in a present-tense description.

"When I come to, I don't know where I am." He stumbled to a nearby barn. "Inside sits a young man, on what looked like a block of wood, his back to me. His skull on the upper right side has been totally torn off by a huge chunk of shrapnel. His brains are showing. The medic kneels, dabbing his skull."

Private Burgett was a couple of hundred yards away, out in the middle of no-man's-land, at the extreme point of A Company's aborted advance. He and several of his squad mates were huddled in a chicken coop, smoking cigarettes, trying to calm down. They had dodged all manner of enemy fire just to get in there. They had seen men killed. Burgett was still thinking about a dead 10th Armored man he had seen, his body hanging out of a jeep, his blood draining into a watery ditch, turning the water "red for a hundred feet back down the ditch."

Now enemy artillery shells began exploding too close for comfort. Private Burgett and the others stubbed out their cigarettes and bolted for the dubious safety of a haystack. Burgett and one of his best buddies, Private Harold Phillips, a blond-haired, blue-eyed Pennsylvanian, saw German tanks edging over the crest of a hill just ahead. One of the tanks rolled forward while the others remained in place, covering the leader.

Burgett and Phillips looked around for a way to escape but saw nothing but open terrain. "If we had a bazooka, we might be able to knock it out, or at least go down trying," Phillips said.

Burgett agreed. "Look at the size of that son of a bitch! It's as big as a house."

The tank's machine gun opened fire, splitting the haystack in the middle and setting the hay on fire. Hugging the ground, they crawled away. Sergeant Don Brininstool, Burgett's squad leader, ordered him to go back, find the captain, and get permission to retreat. "Are you nuts?" Burgett replied. "If I try to cross that field, they'll blow me to bits."

Brininstool glared and repeated his order. Burgett knew he had no choice. He took off at a dead run, literally dodging bullets; he made it to the edge of Noville, where he found the captain. The CO gave him an indecisive order—either go forward or stay in place. Burgett somehow made it back to Brininstool and relayed the order. The squad was under such intense fire that Brininstool decided to retreat. All of them took off at a dead run, back into Noville. Private Burgett made it to a small road and was horrified to realize that the tank was chasing him. "[It] was only a couple hundred or so yards behind and gaining. I didn't try to zigzag; I just wanted to put as much distance as I could between that metal monster and myself. Bursts of machine-gun bullets lanced past me, splattering the pavement around and ahead of me before whining off in different directions. I could see sparks fly where the bullets struck the pavement to my front." Burgett glanced back long enough to see the tank's main gun was pointed right at him, and he felt sick to his stomach. It was like a nightmare brought to life. "Goose bumps rose on my arms, and I could feel the hair crawling on the nape of my neck."

He made it into a house where Phillips and a couple of others were hiding. The body of an old man lay on a brass bed in the corner of one room. The tank pulled alongside the house, rotated its turret, and fired (turning the dead man into mush), just as the Americans ran out of a back door. They managed to escape injury. Soon they received an order to dig in just outside of Noville.

As Burgett dug in, other paratroopers were retreating back into Noville. East of town, Lieutenant Reed and much of C Company were under intense fire. "I yelled to the guys to get off the hill and back to the town, which we did." On the way he sent Private First Class Robert Wiatt and Private Henry Lugo forward to scout for a safe route. The two of them took machine-gun fire and took cover behind a burned-out half-track. Wiatt was senior to Lugo. He ordered him to go back to the company and tell them what was happening. "As Lugo left the cover of the half-track and started back . . . he drew a lot of fire," Wiatt said. "It scared the hell out of him, so he turned back to the half-track and threatened to shoot me for trying to get him killed. I had to do some fast talking to calm him down." With Lugo placated, they and the survivors of C Company made it back to Noville.

With the defeat of the American attack, the battle for Noville turned into a free-for-all. Major Desobry later said it was "like a barroom brawl; no one man could control it or know what was taking place all the time." The major was angry that he was losing so many half-tracks and jeeps to artillery fire. "I would return to the CP, blow my top, and order the vehicles scattered. The order would be obeyed but somebody would move the damned things onto the main streets and the process would be repeated." Finally he ordered his maintenance officer to move all the disabled vehicles back to Bastogne.

The Germans now pressed their tanks forward, generally without infantry support. Some of their armor even got into the foggy, rubble-strewn town. Private Don Addor, the Washington, D.C., native in Headquarters Company, 20th Armored Infantry Battalion, was about to find this out firsthand. He had spent much of the day in and around the farmhouse where the night before he had caught a few hours of sleep on a turnip pile. He and his comrades had been under artillery and sniper fire almost all day. The house was demolished, its windows shattered, and Addor was bathed in the light of burning vehicles. Somewhere in the distance, he could hear the pitiful cries of dying animals that had been caught in burning barns. In the confusion of the fog, Private Addor had actually come face-to-face with German soldiers on two occasions. Both times, the erstwhile enemies had prudently headed in the opposite direction.

Now Private Addor was looking at Desobry's headquarters building, and he noticed paratroopers milling around outside. Curious to know what was going on, he crossed the street but could not find anyone who knew much of anything. A soldier, whom Addor recognized as a member of B Company, 20th Armored Infantry, hustled around the corner and cried: "There's a Tiger tank rolling into town blowing up everything!" Most of the soldiers scrambled into the basement of a nearby house, but Private Addor wanted no part of that. "That was a good place to get buried alive." Instead, Addor went out the back door of the house, looked in one direction, and saw nothing but milky fog. Just when he thought that this was much ado about nothing, he looked the other way and saw the enemy tank no more than twenty-five feet away. "I could have spit on it if my mouth had not gone dry."

Private Addor ducked back into the house and found a bazooka. Another soldier from B Company materialized. He said the bazooka was his, and that he had plenty of experience firing it. Addor gave him the tube, picked up a bag of rockets, and promised to be his loader. The two soldiers left the house, crawled on their bellies up to a wall, right behind a burning half-track, and aimed their weapon at the tank. "I pulled the pin, shoved it to the rear of the barrel and wrapped the little wire around the contact spring." Addor said a quick prayer and patted the other man on the back. He fired. The shell hit the tank, but did no damage. "As I loaded another round the turret started to swing back and forth." They fired and hit the tank "but the shell bounced off without exploding and rolled into the street. The Germans in that tank now knew someone on their right and up close was firing at them."

The enemy tank backed up slightly. Addor and his partner kept firing. They hit the tank several more times but did not destroy it. A German sniper was trying to shoot them, but they were shielded by the corner of the house. "His bullets chiseled away at the stone work, sending showers of dust and chips in front of us." The tank fired and hit the house above the two Americans. Debris collapsed down upon them, but they were unhurt.

They fired again and hit the tank just under its main gun, clearly damaging it. "I think we got the bastard," Addor hollered. "Fire one more in the same place!" He armed a shell and was about to load it when he heard a loud blast from behind him. Concussion knocked him to the ground. "I was out for a couple minutes."

When he awoke, he looked up, and saw the long barrel of an American tank destroyer. It had fired right over their heads and finished off the

German tank. A tank destroyer lieutenant was standing over him talking, but Addor could not hear him. "I could not hear anything at all but a tremendous ringing and roaring in my ears from that muzzle blast." The lieutenant and his men helped Addor and the other soldier to their feet and inside the house. The officer shook their hands, wrote down their names and their units, and promised to put them in for a Silver Star. Shaking the cobwebs from his head, Private Addor walked to a window and watched the German tank burn.

A block to the north, Private Burgett was lying in a ditch, next to a stone wall, on the northeastern edges of Noville, enduring horrendous shell fire. He heard Private Leo Corillo, one of the replacements, screaming for a medic. Corillo ran around the corner of a building "screaming, his guts trailing in the dirt behind him. He was holding most of them in his arms." Burgett and two other men jumped from cover, tackled him, and started to give him first aid. "He lay there sobbing and whimpering, shaking his head from side to side, his eyes wide and glassy, staring at nothing."

Burgett whipped out his raincoat and laid it on the ground. Another soldier took out his canteen and poured some water on the raincoat. They then laid Corillo's guts on the coat and began washing them, "picking off the largest pieces of dirt and stone with our fingers before forcing his guts back into his belly. Then we bound him up tight around the midsection with strips cut from my raincoat, shot him with morphine and dragged him into the ditch to wait for a medic." Having no knowledge of Dr. Prior's barroom aid station, paratrooper medics had set up their own aid station in a barn near the church. They were prowling around Noville, looking for wounded men, but Burgett was not sure if they found Private Corillo, and he had no time to find out. He and his squad soon relocated to foxholes and slit trenches just outside of town.

At this point, the fog grew even thicker, and the situation more inconclusive. With poor coordination between their infantry and armor—not to mention limited visibility—the Germans backed off again, mainly to the ridges. An eerie quiet descended over the town as the shooting tapered off. The air reeked of burning flesh, hair, fuel, and wood. The whole town was thick with plumes of smoke that billowed from a myriad of fires. Only the moans of wounded men and animals, mixed with the ghastly roaring of flames, could be heard.[13]

Just west of Longvilly, not far from St. Michael's grotto, on the N12 highway, Lieutenant Edward Hyduke was pondering his options and coming to realize that they were limited. His combat team, consisting of light tanks, medium tanks, armored cars, and half-tracks, had been there since last night. They had, of course, become intertwined with retreating CCR vehicles. Traffic on the road was monumental. All day long Hyduke had been sitting tight in this relatively quiet area, hearing plenty of shooting in the distance, waiting for word to retreat west to Mageret, and wondering how he would negotiate all this traffic when that order finally came. He figured it was only a matter of time before the Germans found him and attacked him.

Now he heard a call over the radio. One of his tank commanders had just spotted enemy armor southeast of Longvilly. An instant later, Hyduke's column came under devastatingly accurate tank and artillery fire. An armor-piercing shell smashed into the turret of one of the CCR tanks, damaging it beyond repair. At the rear of Hyduke's column, two half-tracks and a light tank were hit and destroyed. At nearly the same time, Lieutenant Colonel Cherry radioed him with the anticipated order to retreat to Mageret. Apparently Captain Ryerson's group had not made contact with the airborne, but the captain and his survivors were holding out in a few houses at the northern section of the little town, keeping the Germans at bay with artillery fire from the 420th Armored Field Artillery Battalion.

Here at Longvilly, Hyduke's tankers fired back at their attackers, destroying two enemy tanks, but still the fire continued. Up and down the line of American vehicles, enemy shells struck home, tearing through armor and flesh alike, setting fires and touching off catastrophic explosions. A panic ensued as vehicles tried desperately to find cover or escape altogether. They sloshed on and off the road, tumbled into ditches, took direct hits, or collided with one another. The traffic problem was now much worse than before. Some of the Americans were abandoning or destroying their vehicles, trying to get away on foot, only to be mowed down by machine guns. Others found cover among the stricken vehicles and worked their way west. Lieutenant Hyduke was among them. He led a small group away from this scene of carnage, west to Mageret. Hyduke's team no longer existed. In less than an hour, he had lost 175 soldiers, seventeen half-tracks, and at least fifteen tanks. But the Germans paid a price too. They also lost fifteen tanks.

Several hundred yards west of this tragic panorama of death, Lieutenant Moot, the forward observer, could hear the shooting and the explosions. There were now no other Americans in the area, only this platoon of Team Cherry tanks, hunkered down in nice defilade positions, out of the line of sight of German armor. Over the last couple of hours, more German infantry soldiers had foolishly attacked them, only to be cut down by machine guns or Lieutenant Moot's artillery. Forty or fifty enemy corpses were lying out there. "Our machine gun ammunition belts contained tracer and incendiary bullets and a lot of the bodies had their clothing burning and smoking from these bullets."

Moot knew that all was not well, though. They were running low on machine-gun ammunition, and everyone was uneasy about their obvious isolation. Moreover, the sounds of battle were coming not just from the front in Hyduke's direction, but from the rear too. "The Lieutenant in command of the tank platoon came over to my tank and we discussed the situation. We both thought that we would soon be cut off from the rear if we did not do something." They were in a difficult spot. For the moment, they were safe, but eventually the Germans would find them. If they did attempt to move, though, the enemy would surely see them and open fire. The narrow road was blocked by all sorts of wrecked vehicles, so it would be difficult just to drive, much less deal with enemy fire.

The other officer went back to his tank and tried to radio Cherry and Hyduke for permission to retreat, but he could not get in touch with either of them. He decided to order a retreat on his own authority. The tanks managed to turn around and roll west, barely slipping past other vehicles. Within five minutes, enemy antitank gunners spotted them and opened fire, destroying the lead tank. The tank platoon leader radioed Moot and told him that his crews were abandoning their Shermans, so Moot and his guys decided to do the same.

They opened the gasoline valve and pitched grenades into the tank, hoping it would explode, and set off on foot, armed with M3 grease guns. Immediately they came under withering small-arms fire. "I decided to run for the knocked out vehicles in the road. As I raised up to run I was hit in the left arm and left buttocks by bullets." He made it behind the vehicles and took cover with one of his crewmen. They rested a minute and then resumed their odyssey, dodging fire, crawling in ditches, taking cover behind destroyed vehicles. A shell exploded nearby, wounding the crewman in the foot, but still they kept moving.

At one spot alongside the road, they saw the tank platoon leader lying wounded along a culvert. "He had been shot through the body and was badly hurt. He said he was too badly wounded to go on and he did not want us to try to help him. He asked us to send the medics for him if we ever caught up with them." Moot and the other soldier hated to leave the lieutenant, but they had to keep going. Somewhere farther west on the road, amidst a tangle of destroyed vehicles, they found an undamaged jeep and drove to Mageret, where they hooked up with Ryerson's people. They told the medics about the wounded lieutenant, but they were never sure if anyone went back to get him.

Two miles to the west, Lieutenant Colonel Cherry's Neffe château was on fire. He and his small band of soldiers had bravely fought off the Germans the entire day, but eventually enemy shells set fire to the roof of the stately building. German grenadiers edged close to the windows and hurled incendiary grenades through them, adding to the conflagration. The flames soon spread, filling the hallways with smoke and detritus.

Only that morning Cherry and his men had promised one another that they were there to stay. Now the colonel knew that was not realistic. If they stayed there much longer, the flames would consume all of them. Cherry radioed Colonel Roberts in Bastogne: "We're not driven out. We were burned out. We are not withdrawing; we are moving." This was mere semantics. Cherry's group was retreating under extreme duress, because they had little choice. He gathered his survivors and set them in motion under cover of smoke and late afternoon shadows. He himself was the last man out. He emptied the magazines of two tommy guns at the Germans, even as their return fire hit an officer riding in the back of Cherry's jeep. In spite of this withering German fire, Cherry and his men made it to the airborne's positions at Mont.

At almost the same time, Lieutenant Colonel Ewell was back in Bastogne. He had just met with General McAuliffe and Lieutenant Colonel Harry Kinnard at the Belgian barracks. Ewell had started the day in an attacking mind-set, but after a long day of combat against an obviously powerful enemy force outside of Bastogne, his attitude had changed. He was now in the process of deploying his battalions on defensible high ground, just east of Bastogne. Moments earlier, he had informed McAuliffe and Kinnard of his plans, and they had approved them.

Now Colonel Ewell was walking through Bastogne, on the way back to his command post, when he saw Sergeant Ammons, an NCO from I Company. With no preamble, the sergeant asked, "Colonel, have you heard about Company I? We have been wiped out."

Ewell was alarmed but skeptical. He returned to his CP, checked out the sergeant's report, and found that he was correct. Company I had been decimated at Wardin. Survivors were trickling in, but it would take many days to rebuild the company. At that moment, Lieutenant Colonel Ewell knew he had made the right decision. It was definitely time to go on the defensive.[14]

A few miles to the south, Lieutenant Colonel Jim O'Hara was thinking the same thing. With his own eyes, he had seen Wardin stragglers and had heard their disquieting story. He knew that he was opposite at least two Panzer Lehr columns. O'Hara wanted to withdraw to high ground around Marvie while still guarding the N34 Wiltz–Bastogne highway. He secured permission from Roberts and was now in the process of setting up in this new spot. "The new position was built with a hasty minefield across the road," O'Hara recalled, "with infantry dug in along side, and the tanks placed in the hedges for concealment. Several tanks were placed to fire to the north." To the south, he now had contact with the newly arrived 327th Glider Infantry Regiment. The 420th Armored Field Artillery provided a nice blanket of covering fire.

A squad of engineers constructed a roadblock on the N34. "Trees were blown so as to interlace, and mines and booby traps were inserted. The block was then covered by machine-gun fire from above and an artillery concentration." Sergeant Holmes, the I and R platoon leader, now had his vehicles set up just northeast of Marvie, hiding behind buildings, but with the highway in sight. He heartily approved of O'Hara's decision to defend here. "He . . . saved our fannies by not being macho."

As the soldiers of Team O'Hara set up along this new ground, the enemy was constantly probing. The whole area was under artillery fire and even some small-arms fire too. Lieutenant Colonel O'Hara set up his headquarters in a stone house, in the middle of a farm just outside of Marvie. He was having trouble with his radios so he summoned a repair team from T/Sergeant John McCambridge's communications section. McCambridge was about a quarter mile away, on a country lane with two of his repairmen, plus a rifleman/guide, heading for the CP. He had left two of his other men in a half-track a couple of hundred yards away.

Now Sergeant McCambridge looked in the distance at a nearby stand of trees. There were men in there, shooting at his group. "We ran like hell and hit the ditch." A few seconds later, a shell screamed in, exploded right above them, and did some major damage. A tree fell over and pinned the two repairmen. They were either dead or unconscious. The rifleman, Private John Behr, caught an enormous hunk of shrapnel that sliced him wide open from his neck to his buttocks. Sergeant McCambridge was bleeding from multiple wounds. "It broke my collar bone, my fingers were hanging off . . . and it took a chunk of meat out of my elbow. The upper left leg and the ankle out of my right leg was missing and I had shrapnel in my right lung."

McCambridge was going into shock, and Behr was near death. The desperately wounded rifleman was lying against his sergeant. McCambridge, with his unwounded right arm, laid Behr's head on his lap and said: "I'll get you out of here." There was no response. Private Behr's head rolled slightly and blood from his massive wound began gushing through his shirt. "[The shrapnel] ripped open his whole spine, all the way down." His warm, crimson blood was soaking through his uniform. He died in Sergeant McCambridge's arms.

The sergeant was groggy with shock and not in much pain, but he knew that he was in bad shape. He needed help and he needed it fast or he would die out there. With all his strength, he started yelling deliriously at one of the men he had left in the half-track, Private Ken Kauffman. "Ken, you Dutch sonofabitch, where are you? Ken? Where the hell are you? Ken, get up here! Where are you? You Dutch sonofabitch!"

Back in the half-track, shells had been landing perilously close, so much so that Private Kauffman, the driver, was struggling with the effects of concussion. He could hear Sergeant McCambridge's distant voice, but he was having trouble focusing on what to do next. For some reason, he thought he needed to fix his flashlight, before going to help the sergeant. Kauffman rummaged around in the half-track, found the flashlight, and started working on it. McCambridge kept screaming, "Ken? Ken? You Dutch SOB, where the hell are you?"

At last Kauffman got his wits together and went to Sergeant McCambridge. Private Kauffman jumped into the ditch and did what he could to help his stricken sergeant. "Help me get Behr out of here," McCambridge said.

Kauffman took one look at Behr and replied, "He's dead."

"Promise me that you'll get his body and take it to Graves Registration," McCambridge implored. Kauffman promised to do so.

Somehow, Kauffman got McCambridge out of the ditch and back to the half-track. He also freed the repairmen from the tree that had pinned them down, and he was glad to see that they were both alive and would be okay. For some reason, Kauffman placed Sergeant McCambridge on the hood of the half-track rather than in the back, and then took off for Bastogne.

McCambridge was cold and uncomfortable during this bumpy ride. He kept yelling, "You Dutch bastard! You're gonna kill me!"

At last Kauffman got him to a Catholic church in Bastogne that was serving as the 501st Parachute Infantry Regiment's hospital. The medics stabilized McCambridge and sedated him. That was about all they could do for now, since he needed serious medical attention and multiple surgeries for his debilitating wounds. He lay on the floor of the church, drifting in and out of consciousness. At one point, he woke up, saw a priest and a nun standing over him, and thought, "I've died and gone to heaven." Private Kauffman, true to his word, retrieved Behr's body and kept it in his half-track until Graves Registration teams could bury it.

In and around Bastogne, the medics were doing the best they could in the face of mounting casualties and constant danger. Battalion surgeons set up their aid stations in houses a few hundred yards behind what they thought were the front lines. The intensity of combat meant that the medics were getting overwhelmed with more cases than they could handle.

Sergeant Wichert, the combat engineer whose right arm had been shattered by an artillery shell that morning, made it to a brick house that was serving as an aid station. Medics put his arm in a splint and loaded him aboard an ambulance. The ambulance tried to make it out of Bastogne, but it took machine-gun fire and crashed. "I went sailing through the air, hit my head on the windshield and slid down behind the steering wheel. My head was so close to the driver's chest that I could hear him breathing through holes in his chest put there by bullets from the machine gun."

The ambulance was a mess of tangled, broken bodies. A diminutive medic managed to remove everyone who was still alive, including Wichert. He put Sergeant Wichert on a stretcher, laid a blanket on top of him, and promised to come back with help. Wichert fell asleep for a while. When he woke up, he was happy to see the face of an officer he had known in the States. "He and his driver loaded me on his jeep . . . and we headed back" to the brick house. The lieutenant left him with a long line of other wounded men who were lying on stretchers just outside the house. Wichert drifted off to sleep, only to awaken later when he felt someone fumbling with his dog tags. Whoever it was, Sergeant Wichert grabbed his leg and heard him say: "Hey, this guy is still alive!" Medics lifted him up and put him in another ambulance that made it to a different aid station house, closer to Bastogne. The house was so crowded with wounded men that Wichert had no place to sit except for right next to an operating table where surgeons were desperately trying to save lives. Finally his turn under the knife came. The doctors were worried that they might have to amputate, but they saved his arm, putting it in a thick cast.

Elsewhere, in an anonymous Bastogne house, Private First Class Neil Garson, a medic from New York City, was experiencing one of the most hectic days of his twenty-one-year-old life. He was a member of the Clearing Platoon, B Company, 80th Medical Battalion, a unit attached to CCB. Garson had volunteered for the army so that his forty-four-year-old father would not get drafted. Young Garson's job, and that of the whole Clearing Platoon, was to stabilize patients, make them as comfortable as possible, and send them back to a field hospital for surgery or more intensive treatment.

Now in Bastogne, Private First Class Garson and his platoon mates were dealing with a steady stream of badly wounded soldiers. "They looked miserable. We had quite a few . . . wounded, of course, principally from shell fire and men who were losing limbs, and a number that just died on our hands. The men who got caught in tanks often were burned to death or suffered tremendous burns. We would smear them with all kinds of jellies and ship them back as fast as we could to the hospitals. We weren't a regular hospital. It was more immediate aid to try to staunch their blood, immobilize their limbs, try to keep them from going into shock, and getting them back . . . as fast as we could. We had blood. We also had saline solutions and a lot of morphine. I would go around jabbing them with morphine syrettes making sure they didn't suffer too much before we sent 'em to the rear." Each time Garson gave a patient a shot of morphine, he noted the dosage and time on a tag, so that medics in other units would know exactly when the patient was due for another shot. This prevented overdoses of the powerful narcotic. Garson and the other medics worked continuously, saving many more lives than they lost.[15]

7

At Noville, the shooting was picking up again. The town was once more under artillery and tank fire. Firefights were going on all over the perimeter. Here and there, the Germans were attempting to get into town. In northeastern Noville, Private Burgett was lying in a slit trench, listening to the ominous sound of approaching German tanks. He could see them just ahead, slowly coming forth out of the fog. "They moved at a slow pace, the long barrels of their cannons looking like huge snouts as they swiveled around." The tanks fired into likely hiding places.

Burgett heard the gears of one tank grinding. It was getting closer by the minute. He and the soldiers in the slit trench had nothing with which to fight the tank. They could feel the heat of the tank's engine as it passed uncomfortably close, "its tracks crumbling bits of earth from the edge of the hole down on top of me." Burgett and the others lay still while the tank passed, and waited for the accompanying infantry. The pervasive fires burning so fiercely in Noville made the enemy soldiers look like "weird shadows . . . as though they were dancing and weaving. They seemed to grow in size, and then blip into nothingness."

The German soldiers were firing their rifles at unseen targets. When they were within range, Burgett and the other paratroopers rose as one and laid down a deadly curtain of fire: "Our small-arms fire lanced into their ranks. I could see them in and out of the flickers and shadows and fired each shot deliberately at individual figures." He was not sure if he hit anyone, though. He fired clip after clip, each time pulling the trigger eight times. When he exhausted the bullets in each clip, the empty stripper clip would pop out of the breech with its distinctive pinging sound. Each time, Private Burgett loaded a new clip and repeated the process. He was starting to run out of targets, because the German infantrymen were retreating over the ridge.

The German tanks, though, immediately reacted. "Engines whined with the surge of power. The huge machines thundered, the ground shuddered under them, high-velocity shells screamed from gun muzzles, and shells exploded indiscriminately amongst us. Screams and shouts broke out and men could be seen running in all directions." Several near misses exploded around Burgett, throwing him out of the trench. He crawled back in, only to have the concussion of more explosions throw him back out. "The left sleeve of my jump jacket was torn from cuff to elbow. The hair on my left arm and the left side of my face were singed. My skin was blackened by burnt powder." To Private Burgett, it seemed like every enemy gun was shooting right at him. Somehow he managed to get out of the ditch and back to Noville, where he found his squad in a cellar.

The Germans were probing around with their tanks, but they could not get a foothold in Noville. In the foggy, smoky shadows, they could not maneuver around the scores of wrecked vehicles that dotted the roads. Their infantry would be too vulnerable attacking with no cover across the open ground outside of Noville. Their tanks needed infantry support in order to survive in Noville at such close proximity to American troops.

Major Desobry was in eastern Noville near the Bourcy road when a soldier told him that Lieutenant Colonel LaPrade wanted to talk to him in the CP. The two men had never really settled the issue of who should assume overall command of the Noville perimeter; they also needed to coordinate their defensive plans for the evening.

Not long after Desobry returned to the schoolhouse headquarters, General Higgins arrived. He was there to see the situation for himself (Colonel Sink, the CO of the 506th, also made a visit). Since LaPrade was senior to Desobry, Higgins designated him as the overall commander. As they spoke, shells were exploding just outside. In an effort to provide some protection for everyone in the room, LaPrade dragged a big armoire several feet across the room and placed it in front of a window that faced north, in the direction of the Germans. Higgins told everyone that for now, at least, they were to remain in Noville: "Nobody's going out of here alive. This is where we halt." But when he left, he went back to Bastogne and recommended to McAuliffe that the Noville garrison be withdrawn to Foy. McAuliffe agreed and asked General Middleton for permission. The corps commander killed the idea: "No, if we are to hold on to Bastogne, you cannot keep falling back."

In the meantime, LaPrade and Desobry were discussing their defensive layouts for the evening. The two officers were standing over a little table, staring downward at a map. They agreed that LaPrade's three rifle companies would station themselves in a ring around the outside of the town, in holes, ditches, slit trenches, or even some buildings. Each company would cover the direction in which it had attacked a few hours earlier—B Company west of the Houffalize road, A Company just east of it, and C Company along the Bourcy road. Desobry's armored infantry and tanks would remain in town as a mobile reserve.

The little room was packed with tables, chairs, telephones, and maps. A few feet away from Desobry and LaPrade, Sergeant Larry Stein, the German Jewish immigrant who had found his American identity in the army, was sitting in a chair, writing in his diary. All day long he had been in and out of the CP, at times roaming around with other soldiers from the intelligence section who were gathering information, engaging in small firefights, and reporting whatever they thought might interest the commanders.

Now Stein was taking a few moments to rest and reflect in the privacy of his diary. He glanced up and noticed the battalion maintenance officer entering the room. The officer reported to Desobry and told him that he had finished towing vehicles to Bastogne and was going to return to his company there. He turned to leave. Stein resumed writing in his diary.

The maintenance officer had parked his recovery vehicle, which looked very similar to a Sherman tank, right in front of the CP. This was a cardinal sin, because it gave away the location of the CP. On one of the ridges northwest of Noville, a German tank crew noticed the recovery vehicle. The loader fed a shell into the breech of his gun. The gunner fired one quick shot and then another.

A millisecond later, their shells zipped past the recovery vehicle, then sliced through the armoire and then into the room. Sergeant Stein saw a flash, heard "an awful crash," and then passed out. The shells exploded, destroying the room and collapsing the building. The tall, strapping LaPrade went down in a heap; his lifeless body was buried beneath a pile of debris. Desobry, lanky and six feet four inches tall, was a hard target to miss. Fragments from the shells, the armoire, and whatever else was nearby tore into him. One of his eyes was nearly ripped from its socket. His face was gashed and lacerated, as was much of his head. He lay unconscious, half buried under the debris.

Soldiers converged on the scene, tossing aside the shattered remains of tables, chairs, timbers, and whatever other rubble was burying those inside the CP. They dragged men out as quickly as possible. Sergeant Stein was stunned and half-conscious but otherwise unhurt. "I don't remember anything until they dug me out." He was lying next to LaPrade's body. He saw a pair of hands grab the dead airborne colonel's legs and pull him into the street. "Then they were pulling me out. My helmet was gone. My rifle was gone." Stein was dazed and probably concussed. He kept thinking over and over that he had lost his rifle and helmet. "It's stupid when I think back, that that's what I was concerned with."

Major Desobry was bleeding badly, but still alive. His soldiers took him to a cellar and bandaged his head. They knew his condition was serious, so they decided to send him to Bastogne for medical treatment. All Desobry could think of was that if he had to go to Bastogne, he wanted to report to Colonel Roberts, fill him in on the situation, and recommend a withdrawal to Foy. He was in shock, bleeding from multiple wounds, and half-demented from concussion, with one of his eyeballs practically rolling onto his cheek. He was obviously in no condition to report to Roberts, but he did not quite understand that yet.

A small group of medics put him in a jeep with other wounded men and told the driver to head for the hospital in Bastogne. At Foy, they ran right into a German patrol. "When they saw the wounded—we were all bloody—they said: 'Aw, go on,'" Desobry later said. They made it to the 506th Parachute Infantry Regiment's aid station. Medics treated Desobry and then sent him to Mande-St-Etienne, where the 326th Airborne Medical Company had just set up a more permanent facility. "This [was] a fairly large complex with . . . surgical tents, surgeons and so on. I remember going into a tent and doctors talking to me." They anesthetized him, operated on him, and managed to save his eye.

Back at Noville, Major Robert Harwick, LaPrade's executive officer, assumed command for the paratroopers. Desobry's deputy, Major Charles Hustead, did the same for the 10th Armored soldiers. Harwick had been in Paris on leave when the 101st left for Bastogne. He had hitched rides to Mourmelon and then Bastogne and walked to Noville on his own, arriving in town earlier that afternoon. Hustead was a competent officer, but he did not quite have Desobry's charisma. "Hustead was sort of like a dried-up individual," Sergeant Stein commented. "I don't think he had much life in him." Stein, like most of the men in the 20th Armored Infantry Battalion, held Desobry in high esteem, but they realized he was gone now. Harwick and Hustead implemented the same plan of defense that their predecessors had devised for that evening. All over Noville, American soldiers took to cellars and foxholes, staying on alert, waiting for the Germans to come again. The fog was so dense and the sun so low in the sky that the only light came from the flicker of fires.[16]

At Wiltz, the situation was getting worse by the minute. Elements of the German 26th Volksgrenadier and 5th Parachute divisions were attacking, steadily closing a ring around the city. At Noertrange, a mile north of Wiltz, a company from the 26th Volksgrenadiers hit a provisional platoon of soldiers from the division band. T/5 John Noon, the percussionist who only a few nights earlier had played drums for Marlene Dietrich, was now in a foxhole, clutching a carbine. "We saw movement in the woods and thought it was the 110th Infantry." T/5 Joe LoCascio, his bandmate and foxhole buddy, excused himself to answer the call of nature behind a haystack. Suddenly, LoCascio hollered, "Hey, Germans are coming!" Noon and the others looked closer at the shapes coming out of the woods. Sure enough, they were German soldiers, and they were opening fire.

Noon and the other bandsmen took off. They slid under a rail fence. One man got stuck. "The Germans shot at him. He was husky. We got him out of there and we went on." They continued through Noertrange while "machine gun bullets ricocheted off stone buildings around us." Noon's group ran all the way back to Wiltz, with the Germans right on their tails. Only concentrated fire from four immobilized Shermans of the 707th Tank Battalion averted a complete debacle. "[They] were able to fire . . . on Notrange [*sic*] and the Village was taken under a severe concentration from the guns of these tanks," one officer later wrote. "No further movement of Germans appeared from the Village itself."

Other Shermans from the 707th were fighting smaller battles on the fringes of Wiltz. Private John Marshall, a New Jersey native, and his three tank crewmates were locked in a terrifying struggle against two Mark V Panthers and one actual Mark VI Tiger. For two days, Marshall and his comrades had steadily been on the move, trying to find Wiltz or friendly lines, whichever came first.

Now Marshall was sighting in on the Tiger, preparing to shoot. "I fired a perfect direct hit with an . . . A.P. shell, and except for the explosion nothing happened. I fired [a] second shot and hit almost the same spot. I might just as well have thrown an orange at the tank, it did no damage." McKnight, the tank commander, ordered Alyea, the driver, to move left just in time, as a near miss from the Tiger zoomed past the Sherman. The American tank retreated. Marshall and his friends then spotted a German column on a road that clearly led into Wiltz. They fired a few shots and destroyed a truck but noticed that German infantry soldiers were stealthily closing in on them. Alyea drove them out of danger, westward to Wiltz.

In the gathering darkness, they were driving parallel to the Wiltz River when seemingly out of nowhere a shell slammed into the treads on the right side of the tank. The Sherman went out of control and slid into the river. Marshall and the two other men in the turret were trapped under water. "Of all the things we went through, we end up drowning," Marshall said to them. But Alyea had gotten free of the tank. He came back and helped them out through the driver's hatch. Soaked and chilled to the bone, they made it to Wiltz and then Bastogne on foot.

In the meantime, the German attacks continued. In the east, they breached the frontline defenses of the 44th Engineer Combat Battalion.

Confused, stuporous groups of engineers were retreating back into the city. They managed to blow up bridges as they retreated, and this slowed the Germans somewhat.[17]

On the southern end of the perimeter, the 687th Field Artillery Battalion was under direct infantry and armor attack—an artilleryman's worst nightmare come to life. For two days, the batteries had been deployed on high ground, firing and displacing, raining shells on the German attackers around Wiltz.

Now the Germans were so close that the cannoneers were lowering their 105-millimeter howitzer muzzles as far as they could go and shooting directly at enemy soldiers or vehicles. This was especially true for Battery A. Lieutenant Les Eames was in a shell hole, close to the Battery A guns, when they came under intense attack. "All hell breaks loose!!" he wrote in his diary. "'A' Battery [was] firing like hell . . . direct fire at approaching *Jerry TANKS!!* Tanks were getting quite a few licks in themselves & were throwing lead all over . . . quite a few of which whizzed over my head. I started to leave my hole twice . . . each time I stuck my head up [an] MG let loose . . . & I could have sworn they were firing only AT ME."

Not far away, T/Sergeant Gene Fleury, the Seattle native who had once worked for the CCC, was in a farmhouse hayloft, with a .50-caliber machine gun in his hands. He and two other soldiers, Bob Stolp and Dick Atkins, had climbed a ladder into the hayloft and set the gun up on a pedestal, with the barrel poking out of a window. Sergeant Fleury peered into the distance, and he saw about two hundred yards away German tanks and dozens of infantry soldiers. "I opened up on 'em. So the Germans fired back, of course." Before long, the whole area echoed with gunfire.

Fleury was using his tracer rounds to aim and choose targets. Stolp and Atkins were loading as fast as they could. Another man a few feet away was supposed to be laying down some cover fire, but he was rolled up in a ball, cowering in fear. "The bullets were flying into the hay," Fleury said. "We could hear 'em. We were hollering at him to shoot," but he could not bring himself to do so.

Enemy rounds were slashing into the hayloft, tearing the hay around them. Each bullet made a distinct *pffft* sound as it impacted. Fleury kept firing and firing, until the .50-caliber barrel was so hot that it was on the verge of melting. "[We] fired the '50' until the barrel [was] overheated, causing a loss of rifling," Atkins recalled. When that happened, the bullets began to spin crazily in every direction. This problem, in combination with the intensity of enemy fire, convinced them that it was time to get out of there. They tossed the machine gun to the first floor, descended the ladder, and piled into a weapons carrier.

The batteries were nearly out of ammunition. At one howitzer in Battery B, Private First Class Lou Dersch's gun crew was down to one shell. Dersch was the gunner, the man who actually pulled the lanyard, and he had been doing that a lot that day as Battery B fired in support of Battery A. "Usually you'd put in three or five powder charges. The more powder charges, the farther you'd shoot. At Wiltz, we put in one. The Germans were so close we could see 'em."

Dersch looked at this last shell and felt sure that it was full of propaganda leaflets. He asked his captain if he should still fire it. The captain said, "What the hell, shoot it and let's get the hell out of here!" With a slight smirk on his face, Dersch pulled the lanyard, watching as the shell scattered leaflets over the target area. "We hitched up our guns, got on our trucks, and got the hell out of there."

Lieutenant Colonel Max Billingsley, the commander of the 687th, now ordered all of his other crews to do the same. Even as the Germans continued their attack, the artillerymen of the 687th loaded up and took off in trucks, trailers, half-tracks, and jeeps. The convoy safely drove southwest about a dozen miles to a crossroads known as Poteau de Harlange. There was nothing much there other than a two-story café building. Billingsley decided to halt at this crossroads for the time being while he went into Bastogne to learn more about the overall situation. Battery A set up west of the road, while B and C dispersed to the north and south, respectively. Headquarters Battery and the fire direction center immediately employed the café as a command post. Vehicles were lined up bumper to bumper on the road or in the adjacent fields. Gun crews unlimbered their howitzers and dispersed them into shooting positions, although they had little or no ammunition. Billingsley thought his batteries were safe, but later that night the Germans ambushed them and came very close to destroying the 687th. The Germans captured between 110 and 125 men from the battalion, many of whom were wounded. Not surprisingly, Headquarters Battery was decimated. Battery A got away to Bastogne. Battery B lost twenty-one men but escaped into Bastogne with most of its vehicles and guns. Battery C lost all of its equipment, including its howitzers, but many of the soldiers got away to Sibret or Bastogne.[18]

After sunset, at Wiltz, Lieutenant Colonel Strickler was in the process of talking to his commanders. He knew that Wiltz was effectively surrounded. In a matter of hours, the Germans would overrun the whole town. It was time to get out if they could.

Strickler and his officers stood together in the cellar that had served as the command post for the last day and a half. They could hear the rumble of shells and the rattle of machine-gun fire outside. "You fellows have done a good job," Strickler said. "Things are tough, and we're not going to get any reinforcements here. It looks like the big stand is to be made at Bastogne by the 101st. We have done all we can do here. Now let's get loose and join our group at Sibret. Get away from Wiltz in small groups."

Grim-faced, they left the room and went their separate ways. Out there in the winter night, the survivors of Wiltz's garrison set about the task of breaking through the enemy ring. Lieutenant Colonel R. W. Ripple tried to get the remnants of his 707th Tank Battalion out on the Wiltz–Roullingen road. In no time, his dilapidated assortment of damaged tanks, assault guns, half-tracks, trucks, and jeeps ran into a German ambush. "A German tank or self-propelled gun scored a hit on an ambulance carrying wounded and set it ablaze," one officer remembered. "The screams of the terrified, helpless wounded were heart-rending. The column was a mass of confusion, unable to break through the roadblock. Flaming vehicles now bathed the area in an eerie flickering light, and enemy machine guns raked the column." Up and down the column, soldiers dismounted and fled on foot. Many were captured, but a few got away.

Driving on the roads was suicide at worst, a captivity wish at best. Most of the retreating Americans were on foot. Private Harold Walter, a support soldier who worked in the headquarters section of the 110th Infantry, was with a group walking the streets of upper Wiltz: "The stillness was timeless, eternal. Only a stray cat, a frightened, barking dog. Single file we went up over [a] hill, into a woods nearby. Machine gun spurts changed our direction." They crossed an open road and saw many wrecked U.S. vehicles. They went into another stretch of woods and kept moving to the west. All of them were hungry, tired, cold, and thirsty. Another soldier, walking alongside Walter, kept saying, "This is just like in the movies." They wandered for miles but eventually made it to American lines.

Sergeant John Forsell, who had been fortunate enough to escape Hosingen two days before, now ran out of luck. He was clinging to the side of a half-track that was trying to drive through a German roadblock. "This is where I got hit by machine-gun fire. I could not hold on, and fell off. The half-track got through." When the shooting died down, the Germans came out from their cover to search the many American bodies lying on the road. "They went from one man to another. If the man was not dead, they shot him."

Now Sergeant Forsell heard their footsteps approaching. He was so frightened that he could hardly breathe. This was it. He was living his last few moments. They were standing over him. "When they lifted my arm, I passed out. My arm dropped and they thought I was dead." When they left, he crawled away and packed his wounds with snow. Unfortunately, another group of Germans found him and captured him.

Lieutenant Colonel Thomas Hoban, the division headquarters commandant, was captured, but Lieutenant Colonel Strickler made it out of Wiltz on foot with about a dozen other soldiers. "We set out, crawling most of the time, and constantly being alarmed by noises in the woods." Navigating with part of a map he had torn from his command post wall, Strickler and his hungry group wandered for three days before finding division headquarters. By then, it had relocated from Sibret to Neufchateau. Strickler was so exhausted that he slumped to the floor and went right to sleep. After more than four days of bitter combat, the 28th Division was finally out of the fight for Bastogne.[19]

8

It was now less than two hours before midnight. The Germans were clearly not going to capture Bastogne anytime soon. Throughout this bloody, decisive day they had failed in every attempt. Their window of opportunity was just about to close. With every passing minute, Bastogne was becoming more a political symbol of American resistance and less a crucial transit point for the German drive to the Meuse. In the process, it was becoming less valuable to the Germans.

To make matters worse, the 705th Tank Battalion had reached Bastogne over the past two hours and was now in position all over the American perimeter. One of Lieutenant Colonel Clifford Templeton's platoons was even now with the beleaguered defenders of Noville. Needless to say, he was quite relieved that his battalion had won its race against time.

Frustrated in their attempts to take Bastogne, the Germans were now bypassing it, steadily closing a ring around the American perimeter. Enemy reconnaissance elements were roaming the night, cutting roads that led out of town. One such unit from the 116th Panzer Division attacked the 326th Airborne Medical Company at Mande-St-Etienne, the crossroads west of Bastogne where much of the 101st Airborne Division had assembled the night before. This medical unit was the closest thing the 101st had to a permanent hospital facility, with the requisite tents, medical equipment, and physicians. The enemy attacked with six tanks and half-tracks, plus about one hundred soldiers (some of whom were clad in civilian clothes). The contest was, of course, one-sided. The shooting lasted fifteen minutes.

Most of the resistance came from a convoy of American supply trucks that happened to be passing through the area. One by one, the enemy picked off the trucks. "The Germans fired on every truck standing there and set them on fire," Private First Class Don Dobbins recalled. He saw an African American truck driver stand up in his cab and start blazing away with his .50-caliber gun. "He didn't last long, for the Germans turned everything they had on him." The enemy fire tore him apart and nearly ripped the cab from the truck. Dobbins took off into a wood line.

Lieutenant Colonel David Gold, the division surgeon and ranking officer, surrendered the unit to Captain Kroll, the enemy commander. Kroll told him to gather his medics and his wounded and be ready to move out in half an hour. Private First Class Elmer Lucas, a medic, was "taken prisoner by Germans in civilian clothes. There were several wounded in the vicinity but the guards didn't pay much attention to them." When the civilian-garbed enemy were not looking, Lucas ran off and escaped. Most were not so lucky. The Germans captured 143 men, including several doctors and many wounded. The 326th comprised the bulk of the 101st Airborne's medical capacity, so this was a significant loss.

The new POWs loaded the wounded into a convoy of trucks and ambulances. When all were ready, the convoy started moving east, toward Germany. "The medical officers and dentists were put on a truck loaded with jerrycans of gasoline," Captain Willis McKee, a physician, recalled. "We spent the next few hours emptying the gasoline over the side. Also, we emptied a few bottles of cognac that we happened to have along." It was not much, but it made them feel a little better.

Farther back in the column, in an ambulance, Major Desobry awoke to the sound of German voices outside. The last thing he remembered was when the doctors of the 326th had put a mask over his face to anesthetize him. In an attempt to orient himself, he looked around the ambulance with his one good eye. "The ambulance would move and then stop, move and then stop." At one of the halts, he again heard German voices. "My gosh, we sure captured a lot of German prisoners," he thought. In a few minutes, when he recognized an obvious tone of command in the German discourse (plus some slurred words from alcohol), he wondered just what on earth was going on. He asked the ambulance driver and learned the awful truth that they were now prisoners of the Third Reich. Desobry sighed and shook his head. He knew he was badly wounded. He wondered if he would ever see out of his damaged eye again. In his heart he felt he had led his soldiers as best he could. He was very proud of the way they had fought at Noville. Now, though, the frigid hopelessness of captivity lay ahead for young Desobry. It had been a long, difficult day indeed for the twenty-six-year-old major. The same was true for every other American at Bastogne.[20]

7

WEDNESDAY, DECEMBER 20

1

At 0030, Colonel William Roberts dictated an order for Lieutenant Colonel Henry Cherry: "Withdraw [Captain William] Ryerson prior to dawn. Suggest route Mageret–Bizory with contact point at Bizory," where the 501st Parachute Infantry Regiment was holding a solid defensive line. The orders filtered down from Cherry in Mont to Ryerson in Mageret. Under cover of darkness, the captain rounded up his remnants and organized a convoy: "The foot soldiers were all dismounted and formed around the tanks to give them what protection they could." Roberts made sure to inform the 501st to expect Ryerson's group.

Just before dawn, Ryerson's column slipped out of Mageret and, taking fire much of the way, made the short trip to Bizory. "Soldiers from the 101st Airborne Division came toward us out of the mist," Lieutenant Carl Moot, the forward observer, recalled. Ryerson's people made it safely into the airborne lines. Some stayed in place to fight with them. Others, like Moot, went to the rear for medical attention: "We proceeded into Bastogne, and all of the wounded were put in a building that was being used for a First Aid Station." Soon medics loaded Lieutenant Moot and the other wounded men into ambulances that somehow made it out of Bastogne to Liège.

In less than a day and a half of bitter fighting, Team Cherry had seriously impeded German attempts to capture Bastogne. The team had been cut off, cut up, and battered, but it was now back in the Bastogne perimeter, ready to continue the fight. Cherry had lost 175 men—a 35 percent casualty rate. He also lost eighteen tanks, twenty-three half-tracks, and numerous other vehicles. Cherry knew he had done his job, but he could not help but resent the way that his unit had been thrown into the battle. "It is not advisable to move an armored column into a situation where no information of either friendly or enemy forces is available without . . . sending out patrols to make contact with adjacent units," he wrote after his command returned to friendly lines. "This Battalion . . . had to fight its way back to Bastogne because of this lack of information." His wrecked vehicles could be replaced, but not his dead soldiers.[1]

At Noville, the Germans were unleashing a titanic artillery barrage. The shelling had started at 0530, and now, nearly two hours later, it was still going strong. Everything from 88-millimeter shells to screaming meemies was smashing into the houses, barns, streets, or the rubble of what had once been a nice town. The noise was immense, overwhelming, like the sound of hundreds of thunderclaps.

In the root cellar of one shattered house, Private Donald Burgett and his squad were sitting around a small, flickering candle, listening to the explosions outside. In the corner, an old woman and three children were sitting atop a pile of sugar beets. The old woman was having a difficult time dealing with the shelling. "When shells landed close to our house, shaking the walls and foundation around us, she would cringe and pull a short blanket up over her head while her body convulsed with wails and sobs."

Burgett's squad leader, Sergeant Vetland, was sitting on a barrel right next to the stairs. He checked his watch. It was almost dawn, and he knew that when the sun rose and the shelling abated, the Germans would attack. A few minutes later, when the sound of explosions finally began to diminish, he stood up and said with complete authority, "Let's go."

The paratroopers climbed the stairs and exited the house. The town was covered with a leaden blanket of fog. Here and there shells were still exploding, but not with their previous intensity. Private Burgett and the other soldiers were returning to the same positions they had occupied the day before. Along the way, he looked around and almost hypnotically surveyed the awful scene of destruction. "The whole city of Noville was in flames; the buildings were in ruins. Great holes gaped in the walls of the houses . . . and the floors were scattered with broken glass and debris. Piles of bricks, stone, and rubble amidst the burning shells of buildings were all that was left of the town. The burning hulks of tanks, half-tracks, jeeps, and trucks were scattered throughout the ruined city. The broken and torn bodies of GIs lay haphazardly throughout the village. Countless German corpses formed a ghostly perimeter around Noville, scattered in uncomfortable, grotesque heaps or cremated in burned-out tanks and other vehicles of war."

Just down the street from Burgett, in a small house, Major Robert Harwick, the new Airborne CO, was indulging in a brief moment of quiet contemplation. "How is it at home?" he wondered. "I'm glad they don't know the spot I'm in."

Harwick was glad that he had written to his family before coming to Noville. He knew that a German attack was imminent, and he silently hoped he possessed the strength to lead his men through the coming battle. He glanced around the little room. "The men were tense, staring out into the darkness. They could see nothing, but it was too quiet." Major Harwick mentally reviewed the placement of his companies, partly to occupy his mind and partly to make sure he had thought of every possible contingency. He sat down and waited. More than anything else, he wished for a good, hot cup of coffee.

In the cellar of a house at the northern edge of Noville, Private James Simms was listening to the ominous sounds of German voices in the darkness outside. Simms was still relatively new to combat. The day before had been his baptism of fire. He had spent much of it in this cellar, serving as an assistant gunner on a bazooka team with a gunner whom he barely knew.

A native of Moulton, Alabama, Simms was the proud possessor of a degree from Auburn University. Before the war, he had been a high school teacher and a football coach. If he could live through today, he would turn twenty-six tomorrow.

But right now, his impending birthday was the farthest thing from his mind. He was leaning forward, peering out of a small window into the foggy darkness, listening to the German voices. "It sounded like a bunch of drunks on Saturday afternoon. They were yelling and whooping, and someone would start up a tank and make it sound like a teenager trying to scratch off at the drive-in." A few minutes later, the tanks were on the Houffalize road, clearly heading for Simms and the defenders of Noville. Simms pulled a bazooka shell out of his bag, yanked off the safety pin, and wired the shell into place. Outside, there were so many tanks that "the ground actually trembled." The same could be said for Private Simms.

Just off the Houffalize road, two enemy tanks aggressively burst into the northern ring of the American perimeter, just behind Private Simms's house but out of his line of sight. There were other American bazooka teams out there, though. The German tanks opened fire on a jeep, blasting it to pieces. In the fog, the enemy crewmen did not see an American bazooka team sneak up on them. The gunner fired. The rocket struck home, and the tank burst into flames. Not far away, Staff Sergeant Lesniak, a tank commander, was on the ground, eyeballing the exact location of the other enemy tank. He ran back to his tank and ordered his driver to edge up Noville's main street until they could see the panzer. The gunner fired a quick shot that destroyed the German tank. An enemy crewman popped out of a hatch, desperately trying to run away. Sergeant Major

Jones (the same man from the Houffalize road OP) spotted him, took aim with his Browning automatic rifle (BAR), and killed him on the spot.

There was another tank right outside of Private Simms's cellar window. He and his gunner could not see it through the fog, but they could hear it. The rumbling sounds grew louder by the minute. The ground and the house continued to shake. The bogey wheels of the tank made their distinct squeaking noises. The gunner kept maneuvering his bazooka every which way, hoping for a good shot, but his field of vision was narrow. Outside, the tank drove right over an American mine, prompting a deafening explosion. The gunner emitted a hysterical, almost maniacal, laugh: "That will fix them sons-of-bitches!"

He was wrong. There were several more explosions as the tank tripped other mines, but it kept coming. Private Simms figured it was about thirty yards away now. In the next instant, it unleashed a main gun round, right into the house. To Simms it seemed as if the whole world was exploding and the house would collapse, but it didn't. His platoon sergeant let out an awful scream as shrapnel tore into his back.

Private Simms thought this was the end. As far as he knew, they were being attacked by an overwhelming armored force, while he and his buddies had no tanks of their own to fight back with. In the next few minutes, he was sure, they would all die in that crummy little basement. Nausea and a deep sense of gloom settled over Simms. He would have no more birthdays, no future of any kind. "I was seized by a terrible sinking feeling that almost knocked me out. I felt physically sick. The main feeling I had was a numb overwhelming dread of oblivion. I thought briefly of home and the good life that may have lay ahead for me. I had the feeling that the solar system would keep spinning forever, but I would not get to see any of it."

Although he was convinced he was about to die, he could not even consider running away. Simms did not want to survive at the expense of his dignity and manhood. "I found myself in the unhappy position of literally choosing to die. If you don't think that is earthshaking, try it sometime. I can promise you that you'll never be the same again."

But much to Private Simms's delight and surprise, the German tank did not close in for the kill. It stayed in place and was soon joined by a couple of others. Together they unleashed machine-gun fire up and down the street. Simms and his gunner still could not get a good shot at them. Elsewhere in the basement, a lieutenant was calling in friendly artillery. The shells were exploding impossibly close; they were probably deterring the enemy tankers from advancing any farther.

Meanwhile, the platoon sergeant was suffering from a wound caused by an inch-square fragment that went all the way through him and was pressing against the skin of his abdomen. He was unconscious, "pale and waxy-looking as a corpse." Nearby, another wounded man was sitting with his back against the cellar wall, fidgeting uncomfortably from the pain of a terrible eye wound. His eyeball was hanging halfway down his cheek in a bloody, viscous mix of goo.

Machine-gun fire from the German tanks was closer now, spattering against the house. Since they still could not get a good bazooka shot off, the lieutenant ordered Simms and another soldier to go upstairs and snipe at the tank commanders. Ever so carefully, they climbed the stairs. One tank was just outside, probably no more than fifteen yards away. Simms covered the rear while the other soldier lined up a shot at a tank commander. He raised his rifle, took a shot, crouched down, and chuckled in disgust: "Missed the son of a bitch." The volume of enemy machine-gun fire grew. A few seconds later, the rifleman took another shot. "Got him." They heard the tank motors revving. Amazingly, the German tanks retreated.

But that was in just one small part of the battlefield. The Germans were attacking from every direction, prompting yet another "barroom brawl" type of fight. The fog limited visibility to ten or twenty yards. German tanks and infantry were all over the place, fighting in small, disjointed groups. Copious amounts of rubble and wrecked vehicles, combined with the fog, made it difficult for the Germans to coordinate their attack.

One Tiger blundered right into the middle of town, ten yards away from Captain Bud Billet's B Company CP. Billet was perhaps the most highly respected officer in the entire 20th Armored Infantry Battalion. "He was so dependable, never shirked responsibility and inspired us to do the right thing," Private Lou Cerutti said. In the estimation of another one of his soldiers, he was "the greatest natural leader of men I have ever known. He was so respected by the men of B Company that if he led the way, they would follow him single file over a cliff."

Now Captain Billet looked out of his window and saw the Tiger's gun muzzle steadily rotating right toward him. At that moment, he knew that he was staring death in the face. Under his breath, he muttered a prayer for deliverance.

Twenty yards down the street, Staff Sergeant Lesniak saw the Tiger, rotated his turret slightly to the right, and told his gunner to fire at will. The gunner fired three shots, all of which hit the Tiger but did not damage it. The enemy crewmen did not wish to press their luck, though. The German driver threw the tank into reverse and backed up blindly. The sixty-eight-ton monster ran over a jeep, crushing it, but then bumped into a half-track. Since the jeep was still caught under its track, like a squashed bug on a shoe, the Tiger was having trouble maneuvering. It crashed into the half-track, careened out of control, and started to tip over. The panicked crew abandoned the tank and escaped into the fog. In the CP, Captain Billet sighed in relief. His prayer for deliverance had been answered.

Just southwest of Noville, a few yards off the N15 highway, Staff Sergeant Bill Kerby's mortar platoon was keeping very busy. His 81-millimeter-gun crews were pumping out shells as fast as they could. Most of the shells were exploding to the northeast, complicating enemy tank movement and perhaps causing casualties among the German infantry soldiers. Now Kerby had a problem. Enemy artillery had knocked out his phone communication with his forward observer, who was holed up in a house deeper into Noville. Kerby and another soldier were on the way to the observer with a new phone line when they saw an American tank pull up. The tank commander, Sergeant Jack Baker, was an old friend of Kerby's. The two men stopped to talk for a moment and then Kerby resumed his journey.

All of a sudden, a German tank appeared from behind a wrecked house, no more than thirty yards away. Kerby and the other man scrambled for cover. The sergeant looked back and saw his friend Baker maneuver his tank into a perfect firing position. *"Boom! Boom!* He knocked the track" off the enemy tank. Kerby continued his original mission, reestablished communications with his observer, and then came back. By that time, some GIs had dropped grenades into the damaged enemy tank. "Everything exploded. All the ammunition in the tank. There was five guys in the tank. Well, that was the end of them. A ball of fire [rose up]. It was unbelievable." In its death throes, the flaming tank came to a stop very close to Kerby's mortar pits. "It heated up our place. We were about twenty yards away and you could feel the heat from it." The rotten, charred stench of the incinerated German crewmen inundated the whole area.

A couple of blocks away, Private First Class Jack Garrity, the Philadelphian from B Company, 20th Armored Infantry, was hunting tanks with a mixed group of airborne and armored infantry soldiers. An airborne captain collared this small group and said: "Follow me to the death." Garrity glanced at his buddy, Private Lou Cerutti from New York, and said, "This guy's nuts!" Even so, they followed him.

They worked their way along the wall of a house. On the other side of the house, they heard a German tank shooting at some unseen target. The captain hoisted Garrity up to the roof so that he could drop a grenade into one of the tank's hatches. Garrity peeked over the edge of the roof and saw an enemy machine gunner pointing his ominous weapon right at the roof. Garrity lowered his head just as the gunner pressed his trigger.

Luckily the bullets were too high. Garrity slid down to the street and related what had happened, and the soldiers moved on.

A few minutes later, Private First Class Garrity saw another German tank in the middle of a street. He grabbed a bazooka from someone, Cerutti loaded him, and he sneaked up on the tank from the side. When Garrity was about twenty-five yards away, he stood upright and aimed. "I fired the bazooka. It hit the tank, but didn't explode. It hit the side." Garrity tossed the bazooka aside, and they all got out of there before the tank could spot them and return fire.

At the same time, in a stone barn in northeastern Noville, Private William Stone was sitting over a radio, relaying instructions for artillery fire from his CO, Lieutenant Francis Canham. By now the Americans had plenty of artillery in place around Bastogne, including Stone's 321st Glider Field Artillery Battalion of the 101st Airborne Division. The battalion's 75-millimeter pack howitzers were firing from positions a few miles to the south.

Canham and a soldier named Plummer were on the second floor of the barn, peering through the fog at the ridges outside of Noville. Those ridges were crawling with German soldiers and tanks. As Canham spotted targets, he called them down to Stone, who in turn radioed them to the fire direction center several miles away. Canham's fire was doing damage to the Germans. His shells blanketed the open areas around Noville, damaging tanks and wounding infantry soldiers.

There was plenty of return fire too. "The Germans were pounding the village . . . with everything they had," Stone wrote. "The piercing whistle of incoming projectiles followed by the sounds of their explosions assaulted our ears. Their blasts buffeted our bodies. The sharp, bitter smell of the exploded powder invaded our nostrils."

At one point, an enemy tank shell slammed into a second-floor window. Plummer called Stone and told him to come upstairs quickly because Canham was hit. "I grabbed the platoon aid man and went upstairs." They were too late. Lieutenant Canham was dead, and Stone was filled with sadness. "He was a skillful, well-trained officer who pushed the fight to the enemy. He never let up." Plummer now did the spotting, and Stone returned to his radio downstairs.

Across the street from the ruined schoolhouse that had been Major William Desobry's CP, Private First Class Jerry Goolkasian was in his Sherman scanning the fog for targets. He could hear scores of German tanks and troops, but he could not see them. In the last couple of hours, since the German attack began, Goolkasian's Sherman had fired at several targets, but he and his fellow crewmen were not sure whether they had hit anything.

Now he and Private First Class Delmer Hildoer—his nominal commander—spotted multiple enemy soldiers coming over a slight rise, right
toward them. "We . . . fired with the .50-caliber 'cause the Germans were
coming up like crazy," Goolkasian said. The fire laced through them,
tearing chunks from their vulnerable bodies, breaking up their attack.

Hildoer fired so continuously that he exhausted his ammo and melted
the machine gun's barrel. "I'll go down and get some more ammunition,"
he told Goolksasian, "you get the barrel off."

Goolkasian popped out of his hatch and stood at the gun. With the
special gloves necessary to change the hot barrel, he unscrewed the old
one and put on the new one. Hildoer was just emerging from the hatch.
Goolkasian turned toward him and then heard a whooshing sound: "There
was this flash in front of me and my left arm was just hanging like a limp
rag and the blood was pouring off it." Goolkasian's arm was barely hanging on to the rest of his body. Fragments also tore into Hildoer, lacerating
his ear and stunning him badly. Goolkasian thought that a mortar shell
had exploded on the back deck of the tank. Hildoer thought it was an
artillery shell.

Goolkasian screamed, "I'm hit!" Hildoer asked him if he could make
it to the 101st Airborne aid station near the church. Goolkasian thought
he could. With his good arm, Private First Class Goolkasian grabbed a
grease gun, slid down the front deck of the Sherman, and landed on his
rump. At that exact moment, the fog lifted like blinds on a window. In the
distance, maybe seventy-five yards away, a German tank saw them and
fired. The shell exploded right in front of the Sherman. "It blew my shoe
off my right foot and I got about ten or twelve pieces [of shrapnel]
through my helmet." Badly wounded though he was, he noticed he was
sitting right next to a dead paratrooper. Just then, an airborne medic came
up to the dead trooper, looked him over, and saw that he was gone. The
medic turned his attention to Goolkasian and helped him up.

The wounded tanker threw an arm around the trooper's neck and
limped on his good foot all the way to the church aid station. The medics
gave him a couple of pints of blood and some morphine and bandaged
him up. His left hand was shot up badly. His arm was still barely attached
to his body. He had nerve damage in his right foot. He lay on a stretcher,
just one of a growing number of wounded, groaning men.

The Germans were swinging around Noville in a pincers movement,
attempting to cut the town off. At the southeastern edge of the village,
Corporal Colby Ricker, the tank destroyer gunner, saw several German
tanks on a ridge some three hundred yards away. "We immediately started
firing. Luckily, my first round . . . was a hit. With the range established, it
was simply a matter of traverse from one target to another." He and his

loader, Private Ellie McManus, had been together since their training in the States. They were a deadly combination. As McManus loaded, Ricker fired. To Ricker, it seemed as if every shot scored a hit. Time after time, he saw enemy crewmen bailing out of their tanks, only to be gunned down by his commander, Sergeant Richard Beaster, who was standing in the turret, blazing away with the destroyer's .50-caliber gun.

Other German attackers, out of Ricker's field of vision, were steadily advancing, closing the ring around Noville. On the eastern edges of town, the paratroopers of A Company, 506th Parachute Infantry, were practically fighting hand-to-hand with the Germans. Enemy tanks were overrunning the American slit trenches and foxholes. Private First Class Steve Polander looked to the right and saw them tearing into a group of paratroopers. "Death struggle screams can be heard." A bazooka team ran around a tank, squeezed off several shots, and destroyed it.

In that same embattled position, Private Burgett and his foxhole buddy, Private Siber Speer, ducked as low into their hole as they could get. They did not have a bazooka, so they planned to wait for the tanks to pass them and then kill the infantry behind them. "A Panther headed straight for our foxhole," Burgett recalled. "Its left track crunched over our hole, tumbling dirt down on us. We didn't dare look up. It stopped."

They were trapped, breathing stale fumes. "If he gets hit and burns, we'll be roasted alive," Burgett said.

"Just pray," Speer replied.

Burgett, an agnostic, was underwhelmed by the idea of praying. Speer was a devoted Catholic. They were lucky. The tank moved on.

So did many others, only to meet determined, accurate fire from the U.S. armor in the town. In the meantime, Burgett and the other foot soldiers rose up and opened fire on the trailing enemy soldiers. "We . . . tore jagged holes in the enemy's lines with rifle and machine-gun fire. All up and down the line I could hear small arms popping. We could see the Germans fire their weapons, work their bolts, and then fire again. We could see them fall as our withering barrage tore through their ranks. Some kicked and thrashed, others screamed, and some just went down hard and lay still." Artillery only added to the carnage. Private Burgett noticed many of the German tanks retreating from the town, back beyond the ridges.

Stalemate once again ruled at Noville. As with their previous attacks, the Germans failed to take Noville. But they had cut the N15 and were slowly establishing a solid perimeter around the American defenders of Noville. Major Charles Hustead was not sure what to do next, because he was out of radio communication with Colonel Roberts. To make matters worse, his tanks were running out of armor-piercing shells.

In the airborne CP, Major Harwick understood that though the Americans were still holding Noville, time was running short for them: "Our aid station was full and we opened another cellar. It was obvious that our losses were making gaps in our line, which could not be plugged. The command post personnel, switchboard operators, clerks—also slightly wounded men, were sent to the companies." Like Hustead, he was out of touch with his superiors and not certain what he should do. His last communication from them had read: "Hold at all costs." Harwick knew that would soon be impossible. "Another attack—surely two—would end the affair for us. We drew up plans to fight a withdrawal." He sent out a jeep with two wounded men and a volunteer messenger. Their orders were to dash south, through the German lines, to General Anthony McAuliffe in Bastogne. The message was curt: "We can hold out, but not indefinitely." There was no reply.[2]

2

Several miles to the south, the Germans were still hoping to take Bastogne with quick, slashing attacks. Already that morning, they had sent a battalion from the 26th Volksgrenadier Division, supported by two tanks and two self-propelled guns, into an attack against Lieutenant Colonel Julian Ewell's lines at Bizory. "They were engaged at long range by . . . machine guns and by all of the artillery which McAuliffe could turn loose on them from Bastogne," Ewell said. "POWs who were later captured from this battalion said that their losses from artillery had been terrific." Ewell also had a platoon of M18 Hellcats from B Company, 705th Tank Destroyer Battalion, at his disposal. The Hellcats destroyed three of the enemy tanks, effectively eliminating the mobility of the failed attack.

At 1115, General Fritz Bayerlein's Panzer Lehr made a push for Marvie with a self-propelled gun, four tanks, and six half-tracks. The town itself was defended by five light tanks from Team O'Hara. Just east of Marvie, E and G Companies of the newly arrived 327th Glider Infantry Regiment were dug into defensive positions.

As artillery shells rained down on Marvie, the enemy came from the woods southeast of town, on the right flank. Led by the tanks, they leapfrogged closer and closer. Soon they spotted Lieutenant Colonel Jim O'Hara's light tanks and opened up on them. The German armor was still well beyond the range of the 37-millimeter peashooters on the little American tanks. Rather than be slaughtered in place, the American tank commander asked O'Hara for permission to withdraw, and the colonel assented.

"The tanks played hide and seek among the falling buildings as they made for the edge of town, but were not entirely successful," O'Hara recalled. An artillery shell set one tank on fire, but it managed to escape. A second one took a direct hit in its suspension system, but it also got away.

Facing such light resistance and sensing that they had found a vulnerable flank, the Germans closed in for the kill. "They were maybe 500 yards away or so," Private First Class John Sherman, a G Company trooper, said. "We could see the infantry moving toward us alongside the tanks and it looked like the whole German army. The incoming fire was heavy." Sherman and his G Company comrades stayed put, shot back, and resisted as best they could. The Germans got closer by the minute.

Not far away, Lieutenant Alfred Regenburg, a G Company officer, was standing at the edge of Marvie, on a road near the battalion command post. He saw four of the light tanks "hell bent for election . . . coming right past us. I ran out to the road, fired a shot to get their attention to stop and form a defensive position with us." They roared past him, paying him no attention at all. "There was no turning back for them. They just went on through the village."

The German tanks and half-tracks smashed through the right flank of the American line and overran many of the E and G Company foxholes. Troopers stubbornly resisted, to the death. The Germans machine-gunned or blasted many of them in their holes. Some of the Americans died from concussion. Others had their guts or chest cavities ripped open by machine-gun bullets. A few were nearly cut in half.

The Germans were in Marvie now, fighting house to house. Private First Class Donald Rich was in a small house with another man, waiting for a good bazooka shot. They heard a Mark IV rolling slowly down the street. Before they could get a shot off, the tank fired at them: "[It] blew a hole about three or four feet in diameter. I went rolling across the floor. I jumped up to see how my buddy made out. He came staggering out of the room. I rushed him to the medics. I never knew if he had serious wounds or if he made it." The bazooka was damaged beyond repair.

Elsewhere in Marvie, another tank shell wounded Lieutenant Colonel Roy Inman, the battalion commander, and one of his company commanders. Major R. B. Galbraieth, Inman's executive officer, took over, but the situation was so chaotic that it was difficult for him to do much.

On a hill to the west, Colonel Joseph Harper, commander of the 327th, was watching the battle unfold. As it happened, he had a perfect view into Marvie. He saw the enemy tanks, half-tracks, and infantry soldiers battering their way along the streets of the little village, shooting up houses. Harper radioed the 2nd battalion CP and got Major Galbraieth, who told the colonel about Inman's wounding. "Are you still in the village?" Harper asked.

"Yes, but the Germans are here also," Major Galbraieth replied. "We expect to drive them out."

To do that, they would need help from U.S. armor, and now they got it. Seven hundred yards north of Marvie, Lieutenant Colonel O'Hara had wisely placed several of his Sherman tanks in a spot where they could cover Marvie. As the German armor plunged deeper into town, steadily moving north, the Sherman crews spotted them and opened fire. In a matter of minutes, they destroyed two Mark IVs and a half-track. A third Mark IV attempted to retreat, only to fall victim to a bazooka. The self-propelled gun got hit simultaneously by tank and bazooka fire. A colossal explosion ripped the vehicle apart, sending chunks of steel and flesh in every direction. Smoke curled from the remains, as ammo cooked off and the crewmen burned to cinders.

With most of the enemy tanks destroyed, the glider troopers now set about the task of winning back the town, house by house. For an hour or two they fought confused, isolated groups of Germans. At the battalion CP, someone collared Private First Class Charles Fisher and told him to get medical help for Lieutenant Colonel Inman. Earlier that morning, Fisher had seen the medics setting up in a barn at the edge of town, so he headed in that direction. Along the way, he came face-to-face with a German soldier. "I looked at him and he looked at me. We both fired at each other; both missed."

Fisher hightailed it to the barn but found it locked. "I pounded on it and yelled for someone to open the door." There was no response, so he worked his way to a house that was attached to the barn. He looked in a window and saw several civilians. "They saw me and began screaming at me and motioning for me to go away." This angered Fisher. What the hell were they talking about? Why weren't they helping him? He broke the window, unlocked it, crawled inside, and began walking toward the barn. All the while, the civilians were clustered around him, yelling at him. "One elderly woman grabbed [my] arm and tried to pull me back. I shook her loose, continued down the hall, and turned into the barn. It was rather dark in the barn but I could make out silhouettes of people coming toward me wearing long overcoats."

The sight of the overcoats caused something to click in Fisher's mind. Paratroopers do not wear overcoats, he realized. He raised his rifle to his shoulder and fired seven quick rounds at the overcoated shapes. "I immediately turned, ran down the hall, through the room of excited civilians, dove back out the window, and crouched down beside a stone wall."

He decided to run back to the battalion CP. "En route, I found the new location of the medics, [and] told them Colonel Inman had been hit . . . which, by this time, they already knew. I was just part of the ten percent who never gets the word."

There were many other such confused skirmishes, but by early afternoon, the Americans had reclaimed Marvie. The Germans had lost three Mark IVs, a self-propelled gun, several half-tracks, and at least thirty dead infantrymen. They had also failed in yet another attempt to knife their way into Bastogne. For them, time had just about run out.[3]

At northeastern Noville, Private Stone, sitting over his little radio, got the withdrawal order first. By now—1300 hours—he was the only one who had any communication with the outside. Majors Harwick and Hustead had both tried to send messengers to Bastogne and back, but this had achieved nothing.

Now Stone listened as the order to withdraw crackled over his radio. General Anthony McAuliffe and Colonel Roberts had decided that Noville could no longer be held—the garrison would have to retreat to Bastogne while it was still possible. The plan was for elements of the 506th and 502nd Parachute Infantry Regiments to attack north toward Foy, diverting German attention while the Noville survivors escaped south on the N15. Stone immediately relayed the order to Major Harwick, who in turn told Hustead.

This set in motion a flurry of activity. At the church, demolition teams wired up heavy ordnance for detonation—81-millimeter mortar shells, mines, or whatever else the hard-pressed Americans could not carry—rather than leave it behind for the Germans. They also wanted to create a rubble-choked roadblock in the middle of town. Officers and NCOs organized the remaining vehicles into a motley convoy. Soldiers drifted to and fro, waiting for the word to hop on their assigned vehicles and leave. Medics gingerly hoisted their patients onto jeeps, half-tracks, or trucks.

At the barroom aid station, Dr. Jack Prior, the young physician from Vermont, was evacuating several of his patients even before he heard about the withdrawal order. One of his drivers backed a medical half-track up to the tavern door and then got out to retrieve something. Prior and Dr. Lee Naftulin, his dentist colleague, helped put four litter casualties into the back of the half-track. There were two litters on each side. "There was a big Red Cross on the back door of the half-track," Prior remembered. "At that point, a German tank came around the corner," out of the fog, "and zeroed in on the half-track. He put a shell right through that Red Cross . . . between the four guys that were in there, through the back of the seat, through the motor and out. The vehicle immediately caught fire."

Prior and Naftulin ran into the street and hauled the wounded men off their litters, out of the burning half-track "right under the gaze of the German tank commander. He didn't fire again." Fortunately, the patients were not burned or hurt further in any way. "They never knew anything had happened."

At this point, someone from Major Hustead's CP ran into the barroom and hollered: "We're leaving, Doc! Come on!"

"I can't go," Prior replied. "No way. I have no wheels anymore."

The man shrugged, told him everyone was supposed to leave Noville in ten minutes, and left.

Lieutenant Prior did not have enough vehicles or litters to transport all of his patients. What on earth was he supposed to do? He could not abandon them. The young doctor thought a moment and then made a decision. He went down to the cellar where most of his men were taking shelter, along with the elderly couple who owned this place. Everyone looked at him expectantly. "I need some help," he said. "I'm gonna surrender these wounded men and I'm gonna stay with 'em. I want some of you volunteers to stay with me."

No one said a thing. At first Prior's men had been staring right at him. Now they were all looking away, as if suddenly they were avidly interested in their shoelaces. The awkward silence continued for several more moments. "At this point my first sergeant seized the initiative." He had a better idea. He ran upstairs, into the street, and asked a group of tankers for some help. Together they ripped every door in the tavern from its hinges and used them as improvised litters. Ever so carefully they strapped each patient to a door and lifted him aboard a tank or some other vehicle, all the while under fire.

In the meantime, Hustead and Harwick had finalized an exodus plan. Dismounted troopers from C Company, 506th Parachute Infantry, would take the lead, along with an M8 armored car, four half-tracks, and five Shermans. There were at least fifty wounded men who could not walk. They would ride on an assortment of vehicles behind this point element. Behind them would be the bulk of the half-tracks and other vehicles. A platoon of Hellcats from C Company, 705th Tank Destroyer Battalion, would bring up the rear. When everyone left the town, an engineer lieutenant would set off a delayed charge to explode the ordnance.

At 1315, as the Americans prepared to leave, a blanket of fog descended over Noville again. The GIs could hardly have asked for anything more desirable. For the last couple of hours, there had been no fog, so visibility was very good. Many of the troops had worried that they would be sitting ducks on the ruler-straight N15. But the fog now afforded them a screen of sorts.

At last, the column moved out, even as German artillery shells still exploded around Noville. One of the tanks soon developed engine trouble. Since the Americans had little time to deal with such things, they destroyed it with thermite grenades and kept going. The M8 took off so fast that it outdistanced the column all the way to Bastogne, against no opposition. The rest of the column was still rolling through the fog. In a half-track at the front of the convoy, Private First Class Don Addor, the communications soldier who had battled a Mark VI the day before, took a last look at Noville. "There was nothing left but a pile of rubble. The last thing I saw of the town was a battered sign sticking up through a pile of rubble. It proclaimed the town's name was Noville." Addor thought that the carcass of the town should be renamed "No-village." The whole spectacle saddened him because only two days earlier, the town had been a pretty little place. Fewer than two days of fighting had reduced it to a shattered husk. The American ammo exploded, collapsing the church steeple into the street, adding to the debris.

In another half-track, Private James Simms, the bazooka man from Alabama, was curiously eyeing a young German prisoner who could speak a little English. The kid said he was only seventeen years old. He had been shot through the calf, but he seemed very relieved to be a prisoner. A paratrooper grabbed the prisoner's wrist and started to yank off his watch. "Leave the damn boy alone!" Simms barked. The other troopers in the track agreed: "Let him keep the damned watch!" The would-be thief backed off.

A few minutes later, the column was about five hundred yards north of Foy. So far, the trip had been quiet. In the lead half-track, an armored shutter accidentally slid over the driver's slit, obscuring his vision. The driver reached up to push it away. Major James Duncan, Hustead's executive officer, was sitting in the passenger seat, next to the driver. Duncan thought that the driver had been wounded, so he pulled the hand brake, halting the half-track. The next one in line had no brakes, so it rammed into the back of Duncan's half-track. At the same moment, German soldiers opened fire from ditches and from a house about ten yards away. A short firefight ensued. Machine gunners in the half-tracks sprayed deadly fire on the Germans in the ditches, killing at least ten and prompting the others to flee. Sergeant Larry Stein and several other soldiers dismounted and fired at the retreating shapes of enemy soldiers. As they did so, Captain Waddell, the battalion operations officer, covered them with a .50-caliber machine gun. The shooting died down. When it did, they mounted up again, and three of the half-tracks went on to Bastogne.

By then, Major Duncan was on the ground farther to the rear of the column, trying to bring up tanks to fire on the German-held house. Major Hustead soon joined him. They had some trouble finding tankers who were willing, or able, to get their Shermans forward.

By the time they got two Shermans into Foy, the Germans were on alert and waiting. They had three tanks on the east side of the road, in perfect ambush positions, plus more infantrymen both in Foy and on either side of the road. Moreover, the American column had lost its forward momentum. The accordion effect set in as vehicles stopped and started, and as troops dismounted, milled around, and wondered what was happening.

At Foy, the two Shermans hosed down the house, set it on fire, and started to back away, but Duncan ordered them forward again. The first Sherman complied and, in the process, rolled right into the kill zone of a waiting enemy tank. "It was a beautiful ambush, if I must say so," one American soldier later wrote. The German fired and scored a direct hit. Private First Class Addor was in his half-track, not far away, and he heard the ugly, torn-metal shriek of the shell slamming into the Sherman. "The silence was shattered by a loud blast. The fog up front turned bright orange. There were a couple more blasts and then all hell broke loose."

The Germans destroyed the other Sherman and then opened fire all up and down the line of American vehicles. In the middle of the column, Private First Class Jerry Goolkasian, the badly wounded tanker, was lying in the back of a half-track, listening to the sound of enemy burp guns. He was semidelirious and could not understand why the driver had stopped the half-track and dismounted. Goolkasian only knew that he wanted to get out of here, back to Bastogne or some other place where they had a nice hospital. "Get this fucking thing going!" he yelled at the half-track driver. "It's only a burp gun!"

As Private First Class Goolkasian screamed ineffectively at the half-track driver, his commander, Captain William Schultz, was in a third Sherman rolling past the two that had been destroyed. Schultz's tank made it into and through Foy. He glanced to the left and noticed Lieutenant Joe Reed and several other airborne troopers along the side of the road. Reed and his platoon from C Company, 506th Parachute Infantry, had been walking point for the whole column. When the shooting started, they had worked their way to this spot just south of Foy.

Captain Schultz looked at Reed and asked, "What the hell is going on?"

Reed and his men had just killed a German machine-gun crew. Not far away, they had also seen German tank crewmen scrambling aboard their vehicles. "Get the hell out of here!" he warned Schultz.

A couple of seconds later, three armor-piercing shells slammed into Schultz's tank. One of them went through the driver's side, killing the driver instantly and setting the tank on fire. Private First Class Delmer Hildoer was sitting on the floor of the turret, right behind the driver. He caught several hunks of shrapnel in his legs. He was already badly wounded, doped up on morphine, and missing an ear from the shell that had wounded his fellow crewman Jerry Goolkasian that morning.

Now he and the captain desperately tried to scramble out of the burning tank. Another man, the loader, got shot in the face as he tried to exit. He slumped back, but Hildoer pushed him out. The captain hurled himself out of the tank and landed right on Lieutenant Reed. Then it was Hildoer's turn: "As I got out on the right hand side of the tank . . . there were three Germans near the tank and I knew I was going to get it. I grabbed a tommy gun from the side of the tank and shot them before they got me. I jumped up and joined Captain Schultz . . . on the other side of the tank."

On the other side of Foy, the volume of enemy fire sweeping up and down the halted column was increasing. Lieutenant Prior, the doctor, had been walking alongside a jeep, monitoring the condition of several of his wounded soldiers when the shooting started. Now he and Naftulin were on their bellies, hugging the bottom of a ditch. "Lying in the ditch and having sniper fire chip away at a fence post beside me was a terrifying experience." It seemed like every time that Prior raised his head even an inch, the unseen enemy soldiers fired and chipped away some more at the fence post, further pinning down the two medical officers.

Prior and Naftulin were lying head to head. Prior peeked from under the rim of his Red Cross–adorned helmet and asked his colleague, "Naf, do you think we're gonna get out of this?"

Naftulin was wearing a regular M1 helmet with no Red Cross. He said, "If you take off the helmet with the Red Cross, we'd be better off. They can see that."

But Prior could not bring himself to get rid of his helmet. Up on the road he could hear many of his wounded soldiers calling for help. "[They] were hollering and screaming to be taken off the vehicles because the Germans were on both sides of the road. They were strafing the road and hitting the vehicles. Two of my men ran out and pulled out one or two people . . . that had been hit." These were men "whose reputation in the unit would have given no clue to the fact that under stress they could meet this challenge."

All up and down the column, American soldiers dismounted, taking cover in ditches and firing back as best they could. The whole area was under intensifying mortar and artillery fire. Private First Class Boyd Etters, a soldier in the Headquarters Company of the 20th Armored Infantry Battalion, was just off the road with a small group of soldiers. They were looking for targets, shooting at whatever seemed threatening, when a mortar shell landed right in their midst. "I caught the concussion of an artillery explosion in my eyes. I was lucky, for the three fellows around me got it for good." He had a nasty headache and was having trouble seeing, but he kept fighting.

Elsewhere, Private First Class Addor dismounted from his half-track and came under withering small-arms fire. A few yards away, a medic was working on an armless man. An artillery shell exploded above them. Addor was unscathed, but the medic was hit. He got up, ran halfway across the road, and said to a buddy: "Hey Charlie! I'm hit!" Then he went down. He had a huge hole through his back and his chest. His blood was pumping onto the road. He was dead in seconds.

Addor took shelter in a snowy ditch. "My feet hit the helmet of the guy right behind me. He was lying there still and dead." It was the same officer who, the day before, had promised to put him in for a Silver Star. Addor looked over the embankment onto the road. "What a mess! Dead were lying all around on the road and in the ditches. Some were hanging out of their vehicles. Trucks and half-tracks were either burning or had been torn to shreds by the enemy fire."

He was seized with an overwhelming impulse to get away from this carnage. He got up, ran to the other side of the road, and heard an explosion. "I was blown into the air. I landed flat on my back." He was unconscious for a few moments. When he regained his senses, he checked himself over and found a piece of shrapnel sticking out of the small of his back. "There was no blood and it didn't hurt."

Still groggy from concussion, Private First Class Addor got up and started walking again. Then he heard the awful sound of a burp gun. Bullets whipped past his nose, so close that he could feel their heat. Two of the bullets struck his right leg, through the shin bone and calf, cutting the artery. "I was sure my time was up and I would soon be joining my dead comrades that lay all around me."

He waited to die, all the while thinking of his parents and his girlfriend. When nothing happened, he heard a voice in his head say, "You're not dead yet!" He looked at the trousers that covered his right leg and saw that they were inundated with blood. He knew that an artery had been cut and that he would have to apply a tourniquet or he would bleed to death. Although he was light-headed, he managed to convert his cartridge belt into a makeshift tourniquet and pull it tight enough for the moment. Relieved, he lay back. But now, in the distance, through the fog, he heard German voices getting closer, and he wondered yet again if he was about to die.

As Private First Class Addor lay by the side of the road struggling to live, the convoy got moving again. Duncan, Hustead, Captain Billet, and a slew of others realized that the best way to get out of this mess would be to skirt around Foy on foot or in vehicles through the fields west of town, and loop around the Germans. With no semblance of any organization, groups of men and vehicles were now doing just that.

Private Burgett had started the journey perched atop a Hellcat at the rear of the column with the TDs. He had seen this platoon of TDs—under the able command of Lieutenant Tom E. Thoms, who would one day be the grandfather of pro golfer David Thoms—ward off several Mark Vs just outside of Noville. In the subsequent fighting, Burgett had gotten separated from the Hellcats.

Now Burgett was in the back of a truck near Foy, roaring away with a .50-caliber. "I was . . . firing, as were the rest of the men of the convoy. Some of the Germans fell kicking, trying to crawl or roll back into the ditch beside the road. Still others went down and lay still, not moving at all. The bodies of friend and foe alike lay scattered about."

American soldiers were scrambling out of ditches, hopping onto moving trucks, jeeps, or half-tracks. The whole area was under intense enemy fire. The key was to keep moving. "What remained of the convoy made its way south through a barrage of exploding shells and streams of tracers and other bullets. The trucks and half-tracks bounced and rocked as they . . . made their way over rough ground. Engines whined and wheels spun." Private Burgett's truck circled through the bumpy fields west of Foy and careened over a ditch, back onto the N15 and toward Bastogne. Many others did the same.

At the same time, Private First Class Addor heard the sounds of German voices gradually recede into the fog. He lay back and contemplated his situation. He was out here, alone, in enemy territory. Every other American who was still alive seemed to be gone. But then he heard a jeep driving down the road. He summoned all of his strength and yelled at whoever was driving the jeep. It skidded to a stop, and Addor was glad to see Corporal Still, the CO's jeep driver. He and an airborne medic were lost, trying to find their way to Bastogne. The medic dumped sulfa powder on his wound and bandaged it.

Corporal Still stepped gently on the gas pedal, and they weaved their way around the burning vehicles along the road. As they drove around one tank, they heard a groan and found a wounded crewman inside. The medic pulled him from the tank and propped him on the hood of the jeep. Addor took one look at the tanker and knew he was in trouble.

"There was a small triangular-shaped wound on his forehead. I thought I could see his brain."

They continued their journey. Somehow they made it through Foy and back to a small aid station in Bastogne, where Dr. Prior was now treating casualties. The tank crewman was dead. Addor was not yet in pain, but he knew that he was badly wounded. Both Naftulin and Prior were bent over him, examining his leg, with obvious looks of concern on their faces. Addor pointed at the leg and said, "It's my right leg . . . Doc. I think I messed it up pretty good this time." Prior and Naftulin nodded in agreement. Addor passed out.

Just south of Foy, Major Harwick was watching the battered survivors as they filed past him into the American perimeter. "They were dirty as only fighting men can get—clothing torn and mud-caked. Two days' beard just made them appear dirtier. They had been in a rough spot. Through their own strength, they had gotten out. They had done a good job and they knew it. That spring in the step of the tired, dirty bodies and the look in the eyes told that." Harwick could hardly have been more proud of them.

The Battle of Noville was finally over. For nearly two days, a mixed group of American infantrymen and tankers had held off an attacking force that outnumbered them by at least five, perhaps even ten, to one. The price of this valor was steep. Team Desobry lost eleven out of its fifteen tanks, one self-propelled gun, eleven half-tracks, and more than a dozen trucks, and at least 63 of its soldiers were killed, wounded, or missing (including Desobry himself), out of an original complement of 325 men. The 1st Battalion, 506th Parachute Infantry, incurred even more devastating losses. The battalion had gone into Noville with 473 soldiers; 212 of them became casualties, a 45 percent rate.

The Germans suffered even more heavily. They lost thirty-one tanks and at least half a regiment of infantry soldiers. From a tactical point of view, the battle was a classic example of the inability of unsupported tanks to secure urban terrain, especially when opposed by another armored force. The Germans never coordinated their tanks and infantry together at Noville. This left their tanks isolated in a foggy urban environment and, thus, quite vulnerable to American bazooka teams and tanks. Only by surrounding Noville and unleashing massive firepower upon the town could the Germans take it. This process was tedious and inefficient. It cost them valuable time, not to mention staggering losses.

Noville itself hardly existed anymore. The town was now a shattered landscape of flaming infernos and boulderlike masonry. The Gestapo soon materialized, rounded up eight people whom they deemed to be American sympathizers, and executed them within the shadow of the church.

With the Noville crossroads now in Colonel Meinrad von Lauchert's pocket, the 2nd Panzer Division commander radioed General Walter Krueger, the CO of the LVIII Panzer Corps: "Request permission to drive on Bastogne."

The answer was prompt, decisive, and illuminating: "Forget Bastogne and head for the Meuse!"

The struggle for Bastogne had now changed from a race to a siege. The Americans had won the race for the town at a time when the Germans most needed it. Now Bastogne still mattered, but in a way different from before. It was no longer a key transit point to the Meuse for the enemy. It was now a political symbol, along with being a major disruption to their communications and resupply efforts. Bastogne now amounted to a veritable bone in their throats.[4]

3

Even as the Americans fled Noville, General McAuliffe was visiting Neufchateau for one last face-to-face meeting with General Troy Middleton. Both of them knew that Bastogne would soon be cut off.

"There are three German divisions in your area," Middleton said, "and the 116th Panzer is on its way." He told McAuliffe that Lieutenant General George Patton's 4th Armored Division was on the way, but with encirclement forthcoming, he wondered if the 101st should stay in Bastogne. "You're going to have a rough time staying there."

McAuliffe was no different from the resolute, tough paratroopers under his command—he was determined to hold Bastogne. He had plenty of artillery support, an excellent tank unit in Combat Command B at his disposal, and a decent logistical situation. "Hell, if we pull out now, we'd be chewed to pieces. I know we can hold out for at least forty-eight hours."

General Middleton assented. The airborne commander, with little more time to spare, got up, shook hands with Middleton, and turned to leave. When McAuliffe reached the doorway, Middleton smiled at him and said in an ironic tone of voice: "Now, Tony, don't get yourself surrounded." The two commanders grinned at each other, and McAuliffe left.

Outside, he climbed into his jeep and his driver took off. On the way to Bastogne, he noticed it was chillier than it had been that morning, with some flurries in the air. He sensed that a snowstorm was about to hit the area. In less than half an hour, McAuliffe's jeep made it to the Belgian barracks. Mere minutes later, as the sun set behind leaden gray clouds, the Germans cut the last road into Bastogne. The siege had begun.[5]

POSTSCRIPT

Several months after the Battle of the Bulge, General Troy Middleton found out that his old friend Colonel Hurley Fuller had been liberated from captivity. For many months, he had worried about Fuller. Was he dead or alive? Middleton did not really know. So for Middleton, the news of Fuller's liberation was welcome indeed. The general picked up his pen and wrote a warm letter to the crusty Texan: "I went over the ground where your unit fought it out with the Krauts, and left with sufficient data to leave no doubt in my mind that your outfit did a magnificent job. Had not your boys done the job they did, the 101st Airborne could not have reached Bastogne in time."

Middleton was exactly right. If Fuller's men and the rest of the 28th Division, Combat Command Reserve (CCR) of the 9th Armored and Combat Command B (CCB) of the 10th Armored, had not fought so well, the Americans would not have won the race for Bastogne. "We had to absorb the first shock and try to slow the enemy," General Norman "Dutch" Cota once explained. "Our troops were like . . . tackles in football. If we could slow up the play until the secondary defense diagnosed it and got set for the tackle, we served our purpose."

This "purpose," or "job," as General Middleton called it, was dirty indeed. It amounted to small, scared groups of poorly informed soldiers fighting tenaciously against overwhelming odds. The cost was considerable. Hundreds were killed; thousands were wounded or taken prisoner. Captivity was a nightmare for those who ended up as POWs. Most lost forty pounds or more because of disease and lack of food. Some did not survive the experience. Among those who did survive, the physical and mental scars endured forever. In exchange for their immense sacrifice, they held off a powerful German offensive for four days, costing the enemy valuable time, terrain, combat power, and, of course, Bastogne.

General Anthony McAuliffe once said, "In my opinion, Combat Command B of the 10th Armored Division never properly was credited with their important role in the Bastogne battle." The same could be said for CCR of the 9th Armored and the 28th Division. Bastogne could not have been held without the contributions of every unit that served there.

In the months and years that followed the battle for Bastogne, the 101st Airborne Division received its deserved share of plaudits, including a Distinguished Unit citation. The division's heroics have endured in popular memory, but that was not necessarily so for the contributions of its partners, for whom the paratroopers had nothing but respect. In early January 1945, General Maxwell Taylor sent a personal telegram to General John Leonard, commander of the 9th Armored Division: "The Officers and Men of the 101st Airborne Division wish to express to your command their appreciation of the gallant support rendered by Combat Command 'R' in the recent defense of Bastogne, Belgium. This division is proud to have shared the battlefield with your command." Taylor even recommended CCR for a unit citation.

Unfortunately, CCR did not get the citation. At the time Taylor made his recommendation, CCR was still on a secret list and not eligible for such a public citation. Later CCR simply got lost in the shuffle.

Nor did the 28th Division get much credit. At the end of the war General Cota submitted a recommendation that the 110th Infantry receive a Distinguished Unit Citation. The recommendation was poorly written. By the time the army bureaucracy reviewed it, neither Cota nor Middleton was around to push for it. Most of the 110th's records had been destroyed in the battle. It had gone through three commanders. Combat historians did very few interviews with soldiers from the outfit for the simple, stark reason that most had been killed, badly wounded, or captured.

To make matters worse, the officers who served on the board that reviewed such recommendations were not very familiar with what the 110th had done. They noted that the 110th had lost two thousand soldiers "missing in action" and wondered if the unit might have capitulated without fighting. The most influential voice on that board, Colonel S. L. A. Marshall, dismissed Cota's recommendation by describing the 110th's action as heroic but "not outstanding above all the others." Marshall ought to have known better, because months before the board met, General Middleton had written to him and expressed sentiments similar to what he had told Fuller: "This regiment [the 110th] . . . put up stiff resistance for three days. Had not this regiment put up the fight it did, the Germans would have been in Bastogne long before the 101st Airborne reached the town."

With no such information at their fingertips, the board turned down the citation. The 112th Infantry Regiment did receive a citation in 1947, but all subsequent attempts to award one to the 110th, including one initiated by Middleton, failed. "The bureaucratic Army awards system insists on reinforcing earlier poor decisions and refuses to go back and study the record," Colonel James Bradin, a 28th Division officer and historian of the Bulge, wrote many years after World War II. To this day, there is no official army recognition of what the 110th Infantry, the 28th Division as a whole, or CCR did east of Bastogne. Perhaps, instead, there will be some recognition in popular memory.[1]

The Bastogne corridor is peaceful now. Monuments, statues, museums, and markers adorn the region in mute testimony to the momentous events that occurred there. The ghosts are never far away, though. Somehow they are always there—in rebuilt churches, barns, homes, castles, and roads. They are there in the lonely woods that are thick with fir trees, or in the pine-needle-encrusted remnants of old foxholes. May the ghosts never be forgotten.

NOTES

Introduction

1. 28th Infantry Division, G3 Journal, December 17, 1944, Record Group (RG) 407, Entry 427, Box 8518, National Archives, College Park, Maryland (all subsequent National Archives citations are also from Entry 427); "History of the 110th Infantry Regiment," RG 407, Box 8596; 110th Infantry After Action Report, December 1944, RG 407, Box 8601; *History of the 110th Infantry Regiment, World War II*, no pagination, self-published; 28th Infantry Division Historical Record, Pennsylvania National Guard Museum, Historical Archives, Indiantown Gap, Pennsylvania (hereafter referred to as PA Guard Museum); Edwin Rensmeyer, "The Story of a Civilian Soldier," unpublished memoir, p. 15, PA Guard Museum (Rensmeyer was the intelligence officer wondering whether or not to burn the codes and signals); Colonel Hurley Fuller, "Report of Operations of the 110th Infantry Combat Team, 16–18 December," copy in author's possession; Colonel Hurley Fuller, personal background research paper by Scott S. at www.scottstrance .com; Henry Grady Spencer, *Nineteen Days in June 1944* (Kansas City, MO: Lowell Press, 1984), pp. 171–173 (Spencer was a battalion commander in the 23rd Infantry and witnessed Fuller's relief); Hugh Cole, *The United States Army in World War II: The Ardennes, Battle of the Bulge* (Washington, DC: Center of Military History, United States Army, 1994, reprint of 1965 edition), pp. 190–191; Charles B. MacDonald, *A Time for Trumpets: The Untold Story of the Battle of the Bulge* (New York: Bantam Books, 1984), pp. 134–135, 275–277; Robert F. Phillips, *To Save Bastogne* (Burke, VA: Borodino Books, 1996; reprint of 1983 edition), pp. 136–138; Frank James Price, *Troy H. Middleton: A Biography* (Baton Rouge: Louisiana State University Press, 1974), pp. 204–206 (after Fuller's Normandy relief, he disingenuously intimated to his old friend Middleton that he had been relieved for mouthing off to General Robertson).

1. Before the Fury

1. "History of Company F, 2nd Battalion, 112th Infantry," RG (Record Group) 407, Entry 427, Box 8618, National Archives, College Park, Maryland (all subsequent National Archives citations are also from Entry 427); Herman "Ham" Kramer, interview with the author, March 14, 2005.

2. Bob Bradicich, unpublished memoir, listed at his personal Web site, www.mypcpro.com/ww2/Bradicich; "Clearing Combat Diary, Co. 'D' 103rd Medical Btn. 28th Infantry Division," pp. 17–18, copy in author's possession; J. Paul Luther, unpublished memoir, p. 11, copy in author's possession. I am grateful to J. Paul Luther for giving me a copy of both diaries.

3. Roland Gaul, *The Battle of the Bulge in Luxembourg, Volume II, The Americans* (Atglen, PA: Schiffer Military, 1995), p. 80; Bernard Quinn, "The Private Who Lost and Won," *American Legion Magazine*, February 1963, pp. 14–15; "George Mergenthaler," *After the Battle*, pp. 18–20, date and author unavailable.

4. "Co. D, 103rd Medical Btn. Diary," p. 18; E. C. Wilson, interview with the author, February 4, 2005; Dorothy Chernitsky, *Voices from the Foxholes*, self-published, 1991, pp. 26–28.

5. William Pena, *As Far as Schleiden: A Memoir of World War II*, self-published, 1992, pp. 94–98; Les Eames, personal diary, December 10, 1944, copy in author's possession, courtesy of Lou Dersch.

6. "Operations of the 28th Division 16 December to 31 December 1944" (AAR), RG 407, Box 8480, National Archives; Colonel Gustin Nelson to his father, May 1945, copy of the letter in author's possession, courtesy of Pierre Eicher; Fuller, "Report of Operations"; Trevor Dupuy, David Bongard, and Richard Anderson, *Hitler's Last Gamble: The Battle of the Bulge, December 1944–January 1945* (New York: HarperCollins Publishers, 1994), pp. 103–104.

7. Charles Haug, unpublished memoir, pp. 8–11, and Veterans Questionnaire, 28th Infantry Division Survey Material, Murray Shapiro, unpublished memoir, no pagination, 28th Infantry Division Survey Material, both at United States Army Military History Institute, Carlisle, Pennsylvania (hereafter referred to as USAMHI); Charles Hogzett, "Recollections of an Infantry Lieutenant, WWII," unpublished memoir, pp. 29–31, Pennsylvania National Guard Museum, Historical Archives, Indiantown Gap, Pennsylvania (hereafter referred to as PA Guard Museum); Alexander Hadden, *Not Me! The World War II Memoir of a Reluctant Rifleman* (Bennington, VT: Merriam Press, 2003), pp. 51–54.

8. Harry Kemp, "The Operations of the 3rd Battalion, 109th Infantry Regiment, 28th Infantry Division in the Vicinity of Diekirch, Luxembourg, 16 December–23 December 1944. Experiences of a Battalion Executive Officer," Box 3, Charles B. MacDonald Papers, USAMHI (paper originally prepared for the Infantry School, Fort Benning, in 1949); Bedford Davis, *Frozen Rainbows: The World War II Adventures of a Combat Medical Officer* (Elk River, MN: Meadowlark Publishing, 2003), pp. 204–205; Chernitsky, *Voices from the Foxholes*, p. 208.

9. John Allard, "A Replacement in the Bloody Bucket," unpublished memoir, p. 6, Box 3, Charles B. MacDonald Papers, USAMHI; "History of Company F," RG 407, Box 8618, National Archives; Hadden, *Not Me!*, pp. 51–52; Chernitsky, *Voices from the Foxholes*, pp. 208–209.

10. Charles T. Johnson, unpublished memoir, p. 2; and Ralph Larson, unpublished memoir, pp. 3–4, both in Box 3, Charles B. MacDonald Papers, USAMHI; Haug, unpublished memoir, pp. 11–12, USAMHI; Vernon "Buck" Bloomer, interview with the author, February 14, 2005; First Lieutenant Randall Patterson, "K Company Diary," December 1944, RG 407, Box 8619, National Archives; Gaul, *Battle of the Bulge in Luxembourg, Volume II*, p. 85; Clarence Blakeslee, "A Personal Account of WWII by Draftee #35887149," self-published, 1998, pp. 61–63.

11. Joe Norris, interview with the author, March 28, 2005; Amos Meyers, unpublished memoir, p. 2, and Edwin Cornell, Veterans Questionnaire, both in 28th Infantry Division Survey Material, USAMHI; Chernitsky, *Voices from the Foxholes*, pp. 64, 209.

12. Hogzett, unpublished memoir, p. 33, PA Guard Museum; Edward Gasper, interview with the author, December 30, 2004.

13. Stephen Prazenka to John Toland, no date, Box 34, John Toland Papers, Library of Congress, Manuscript Division, Washington, DC (hereafter referred to as LOC) (Prazenka was one of the I and R soldiers who interrogated Elise Dele), 28th Division AAR; Gaul, *Battle of the Bulge in Luxembourg, Volume II*, p. 77; Lindenmeyer is quoted in "The American Experience: Battle of the Bulge," Public Broadcasting System documentary transcript, p. 2, and in Roland Gaul, *The Battle of the Bulge in Luxembourg, Volume I: The Germans* (Atglen, PA: Schiffer Military History, 1995), pp. 46–48; Charles B. MacDonald, *A Time for Trumpets: The Untold Story of the Battle of the Bulge* (New York: Bantam Books, 1984), pp. 11–14; Harry Kemp, *The Regiment: Let the Citizens Bear Arms! A Narrative History of an American Infantry Regiment in World War II* (Austin, TX: Nortex Press, 1990), pp. 227–228; G2 Period Report #189, First U.S. Army, copy in author's possession.

14. JJ Kuhn, *I was Baker 2: Memoirs of a World War II Platoon Sergeant* (West Bend, WI: DeRaimo Publishing, 1994), pp. 176–182; Frank Kusnir, interview with the author, January 3, 2005.

15. Colonel Hurley Fuller, "Report of Operations of the 110th Infantry Combat Team, 16–18 December," copy in author's possession; G2 notes for the commanding general, September 21, 1945, PA Guard Museum; 28th Division AAR; Major General Norman Cota, combat interview with Lieutenant Jack Shea, no date, World War II Combat Interviews #78, microfiche copy of the entire collection in the author's possession (hereafter referred to as CI); 28th Division G2 AAR, PA Guard Museum; VIII Corps AAR, CI #350; Major General Troy Middleton, combat interview with Captain L. D. Clark, January 19, 1945, CI-350; Troy Middleton, interview with John Toland, notes, no date, Box 36, Toland Papers, LOC; Malcolm Wilkey, unpublished memoir, p. 12, Box 1, Charles B. MacDonald Papers, USAMHI; Robert Miller, *Division Commander: A Biography of Major General Norman D. Cota* (Spartanburg, SC: Reprint Company Publishers, 1989), p. 138; Omar Bradley, *A Soldier's Story* (New York: Holt, 1951), p. 453; MacDonald, *Time for Trumpets*, p. 75.

16. "The G2 Battle of the Bulge," p. 4, paper probably authored by Colonel Benjamin "Monk" Dickson, Box 36, Toland Papers, LOC; Department of the Air Force, "Summary of Weather Conditions and Their Effects during the Ardennes Offensive," Box 7, Charles B. MacDonald Papers, USAMHI; VIII Corps AAR, CI-350.

17. General Edwin Sibert, interview with Forrest Pogue, 1951, notes; General Kenneth Strong, Supreme Headquarters, Allied Expeditionary Force (SHAEF) G2, interview with Forrest Pogue, 1946, notes; General Bedell Smith, SHAEF Chief of Staff, interview with Forrest Pogue, 1947, notes; General E. T. Williams, Twenty-First Army Group G2, interview with Forrest Pogue, 1947, notes; Adolf Rosengarten, G2 section of the First Army, interview with Forrest Pogue, 1949, notes; Colonel Monk Dickson, interview with Forrest Pogue, 1952; Malcolm Wilkey, VIII Corps G2 section, to Charles B. MacDonald, March 7, 1983; all interviews and notes are in Box 1, Charles B. MacDonald Papers, USAMHI; General

Edwin Sibert to John Toland, February 1, 1958, Box 39, Toland Papers; Monk Dickson and Sy Peterman, "We Wouldn't Be Warned in the Bulge," Box 36, Toland Papers, LOC; Dickson, "G2 Battle of the Bulge," LOC; VIII Corps AAR, CI-350; MacDonald, *Time for Trumpets*, pp. 62–79. MacDonald's discussion of Allied intelligence failures is the best single treatment of the topic.

2. Friday, December 15

1. Hugh Cole, *The United States Army in World War II: The Ardennes, Battle of the Bulge* (Washington, DC: Center of Military History, United States Army, 1994, reprint of 1965 edition), pp. 19–47, 63–74; Charles B. MacDonald, *A Time for Trumpets: The Untold Story of the Battle of the Bulge* (New York: Bantam Books, 1984), pp. 17–38; Gary Schreckengost, "Buying Time at the Battle of the Bulge," *World War II*; Roger Cirillo, "Forgotten Glory: The 110th Infantry in the Battle of the Bulge," *Officer Review*, January 1998. I have given only a brief overview of the German plan. For a more in-depth discussion, consult MacDonald or Cole, or see John S. D. Eisenhower, *The Bitter Woods* (New York: G. P. Putnam's Sons, 1969), pp. 105–161.

2. Charles Haug, unpublished memoir, p. 13, Ralph Larson, unpublished memoir, p. 4, both in 28th Division Survey Material, United States Army Military History Institute, Carlisle, Pennsylvania (hereafter referred to as USAMHI); William Kelley, unpublished memoir, p. 1, copy in author's possession; Cecil Hannaford, unpublished memoir, p. 5, copy in author's possession, interview with the author, June 1, 2005; Frank Olsen is quoted in "Men of War: Untold Stories of the Battle of the Bulge," documentary, 28th Infantry Division Association, 1988; Vernon "Buck" Bloomer, interview with the author, February 14, 2005; First Lieutenant Randall Patterson, "K Company Diary," December 1944, Record Group 407, Entry 427, Box 8619, National Archives, College Park, Maryland. Interestingly enough, Patterson's on-the-spot diary mirrors the latter-day recollections of both Larson and Bloomer.

3. Thomas Hickman, diary, December 15, 1944, Pennsylvania National Guard Museum, Historical Archives, Indiantown Gap, Pennsylvania (hereafter referred to as PA Guard Museum); Greg Mazza to the author, February 2, 2005; Tom Beadel, interview with the author, February 15, 2005; John Noon, interview with John Toland, notes, Box 35, Toland Papers, Library of Congress, Manuscript Division, Washington, DC; Dietrich's performance is briefly discussed in John Toland, *Battle: The Story of the Bulge* (Lincoln: University of Nebraska Press, 1959), p. 8, and MacDonald, *Time for Trumpets*, pp. 96–97, 199.

4. Bradicich, personal Web site, www.mypcpro.com/ww2/Bradicich; Rensmeyer, unpublished memoir, pp. 12–13, PA Guard Museum; 110th Infantry Regiment, Unit Diary, December 15, 1944, RG 407, Box 8597, National Archives; Professor Joseph Maertz of Clervaux, Luxembourg, interview with Charles B. MacDonald, August 22, 1981, notes, Box 6, MacDonald Papers, USAMHI; MacDonald, *Time for Trumpets*, p. 137.

5. Wilkey to MacDonald, Wilkey, unpublished memoir, pp. 5–10, Box 1, MacDonald Papers, USAMHI; VIII Corps AAR, CI-350.

6. Company K, 110th Infantry, combat interview, May 8, 1945, CI-78; Leroy "Whitey" Schaller, unpublished memoir, p. 1, copy provided to author by Mr. Schaller; Allard, unpublished memoir, pp. 1–7, Allard to Charles B. MacDonald,

May 17, 1982, Box 3, MacDonald Papers; Robert Jackson survey, 28th Division Survey Material, both at USAMHI; Jackson, *Kriegie: Prisoner of War*, self-published, 1995, pp. 43–45.

3. Saturday, December 16

1. 112th Infantry S2 Journal, December 16, 1944, Record Group (RG) 407, Entry 427, Box 8611, National Archives, College Park, Maryland (all subsequent National Archives citations are also from Entry 427); Lieutenant Saad Khalil, Weapons Platoon Leader, Company B, 112th Infantry, World War II Combat Interviews #78, microfiche copy of the entire collection in the author's possession (hereafter referred to as CI); Frank Olsen is quoted in "Men of War; Untold Stories of the Battle of the Bulge," documentary, 28th Infantry Division Association, 1988, and John Guerriero, *Erie Morning News*, no date; Charles Haug, unpublished memoir, and Murray Shapiro, unpublished memoir, United States Military History Institute, Carlisle, Pennsylvania (hereafter referred to as USAMHI); Charles Hogzett, "Recollections of an Infantry Lieutenant, WWII," unpublished memoir, p. 35, Pennsylvania National Guard Museum, Historical Archives, Indiantown Gap, Pennsylvania (hereafter referred to as PA Guard Museum); Dorothy Chernitsky, *Voices from the Foxholes*, self-published, 1991, pp. 41–42; Alexander Hadden, *Not Me! The World War II Memoir of a Reluctant Rifleman* (Bennington, VT: Merriam Press, 2003), pp. 60–61; Clarence Blakeslee, "A Personal Account of WWII by Draftee #35887149," self-published, 1998, pp. 65–66. The searchlights were most prevalent in the 112th Infantry sector, where Manteuffel was relying heavily on infiltration. However, the lights could be seen elsewhere around the 28th Division. One account, the combat interview of K Company, 110th Infantry (CI-78), even claims that the lights could be seen in Hosingen and Clervaux late in the evening on December 15.

2. 3rd Battalion, 110th Infantry AAR, RG 407, Box 8601, National Archives; Company K, 110th, combat interview, CI-78; Chernitsky, *Voices from the Foxholes*, p. 73; Allyn Vannoy and Jay Karameles, *Against the Panzers: United States Infantry Versus German Tanks, 1944–1945* (Jefferson, NC: McFarland & Company, 1996), pp. 201–202.

3. 109th Infantry Regiment, Unit Journal, December 16, 1944, RG 407, Box 8593, National Archives; Jackson, *Kriegie*, p. 45; Harry Kemp, *The Regiment: Let the Citizens Bear Arms! A Narrative History of an American Infantry Regiment in World War II* (Austin, TX: Nortex Press, 1990), pp. 210–218.

4. 687th Field Artillery Battalion, AAR and Unit Journal, December 1944, RG 407, Box 20109; 107th Field Artillery Battalion, Unit Journal, December 16, 1944, RG 407, Box 8580; 108th Field Artillery AAR, all are located in the National Archives; Gene "Jock" Fleury, interview with the author, March 7, 2005; "687th Field Artillery Battalion Memoirs," unpublished, Veterans Oral History Project, Library of Congress (hereafter referred to as VOHP), 2001/001/19036; Les Eames, personal diary, December 16, 1944, copy in author's possession, courtesy of Lou Dersch.

5. 1st Battalion, 110th Infantry AAR, RG 407, Box 8601, National Archives; Leroy "Whitey" Schaller, unpublished memoir, p. 1, copy provided to the author by Mr. Schaller; Stanley Showman, interview with the author, January 28, 2005; JJ Kuhn, *I Was Baker 2: Memoirs of a World War II Platoon Sergeant* (West Bend,

WI: DeRaimo Publishing, 1994), pp. 184–185; Chernitsky, *Voices from the Foxholes*, pp. 76–77, 109–110, 144–146; diagram of Marnach, provided to the author by Pierre Eicher. Eicher is a native of Marnach and lived there during the war. His house was located next to the church, in the center of town. During the barrage, German *nebelwerfer* rockets destroyed the Eicher home. After the war, the family rebuilt the house, and Pierre lives there today.

6. 28th Division AAR, RG 407, Box 8480; "History of the 110th Infantry," RG 407, Box 8596; both in the National Archives; 110th Infantry AAR, PA Guard Museum; Colonel Hurley Fuller, "Report of Operations of the 110th Infantry Combat Team, 16–18 December," copy in author's possession; Daniel Strickler, "The Battle of the Bulge," unpublished memoir, pp. 3–5, Box 3, Charles B. Mac-Donald Papers, USAMHI; Strickler, "The Breakthrough as I Saw It," unpublished memoir, pp. 1–2, Box 39, Toland Papers, Library of Congress, Manuscript Division, Washington, DC (hereafter referred to as LOC); Frank LoVuolo, *The Bulge Bugle*, February 1990, p. 12; Jack Chavez, personal diary, December 16, 1944, PA Guard Museum; Chernitsky, *Voices from the Foxholes*, pp. 229–230.

7. 3rd Battalion, 110th Infantry AAR, RG 407, Box 8601, National Archives; 110th Infantry Regiment, AAR, PA Guard Museum; Hugh Cole, *The United States Army in World War II: The Ardennes, Battle of the Bulge* (Washington, DC: Center of Military History, United States Army, 1994; reprint of 1965 edition), p. 182; Charles B. MacDonald, *A Time for Trumpets: The Untold Story of the Battle of the Bulge* (New York: Bantam Books, 1984), pp. 138–139; Robert F. Phillips, *To Save Bastogne* (Burke, VA: Borodino Books, 1996; reprint of 1983 edition), pp. 33–35.

8. 3rd Battalion, 110th Infantry AAR, RG 407, Box 8601, National Archives; "History of the 110th Infantry Regiment," RG 407, Box 8596, National Archives; William Meller, "The Young Warrior," unpublished memoir, pp. 6–10, Box 1, William Meller Papers, USAMHI; Fred Pruett, oral history, Fred Pruett Collection, VOHP, AFC/2001/001/18581; Chernitsky, *Voices from the Foxholes*, pp. 28–29.

9. 112th Infantry S2 Journal, December 16, 1944, RG 407, Box 8611; Patterson, K Company Diary, RG 407, Box 8619; both in the National Archives; "The 112th Infantry Regiment and the German Winter Offensive during the Period 16 December through 24 December 1944" (AAR), by First Lieutenant George Tuttle, CI-78; Colonel Gustin Nelson and Major Justin Brainard, S3, combat interview, January 14, 1945, CI-78; 3rd Battalion, 112th Infantry AAR, CI-78; Ray Carpenter, "112th on 12/16 and After," Box 39, Toland Papers, LOC (Carpenter was in the I and R section of the 112th); Colonel Gustin Nelson to his father, May 1945, copy of the letter in author's possession, courtesy of Pierre Eicher; Ralph Larson, unpublished memoir, pp. 5–6, and Shapiro, unpublished memoir, both in Box 3, Charles B. MacDonald Papers, USAMHI; Vernon "Buck" Bloomer, interview with the author, February 14, 2005; Blakeslee memoir, pp. 68–70.

10. 112th Infantry S2 and S3 Journals, December 16, 1944, RG 407, Box 8611, National Archives; Lieutenant Colonel William Allen and 1st Lieutenant Joseph W. Morgan, combat interview, January 16, 1945, CI-78; Lieutenant L. Franco and Lieutenant Frances Smysor, combat interview, May 4, 1945, CI-78; "Men of War"; William Kelley, unpublished memoir, pp. 1–2, copy in author's possession; Lynford Lilly, interview with the author, February 1, 2005; Peter Friscan to Mr. Johnson, circa 1949, Pennsylvania Military Museum, Boalsburg, Pennsylvania, courtesy of Joe Horvath.

11. 112th Infantry, S2 and S3 Journals, December 16, 1944, RG 407, Box 8611, National Archives; Khalil, combat interview, CI-78; Hogzett, unpublished

memoir, pp. 35–36, PA Guard Museum; Haug, unpublished memoir, pp. 16–17, USAMHI; Hadden, *Not Me!*, pp. 61–63.

12. 112th Infantry AAR, CI-78; Major Walden Woodward, CO, 3rd Battalion, Captain Guy Piercey, CO, M Company, Captain William Cowan, S1, 3rd Battalion, combat interview with T/3 William Henderson, CI-78; Lieutenant Robert Black, CO, Cannon Company, Lieutenant Richard Purcell, XO, First Sergeant George Mortimer, combat interview with T/3 William Henderson, January 23, 1945, CI-78; First Sergeant George Mortimer, personal diary, December 16, 1944, CI-78; Wayne Kugler, personal diary, December 16, 1944, Veterans of the Battle of the Bulge Collection, 28th Division donations, USAMHI; William Train, "My Memories of the Battle of the Bulge," unpublished memoir, pp. 6–7, PA Guard Museum.

13. 112th Infantry, S3 Journal, December 16, 1944, RG 407, Box 8611, National Archives; 112th Infantry, AAR, CI-78; Nelson, Brainard, combat interview; Woodward et al., combat interview; Lieutenant Colonel Joseph Macsalka and 2nd Battalion, 112th Infantry, combat interview, January 22, 1945, all in CI-78; Nelson to father; Headquarters Company, 2nd Battalion, 112th Infantry, Unit History, RG 407, 2nd Battalion, S3 Journal, December 16, 1944, both in Box 8616, National Archives; F Company, G Company, 112th Infantry, Unit Histories, both in RG 407, Box 8618; H Company, 112th Infantry, Unit History, RG 407, Box 8620, National Archives.

14. 1st Battalion, 110th Infantry, AAR, RG 407, Box 8601, National Archives; 110th Infantry, AAR, PA Guard Museum; Schaller, unpublished memoir, p. 1; Showman interview; Joe Norris, interview with author, March 28, 2005; Chernitsky, *Voices from the Foxholes*, p. 76; Kuhn, *I Was Baker 2*, pp. 185–186. Maria Eicher was Pierre Eicher's younger sister. She told me that when she and the other residents of Marnach were evacuated in the fall of 1944, she left the doll in her house at Marnach. Later, by sheer coincidence, after the Battle of the Bulge, she saw the doll, and the Americans returned it to her.

15. 3rd Battalion, 110th Infantry, AAR, RG 407, Box 8601; 687th Field Artillery Battalion, AAR, RG 407, Box 20109; 109th Field Artillery Battalion, Unit Journal, December 16, 1944, RG 407, Box 8586, all at the National Archives; 110th Infantry AAR, PA Guard Museum; Fuller, "Report of Operations"; Meller, unpublished memoir, pp. 10–17, USAMHI; Jacob Welc, Bronze Star Citation, PA Guard Museum; Phillips, *To Save Bastogne*, pp. 34–42.

16. 3rd Battalion, 110th Infantry, AAR, RG 407, Box 8601; 109th Field Artillery Battalion, Unit Journal, December 16, 1944, RG 407, Box 8586; 103rd Engineer Combat Battalion, AAR, RG 407, Box 8571; Captain Bill Jarrett to Jim, May 23, 1945, RG 407, Box 8575; all at the National Archives; K Company, 110th Infantry, combat interview, CI-78; 103rd Engineer Combat Battalion, Notes, CI-78; James Arbella, interview with author, January 6, 2005; Edward Gasper, interview with author, December 30, 2004; George Stevenson, oral history, VOHP, 2001/001/10320; Vannoy and Karameles, *Against the Panzers*, pp. 202–204.

17. VIII Corps, AAR, CI-350; "Questions Answered by Lieutenant General Troy H. Middleton," in a letter to the theater historian, July 30, 1945, CI-350; General Troy Middleton, combat interview with Captain L. B. Clark, January 19, 1945, CI-350; Middleton, combat interview with Clark, April 20, 1945, CI-229; Colonel Walter Stanton, deputy chief of staff, VIII Corps, combat interview with Captain L. B. Clark, January 16, 1945, CI-229; Malcolm Wilkey, unpublished memoir, pp. 10–11, Box 1, Charles B. MacDonald Papers, USAMHI; Frank James

Price, *Troy H. Middleton: A Biography* (Baton Rouge: Louisiana State University Press, 1974), pp. 215–217.

18. 28th Infantry Division, G3 Journal, December 16, 1944, RG 407, Box 8518, National Archives; 28th Infantry Division, Unit Report, Box 3, Charles B. MacDonald Papers, USAMHI; Major General Norman D. Cota, combat interview, CI-78; Major R. S. Garner, combat interview with Captain William Dunkersley, May 3, 1945, CI-78; Raymond Fleig, "The 707th Tank Battalion in World War II," self-published, pp. 137–140; Harold Snedden to Carl Montgomery, February 9, 1945, Box 7, Carl Montgomery Papers, USAMHI; Strickler, "Battle of the Bulge," pp. 5–11, USAMHI; Fuller, "Report of Operations"; Robert Miller, *Division Commander: A Biography of Major General Norman D. Cota* (Spartanburg, SC: Reprint Company Publishers, 1989), pp. 138–142; Peter Schrijvers, *Unknown Dead: Civilians in the Battle of the Bulge* (Lexington: University Press of Kentucky, 2005), p. 97.

19. 1st Battalion, 110th Infantry, AAR, RG 407, Box 8601, National Archives; 110th Infantry, AAR, PA Guard Museum; 707th Tank Battalion, S3 Journal, December 16, 1944, RG 407, Box 16680; 109th Field Artillery Battalion, Unit Journal, December 16, 1944, RG 407, Box 8586; both at National Archives; Fleig, "707th Tank Battalion in World War II," pp. 140–142; Garner, combat interview, CI-78; Frank Richwine, interview with the author, January 12, 2005. Richwine, a communications officer in the 1st Battalion headquarters, related the phrase "What do we do now, Jimmy?"; John Maher, unpublished memoir, pp. 1–3, 28th Infantry Division Survey Material, USAMHI; Chernitsky, *Voices from the Foxholes*, pp. 91, 147–149; Charles T. Johnson, unpublished memoir, Box 3, Charles B. MacDonald Papers, USAMHI, pp. 3–4; conversations with Pierre Eicher, July 2005.

20. 1st Battalion, 3rd Battalion, AARs, RG 407, Box 8601, National Archives; Fuller, "Report of Operations"; Schreckengost, "Buying Time at the Battle of the Bulge"; MacDonald, *Time for Trumpets*, p. 142.

21. 3rd Battalion, 110th Infantry, AAR, RG 407, Box 8601, National Archives; Fleig, "707th Tank Battalion in World War II," p. 143; Company K, 110th Infantry, combat interview, CI-78; Stevenson, oral history, LOC; Ralph Obuchowski, veterans questionnaire, 28th Infantry Division Survey Material, USAMHI; Chernitsky, *Voices from the Foxholes*, pp. 64–65; Vannoy and Karameles, *Against the Panzers*, pp. 205–207.

22. 112th Infantry, S3 Journal, December 16, 1944, RG 407, Box 8611, National Archives; Allen interview, CI-78; Haug, unpublished memoir, pp. 18–20, USAMHI; Shapiro, unpublished memoir, USAMHI; Hadden, *Not Me!*, pp. 63–64; Cole, *The Ardennes*, pp. 197–198.

23. 3rd Battalion, 110th Infantry, AAR, RG 407, Box 8601, National Archives; 110th Infantry, AAR, PA Guard Museum; Meller, unpublished memoir, pp. 20–24, USAMHI; Pruett, oral history, LOC; Chernitsky, *Voices from the Foxholes*, p. 42.

24. 28th Infantry Division, G3 Journal, December 16, 1944, RG 407, Box 8518; 1st Battalion, 110th Infantry, AAR, RG 407, Box 8601; 109th Field Artillery, Unit Journal, RG 407, Box 8586; all in National Archives; 28th Infantry Division, AAR, CI-78; Cota, combat interview, CI-78; Fuller, "Report of Operations"; Schaller, unpublished memoir, p. 1; Showman interview; Johnson, unpublished memoir, pp. 4–5; Miller, *Division Commander*, p. 142; Chernitsky, *Voices from the Foxholes*, pp. 76–77, 19–110.

4. Sunday, December 17

1. 2nd Battalion, 110th Infantry, AAR, 1st Battalion, 110th Infantry, AAR, Record Group (RG) 407, Entry 427, Box 8601; "History of Company F . . . 112th Infantry," RG 407, Box 8618; all in the National Archives, College Park, Maryland (all subsequent National Archives citations are also from Entry 427); 110th Infantry, AAR; "History of the 109th Field Artillery Battalion," both in Pennsylvania National Guard Museum, Historical Archives, Indiantown Gap, Pennsylvania (hereafter referred to as PA Guard Museum); Joseph Maertz, "Luxembourg in the Rundstedt Offensive," paper found in Box 39, John Toland Papers, Library of Congress, Manuscript Division, Washington, DC (hereafter referred to as LOC); Charles T. Johnson, unpublished memoir, pp. 5–6, Box 3, Charles B. MacDonald Papers, United States Military History Institute, Carlisle, Pennsylvania (hereafter referred to as USAMHI); Dorothy Chernitsky, *Voices from the Foxholes*, self-published, 1991, pp. 152–153; Frank Stepnick, interview with the author, March 31, 2005; Manteuffel's quote was related to me by Bob Phillips, interview, December 29, 2004. Bob is the preeminent historian of the 110th Infantry in the Bastogne corridor and the author of *To Save Bastogne*. He interviewed Manteuffel extensively. I would like to thank Bob for sharing his wealth of knowledge, and so much of his time, with me.

2. 112th Infantry Regiment, S3 Journal, December 17, 1944, RG 407, Box 8611, National Archives; 112th Infantry, Combat Interviews #78, microfiche copy of the entire collection in the author's possession (hereafter referred to as CI); 112th Infantry, AAR, CI-78; Gustin Nelson interview, CI-78; Charles Haug, unpublished memoir, pp. 20–21, USAMHI; Peter Friscan to Mr. Johnson, Pennsylvania Military Museum; William Kelley, unpublished memoir, pp. 3–5, e-mail to author, September 23, 2005.

3. 110th Infantry, AAR; "History of the 109th Field Artillery Battalion"; both in PA Guard Museum; 2nd Battalion, 110th Infantry, AAR, RG 407, Box 8601; 707th Tank Battalion, S3 Journal, December 17, 1944, RG 407, Box 16680; both in the National Archives; Raymond Fleig, "707th Tank Battalion in World War II," self-published, pp. 142–146; Major R. S. Garner, combat interview, CI-78; Lieutenant Jack Haisley, 2nd Platoon Leader, C Company, 110th Infantry, combat interview with M/Sergeant Monroe Ludden, May 4, 1945, CI-78; John Anderson, "Company D. 707 Tank Battalion," and Howard Thomsen, "History of Company 'B' 707th Tank Battalion," both at www.707tkbn.org; Colonel Hurley Fuller, "Report of Operations of the 110th Infantry Combat Team, 16–18 December," copy in author's possession; Stepnick interview; Phillips interview; Joe Norris, interview with the author, March 28, 2005; Leroy "Whitey" Schaller, unpublished memoir, p. 1, copy provided to author by Mr. Schaller; James Smith interview with John Toland, Notes, Box 39, Toland Papers, LOC; Chernitsky, *Voices from the Foxholes*, pp. 77–78; Gerald Astor, *A Blood Dimmed Tide* (New York: Dell Publishing, 1992), pp. 123–124. In the summer of 1945, Pierre Eicher took photographs and documented the locations of the destroyed D Company, 707th Tank Battalion, tanks. He was kind enough to share this information with me.

4. 28th Infantry Division, G3 Journal, December 17, 1944, RG 407, Box 8518; 707th Tank Battalion, S3 Journal, December 17, 1944, RG 407, Box 16680; 9th Armored Division, CCR, G3 Journal, December 17, 1944, RG 407, Box 15787; 2nd Tank Battalion, AAR, S3 Journal, December 17, 1944, RG 407, Box 15896; all in National Archives; 28th Division AAR, CI-78; Major General Norman

Cota, combat interview with Lieutenant Jack Shea, CI-78; Fuller, "Report of Operations"; 110th Infantry, AAR, PA Guard Museum; Colonel Gustin Nelson to his father, May 1945, copy of the letter in author's possession, courtesy of Pierre Eicher; Fleig, "707th Tank Battalion in World War II," pp. 146–147; Maertz, "Luxembourg in the Rundstedt Offensive," LOC; James Pelletier to Frank Kieffer, August 21, 1997, letter on display at the Battle of the Bulge Museum, Clervaux, Luxembourg; Donald Fink, unpublished memoir, p. 1; Don Fink to Robert Peterson, May 7, 2003; Robert Peterson, "A Memorial Tribute to the 2nd Tank Battalion, 9th Armored Division"; copies of Fink's memoir, letter, and this paper were all provided to me courtesy of Bob Peterson; Walter Reichelt, *Phantom Nine: The 9th Armored (Remagen) Division, 1942–1945* (Austin, TX: Presidial Press, 1987), pp. 127–128.

    5. 112th Infantry, S3 Journal, December 17, 1944, RG 407, Box 8611; 229th Field Artillery Battalion, AAR, RG 407, Box 8588, both at the National Archives; Colonel Gustin Nelson and Major Justin Brainard, S3, combat interview, January 14, 1945, CI-78; Lieutenant L. Franco and Lieutenant Frances Smysor, combat interview, May 4, 1945, CI-78; Major Walden Woodward, CO, 3rd Battalion, Captain Guy Piercey, CO, M Company, Captain William Cowan, S1, 3rd Battalion, combat interview with T/3 William Henderson, CI-78; Lieutenant Robert Black, CO, Cannon Company, Lieutenant Richard Purcell, XO, First Sergeant George Mortimer, combat interview with T/3 William Henderson, January 23, 1945, CI-78; First Sergeant George Mortimer, personal diary, December 16, 1944, CI-78; Lieutenant Leo Kodzerski, CO, 1st Platoon, Company C, 630th TD (towed) Battalion, and First Sergeant Joseph McKenna, combat interview, January 21, 1945, CI-78; Nelson to father; General Walter Krueger, LVIII Panzer Corps, 5th Panzer Army, "Concerning Our Offensive in the Ardennes," Box 8, Charles B. MacDonald Papers; Major Fritz Vogelzang, "The Battle of Ouren," 28th Infantry Division Survey Material; Wayne Kugler, personal diary, December 16, 1944, Veterans of the Battle of the Bulge Collection (VBOB), 28th Division donations; Murray Shapiro, unpublished memoir; all at USAMHI; Ray Carpenter, "112th on 12/16 and After," Box 39, Toland Papers, LOC; Clarence Blakeslee, "A Personal Account of WWII by Draftee #35887149," self-published, 1998, pp. 76–78; Hugh Cole, *The United States Army in World War II: The Ardennes, Battle of the Bulge* (Washington, DC: Center of Military History, United States Army, 1994, reprint of 1965 edition), pp. 198–202; Charles Crain, *Stories from Three Wars: One Soldier's Memories* (Spartanburg, SC: The Reprint Company Publishers, 2005), p. 80.

    6. 109th Infantry, Unit Journal, RG 407, Box 8593, National Archives; 109th Infantry, AAR, CI-78; John McDonald, "History of the 109th Infantry Regiment," USAMHI; Harry Kemp, "The Operations of the 3rd Battalion, 109th Infantry Regiment, 28th Infantry Division in the Vicinity of Diekirch, Luxembourg, 16 December–23 December 1944. Experiences of a Battalion Executive Officer," Box 3, Charles B. MacDonald Papers, USAMHI (paper originally prepared for the Infantry School, Fort Benning, in 1949); Robert Jackson, *Kriegie: Prisoner of War*, self-published, 1995, pp. 49–54; Harry Kemp, *The Regiment: Let the Citizens Bear Arms! A Narrative History of an American Infantry Regiment in World War II* (Austin, TX: Nortex Press, 1990), pp. 239–246; Bedford Davis, *Frozen Rainbows: The World War II Adventures of a Combat Medical Officer* (Elk River, MN: Meadowlark Publishing, 2003), pp. 212–213.

    7. 1st Battalion, 3rd Battalion, 110th Infantry, AARs, RG 407, Box 8601; 707th Tank Battalion, S3 Journal, December 17, 1944, RG 407, Box 16680; 2nd

Tank Battalion, AAR, RG 407, Box 15896; all in the National Archives; Willie Dayhuff, unpublished memoir, p. 1, copy in author's possession; Willie Dayhuff, interview with the author, November 26, 2004; Cecil Hannaford, unpublished memoir, copy in author's possession, interview with author, June 1, 2005; Josef Reush, "German Veteran Voices," *The Gravel Agitator: The Newsletter of the 27th Armored Infantry Battalion*, Spring 2001. Reush was part of a German 75-mm PAK crew at Heinerscheid; Walter Reichelt, *Phantom Nine: The 9th Armored (Remagen) Division, 1942–1945* (Austin, TX: Presidial Press, 1987), pp. 128–129; Robert F. Phillips, *To Save Bastogne* (Burke, VA: Borodino Books, 1996; reprint of 1983 edition), pp. 106–109.

8. 3rd Battalion, 110th Infantry, AAR, RG 407, Box 8601; 707th Tank Battalion, S3 Journal, December 17, 1944, RG 407, Box 16680; 103rd Engineer Combat Battalion, AAR, RG 407, Box 8571; Jarrett letter, RG 407, Box 8575; all in the National Archives; Company K, combat interview, CI-78; Fleig, "707th Tank Battalion in World War II," p. 149; Edward Gasper, interview with author, December 30, 2004; James Arbella, interview with author, January 6, 2005; Allyn Vannoy and Jay Karameles, *Against the Panzers: United States Infantry Versus German Tanks, 1944–1945* (Jefferson, NC: McFarland & Company, 1996), pp. 207–211.

9. 28th Infantry Division, G3 Journal, December 17, 1944, RG 407, Box 8518; 1st Battalion, 110th Infantry, AAR, RG 407, Box 8601, both at the National Archives; 110th Infantry, AAR, PA Guard Museum; Fuller, "Report of Operations"; John Maher, unpublished memoir, pp. 3–4, William Fox, memoir statement, 28th Infantry Division Donations, VBOB Collections, both at USAMHI. Fox was a service company truck driver in Munshausen who encountered Captain Irving Warden after his close call with the Germans. Rudolph Siebert, "Ardennes Offensive 1944," pp. 2–4, copy provided to me by Pierre Eicher; Eicher, interview with the author and tour of Munshausen, July 27, 2005. Eicher is the leading local expert on the Bastogne corridor. He has spent sixty years studying the battle, interviewing veterans of both sides, talking to local citizens who experienced the Bulge, and compiling primary source information; Chernitsky, *Voices from the Foxholes*, pp. 91–92; Phillips, *To Save Bastogne*, p. 89.

10. 28th Division, G3 Journal, December 17, 1944, RG 407, Box 8518, National Archives; 28th Division, AAR, CI-78; Cota interview, CI-78; 110th Infantry, AAR; Edwin Rensmeyer, "The Story of a Civilian Soldier," unpublished memoir, pp. 13–15; both at PA Guard Museum; Frank Kusnir, interview with author, January 3, 2005; "Men of War: Untold Stories of the Battle of the Bulge," documentary, 28th Infantry Division Association, 1988; Phillips interview; Maertz, "Luxembourg in the Rundstedt Offensive," LOC; Fuller, "Report of Operations"; Jean Serve, interview with Charles B. MacDonald, Notes, Box 6, Charles B. MacDonald Papers, USAMHI; Peter Schrijvers, *The Unknown Dead: Civilians in the Battle of the Bulge* (Lexington: University Press of Kentucky, 2005), pp. 97–98.

11. 1st Battalion, 3rd Battalion, 110th Infantry, AAR, RG 407, Box 8601; 2nd Tank Battalion, AAR, S3 Journal, December 17, 1944, RG 407, Box 15896; both at the National Archives; Fuller, "Report of Operations"; Rensmeyer, unpublished memoir, pp. 14–15; 110th Infantry Medical Personnel, combat interview with Captain H. P. Hudson, May 4, 1945, CI-78; "Dramatic Battle Around Clerf," paper found in Box 39, Toland Papers, LOC; Stanley Showman, interview with author, January 28, 2005; Carl Montgomery to his mother, May 1945, Box 2, Carl Montgomery Papers; CCR, 9th Armored Division AAR, "History of the 9th Armored Division," John Leonard Papers; both collections at USAMHI; Carl

Montgomery, interview with the author, July 21, 2005, plus subsequent conversations with the author; Schrijvers, *The Unknown Dead*, p. 96; Reichelt, *Phantom Nine*, pp. 129–130; Chernitsky, *Voices from the Foxholes*, pp. 154–157.

12. 1st Battalion, 2nd Battalion, 110th Infantry, AAR, RG 407, Box 8601; 2nd Tank Battalion, AAR, S3 Journal, December 17, 1944, RG 407, Box 15896; 707th Tank Battalion, S3 Journal, December 17, 1944, RG 407, Box 16680; all at the National Archives; 110th Infantry, AAR, PA Guard Museum; Fuller, "Report of Operations"; Major R. S. Garner, combat interview with Captain William Dunkersley, May 3, 1945, CI-78; Fleig, "707th Tank Battalion in World War II," pp. 146–147; "5th Company, Panzer Regiment 3, 2nd Panzer Division" combat record, 28th Division Survey Material, USAMHI; Frank Richwine, interview with author, January 12, 2005; Phillips interview; "Men of War"; Bradicich, unpublished memoir, at his personal Web site; Chernitsky, *Voices from the Foxholes*, pp. 126–128, 153–158; Reichelt, *Phantom Nine*, pp. 129–130. The CCR tanks that survived the day's combat in Reuler attempted to retreat cross-country in the evening. They got bogged down and had to be destroyed.

13. 28th Infantry Division, G3 Journal, December 17, 1944, RG 407, Box 8518; 1st Battalion, 2nd Battalion, 110th Infantry, AAR, RG 407, Box 8601; all at the National Archives; 28th Infantry Division, AAR, CI-78; Cota, combat interview, CI-78; 110th Infantry Medical Personnel, combat interview, CI-78; Haisley, combat interview, CI-78. Haisley survived his wounds and became a POW; 110th Infantry, AAR; Rensmeyer, unpublished memoir, pp. 15–16; Jack Chavez, personal diary, December 17, 1944; all at PA Guard Museum; Fuller, "Report of Operations"; Siebert, "Ardennes Offensive," p. 4; "5th Company, Panzer Regiment 3"; Ralph Johnson, unpublished memoir, pp. 3–5; both at 28th Division Survey Material, USAMHI; "Men of War"; Clarence Johnson, interview with author, August 21, 2005; Phillips interview; Maertz, "Luxembourg in the Rundstedt Offensive"; Phillips, *To Save Bastogne*, pp. 135–140; Chernitsky, *Voices from the Foxholes*, pp. 92–93, 126–128; Cole, *Ardennes*, pp. 190–191; JJ Kuhn, *I Was Baker 2: Memoirs of a World War II Platoon Sergeant* (West Bend, WI: DeRaimo Publishing, 1984), pp. 7–8, 187–188.

14. 28th Division, G3 Journal, December 17, 1944, RG 407, Box 8518; 112th Infantry, S3 Journal, December 17, 1944, December 18, 1944, RG 407, Box 8611; K Company Diary, RG 407, Box 8619; F Company Unit History, RG 407, Box 8618; all at the National Archives; 28th Division, AAR, CI-78; 112th Infantry, AAR, CI-78; Nelson, Brainard, combat interview, CI-78; Lieutenant James Sharpe, combat interview, CI-78; Nelson, letter to father; Larson, unpublished memoir, pp. 7–9, MacDonald Papers, USAMHI; Vernon "Buck" Bloomer, interview with author, February 14, 2005; Kelley, unpublished memoir, p. 5, e-mails. Kelley later found out that his friend Pete was captured.

15. 10th Armored Division, G3 Journal, December 16, 1944, and December 17, 1944, RG 407, Box 15915; Combat Command B (CCB), S3 Journal, December 16, 1944, and December 17, 1944, RG 407, Box 15974; all at National Archives; William Roberts to John Toland, January 1957, Box 33, Toland Papers, LOC; William Desobry, oral history, William Desobry Papers, USAMHI; Spurgeon Van Hoose, interview with the author, November 24, 2004; Lester Nichols, *Impact: The Battle Story of the Tenth Armored Division* (Nashville, TN: Battery Press, 1954), pp. 79–80.

5. Monday, December 18

1. 101st Airborne Division, AAR, Record Group (RG) 407, Entry 427, Box 14332; G3 Journal, December 17–18, 1944, RG 407, Entry 427, Box 14360; both at the National Archives, College Park, Maryland (all subsequent National Archives citations are also from Entry 427); Arlo Butcher to his mother, May 22, 1945, Collection Number 68, World War II Letters, Western Historical Manuscript Collection, University of Missouri–Columbia (hereafter referred to as WHMC); Leonard Rapport and Arthur Northwood, *Rendezvous with Destiny: A History of the 101st Airborne Division* (Nashville, TN: Battery Press, 1948; reprinted in 2000), pp. 428–431; George Koskimaki, *The Battered Bastards of Bastogne* (Havertown, PA: Casemate, 2003), pp. 5–6, 20–26; Donald Burgett, *Seven Roads to Hell: A Screaming Eagle at Bastogne* (Novato, CA: Presidio Press, 1999), pp. 14–17.

2. 3rd Battalion, 110th Infantry AAR, RG 407, Box 8601; Jarrett letter, RG 407, Box 8575; both at the National Archives; K Company, World War II Combat Interviews #78, microfiche copy of the entire collection in the author's possession (hereafter referred to as CI); Raymond Fleig, The "707th Tank Battalion in World War II," self-published, pp. 149–150; Edward Gasper, interview with author, December 30, 2004; Bernie Porter, interview with the author, January 4, 2005; George Stevenson, oral history, Veterans Oral History Project, Library of Congress (hereafter referred to as VOHP), 2001/001/10320; Allyn Vannoy and Jay Karameles, *Against the Panzers: United States Infantry Versus German Tanks, 1944–1945* (Jefferson, NC: McFarland & Company, 1996), pp. 210–214.

3. 112th Infantry, S3 Journal, December 18, 1944, RG 407, Box 8611, National Archives; 112th Infantry AAR, CI-78; Gustin Nelson, combat interview, CI-78; Colonel Gustin Nelson to his father, May 1945, copy of the letter in author's possession, courtesy of Pierre Eicher; "Men of War: Untold Stories of the Battle of the Bulge," documentary, 28th Infantry Division Association, 1988; John Guerriero at www.erieveterans.com. In the days ahead, the 112th Infantry more or less held together. Nelson conducted a fighting retreat under the command of the 106th Infantry Division, and eventually linked up with the 82nd Airborne Division on the northern shoulder of the Bulge. In two short days, the 112th did an excellent job of holding the Ouren bridges.

4. 28th Division, G3 Journal, December 18, 1944, RG 407, Box 8518; 3rd Battalion, 110th Infantry AAR, RG 407, Box 8601; both at the National Archives; 28th Division AAR, CI-78; 110th Infantry AAR, Pennsylvania National Guard Museum, Historical Archives, Indiantown Gap, Pennsylvania (hereafter referred to as PA Guard Museum); Daniel Strickler, "The Battle of the Bulge," unpublished memoir, pp. 12–17, Box 3, Charles B. MacDonald Papers, United States Army Military History Institute, Carlisle, Pennsylvania (hereafter referred to as USAMHI); "Memories of LTC Strickler," Box 35, John Toland Papers, Library of Congress, Manuscript Division, Washington, DC (hereafter referred to as LOC); Robert Miller, *Division Commander: A Biography of Major General Norman D. Cota*, Spartanburg, SC: Reprint Company Publishers, 1989), p. 145; Robert F. Phillips, *To Save Bastogne* (Burke, VA: Borodino Books, 1996, reprint of 1983 edition), pp. 161–163.

5. 28th Division, G3 Journal, December 18, 1944, RG 407, Box 8518; 109th Field Artillery Battalion, Unit Journal, RG 407, Box 8586; "History of the 110th

Infantry," RG 407, Box 8596; all at the National Archives; 28th Division AAR, CI-78; "History of the 109th Field Artillery," PA Guard Museum; Charles T. Johnson, unpublished memoir; Jean Serve, interview with Charles B. MacDonald, Notes, Box 6, Charles B. MacDonald Papers; both at USAMHI; Jean Serve, "Defense of Castle Clerf," Box 39, Toland Papers; Georges Paul, interview with John Toland, notes, Box 37, Toland Papers, both at LOC; "Men of War"; Bob Kalish, interview with author, January 19, 2005; Frank Kusnir, interview with author, January 3, 2005; Bob Phillips, interview with author, December 29, 2004; Pierre Eicher, interview with author, July 27, 2005; Donald Fink, unpublished memoir, pp. 1–2; Hugh Cole, *The United States Army in World War II: The Ardennes, Battle of the Bulge* (Washington, DC: Center of Military History, United States Army, 1994, reprint of 1965 edition), pp. 191–192; Phillips, *To Save Bastogne*, pp. 142–144; Charles B. MacDonald, *A Time for Trumpets: The Untold Story of the Battle of the Bulge* (New York: Bantam Books, 1984), pp. 278–279, 284–285. Today Clervaux castle is rebuilt. It houses an art museum, a war museum, a castle museum, a restaurant, and Luxembourg government offices. In the castle courtyard, there is a Sherman tank from the 9th Armored Division and a German PAK gun. There is a plaza and a bandstand where the bodies of German soldiers once lay.

6. 28th Division, G3 Journal, December 18, 1944, RG 407, Box 8518, National Archives; 28th Division AAR, CI-78; 28th Division Mechanized Reconnaissance Troop, AAR, Unit Histories, USAMHI; Richard Sheesley, unpublished memoir, pp. 2–3, PA Guard Museum; Gene McHale to Pierre Eicher, June 20, 2000, Gene McHale, unpublished memoir, pp. 1–3, both documents given to me by Pierre Eicher; Bernard Quinn, "The Private Who Lost and Won," *American Legion*, February 1963, pp. 14–15; "George Mergenthaler," *After the Battle*.

7. 28th Division, G3 Journal, December 18, 1944, RG 407, Box 8518; 3rd Battalion, 110th Infantry, AAR, RG 407, Box 8601; 687th Field Artillery, Unit Journal, RG 407, Box 20109; 707th Tank Battalion, S3 Journal, December 18, 1944, RG 407, Box 16680; all at the National Archives; 28th Division, AAR, CI-78; Major General Norman Cota, combat interview with Lieutenant Jack Shea, CI-78; Strickler, "Battle of the Bulge," pp. 15–19; "The American Experience: Battle of the Bulge," Public Broadcasting System documentary transcript; *History of the 110th Infantry Regiment, World War II*, no pagination, self-published, PA Guard Museum; Saul Levitt, "The Thin Line," *Yank*, February 18, 1945; Ivan Peterman, "They Took the Nazis' Sunday Punch," *Saturday Evening Post*, September 28, 1946; Strickler, "Memories of LTC Strickler"; Joseph Maertz, "Luxembourg in the Rundstedt Offensive," Box 39, Toland Papers; Thomas Hoban interview with John Toland, Notes, Box 35, Toland Papers; Hoban, Report of Action at Wiltz, written on July 14, 1945, Box 35, Toland Papers; all at LOC; Company A, 44th Engineer Combat Battalion, "Record of Events," December 18, 1944, 2001/001/18048; *44th Engineer Combat Battalion: We Clear the Way*, self-published, pp. 51–52, both at VOHP, LOC; Miller, *Division Commander*, pp. 144–146; Phillips, *To Save Bastogne*, pp. 217–222.

8. 9th Armored Division, G3 Journal, December 18, 1944, RG 407, Box 15787; 52nd Armored Infantry Battalion, AAR, RG 407, Box 15886; 2nd Tank Battalion, AAR, RG 407, S2/S3 Journals, December 18, 1944, Box 15896; 73rd Armored Field Artillery Battalion, AAR, RG 407, Box 15879; all at the National Archives; CCR, 9th Armored Division, AAR, John Leonard Papers, USAMHI; Major General Troy Middleton, combat interview with Captain L. D. Clark, Jan-

uary 19, 1945, CI-350; VIII Corps, AAR, CI-350; Cole, *The Ardennes*, pp. 249–296; Frank James Price, *Troy H. Middleton: A Biography* (Baton Rouge: Louisiana State University Press, 1974), pp. 224–225; Walter Reichelt, *Phantom Nine: The 9th Armored (Remagen) Division, 1942–1945* (Austin, TX: Presidial Press, 1987), pp. 130– 134; Phillips, *To Save Bastogne*, pp. 175–177.

9. 112th Infantry, S3 Journal, December 18, 1944, RG 407, Box 8611; F Company Diary, RG 407, Box 8618, both at the National Archives; 112th Infantry, AAR, CI-78; Colonel Gustin Nelson and Major Justin Brainard, S3, combat interview, January 14, 1945, CI-78; Nelson to his father; Cecil Hannaford, interview with the author, June 1, 2005, and unpublished memoir, copy in author's possession.

10. CCB, S3 Journal, December 18, 1944, RG 407, Box 15974; 101st Airborne Division, AAR, RG 407, Box 14332; G3 Journal, December 18, 1944, RG 407, Box 14360; all at the National Archives; CCB, AAR, CI-305; William Roberts to S. L. A. Marshall, February 18, 1945, "Reflections and Impressions of Bastogne," CI-305; William Roberts to John Toland, January 1957, Box 33, Toland Papers, LOC; "American Experience: Battle of the Bulge"; 101st Airborne Division, Summary, CI-227; Brigadier General Anthony McAuliffe, combat interview, CI-229; Rufus Lewis, interview with the author, April 4, 2005; 420th Armored Field Artillery Battalion, AAR, copy provided to me by Rufus Lewis and at CI-305; Don Addor, *Noville Outpost to Bastogne: My Last Battle* (Victoria, British Columbia: Trafford, 2004), pp. 9–10; S. L. A. Marshall, *Bastogne: The Story of the First Eight Days* (Washington, DC: Infantry Journal Press, 1946), pp. 12–18; Guy Arend, *The Battle for Bastogne* (Bastogne: Bastogne Historical Center, no date), pp. 47–55; Price, *Middleton*, pp. 224–228; Cole, *Ardennes*, pp. 304–307.

11. 28th Division, G3 Journal, December 18, 1944, RG 407, Box 8518; "History of the 110th Infantry Regiment," RG 407, Box 8596; 2nd Tank Battalion, AAR, S2/S3 Journals, December 18, 1944, RG 407, Box 15896, all at National Archives; CCR, 9th Armored Division, AAR, "History of the 9th Armored Division," Leonard Papers; Charles Johnson, unpublished memoir, pp. 13–14, MacDonald Papers; Ralph Johnson, unpublished memoir, pp. 7–10, 28th Division Survey Material; Harry Mason, unpublished diary, 28th Division Donations, Veterans of the Battle of the Bulge Collection, all at USAMHI; Colonel Hurley Fuller, "Report of Operations of the 110th Infantry Combat Team, 16–18 December," copy in author's possession; Seely is quoted in *History of the 110th Infantry*; Reichelt, *Phantom Nine*, pp. 134–136; Dorothy Chernitsky, *Voices from the Foxholes*, self-published, 1991, pp. 158–164; Phillips, *To Save Bastogne*, pp. 140–142, 151–154; MacDonald, *Time for Trumpets*, pp. 287–288. During the Battle of the Bulge, the 9th Armored Division was split up into three combat commands that fought separately over a 95-mile front. For much of the Bulge, the high command designated the 9th Armored for the "secret list," meaning that correspondents could not report on its exploits. The Allies were not fooling anyone, though. The Germans knew all about the presence of the 9th Armored and believed three separate times that they had destroyed it. They were wrong. The resilient 9th was never destroyed. This earned the unit the nickname "Phantom Nine." Only in early January, after intense lobbying from CO Major General John Leonard, did the high command remove the 9th Armored from the secret list. By then, the division's story was lost in the shuffle of many other stories. Thus the division never got the credit it deserved for fighting so well in the battle. This is especially true for CCR, which basically fell on its sword to earn Middleton a few more hours to set up the defense of Bastogne.

12. 9th Armored Division, AAR; CCR, 9th Armored Division, AAR; "History of the 9th Armored Division," all in the Leonard Papers; Eugene Watts to Charles B. MacDonald, February 28, 1985, Box 1, Charles B. MacDonald Papers, all at USAMHI; 52nd Armored Infantry Battalion, AAR, RG 407, Box 15886, National Archives; Eugene Watts, interview with author, April 12, 2005; Carlton Willey, interview with author, March 1, 2005; Reichelt, *Phantom Nine*, pp. 136–139; Cole, *The Ardennes*, pp. 295–298; MacDonald, *Time for Trumpets*, pp. 288–289.

13. CCB, S3 Journal, December 18, 1944, RG 407, Box 15974; 3rd Tank Battalion, AAR, RG 407, Box 16037; S3 Journal, December 18, 1944, RG 407, Box 16039, all at National Archives. Henry Cherry was the commander of the 3rd Tank Battalion; "History of the 9th Armored Division," Leonard Papers, USAMHI; Lieutenant Colonel Henry Cherry, Major William McChesney, Captain William Ryerson, and Lieutenant Edward Hyduke, combat interview with Captain John Westover, January 18, 1945, CI-305; Roberts to Toland; William Roberts, Notes on Team Cherry, both in Box 33, Toland Papers, LOC; "The 420th at War," unpublished unit history, p. 74, copy provided by Rufus Lewis; 420th AAR; Mike Heyman, *Christmas in Bastogne: A Personal Story of World War II*, self-published, 1994, pp. 301–304; "The Battle of the Bulge," *After the Battle*, 1974, pp. 3–4; Reichelt, *Phantom Nine*, pp. 136–139; Arend, *Bastogne*, pp. 56–57; MacDonald, *Time for Trumpets*, pp. 288–291; Cole, *The Ardennes*, pp. 298–301; Marshall, *Bastogne: First Eight Days*, pp. 22–24, 176–182.

14. CCB, S3 Journal, December 18, 1944, RG 407, Box 15974; 20th Armored Infantry Battalion, S3 Journal, December 18, 1944, RG 407, Box 16008; 54th Armored Infantry Battalion, AAR and Historical Record, RG 407, Box 16016; S3 Journal, December 18, 1944, RG 407, Box 16019; all at the National Archives; Lieutenant Colonel James O'Hara, combat interview (and AAR) with Captain John Westover, CI-305; Desobry oral history, William Desobry to Charles B. MacDonald, August 24, 1983, Box 2, Charles B. MacDonald Papers; William Desobry, miscellaneous notes, Box 2, S. L. A. Marshall Papers, all at USAMHI; Bill Kerby, interview with author, May 3, 2005; S. L. A. Marshall claims in *Bastogne: The First Eight Days*, p. 14, that Colonel Roberts referred to Desobry's youth while giving him orders: "You are young, and by tomorrow morning you will probably be nervous." This has been repeated in nearly every subsequent account of their meeting. However, Desobry denies that Roberts ever said this. He claims that this reference to his youth was "dreamed up by Marshall."

15. 28th Division, G1 Journal, RG 407, Box 8481; 110th Infantry, Unit Diary, RG 407, Box 8597; 101st Airborne Division, AAR, RG 407, Box 14332; G3 Journal, RG 407, Box 14360; 506th Parachute Infantry Regiment, S3 Journal, December 18, 1944, RG 407, Box 14438; all at the National Archives; S. L. A. Marshall, combat interviews with Colonel Tom Sherburne and Captain Cecil Dillon; Statement by Colonel Tom Sherburne, both in Box 1, Marshall Papers, USAMHI; Butcher to his mother, WHMC; "American Experience: Battle of the Bulge"; Francis Sampson, *Look Out Below! A Story of the Airborne by a Paratrooper Padre* (Washington, DC: Catholic University of America Press, 1958), p. 104; Cole, *The Ardennes*, p. 192; Arend, *Bastogne*, pp. 59–61; Rapport and Northwood, *Rendezvous with Destiny*, p. 437; Koskimaki, *Battered Bastards of Bastogne*, p. 34; Burgett, *Seven Roads to Hell*, pp. 32–39.

16. 20th Armored Infantry Battalion, S3 Journal, December 18, 1944, RG 407, Box 16008; S2 Journal, December 18, 1944, RG 407, Box 16013, both at National Archives; Team Desobry, combat interview (and AAR) with Captain

John Westover, January 1945, CI–305; Desobry oral history; Desobry to MacDonald, MacDonald Papers; Desobry, miscellaneous notes, Marshall Papers, both at USAMHI; *After the Battle*, p. 4; Kerby interview; Ludwig "Larry" Stein, interview with author, April 29, 2005; Addor, *Noville Outpost to Bastogne*, pp. 12–16.

6. Tuesday, December 19

1. CCB, S3 Journal, December 19, 1944, Record Group (RG) 407, Entry 427, Box 15974; 3rd Tank Battalion, S3 Journal, RG 407, Box 16039; 73rd Armored Field Artillery Battalion, RG 407, Box 15879; Casualty Report, Box 15881; all at the National Archives, College Park, Maryland (all subsequent National Archives citations are also from Entry 427); CCR, AAR; "History of the 9th Armored Division"; both in John Leonard Papers, United States Military History Institute, Carlisle, Pennsylvania (hereafter referred to as USAMHI); 58th Armored Field Artillery Battalion, AAR, Box 5, Charles B. MacDonald Papers, USAMHI; William Roberts to John Toland, Notes on Team Cherry, January 1957, Box 33, John Toland Papers, Library of Congress, Manuscript Division, Washington, DC (hereafter referred to as LOC); Henry Cherry, combat interview, World War II Combat Interviews #305, microfiche copy of the entire collection in the author's possession (hereafter referred to as CI); *After the Battle*, p. 4; Spurgeon Van Hoose, interview with author, November 24, 2004; Walter Reichelt, *Phantom Nine: The 9th Armored (Remagen) Division, 1942–1945* (Austin, TX: Presidial Press, 1987), pp. 140– 142; Hugh Cole, *The United States Army in World War II: The Ardennes, Battle of the Bulge* (Washington, DC: Center of Military History, United States Army, 1994, reprint of 1965 edition), pp. 296–297; S. L. A. Marshall, *Bastogne: The Story of the First Eight Days* (Washington, DC: Infantry Journal Press, 1946), pp. 181–183; Charles B. MacDonald, *A Time for Trumpets: The Untold Story of the Battle of the Bulge* (New York: Bantam Books, 1984), pp. 289, 293–294.

2. VIII Corps, AAR, CI-350; Major General Troy Middleton, combat interview with Captain L. D. Clark, January 19, 1945, CI-350; Troy Middleton interview with John Toland, notes, no date, Box 36, Toland Papers, LOC; Malcolm Wilkey, unpublished memoir, pp. 18–24, Box 1, Charles B. MacDonald Papers, USAMHI; Frank James Price, *Troy H. Middleton: A Biography* (Baton Rouge: Louisiana State University Press, 1974), pp. 234–235.

3. 101st Airborne Division, AAR, RG 407, Box 14332; G3 Journal, December 19, 1944, RG 407, Box 14360; both at the National Archives; 101st Airborne Division Summary, CI-227; G3 Report, CI-230; Brigadier General Anthony McAuliffe, combat interview with S. L. A. Marshall, CI-229; Lieutenant Colonel Julian Ewell, combat interview with S. L. A. Marshall, CI-229; Lieutenant Colonel Julian Ewell to S. L. A. Marshall, March 14, 1945, CI-229; Julian Ewell, oral history, Julian Ewell Papers, USAMHI; Laurence Critchell, *Four Stars of Hell: The U.S. Paratroopers in Combat from the Night Drop at Normandy to the Battle of the Bulge* (New York: Ballantine Books, 1947), pp. 212–216; Francis Sampson, *Look Out Below! A Story of the Airborne by a Paratrooper Padre* (Washington, DC: Catholic University of America Press, 1958), pp. 104–105; MacDonald, *Time for Trumpets*, p. 491; Marshall, *Bastogne: The First Eight Days*, pp. 31–33.

4. 20th Armored Infantry Battalion, S3 Journal, December 19, 1944, RG 407, Box 16008; S2 Journal, December 19, 1944, RG 407, Box 16013; both at the National Archives; William Desobry to Charles B. MacDonald, August 24, 1983, Box 2, MacDonald Papers; Desobry, miscellaneous notes, S. L. A. Marshall

Papers; Oral History, Desobry Papers, all at USAMHI; Team Desobry, combat interview, CI-305; Jack Garrity, interview with author, April 22, 2005.

5. 3rd Tank Battalion, S3 Journal, RG 407, Box 16039; Unit Citation Recommendation, RG 407, Box 16038; 101st Airborne Division, G3 Journal, December 19, 1944, RG 407, Box 14360, all at the National Archives; Cherry, combat interview, CI-305; Ewell, combat interview, CI-229; Ewell to Marshall, CI-227; Barry Veden, editor, *My Heroes: The Men of Northern Indiana Chapter XXX Veterans of the Battle of the Bulge* (Charleston, SC: BookSurge LLC, 2004), p. 174; Guy Arend, *The Battle for Bastogne* (Bastogne: Bastogne Historical Center, no date), pp. 79–83; Mike Heyman, *Christmas in Bastogne: A Personal Story of World War II*, self-published, 1994, pp. 304–307; Sampson, *Look Out Below!* pp. 105–106; George Koskimaki, *The Battered Bastards of Bastogne* (Havertown, PA: Casemate, 2003), pp. 45–52.

6. 52nd Armored Infantry Battalion, RG 407, Box 15886, National Archives; 9th Armored Division, AAR; CCR, AAR; "History of the 9th Armored Division"; Eugene Watts to Colonel James Van Straten, all in Leonard Papers; Eugene Watts to Charles B. MacDonald, Box 1, MacDonald Papers, USAMHI; Eugene Watts to Pierre Eicher, December 13, 1985, copy of the letter provided to me by Pierre Eicher; Eugene Watts, interview with author, April 12, 2005; Carlton Willey, interview with author, March 1, 2005; Frank Richwine, interview with author, January 12, 2005; Ray Stoker, interview with author, March 29, 2005; Elmer Oakes, interview with author, March 21, 2005; Reichelt, *Phantom Nine*, pp. 144–148.

7. 54th Armored Infantry Battalion, Unit History; AAR, Historical Record, RG 407, Box 16016; S2 Journal, December 19, 1944, RG 407, Box 16019, all at the National Archives; Lieutenant Colonel James O'Hara, combat interview with Captain John Westover, CI-305; John Devereaux, interview with John Toland, Notes, Box 33, Toland Papers, LOC; Tom Holmes, interview with author, May 24, 2005; John Toland, *Battle, the Story of the Bulge* (New York: New American Library, 1985), p. 140; Peter Schrijvers, *The Unknown Dead: Civilians in the Battle of the Bulge* (Lexington: University Press of Kentucky, 2005), p. 106.

8. 52nd Armored Infantry, AAR, RG 407, Box 15886; CCB, S3 Journal, December 19, 1944, RG 407, Box 15974; 3rd Tank Battalion, AAR, RG 407, Box 16037; Unit Citation Recommendation, RG 407, Box 16038; S3 Journal, December 19, 1944, RG 407, Box 16039; 73rd AFA, AAR, RG 407, Box 15879, all at the National Archives; Cherry, combat interview, CI-305; CCR, AAR; "History of the 9th Armored Division," both at Leonard Papers; Ralph Johnson, unpublished memoir, pp. 10–11, 28th Division Survey Material; Wayne Wichert, unpublished memoir, pp. 1–3, Box 2; 58th Armored Field Artillery Battalion, AAR, Box 5, both in Charles B. MacDonald Papers; all at USAMHI; "The History of the 58th Armored Field Artillery Battalion," self-published, 1945, pp. 34–36; Edwin Rensmeyer, "The Story of a Civilian Soldier," unpublished memoir, pp. 18–19, PA Guard Museum; Roberts to Toland, Notes on Team Cherry, Toland Papers, LOC; 420th Armored Field Artillery Battalion, AAR, copy provided by Rufus Lewis; "The 420th at War," unpublished unit history, pp. 19, 74–75, copy provided by Rufus Lewis; Willis Crittenberger, "Bastogne: From the Gunner's Observation Post," *Bulge Bugle*, November 1994, p. 24; The hill from which the 420th fired on December 19 is where the Mardasson monument and Bastogne Historical Center are located today; Van Hoose interview; Reichelt, *Phantom Nine*, pp. 140–143; Marshall, *Bastogne: The First Eight Days*, pp. 27–29.

9. CCB, S3 Journal, December 19, 1944, RG 407, Box 15974; 20th Armored Infantry Battalion, AAR, RG 407, Box 16007; S3 Journal, December 19, 1944, RG 407, Box 16008; S2 Journal, December 19, 1944, RG 407, Box 16013; 101st Airborne Division, AAR, RG 407, Box 14332; Division Narrative, RG 407, Box 14335; 506th Parachute Infantry Regiment, Daily Report, RG 407, Box 14340; S2 Journal, December 19, 1944, RG 407, Box 14443; AAR, RG 407, Box 14438; S3 Journal, December 19, 1944, RG 407, Box 14445; all at the National Archives; Team Desobry, combat interview, CI-305; 101st Airborne Summary, CI-227; McAuliffe, combat interview, CI-229; Desobry, oral history, Desobry Papers; Desobry, Notes, Marshall Papers; Desobry to MacDonald; Captain Jean Holstein, "Operations of the 506th Parachute Infantry Regiment, 101st Airborne Division at Bastogne, Belgium, 19–20 December 1944," paper prepared for the Infantry School, 1949, Box 5, Charles MacDonald Papers; all at USAMHI; Roberts to Toland, Toland Papers; Delmer Hildoer, interview with John Toland, Notes, Box 33, Toland Papers, both at LOC; Garrity interview; Jerry Goolkasian, interview with author, June 1, 2005, and August 29, 2005; Jack Prior, interview with author, April 15, 2005; Jack Prior, "The Night Before Christmas: Bastogne, 1944," *Onendaga County Medical Society Bulletin*, December 1972, p. 42; Lonnie Gill, *Tank Destroyer Forces, WWII—Seek-Strike-Destroy* (Paducah, KY: Turner Publishing, 1992), no pagination; Marshall, *Bastogne: The First Eight Days*, pp. 55–61.

10. 54th Armored Infantry, Unit History; AAR, Historical Record, all in RG 407, Box 16016; S2 Journal, December 19, 1944, RG 407, Box 16019; 101st Airborne Division, AAR, RG 407, Box 14332, all at the National Archives; O'Hara, combat interview, CI-305; Ewell, combat interview, CI-229; Ewell to Marshall, CI-227; Mickey Finn et al., "I Company, 501st Parachute Infantry, December 19, 1944," unpublished paper, 101st Airborne Division Survey Material, USAMHI; Koskimaki, *Battered Bastards of Bastogne*, pp. 54–65; Patrick O'Donnell, *Beyond Valor: World War II's Ranger and Airborne Veterans Reveal the Heart of Combat* (New York: The Free Press, 2001), pp. 241–244; Mark Bando, *Vanguard of the Crusade: The 101st Airborne Division in World War II* (Bedford, PA: Aberjona Press, 2003), pp. 227–229.

11. 3rd Tank Battalion, AAR, RG 407, Box 16037; Unit Citation and Recommendation, RG 407, Box 16038; S3 Journal, December 19, 1944, RG 407, Box 16039; 28th Division, G3 Journal, December 19, 1944, RG 407, Box 8518; all at the National Archives; Cherry, combat interview, CI-305; Ewell, combat interview, CI-229; Ewell to Marshall, CI-227; Thomas Hoban, Report of Action at Wiltz, written on July 14, 1945, Box 35, Toland Papers, LOC; Holmes interview; Koskimaki, *Battered Bastards of Bastogne*, pp. 66–67; Marshall, *Bastogne: The First Eight Days*, pp. 37–41, 49–50, 184–187; MacDonald, *Time for Trumpets*, p. 295; Robert Miller, *Division Commander: A Biography of Major General Norman D. Cota* (Spartanburg, SC: Reprint Company Publishers, 1989), p. 147–149; Robert F. Phillips, *To Save Bastogne* (Burke, VA: Borodino Books, 1996; reprint of 1983 edition), pp. 223–226.

12. 705th Tank Destroyer Battalion, AAR; "History of the 705th Tank Destroyer Battalion"; S3 Reports, December 19, 1944; Citation Recommendation, all in RG 407, Box 23718; S2 Journal, December 19, 1944, RG 407, Box 23719; all at the National Archives; 705th Tank Destroyer Battalion, combat interview with Lieutenant Joe Webber, CI-229; Lieutenant Claude Duvall, combat interview with Lieutenant Joe Webber, CI-229; Lois Pawley Wick, "History

of the 705th Tank Destroyer Battalion," unpublished manuscript, pp. 882–891. I thank John Andrew for lending me a copy of this history; Larry Tanber to author, April 2, April 10, and August 5, 2005; Veden, *My Heroes*, pp. 181–184.

13. CCB, S3 Journal, RG 407, Box 15974; 20th Armored Infantry Battalion, AAR, RG 407, Box 16007; S3 Journal, December 19, 1944, RG 407, Box 16008; S2 Journal, December 19, 1944, RG 407, Box 16013; S4 AAR, RG 407, Box 16015; 506th Parachute Infantry Regiment, Daily Report, RG 407, Box 14340; S2 Journal, December 19, 1944, RG 407, Box 14443; AAR, RG 407, Box 14438; S3 Journal, December 19, 1944, RG 407, Box 14445; all at the National Archives; Team Desobry, combat interview, CI-305; Desobry, oral history, Desobry Papers; Desobry, miscellaneous notes, Marshall Papers; Desobry to MacDonald; Holstein, "Operations of the 506th Parachute Infantry Regiment," both in MacDonald Papers; all at USAMHI; Hildoer interview with Toland, LOC; 420th Armored Field Artillery Battalion, AAR; Goolkasian interviews; Marshall, *Bastogne: The First Eight Days*, pp. 60–64; Koskimaki, *Battered Bastards of Bastogne*, pp. 70–82; Donald Burgett, *Seven Roads to Hell: A Screaming Eagle at Bastogne* (Novato, CA: Presidio Press, 1999), pp. 49– 74; Don Addor, *Noville Outpost to Bastogne: My Last Battle* (Victoria, British Columbia: Trafford, 2004), pp. 29–36.

14. CCB, S3 Journal, December 19, 1944, RG 407, Box 15974; 3rd Tank Battalion, AAR, RG 407, Box 16037; Citation Recommendation, RG 407, Box 16038; S3 Journal, December 19, 1944, RG 407, Box 16039; all at the National Archives; 420th Armored Field Artillery Battalion, AAR; "420th at War," pp. 75–77; Roberts, Notes on Team Cherry, Toland Papers, LOC; Ewell, oral history, Ewell Papers, USAMHI; Ewell, combat interview, CI-229; Ewell to Marshall, CI-229; Cherry, combat interview, CI-305; Major Gary Evans, "The 501st Parachute Infantry Regiment at Bastogne, Belgium, December 1944," Historical Resources Collection 2, U.S. Army Center of Military History, Washington, DC; Critchell, *Four Stars of Hell*, pp. 221–225.

15. 54th Armored Infantry Battalion, Unit History; AAR, Historical Record, all at RG 407, Box 16016, National Archives; Colonel William Roberts, combat interview with Captain John Westover, January 12, 1945, CI-305; O'Hara, combat interview; Wichert, unpublished memoir, MacDonald Papers, USAMHI; John McCambridge, interview with author, April 26, 2005; Joe Bonner, interview with author, April 11, 2005 (Bonner was a rifleman in McCambridge's squad); Neil Garson, interview with author, February 22, 2005; Holmes interview. Wichert made it out of Bastogne before the siege and eventually to a hospital in England. McCambridge spent the whole siege in a state of semiconsciousness in Bastogne. He was permanently disabled from his wounds and endured substantial pain every day of his life.

16. CCB, S3 Journal, December 19, 1944, RG 407, Box 15974; 20th Armored Infantry Battalion, AAR, RG 407, Box 16007; S3 Journal, December 19, 1944, RG 407, Box 16008; S2 Journal, December 19, 1944, RG 407, Box 16013; 101st Airborne Division, Narrative, RG 407, Box 14335; G3 Journal, December 19, 1944, RG 407, Box 14360; 506th Parachute Infantry Regiment, Daily Report, RG 407, Box 14340; S2 Journal, December 19, 1944, RG 407, Box 14443; S3 Journal, December 19, 1944, RG 407, Box 14445; all at the National Archives; Desobry, oral history, Desobry Papers; Desobry, miscellaneous notes, Marshall Papers; Desobry to MacDonald; Holstein, "Operations of the 506th Parachute Infantry Regiment," both in MacDonald Papers, all at USAMHI; Team Desobry, combat interview, CI-305; Roberts, combat interview, CI-305; McAuliffe, combat inter-

view, CI-229; Lieutenant Colonel Harry Kinnard, G3 Report, CI-230; Ludwig "Larry" Stein, interview with author, April 29, 2005; Koskimaki, *Battered Bastards of Bastogne*, pp. 82–85; Burgett, *Seven Roads to Hell*, pp. 74–81; Marshall, *Bastogne: The First Eight Days*, pp. 64–66; MacDonald, *Time for Trumpets*, pp. 495–496.

17. 28th Division, G3 Journal, December 19, 1944, RG 407, Box 8518; 707th Tank Battalion, S3 Journal, December 19, 1944, RG 407, Box 16680, all at the National Archives; *44th Engineer Combat Battalion: We Clear the Way*, self-published, at Veterans Oral History Project, Library of Congress (hereafter referred to as VOHP); Thomas Hoban interview with John Toland, Notes, Box 35; Hoban, Report of Action at Wiltz, written on July 14, 1945, Box 35; Joseph Maertz, "Luxembourg in the Rundstedt Offensive," paper found in Box 39; John Noon, interview with John Toland, notes, Box 35; all in Toland Papers, LOC; Raymond Fleig, "The 707th Tank Battalion in World War II," self-published, pp. 157–158; John Marshall, "A Fighter Tanker's Story," unpublished memoir, pp. 54–62, both at USAMHI; John Marshall, interview with author, January 5, 2005; Phillips, *To Save Bastogne*, pp. 225–229.

18. 687th Field Artillery Battalion, AAR and Unit Journal, RG 407, Box 20109, National Archives; "History of 687th Field Artillery Battalion," Unit Citation, copy in author's possession, courtesy of Lou Dersch; "World War II: 687th Field Artillery Battalion Memoirs," 2001/001/19036, VOHP, LOC; Arch Jack, personal diary, pp. 11–12, copy in author's possession, courtesy of Lou Dersch; Les Eames, personal diary, December 19, 1944, pp. 15–16, copy in author's possession, courtesy of Lou Dersch; Lou Dersch, interviews with author, December 6, 2004, January 17, 2005, combined with copy of Bronze Star Citation; Gene "Jock" Fleury, interview with author, March 7, 2005; Phillips, *To Save Bastogne*, pp. 239–243. For many years after the war, historians believed that the 687th was ambushed at Café Schumann, just outside of Wiltz. Indeed, the official records even make this claim. But, in the 1990s, veterans of the 687th, led by Les Eames (and aided by Pierre Eicher), verified that the action really happened several miles to the southeast at Poteau de Harlange. Bob Phillips was the first historian to redress this error in the revised edition of his book cited above.

19. 28th Division, G3 Journal, December 19, 1944, RG 407, Box 8518; 707th Tank Battalion, S3 Journal, December 19, 1944, RG 407, Box 16680; 3rd Battalion, 110th Infantry, AAR, RG 407, Box 8601; all at the National Archives; 28th Division, AAR, CI-78; General Norman Cota, combat interview with Lieutenant Jack Shea, CI-78; 110th Infantry, AAR, PA Guard Museum; Maertz, "Luxembourg in the Rundstedt Offensive"; Hoban, interview with Toland; Report of Action at Wiltz; Daniel Strickler, "Memories of LTC Strickler"; all at Toland Papers, LOC; Strickler, "The Battle of the Bulge," unpublished memoir, pp. 22–33, MacDonald Papers; Harold Walter to Carl Montgomery, May 4, 1945, Box 7, Carl Montgomery Papers; both at USAMHI; Fleig, "707th Tank Battalion in World War II," pp. 157–160; Phillips, *To Save Bastogne*, pp. 233–238, 251–259; Chernitsky, *Voices from the Foxholes*, p. 65.

20. 705th Tank Destroyer Battalion, AAR; S3 Reports, December 19, 1944, RG 407, Citation Recommendation, all at RG 407, Box 23718; 326th Airborne Medical Company, AAR, RG 407, Box 14447; Don Dobbins, unpublished memoir, RG 407, Box 14441; all in the National Archives; Wick, "History of the 705th Tank Destroyer Battalion," pp. 892–897; 705th Tank Destroyer Battalion, combat interview, CI-229; Statement by PFC Elmer C. Lucas, CI-229; Desobry, oral history, Desobry Papers; Desobry, miscellaneous notes, Marshall Papers, both at

USAMHI; Koskimaki, *Battered Bastards of Bastogne*, pp. 96–105; Arend, *Bastogne*, pp. 105–107.

7. Wednesday, December 20

1. CCB, S3 Journal, December 20, 1944, Record Group (RG) 407, Entry 427, Box 15974; 3rd Tank Battalion, AAR and Strength Report, RG 407, Box 16037; Unit Citation and Recommendation, RG 407, Box 16038; S3 Journal, December 20, 1944, RG 407, Box 16039; 101st Airborne Division, G3 Journal, RG 407, Box 14360, all at the National Archives, College Park, Maryland (all subsequent National Archives citations are also from Entry 427); Henry Cherry, combat interview, World War II Combat Interviews #305, microfiche copy of the entire collection in the author's possession (hereafter referred to as CI); "The 420th at War," unpublished unit history, p. 77, copy provided by Rufus Lewis; Hugh Cole, *The United States Army in World War II: The Ardennes, Battle of the Bulge* (Washington, DC: Center of Military History, United States Army, 1994; reprint of 1965 edition), p. 303.

2. CCB, S3 Journal, December 20, 1944, RG 407, Box 15974; 20th Armored Infantry Battalion, S3 Journal, December 20, 1944, RG 407, Box 16008; S2 Journal, December 20, 1944, RG 407, Box 16013; 506th Parachute Infantry Regiment, Daily Report, December 20, 1944, RG 407, Box 14340; AAR, RG 407, Box 14438; S2 Journal, December 20, 1944, RG 407, Box 14443; S3 Journal, December 20, 1944, RG 407, Box 14445; Headquarters Company, Unit Report, RG 407, Box 14438; 705th Tank Destroyer Battalion, AAR, Citation Recommendation, RG 407, Box 23718; all at the National Archives; Captain Jean Holstein, "Operations of the 506th Parachute Infantry Regiment, 101st Airborne Division at Bastogne, Belgium, 19–20 December 1944," paper prepared for the Infantry School, 1949, Box 5, Charles MacDonald Papers, all at United States Military History Institute, Carlisle, Pennsylvania (hereafter referred to as USAMHI); Lieutenant Tom E. Thoms, combat interview with Lieutenant Joe Webber, CI-229; Team Desobry, combat interview with Captain John Westover, January 1945, CI-305; Delmer Hildoer, interview with John Toland, Notes, Box 33, John Toland Papers, Library of Congress, Manuscript Division, Washington, DC (hereafter referred to as LOC); William Stone, unpublished memoir at www.thedropzone.org; Jerry Goolkasian, interviews with the author, June 1, 2005, and August 29, 2005; Goolkasian to family, December 23, 1944, copy provided to me by Goolkasian; Jack Garrity, interview with author, April 22, 2005; Bill Kerby, interview with author, May 3, 2005; Ray Moore, "Remembering the 'Bravest' Leader—Capt. Omar 'Bud' Billet," *Tiger Tales*, Fall/Winter 2003, pp. 40–41; *Tank Destroyer Forces, WWII-Seek-Strike-Destroy* (Paducah, KY: Turner Publishing, 1992); James Simms, *A Soldier's Armageddon* (Manhattan, KS: Sunflower University Press, 1999), pp. 20–29; George Koskimaki, *The Battered Bastards of Bastogne* (Havertown, PA: Casemate, 2003), pp. 106–112; Donald Burgett, *Seven Roads to Hell: A Screaming Eagle at Bastogne* (Novato, CA: Presidio Press, 1999), pp. 80–89.

3. 54th Armored Infantry Battalion, Unit History; AAR; Historical Record, RG 407, Box 16016; S2 Journal, December 20, 1944, RG 407, Box 16019; 327th Glider Infantry Regiment, AAR; S3 Periodic Report, December 20, 1944; S2 Periodic Report, December 20, 1944; S2 Journal, December 20, 1944, RG 407, Box 14424, all at the National Archives; Colonel Joseph Harper, combat interview

with Colonel S. L. A. Marshall; 2nd Platoon, Company B, 705th Tank Destroyer Battalion, combat interview with Lieutenant Joe Webber, CI-229 and CI-230; Lieutenant Colonel James O'Hara, combat interview with Captain John Westover, CI-305; Lieutenant Colonel Julian Ewell, combat interview with S. L. A. Marshall, CI-229; Cole, *The Ardennes*, pp. 456–457; Laurence Critchell, *Four Stars of Hell: The U.S. Paratroopers in Combat from the Night Drop at Normandy to the Battle of the Bulge* (New York: Ballantine Books, 1947), pp. 224–227; Guy Arend, *The Battle for Bastogne* (Bastogne: Bastogne Historical Center, no date), pp. 113–121; Koskimaki, *Battered Bastards of Bastogne*, pp. 133–140. In 1951, Charles Fisher returned to Marvie and was reunited with the civilians who had tried to warn him of the Germans' presence in the barn. He shared coffee and cakes with these folks and reminisced. They told him that in an effort to hinder the Germans who were chasing him, they closed the broken window after he dived out of it.

4. CCB Strength Reports, RG 407, Box 15964; 20th Armored Infantry Battalion, AAR, RG 407, Box 16007; S3 Journal, December 20, 1944, RG 407, Box 16008; S2 Journal, December 20, 1944, RG 407, Box 16013; 506th Parachute Infantry Regiment, Daily Report, December 20, 1944, RG 14340; S2 Journal, December 20, 1944, RG 407, Box 14443; AAR, RG 407, Box 14438; S3 Journal, December 20, 1944, RG 407, Box 14445; 705th Tank Destroyer Battalion, AAR, Citation Recommendation, RG 407, Box 23718; S2 Journal, December 20, 1944, RG 407, Box 23719; all at the National Archives; Team Desobry, combat interview, CI-305; Thoms, combat interview, CI-229; Boyd Etter to Kath, Lill, George & Bob, no date, 10th Armored Division Questionnaire Material; Walter Kreuger, "Concerning the Offensive in the Ardennes," Box 8, Charles B. MacDonald Papers; Holstein, "Operations of the 506th Parachute Infantry Regiment," MacDonald Papers; all at USAMHI; Stone, unpublished memoir, www.thedropzone .org; Goolkasian interviews; Jack Prior, interview with the author, April 15, 2005; Jack Prior, "The Night before Christmas: Bastogne, 1944," *Onendaga County Medical Society Bulletin*, December 1972, pp. 42–43; Delmer Hildoer, interview with John Toland, Notes, Box 33, John Toland Papers, LOC; Simms, *A Soldier's Armageddon*, pp. 40–41; Don Addor, *Noville Outpost to Bastogne: My Last Battle* (Victoria, British Columbia: Trafford, 2004), pp. 42–59; Burgett, *Seven Roads to Hell*, pp. 97–109; Koskimaki, *Battered Bastards of Bastogne*, pp. 112–123; Cole, *The Ardennes*, pp. 455–456; Peter Schrijvers, *The Unknown Dead: Civilians in the Battle of the Bulge* (Lexington: University Press of Kentucky, 2005), pp. 101–103. Addor ended up losing part of his right leg. Goolkasian lost a finger but after multiple surgeries kept his left arm.

5. Troy Middleton interview with John Toland, notes, no date, Box 36, Toland Papers, LOC; Major General Troy Middleton, combat interview with Captain L. D. Clark, January 19, 1945, CI-350; VIII Corps, AAR, CI-350; Brigadier General Anthony McAuliffe, combat interview, CI-229; 101st Airborne Summary, CI-227; Frank James Price, *Troy H. Middleton: A Biography* (Baton Rouge: Louisiana State University Press, 1974), p. 253; Toland, *Battle*, pp. 163–164; John S. D. Eisenhower, *The Bitter Woods* (New York: G. P. Putnam's Sons, 1969), p. 320.

Postscript

1. General Maxwell Taylor's letter is in 9th Armored Division Commendation Letters, John Leonard Papers, United States Military History Institute, Carlisle, Pennsylvania; Major General Troy Middleton, combat interview with

Captain L. D. Clark, January 19, 1945, CI-350; Brigadier General Anthony McAuliffe, combat interview, CI-229; Major General Norman Cota, combat interview with Lieutenant Jack Shea, CI-78; McAuliffe's quote can be seen at www .tigerdivision .com; James Bradin, "The Forgotten Pennsylvanians," *Army*, August 1987, pp. 63–67; Ivan Peterman, "They Took the Nazis' Sunday Punch," *Saturday Evening Post*, September 28, 1946; Frank James Price, *Troy H. Middleton: A Biography* (Baton Rouge: Louisiana State University Press, 1974), p. 222; Roger Cirillo, "Forgotten Glory: The 110th Infantry in the Battle of the Bulge," *Officer Review*, January 1998; Roger Cirillo, conversation with the author, June 13, 2005. Roger is very knowledgeable about the 28th Division in the Bulge (and, in a larger sense, the U.S. Army in World War II). I thank him for providing me with valuable information on the citation issue and many other topics relevant to the struggle for Bastogne.

PHOTO CREDITS

Pages 123 (top) and 132 (top), United States Army Military History Institute; pages 123 (bottom), 124, 125, 126, 129 (bottom), 130, 131, and 132 (bottom), National Archives; pages 127, 128, and 129 (top), Nancy McManus

INDEX

Page numbers in *italics* refer to illustrations.